The Canadian Cycling Association's Complete Guide to Bicycle Touring in Canada

Elliott Katz

Doubleday Canada Limited
Great North Books

Canadian Cataloguing in Publication Data
Katz, Elliott
        The Canadian Cycling Association's complete
guide to bicycle touring in Canada

Includes index.
Canada ISBN 0-385-25415-6

1. Bicycle touring - Canada - Guidebooks.
2. Canada - Guidebooks.   I.   Canadian Cycling Association.
II.   Title.   III.   Title: Complete guide to bicycle touring in Canada.

GV1046.C2K38 1993   796.6'4'0971   C93-093042-8

U.S. edition ISBN 0-920361-04-8

Cover and text design by Tania Craan
Cover photo by Don Hollingshead/Velographics
Maps by Rodney Frost
Printed and bound in Canada

Published in Canada by
Doubleday Canada Limited
105 Bond Street
Toronto, Ontario
M5B 1Y3

Published in the United States by
Great North Books
60 Bayhampton Crescent
Thornhill, Ontario, Canada
L4J 7G9

Distributed in the United States by
Firefly Books Limited
250 Sparks Avenue
Willowdale, Ontario, Canada
M2H 2S4

Contents

Acknowledgements

Reading this book is like joining a club, where cyclists from every part of Canada share secrets about their favorite tours. I owe much to the people who contribute such information. The Canadian Cycling Association, including Interim Director General Charles Laframboise, along with assistants Gayle Kean and Christine Jenkins, co-ordinated the material sent in from tour leaders across Canada. I would like to thank the following people for their assistance: Sara Darling and Garry Wilson, The Yukon; Volker Bodegom and Roy Smyth, British Columbia; Don Hollingshead, and authors Gail Helgason and John Dodd of *The Canadian Rockies Bicycling Guide* and *Bicycle Alberta*, Alberta; Noreen Hetherington, Saskatchewan; Robert Thom, Manitoba; Tom Sylvester and Bruce Timmermans, Ontario; Jean-Pierre Maisonneuve, Québec; Jerri Burke and Jim Carter, New Brunswick; Walton Watt, and Bicycle Nova Scotia and their publication *Bicycle Tours in Nova Scotia*, Nova Scotia; Colleen Walton, Prince Edward Island; and Tom Sandland and Gerry Stone, and the Newfoundland and Labrador Cycling Association and their publication *Newfoundland by Bicycle*, Newfoundland and Labrador.

Finally, I would like to thank my editor at Doubleday, Maggie Reeves, for her enthusiasm and determination during the making of this book.

Forewords

Cycling in Canada is not new. Since the late 1800s, this country has been recognized internationally as a great place to cycle, and the reputation is well earned. More and more Canadians are discovering that one of the best adventures of their lives is waiting on their own doorstep.

Oh, Canada is a wonderful place to cycle! Many of the roads carry light traffic and are sufficiently wide to accommodate cyclists. An increasing number of towns and cities are providing cyclists with recreational bike paths and bike racks for secure parking. In rural areas, campgrounds and hostels cater to the long-distance cyclist.

The Canadian Cycling Association (CCA), the recognized governing body for cycling in Canada since the 1800s, has been actively improving the environment for cyclists. Initially formed to lobby for better roads, the CCA today enjoys working with Highways, Tourism and other government agencies to ensure that wherever cyclists choose to ride, they are able to do so safely and pleasurably.

As long as there are cyclists, the CCA will continue to provide programs and services to foreigners and Canadians alike. We recognize the many benefits of cycling and encourage all individuals to join this active lifestyle.

Happy cycling, and may the wind always be at your back!

Danelle Laidlaw
Vice-president, Recreation and Transportation
Canadian Cycling Association

Canada is renowned around the world for the spectacular features of its natural scenery, the exceptional diversity of its cultural heritage and the proverbial hospitality of its inhabitants. Cycling is certainly the best way to witness the beauty of the Canadian landscape and to interact with its citizens. Peaceful wooded valleys, tree-framed riverbanks, picturesque villages, rustic islands, snow-capped mountains and ocean beaches can be discovered and enjoyed by bicycle.

According to the 1992 Canadian Sport and Fitness Marketing Survey, cycling ranks in Canada as the third most popular year-round sport/fitness activity for ages 18 years and over, after walking and swimming.

In 1984 when I attended a national symposium on bicycle touring in Canada, organized by the Canadian Cycling Association, I realized then just how much this environmentally friendly way of traveling was still vastly underutilized. Public transportation—airlines, buses, trains and ferries—were not responding fast enough to support the cyclist's desire to travel. Basic touring information required by cyclists then was somewhat difficult to obtain.

Cyclists interested in experiencing the pleasures of touring have been witnessing significant developments. Policies relevant to cyclists have been enacted and services are now uniformly provided by public carriers. Numerous towns and cities are providing cyclists with route maps and developing recreational cycling facilities and events. A growing number of professional tour operators are offering a wide range of itineraries all across Canada. And talented writers such as Elliott Katz are sharing their expertise in the field of bicycle touring.

From individual touring to larger groups, *The Canadian Cycling Association's Complete Guide to Bicycle Touring in Canada* will provide you with the most up-to-date information required by cyclists wishing to experience a trip of a lifetime in Canada. The first part of the book offers advice on the purchase of a bicycle, equipment you need to take with you, tips on safe cycling and the transportation of bicycles on public carriers. The second part will guide you through Canada's most scenic and enjoyable cycling routes. Each chapter provides a number of leisurely and challenging tours, varying in length from one to ten days or more. Route descriptions include the tour length, starting point, sites of general and historical interest, provincial and federal parks, and accommodations and campgrounds. And for ambitious cyclists who want to ride across Canada, each chapter provides an across-the-province tour. These provincial tours link up to form a continuous route, generally following scenic roads with light traffic.

Jean-Pierre Maisonneuve
Chair, Touring Committee
Canadian Cycling Association

Preface

This book is designed to provide you with the best information and the best bicycle tours in all ten provinces and the Yukon.

More than 125 tours are described, ranging from one day to several weeks. You can also ride right across Canada by linking the last tour in each province—an across-the-province route. These routes begin in British Columbia and end in Newfoundland, and most routes follow county roads off the beaten track.

To help you select a tour, we begin each route with a list of key points: length, time, rating, terrain, roads, traffic and starting point. Other bike tours that connect with the route and a brief overview are also provided. A distance log, in both kilometers and miles, is a feature part of the route descriptions.

New maps have been added for each tour. To help guide you, the maps show features that are important to cyclists such as campgrounds, major hills, hostels, historic parks, and ferry routes.

Roads and facilities change. Since this book is an ongoing project, we welcome comments and news of changes for future editions. Please write: Elliott Katz, 60 Bayhampton Crescent, Thornhill, Ontario, Canada L4J 7G9.

Legend

The maps in this book contain the following symbols. Please note that these maps are not to scale, and are intended for use with the tour distance log descriptions and provincial road maps.

▬▬▬	bicycling route
▬▬▬	roads
❁	beginning of tour
⋯🚢⋯	ferry route
■	provincial park
🏛	historic monument or park
▲	steep hill
⋀	campground
🏠	hostel
⑰	road number
—·—	park or provincial boundary
- - -	recreational trail
●	mountain peak
⌣	mountain pass
▨	urban area
⊼	picnic area
ⅠⅠⅠⅠⅠⅠⅠ	railway line

Canada
A Cyclist's Overview

THE LAND, THE PEOPLE

Canada is Big: The second-largest country in the world (after the Confederation of Independent States—the former Soviet Union), Canada covers more than 9.8 million square km (3.8 million square miles). The country is divided into ten provinces (eight are along the U.S. border, the other two are islands) and two territories, in northern Canada. The majority of Canada's 26 million people (one-tenth the population of the United States) live within 320 km (200 miles) of the U.S. border.

Language: English and French are Canada's official languages. French is concentrated in Québec, eastern Ontario, and New Brunswick, although French-speaking communities are found in most of the country. But even in Québec, you can generally find someone who can speak some English. If you don't speak any French, bring a small phrase book. Your effort to speak French is appreciated.

Distances: Major cities are generally far apart. For example, cycling between Ottawa and Toronto could take three to six days. Riding across Canada west to east—from British Columbia to Newfoundland—may take several months.

TOURIST INFORMATION

The addresses and telephone numbers (most of them toll-free) for tourist information centers operated by each province are listed at the beginning of each chapter in this book. If you live outside Canada, you can also contact the tourism department of the nearest Canadian consulate or embassy for information about Canada. In addition, many provinces operate information centers in major cities in the United States and other countries. Check your local directory.

Canada's Bicycling Magazine: *Pedal* provides news and information on recreational and competitive cycling in Canada. Published monthly from March to November, the magazine has articles on bicycle touring and all-terrain biking, as well as buyer's guides on bikes and related products. It's available at newsstands and bike shops, at $2.50 per issue. Subscriptions (9 issues per year) are $19.26 (including GST) in Canada, $26 (U.S.) in the United States and $30 (U.S.) for other countries. Contact: Pedal Magazine, 2 Pardee Avenue, Suite 204, Toronto, Ontario M6K 3H5, telephone (416) 530-1350, fax (416) 530-4155.

The Canadian Cycling Association: CCA is the national organization responsible for cycling in Canada. It's the most extensive source of information for cyclists in Canada. The CCA also offers bicycle touring leadership courses as part of its CAN-BIKE program. Contact: Canadian Cycling Association, 1600 James Naismith Drive, Suite 810, Gloucester, Ontario K1B 5N4, telephone (613) 748-5629, fax (613) 748-5692.

RENTING BIKES

Bicycle rentals are available in many popular bicycle touring areas. For example, in Alberta you can rent a bike for a one-way trip on the Icefields Parkway between Jasper and Banff.

If you've rented bikes in Europe, you'll find the bikes available for rental in Canada are usually lighter-weight. For a current list of bike rental outlets, contact the provincial cycling association and tourism office listed at the beginning of each chapter.

LAWS RELATING TO BICYCLES

Highway traffic and vehicle laws are set by each province. Laws concerning bicycles vary but most provinces have some rules in common:

• Cyclists should ride as near to the right of the road as practicable.

• Don't ride two or more abreast in British Columbia, Alberta, Manitoba, Nova Scotia, Prince Edward Island, Newfoundland, Yukon and Northwest Territories. Double riding is not prohibited in Saskatchewan and Ontario. In New Brunswick riding two abreast is permitted only on bike lanes and paths.

• Keep one or both hands on handlebars except when signaling.

• Don't carry more people than the bike is designed and equipped to carry. A correctly attached child seat or a trailer is usually a permissible modification.

• Don't carry packages in a way that interferes with the proper operation and control of the bicycle.

• Use hand signals when turning, changing lanes or slowing down, if your movement affects other road-users.

• Use lights and reflectors when riding at night.

IN CASE OF AN ACCIDENT

Call the police. Although laws vary among the provinces, there is usually an obligation to report an accident to the police if there are physical injuries, or property damage of more than a specified amount.

Record as many details about the accident as possible, including the date, time, location, what happened in the accident, weather and road conditions, names and addresses of motorists involved and witnesses and what they said, as well as the name and badge number of the police officer. Draw a map of the accident scene and, if you have a camera, take photographs. This information may be helpful in any further action or claim in connection with the accident.

The Canadian Cycling Association offers insurance to members. Contact a provincial cycling association for more information.

MEASUREMENTS

Canada is Officially Metric: Road signs are in kilometers, weather temperatures are given in degrees Celsius, and gas is sold by the liter. In most grocery stores, the prices of items sold by weight, such as produce and meat, are often given in both cost per kilogram and cost per pound. In this book, we've given measurements in metric, followed by imperial equivalents in parentheses.

Speed: 50 km/hour is approximately 30 m.p.h
80 km/hour is approximately 50 m.p.h.
100 km/hour is approximately 60 m.p.h.
(Multiply distance in kilometers by 5/8 to get the approximate number of miles.)

Temperature: To convert Celsius to Fahrenheit:
degrees Celsius $\times$ 9/5 + 32 = degrees Fahrenheit
(Or for a simple approximation: double the degrees Celsius and add 30.)
To convert Fahrenheit to Celsius:
degrees Fahrenheit – 32 $\times$ 5/9 = degrees Celsius

Some Metric Equivalents:
1 kilometer (km) = 0.62 mile
1 mile = 1.6 kilometers (km)
1 meter = 1.09 yards
1 yard = 0.91 meter (m)
1 meter = 3.28 feet
1 meter = 39.4 inches
1 foot = 0.3 meter
1 yard = 90 centimeters
1 inch = 2.54 centimeters
1 centimeter = 0.39 inch

1 square kilometer = 0.386 square mile
1 hectare = 2.47 acres
1 tonne (1,000 kilograms) = 1.10 tons
1 kilogram = 2.2 pounds
1 pound = 2.2 kilograms (kg)
1 liter = 0.264 U.S. gallons
1 liter = 0.22 imperial gallon
1 imperial gallon = 4.5 liters (L)
1 American gallon = 3.8 liters

WEATHER

Canada has a northern temperate climate with warm summers and cold winters. The chapters on each province provide more specific weather information.

Weather Reports: Environment Canada, a department of the federal government, provides recorded weather reports and forecasts by telephone. Look under "Environment Canada" in the government listings in the local telephone directory. Weather information is also broadcast regularly on the radio and television and is published in daily newspapers.

Six Time Zones: Newfoundland Standard Time, covering Newfoundland and Labrador, is 3-1/2 hours earlier than Greenwich Mean Time (GMT)—the world's time zones are measured from Greenwich, England, at 0 longitude.

Atlantic Standard Time, 4 hours earlier than GMT, includes Nova Scotia, New Brunswick, Prince Edward Island and Québec east of Baie Comeau.

Eastern Standard Time, 5 hours earlier than GMT, includes the rest of Québec, and Ontario except for the northwestern part of the province.

Central Standard Time, 6 hours earlier than GMT, covers northwestern Ontario, Manitoba and southeastern Saskatchewan.

Mountain Standard Time, 7 hours earlier than GMT includes the rest of Saskatchewan, Alberta and northeastern British Columbia.

Pacific Standard Time, 8 hours earlier than GMT, includes the remainder of British Columbia.

Daylight Saving Time is in effect in most of Canada from the last Sunday in April to the last Saturday in October.

HOW TO GET THERE

Airlines: Most international air carriers serve Canada's major cities. Within Canada are a number of national and regional airlines. See the chapter on planning your tour for information on transporting bikes on airplanes and trains.

Railways: VIA Rail is the national passenger train service. It connects with Amtrak (the U.S. passenger rail service) at several border crossings. For information on Amtrak, call tollfree from the United States 1-800-USA-RAIL. Newfoundland and Prince Edward Island have no passenger rail service.

VIA Rail handles bicycles as checked personal baggage at a minimal charge. Bikes must be packaged in boxes. If you don't have a box, VIA will supply one free. You have to turn the handlebars and remove the pedals. Bring your own tools to do it, as VIA doesn't provide them.

Many of the bicycle tours in this book can be reached by VIA Rail. Telephone numbers for contacting VIA Rail within each province are given in the chapters.

For VIA Rail information in the United States, contact your travel agent. In the United Kingdom, contact Compass Travel, 527 Priest Gate, 3rd Floor, Peterborough, England PE1 1LE, telephone (0733) 53809. VIA Rail also has sales agents in 22 other countries. For information, write: VIA Rail Canada, P.O. Box 8116, Station A, Montréal, Québec H3C 3N3.

By Car: Canada is easily reached by highway and is within a day or two's drive of much of the United States. An extensive highway network links it with the United States. Highways also take you to the start of the bicycle tours in this book.

The highway speed limit is usually 100 kilometers per hour, which is approximately 60 miles per hour. In Canada, motorists drive on the right as they do in the United States.

Driver's licenses from the United States and most foreign countries are valid in Canada for varying periods of time depending on the province or territory.

Most major oil company credit cards are accepted at their own gas stations in Canada. Most of the major car rental companies operate throughout Canada. It's also possible to get lower rates from smaller car rental companies.

Ferries: The provinces of Prince Edward Island and Newfoundland are islands that are reached by ferries. On Vancouver Island, the Gulf Islands and the Sunshine Coast—all in British Columbia—ferries are the main transportation link. Many of the tours in this book involve taking a ferry. Ferries permit bicycles; but may charge a fee.

HEALTH

Food and Water: Tap water and food from stores are safe to consume. Fruits and vegetables should be washed before eating. If you're taking water from a stream, river or lake that is safe to drink from, take the precaution of purifying it by boiling. Carry a basic first aid kit.

Health Insurance: Canada has a high standard of hospital and medical services. However, if you're hospitalized, it can be extremely costly. Find out if your present health insurance covers you outside your resident country or province and, if it does, to what extent. If it doesn't, you should obtain travel health insurance before leaving home. Be sure the plan covers you while you're bicycle touring.

Medical Services: If you need medical services, ask at a tourist information center for directions to a public hospital, or call the emergency assistance number listed inside the front cover of any telephone directory.

MONEY MATTERS

Canadian Money: There are 100 cents in one Canadian dollar. Bank-notes are available in denominations of $2, $5, $10, $20, $50 and $100. Coins in use are: 1 cent (penny), 5 cents (nickel), 10 cents (dime), 25 cents (quarter), and $1 (known as a loonie).

At time of writing, one U.S. dollar is worth approximately $1.35 Canadian, and one British pound is worth approximately $2.00 Canadian. Call a bank for current exchange rates.

Travelers checks: Accepted by most hotels, restaurants and stores. If you'll be traveling through rural areas and small towns, you may want to cash some travelers checks beforehand at a currency exchange service or bank. For security, carry your travelers checks in a money pouch under your clothing.

Credit Cards: Commercial establishments in Canada accept most major credit cards, including American Express, MasterCard, Visa and Diners Club.

Automatic Teller Machines (ATMs): ATMs, operated by banks and trust companies, are widely available in cities and smaller centers. Many of Canada's ATMs are part of the Cirrus and Plus System networks, which enable visitors from the U.S. to withdraw Canadian funds from the machine.

Banks: Hours vary by branch, but they're generally open from 10:00 a.m. to 3:00 p.m. Monday to Thursday and until 6:00 p.m. on Friday. Most trust companies are open from 9:00 a.m. to 5:00 p.m. Monday to Saturday.

Exchanging Money: If you're coming

from the United States, you'll usually get a better rate if you exchange your American dollars in Canada.

Currency exchange services (found in international airports and major cities), banks and trust companies give better rates than stores or restaurants.

COSTS

Campgrounds: Provincial and national park campgrounds usually have better campsites with more space between them, and lower fees than commercial campgrounds. Many offer washrooms with hot showers, and picnic shelters where you can cook and eat during wet weather. Costs range from $7 to $15 per night.

Commercial campgrounds, like those operated by KOA, usually offer more facilities, such as game rooms and grocery stores. They also cost more.

Hotels and Motels: If you're staying in hotels, you have a wide choice. Canada has a whole range of medium-priced and inexpensive accommodations, including resorts, small hotels and roadside motels. The major hotel chains have standard accommodation and toll-free telephone reservation lines.

A double room at an inexpensive hotel can cost $40 to $80, a moderate hotel $80 to $130, and at an expensive hotel $130 to $180 depending on location. Prices are usually higher during the peak summer tourist season than during the off-season.

Bed-and-Breakfasts: Bed-and-breakfasts are available in cities, small towns and rural areas. Many farms also offer bed-and-breakfast accommodation. Each province's tourist information center can give you listings of bed-and-breakfasts. Rates range from $20 to $60 a night and include breakfast.

Hostels: Canadian hostels are open to people of all ages, both families and singles. Costs for lodging range from $7 to $15. For more information, contact the Canadian Hostelling Association, National Office, 1600 James Naismith Drive, Suite 608, Gloucester, Ontario K1B 5N4, telephone (613) 748-5638.

FOOD

Restaurants: Although Canada has many fast food chains that sell hamburgers, pizza, chicken and more, a wide selection of restaurants are available. A fast food meal is usually $5 to $10. A meal at an inexpensive restaurant usually costs under $20, at a moderate restaurant $20 to $35 and at an expensive restaurant $35 to $100. These prices do not include alcoholic drinks, taxes and tip.

Groceries: Food is usually cheaper in supermarkets than in the smaller convenience stores. Stock up when you can. Overall, food prices are slightly higher than in the United States but lower than in western Europe.

SHOPPING HOURS

Store hours vary, but they're generally Monday through Saturday 9:00 a.m. to 6:00 p.m. Many supermarkets are open to 9:00 p.m. or 10:00 p.m. Some provinces allow Sunday shopping. In provinces where Sunday shopping isn't allowed, supermarkets are closed on Sundays. Most small convenience stores are open seven days a week. In major cities, there are usually several pharmacies open until 11:00 p.m. or midnight.

PUBLIC HOLIDAYS

Most stores and banks are closed on: New Year's Day—January 1; Good Friday; Victoria Day—Monday just before or on May 24; Canada Day—July 1; Labour Day—first Monday in September; Thanksgiving—second Monday of October; Christmas—December 25; and Boxing Day—December 26.

In addition, banks and government offices may also be closed on Easter Monday in April and Remembrance Day, November 11.

Other Holidays: Alberta, British Columbia, New Brunswick, Manitoba, Ontario and Saskatchewan observe a mid-summer holiday on the first Monday in August. (It has a different name in each province.) Most stores and banks are closed on those days.

Québec takes public holidays on January 2, and on June 24 for St. Jean Baptiste Day.

COMMUNICATIONS

Telephones: Canada's telephone system is one of the most modern in the world. Pay telephones are found in most public locations. Local calls cost 25 cents.

Long-distance Calls: Travelers can use a telephone credit card or major credit card, call collect, or deposit money into a pay telephone.

Hotels often charge an extra fee for long-distance calls placed from telephones in their rooms. You would probably save money using a public telephone.

Fax: Service is available at many hotels as well as many stationery stores and private mail box outlets.

Mail and Courier: To send or receive letters and packages, Canada Post offers a variety of services, including its own courier service, known as Priority Post. Use Canadian postage stamps on mail posted in Canada.

Receiving Mail: If you want to send mail to yourself to be picked up en route on your tour, or otherwise receive mail, you can have it sent to your name, c/o General Delivery, Main Post Office, town, province and postal code.

General Delivery mail must be picked up within 15 days, or it will be returned to sender. Look up the postal code in a directory available in post offices, or if you're outside the country, you can call Canada Post at (613) 993-1296.

Couriers: Canada is also served by major couriers offering next-day service within Canada, and between Canada and the United States, as well as express service to and from other countries.

ENTERING CANADA

Americans may be asked for proof of citizenship such as a passport or a birth or baptismal certificate. Naturalized U.S. citizens should carry a naturalization certificate. Permanent U.S. residents who are not citizens are advised to bring their Alien Registration Receipt Card (Green Card).

Citizens of all other countries, except Greenland and residents of St. Pierre and Miquelon, must have a valid passport and some also require a visitor's visa to enter Canada. Travelers under 18 and unaccompanied by an adult need a letter of permission to travel in Canada from a parent or guardian.

Visitors to Canada are allowed to bring in any reasonable amount of personal effects, food and a full tank of gas. Gifts up to $40 (Canadian funds) each in value are duty free provided they do not contain alcohol, tobacco or advertising material.

Visitors 19 years or over may import 1.1 liters (40 ounces) of liquor or wine, or twenty-four 355-mL (12-ounce) cans or bottles of beer. For detailed information, contact: Revenue Canada, Customs and Excise, Communications Branch, Ottawa, Ontario K1A 0L5.

GOODS AND SERVICES TAX REFUNDS

The Goods and Services Tax (GST) is a 7 per cent tax charged on most goods and services sold or provided in Canada. (The tax is not charged on most food bought in grocery stores.)

If you're a visitor to Canada, you pay the GST but can get a refund of the tax paid on certain goods that you take out of Canada and GST paid on accommodation if you stay less than one month.

You can get more information and application forms from: Revenue Canada, Customs and Excise, Visitors' Rebate, Ottawa, Ontario K1A 1J5, or call toll-free in Canada 1-800-66VISIT (1-800-668-4748), from outside Canada (613) 991-3346, TDD (hearing/speech disabled) in Canada 1-800-465-5770.

Buying a Bicycle

The best bicycle for you is one that suits your needs. But how do you choose from the many types of bikes now available? If you're going on overnight or longer trips on paved roads, you need a multi-speed touring bike. If you want to explore backcountry trails or other unpaved areas, shop for an all-terrain (mountain) bike.

Touring: The multi-speed touring bicycles have a large range between low and high gears to let you pedal steadily up steep hills, against the wind or cruise over level terrain at a good pace. Touring bikes now generally come in 10, 12, 15, 18 or 21 speeds.

A range of gears on your bike allows your feet to go around on the pedals at the same speed. This makes your body more efficient. Your pedalling should be quick and easy. The number of speeds refers to the total gearing combinations possible between the chain ring (on the crank or pedals) and the freewheel (on the rear axle). For example, a 21-speed bike with 3 gears on the chain ring and 7 gears on the freewheel has 21 possible gearing combinations.

If you're new to multi-speed bikes, remember using the smaller diameter gears in the front make pedalling easier. It's the opposite in the rear: the larger the gear you shift the chain onto, the easier the pedalling.

The best way to know the ranking of each gearing combination is count the teeth on each gear. Divide the number of teeth on the front chain ring gear by the number of teeth on the gear on the rear freewheel. This will give you the ratio of turns.

For instance, on a 21-speed touring bike, the three gears on the front have 28, 38 and 48 teeth. The 7 gears on the freewheel could range from 13 to 28 teeth.

First gear (the easiest to pedal) would use the 28-tooth gear in the front (the one with the smallest diameter) and the 28-tooth gear on the freewheel (the one with the largest diameter). Divide 28 by 28 equals 1 to 1. This means one complete turn on your pedals makes the rear wheel go around once.

The 21st gear would use the 48-tooth gear in front (the one with the largest diameter) and the 13-tooth gear (the smallest diameter) on the freewheel. So $48 \div 13 = 3.69$. With one complete turn of the pedals, the rear wheel goes around 3.69 times.

Calculate the ratios for each possible combination of gears. In our example the results for the second to the twentieth gear would range between 1 to 1 and 3.69 to 1.

Racing bicycles, though they look similar to touring bikes, are more fragile and are not meant for riding with any extra load. Touring bicycles have lower-pressure tires and more durable rims and wheels.

Lighter is Better: The lighter your touring bicycle, the better. Even a small amount of weight makes a big difference on a tour. The more expensive lighter bikes usually have higher-quality components that are not only lighter but more durable.

A touring bike with dropped handlebars is best suited to long-distance cycling. Dropped handlebars put your body in the best position to pedal. By leaning forward, you cut down on wind resistance. This dropped position may initially give you a stiff neck, but as your neck muscles strengthen this feeling will go away.

Handlebar Comfort: One way to make dropped handlebars more comfortable on your hands is to put a foam-padding covering on them, or wear cycling gloves with padded palms.

Upright Handlebars: Three-speed, five-speed and six-speed bicycles are also suitable for day-long tours or overnight tours. Some have dropped handlebars but most come with upright handlebars and spring saddles. Both are easier to get used to than the dropped handlebars and hard seat. If you plan to tour at a leisurely pace and don't want the dropped handlebars, one of these bicycles should be fine.

Sitting upright does mean you have more wind resistance, but if you're interested not in covering distance but rather in savoring short tours of less than 40 or 50 kilometers (25 or 30 miles) per day, and you want to sit upright, by all means get one of these bikes. Several around-the-world cyclists have done their multi-year tours on these kinds of bikes.

All-Terrain Bikes: Also called mountain bikes, these are designed to withstand the rough handling of dirt roads and backcountry trails. They combine some of the features of the one-speed coaster-brake bicycle and the multi-speed touring bike. All-terrain bikes have fat tires up to 6.5 centimeters (2-1/2 inches) wide, wide-range gears—up to 24 speeds—to get up and down hills, upright handlebars for better control, a wide seat and heavy-duty brakes.

All-terrain bikes are easier to ride on the gravel shoulder of a highway. However, for regular riding on paved roads, all-terrain bikes tend to be slower and heavier than most touring bikes. It's a trade-off—your choice depends on the kind of riding you're going to be doing.

Where to Shop: The best place to buy a bicycle is at a reputable bicycle shop that guarantees bikes and has trained mechanics who service the bikes on the premises. The sales staff are usually knowledgeable and can help you choose the best bike for your needs in your price range.

Bikes are like most consumer products: you get what you pay for: the cheaper brands may give you problems soon after they're out on the road.

Shop around and compare bicycles and prices. When you've decided on a bicycle, try to purchase it from a shop near your home. Even if the bike costs a few dollars more, the extra convenience may be worth it. When the bike needs adjustment it's a lot easier to take it a few blocks than to haul it across town.

GETTING THE RIGHT SIZE

Most important when buying a bike is ensuring that it fits you properly. Frame size is your primary consideration. The standard adult bicycle frame ranges from 58 to 66 centimeters (19 to 26 inches), which is the distance between the top of the frame where the seat post slides into the frame and the center of the crank where the pedals revolve. Your frame size is roughly 28 centimeters (11 inches) shorter than your inseam measurement.

Get on the bicycle. With both feet flat on the ground you should be able to straddle the top tube of the frame of a touring bike with about 5 centimeters (2 inches) to spare, or 7.5 centimeters (3 inches) or more on an all-terrain bike.

The Seat: A badly adjusted saddle can cause neck pain and soreness in the upper arms and lower back.

The seat is the proper height when you can sit on it with one foot touching the ground. When the heel of your foot is on the pedal in the down position, your knee should be slightly bent.

Handlebars: With one elbow touching the tip of the saddle, the handle-bars should be no more than 25 millimeters (1 inch) from your fingertips. If the handlebars are too far forward, too low or too high, they will cause wrist strains; ask the shop to make adjustments.

It may be necessary to change the handlebar extension (which connects the handlebars and the stem) for one of a different size. The handlebar should be a bit lower than the saddle.

SECONDHAND BICYCLES

Ads for used bicycles can be found in newspapers as well as on bulletin boards in supermarkets, universities and some bike shops. The old saying that buying a used car is buying someone else's troubles is sometimes true for bicycles, so you have to be careful.

Buying a secondhand bicycle is like buying other mechanical devices. Know what you are buying or it may end up costing you a lot more than you anticipated. Some bike shops sell used bicycles, usually bikes that were traded in by their owners to purchase a new bike. If the bike shop overhauls their used bikes, there probably is less risk in buying one.

Test Rides: When you are shopping for a used bicycle, ride it to see how it handles at slow and fast speeds. If the bike fits you and is comfortable, do the safety check described in Chapter 5, "Safe Cycling," and examine the bike carefully for mechanical defects.

Here are some things to look for:

- Look at the bicycle from the front and back to check that the frame is straight and the wheels are in line. Turn the bike upside down, letting it rest on the seat and handlebars. The wheels should spin freely and be centered between the forks.
- Spin the wheel and hold a pencil beside the brake shoe to measure side to side movement; it should be no more than 3 millimeters (1/8 inch).
- Hold the wheel and push it firmly from side to side. The wheel should be firmly secured at the dropouts and not move sideways. Pluck each of the spokes; they should be tight and have the same twanging sound.
- Turn the pedals. When the wheels spin there shouldn't be any clicking noises. Put on the brakes; the wheels should stop instantly. Brake shoes should hit the rim squarely and release it without sticking.
- Examine the frame carefully, particularly the forks and where the tubes of the frame join. Wrinkled paint may indicate that the bicycle was in an accident. A fresh paint job may indicate the same thing.
- The pedals and cranks should turn freely with little or no sideways play. Cranks should be straight. Bent cranks may be a sign that the bike was in an accident.

- Gears should change smoothly, without slipping and without a chunking noise. Try the gears both with the bike upside down and during your test ride.
- With the bicycle right side up, put the front brake on and try to move the handlebars back and forth. If there is a lot of play, the headset (the part that connects the handlebar stem with the frame) may be worn or need adjustment.

The used bicycle you look at may not be in perfect condition. Before you purchase the bike, take it into a repair shop and find out how much repairs will cost.

RENTING A BICYCLE

In a lot of cities, as well as in national and provincial parks and other areas offering good cycling, many bike shops rent touring bicycles. If you're traveling to an area and find it too difficult to transport your bike, or don't own one, contact a bicycle rental outlet in advance and reserve a bike for your trip. Some rental outlets also rent helmets, panniers and other accessories. To find out about shops that rent bicycles, contact the provincial tourism departments and the provincial cycling associations.

What to Take with You

In bike touring, less is more. The exhilarating freedom of bicycle touring comes from traveling with just your bike and what you're carrying on it. To travel freely means bringing only the essentials. Weighing down your bike slows you down and makes a grueling ordeal of cycling uphill or against the wind.

Your Touring Plans: The amount of gear you need depends on your touring plans. If you're cycling from motel to inn and planning to eat only in restaurants, you can travel very light. Just pack some clothing and toiletries and you're off. Not having to carry a sleeping bag, tent and cooking gear leaves you with a fairly light load.

Camping out and cooking your meals requires more gear but can give you a greater sense of freedom. You're self-sufficient. You can stop anywhere and be self-reliant with just a few essentials.

PANNIERS

The bags that attach to a carrier and hang alongside the wheel are called panniers. Both front and rear panniers are available. Front panniers are generally smaller and are used only when the extra capacity is needed for a long camping tour.

Shop around before you buy. The cheaper panniers tend to be smaller and less sturdy than the better quality bags. They might be good enough for doing errands around town, but for touring you'll have fewer problems (and usually more space).

Get panniers with a capacity of around 40 liters (2,500 cubic inches). Each pannier usually consists of one large main pocket and one or two smaller outside pockets.

The better pannier bags are made of a sturdy and waterproof material such as Cordura nylon, and come with safety reflectors. Inside each pannier there must be a stiff frame or strong backing, so the panniers won't get caught in the rear wheel spokes.

The panniers' suspension systems should attach very securely to the carrier. Some of the cheaper systems don't. If the panniers are loose, they can get caught in the spokes or fall off the carrier. Bring your bike with you when you're shopping and try the panniers on. If you have cantilever brakes, make sure the panniers don't interfere with their operation.

You should be able to remove panniers from your bicycle fairly quickly so you don't have to leave them unattended. When off the bike, some pairs of panniers can be joined with snaps or Velcro and have an adjustable shoulder strap for easy carrying when you're walking.

Day packs or backpacks that you

carry on your bike when you ride are really only useful on day tours. If you're traveling for longer than a day, you won't want to be carrying any weight on your back.

CARRIERS

To attach panniers to the bike you need you need a carrier (also called a rack). Get the best you can afford.

Quality Rear Carriers: These attach to both seat stays and have two or more supports on each side to support the weight of the panniers. Among the best-known rack makers are Blackburn, Minoura and Vetta. Most quality carriers are made of aluminum.

Front Carriers: These attach to the front forks and are designed to lower the center of gravity to keep your bike more stable. Try to keep your baggage to a minimum so you use only rear panniers and don't weigh down your bike with both front and rear panniers. If you need to use both, put 40 per cent of the weight forward and 60 per cent to the rear.

Center of Gravity: The lower the weight on the bicycle, the lower the center of gravity and the easier and safer the riding. Pack heavy items such as stoves and canned food in the bottom of the pannier. Put light items such as a sleeping bag on top of the carrier.

HANDLEBAR BAGS

A handlebar bag is handy for items that you want to reach quickly without dismounting from your bike. A clear plastic map case on the top of the handlebar bag lets you refer to the map while riding. Handlebar bags range from 8 to 11.5 liters (500 to 700 cubic inches). The handlebar bags designed for all-terrain bikes are generally smaller, in the 2-liter (130-cubic-inch) size.

Strong shock cords from the bottom of the handlebar bag to the front wheel forks prevent the bag from bouncing around when you go over bumps. Buy a bag made of sturdy material so it won't sag when it's full and rub your front wheel.

Handlebar bags should be easily removable from the bike. Some come with a shoulder strap to convert them to shoulder bags.

Put only light items in the handlebar bags. Heavy gear raises the bike's center of gravity, affecting balance.

WATER BOTTLES

Plastic bottles for cyclists come with wire frames that attach to the handlebars or the frame of the bicycle. Their double caps have a small opening that let you drink while pedaling. Many bike frames have threaded holes for mounting water bottle holders.

TOOLS AND SPARE PARTS

Always carry a small tool kit when you're touring. If you don't have the tools needed to fix a flat or other problem you may have a long walk to a bike shop. Get a dependable pump that can inflate your tire hard enough for you to be able to ride on it. Some of the cheap pumps can't do this. Make sure the pump you have fits the valves (either Presta or Schraeder) on your bike's tires.

A suggested kit contains:
- [ ] Tire levers
- [ ] Spare inner tubes
- [ ] Tire pump
- [ ] Tire patch kit
- [ ] Pressure gauge
- [ ] Extra spokes and spoke wrench
- [ ] Spare brake and gear cables
- [ ] Spare brake pads
- [ ] Bicycle wrenches
- [ ] Adjustable crescent wrench (8 to 16 millimeter range)
- [ ] Allen keys (usually 4, 5, and 6 millimeter)
- [ ] Screwdriver
- [ ] Pliers
- [ ] Penknife or scissors
- [ ] Chain rivet remover and spare links
- [ ] Freewheel removal tool
- [ ] Spare bulb and batteries for your lights
- [ ] Can of spray lubricant

LOCKS

Every time you leave your bicycle, even for a few minutes, lock it to something secure such as a lamppost, bicycle rack or other immovable object. Take your panniers and handlebar bag with you. If your gear is stolen from your bike, the trip is ruined.

Keep Bike Thieves Away: You may think you're only going to be gone for a moment, but it takes less than a minute for a thief to make off with your bicycle or panniers. You've probably spent a fair amount of money on your bicycle, so protect it with a dependable lock.

Always lock the frame and both the front and rear wheels, or, if you have quick-release wheels, take the front wheel with you. Never lock your bicycle by the front or rear wheel alone.

Cable Locks: If you use a cable with a regular lock, position the lock so it's high off the ground. That way, bike thieves can't put one side of their bolt cutters on the ground, which would give them better leverage to cut the lock.

There's nothing like that empty, sinking feeling when you discover a thief has made off with your bike. I once came out of a shop in the middle of the day on a busy street and found two thieves with bolt cutters trying to cut the cable lock on my bicycle. None of the passersby did anything. Fortunately when I yelled at them they ran. I immediately bought a large U-shaped lock.

U-shaped Locks: It's definitely worthwhile to invest in one of those virtually indestructible heavy-duty U-shaped locks, such as the Kryptonite, Citadel or Bike Guard. All of them include a guarantee of several hundred dollars if your bike is stolen. Make sure the guarantee applies in Canada.

Combined Locks: To overcome the inconvenience of having to take off your front wheel every time you lock the bike with a U-shaped lock, use a cable and lock to lock the wheels to the frame while using the U-shaped lock to lock the frame to an immovable object.

Safeguarding Your Bike: Here are some other measures you can take to safeguard your bike:

• Record the bike's serial number and register the bike at a police station.
• Scratch your name and telephone number on the frame.
• Take a color photo of your bicycle (with accessories) so you can identify it in case it is stolen.
• Get theft insurance for your bicycle. It can be included in your household policy. Bring the receipt for your bike to your insurance agents and have them add it to your policy.

CLOTHING

Less is More: Bring the least amount of clothing possible. Choosing the right clothing lets you do more with less. For most bicycle touring on summer days you'll probably be most comfortable wearing a T-shirt and shorts. Even in cool weather, shorts are usually more comfortable than long pants, which can constrict knee movement. If you do wear long pants, choose a light cotton pair. Avoid jeans, as they have thick folded-over seams that can chafe your skin. Use pant clips to keep cuffs out of the chain.

Layering: On your torso wear layers of light clothing. This lets you regulate your comfort by adding or removing layers as the weather changes. A cotton T-shirt is the first layer. Cotton absorbs perspiration without feeling clammy. The next layer can be a shirt, followed by a wool sweater and then a nylon windbreaker for cool temperatures. As you warm up, stop and remove a layer of clothing.

Rain and Cold: In case of rain, pack a poncho or cycling rainsuit. (Rainwear of Goretex or other microporous fabric keeps you dry while letting the perspiration out). During spring or fall, or at high elevations, the weather can be cool and windy, and your hands can get pretty cold. Bring a pair of gloves or mitts.

Headwear: Never ride anywhere without a helmet. On cold days wear a wool hat or ear muffs under your helmet. On hot days, you can wear a cycling cap under your helmet and dampen it to keep your head cool.

Packing: To pack your clothes, put each item in a clear plastic bag. Roll up the bag and slip it vertically into the pannier. This way, when you want to retrieve something, you can see the top of each bag and don't have to dig to the bottom of the pannier to find it.

SUN AND INSECTS

In hot weather make sure you wear a sunhat with a visor that fits under your helmet. You may also want to wear sunglasses to protect your eyes from wind and insects. If your skin tends to burn in the sun, use a sunscreen to block the harmful effects of the sun's rays. Use a suntan lotion if you want to tan.

Repellents: Mosquitoes and blackflies can be a problem for cyclists, especially when you stop for a break or to camp. Use an insect repellent with a high percentage of active ingredient. The most effective is M-diethyl-meta-toluamide (diethyl toluamide or DEET for short).

Scents: Floral scents attract bugs, so don't use scents, colognes or scented soaps or shampoos while in the outdoors. Do wash, though, as mosquitoes like warmth and humidity and are more attracted to people who perspire a lot.

Choosing a Campsite: Look for a dry and open area that has a breeze to keep insects from clustering. Avoid tall grass and thick woods that break the wind. Most important, stay away from areas with stagnant water, where mosquitoes breed.

FOOD

On a bicycle tour you can shop at local stores every day for fresh food. Not having to carry a lot of food saves a lot of weight. Of course, the easiest way to get your daily nourishment when bicycle touring is to stop at restaurants. But this can be expensive, and you miss the pleasure of eating in the outdoors.

Buy the foods you like and determine your needs from experience. How you feel is the best measure of how well you are eating.

Carbohydrates are the quick-energy foods. Snacks consumed during rest stops should be high in carbohydrates. Good snacking foods are granola bars, fruit bars, raisins and other dried fruits, chocolate, nuts and shredded coconut. Some stores sell "trail mix" containing a variety of dried fruits, raisins and nuts.

Fat, found in meat, butter, margarine and nuts, is another source of energy. The body stores fat and can convert it into heat energy very quickly when needed. On cold days, adding extra butter or margarine to your morning oatmeal will help keep you warm.

Protein, found in meat, fish, eggs, milk and cheese, produces energy that lasts longer. However, protein consumes calories in its conversion into energy.

Water is the best liquid to drink to prevent dehydration. Your body loses moisture in perspiration and urine. When you exert yourself cycling and perspire more than usual, you should drink water regularly, at least eight to ten glasses a day.

Non-perishables: If you're touring through the backcountry or a remote area where you will not be able to buy food, stock up on non-perishables, such as dehydrated soup mixes, canned meat or fish, and macaroni.

Salt and Sugar: It's a good idea to bring along small amounts of salt, pepper, spices, sugar, peanut butter and jam in tightly closed plastic containers. These items are usually sold in volumes larger than you need for your trip, and if you buy them on the road, they will add extra weight and volume.

Breakfast: To get an early start in the morning, eat a quick and simple breakfast such as eggs, oatmeal, granola, or peanut butter and jam on bread, with juice and fruits.

Quick Lunches: Can be made with bread and cheese, salami, canned meat or fish, or peanut butter and jam, fruit and juice.

Supper: After riding all day you're hungry, and you have more time to prepare the meal. Try to plan a meal that takes about half an hour to prepare so you can cook and set up camp while it's still daylight. Cook fresh meat, fish or anything else that you can buy at a local grocery store.

STOVES

The lighter your cooking gear, the better.

Butane Stoves: These are the simplest to operate. The cartridges contain pressurized butane gas that vaporizes instantly when vented to atmospheric pressure. Just open the valve and light. The cartridges weigh more than white gas for the same amount of heating energy, but they're more convenient.

The Bleuet S200-S stove is the most widely available butane stove. It costs about $25 and weighs 420 grams (15 ounces). A butane cartridge lasts about three hours, weighs 190 grams (7 ounces) and costs about $2.50.

White Gas: These stoves burn hotter than butane stoves and the fuel is cheaper. The most popular of the lightweight white gas stoves are the Coleman Peak 1, which weighs 800 grams (1 pound, 12 ounces) and sells for $60; the Svea 123, which weighs 510 grams (1 pound, 2 ounces) and

sells for $60, and the Optimus 8R weighing 670 gm (1 pound, 8 ounces) and also costs around $60. The MSR WhisperLite uses a fuel bottle as the stove's reservoir and is very light, weighing in at only 350 grams (12 ounces). It sells for around $70.

Safety: White gas is very flammable and should be carried in a metal leakproof container such as a Sigg or similar fuel bottle.

Practice operating the stove at home so you won't have any problems when you're out on the road. Never use the stove inside a tent. Make sure it's stable and that there is adequate air circulation.

Cook-sets: For cooking and eating, get a lightweight aluminum cook-set consisting of a pot with a lid that doubles as a frying pan and a dish. Sigg offers sets of nesting pots designed to fit a Coleman Peak 1 or Svea 123 stove inside the cook-set, which will save space in your panniers. Don't forget a spoon, fork and knife.

TENTS

The lightest shelter is a coated rip-stop nylon tarp measuring approximately 2.7- by 3.6 meters (9 by 12 feet), with grommets along the edges. Tarps protect you from rain and sun, but not from biting mosquitoes and blackflies. For complete protection, get a tent. In recent years, tents designed for bicycle touring have come out. They're lighter, usually under 2 kilograms (4.4 pounds) and smaller than most lightweight tents. They fit into panniers where space is at a premium.

Pack the tent and pegs at the bottom of a pannier. If the tent poles don't fit in the panniers, secure them with shock or bungee cords to the carrier or the top tube of your bicycle.

SLEEPING BAGS

Don't scrimp on a sleeping bag. There is nothing worse than a miserable night awake and shivering in a bargain-basement sleeping bag. Buy a bag that will keep you warm at the coldest temperatures that you're likely to encounter in the region and time of year you'll be cycling. But don't go overboard either. A winter sleeping bag is too much weight and is too hot for the summer.

Down: Get a quality bag from a good camping equipment store. Mummy bags are generally warmer and lighter than rectangular bags. Synthetic-filled bags cost less than down bags rated to the same temperature, but down has the advantage of compressing to a smaller size for packing, an advantage in the limited space on your bike.

Synthetic: On the other hand, the top-quality synthetics, such as Polarguard, Hollofil II and Quallofil, dry faster when wet. But if you're careful with a down bag you should be able to keep it dry. When riding, always cover your stuff-sack with a large plastic bag in case you get caught in a sudden downpour.

Backpacking Hammocks: These are light, compact to pack and comfortable to sleep in. Just find two trees spaced the correct distance apart and tie one end of the hammock to each tree. If there's a possibility of rain, rig a tarp over the hammock.

CHECKLIST

Here's a suggested checklist. Modify it to suit your plans and needs.

Bicycle Gear
- [ ] Helmet
- [ ] Panniers and carrier
- [ ] Handlebar bag
- [ ] Battery-operated light to double as flashlight
- [ ] Cycling gloves or wool gloves
- [ ] Water bottle
- [ ] Tool kit and spare parts (see list on page 15)
- [ ] Lock

Clothing
- [ ] T-shirt
- [ ] Long-sleeved shirt (polypropylene)
- [ ] Sweater
- [ ] Nylon windbreaker
- [ ] Cycling shorts
- [ ] Long pants
- [ ] Underwear
- [ ] Socks
- [ ] Shoes
- [ ] Swimsuit
- [ ] Towel
- [ ] Sun hat
- [ ] Wool hat
- [ ] Poncho or rain suit

Toiletries
- [ ] First aid kit

☐ Toothbrush and toothpaste
☐ Biodegradable soap and shampoo
☐ Toilet paper

Cooking Gear

☐ Stove, fuel and matches
☐ Pot and pan set
☐ Dish and cup
☐ Spoon, fork and knife
☐ Food containers
☐ Can opener
☐ Bottle opener

Shelter

☐ Tent
☐ Sleeping bag

Miscellaneous

☐ Insect repellent
☐ Sun screen
☐ Candles
☐ Map

Books and pamphlets are available from the Canadian Cycling Association. For a catalog, contact: Canadian Cycling Association, 1600 James Naismith Drive, Suite 810, Gloucester, Ontario K1B 5N4, telephone (613) 748-5629, fax (613) 748-5692.

Planning Your Tour

Start enjoying the freedom of bicycling by taking day trips or short tours to learn what equipment you need and what's extra weight. Chances are, on your first trip you'll burden yourself with too much gear. After a few short tours you'll know how to operate your equipment and exactly what you need to bring for the length of your trip.

Beginning with short trips also gives you an idea of how far you can ride each day. Don't try to cover too much distance; a good average for your first trip is 65 to 80 kilometers (40 to 50 miles) each day. This allows you time to stop for a swim and still arrive at your overnight destination in time to cook supper and—if you're camping—to put up the tent in daylight.

When you've chosen a tour, look at the road map and choose a goal for each day. Design the tour to suit your own tastes.

Accommodation Reservations: On a weekend trip, you don't want to spend precious time looking for accommodation. Reserve ahead. Many campgrounds accept reservations for a number of their campsites. The remainder are given out on a first-come, first-served basis.

Reservations can be more important for cyclists than for motorists. If it's late in the afternoon and there's no room at the campground, a motorist won't mind driving 100 kilometers (60 miles) to another. For a cyclist, it's not that easy.

When making reservations, say what time you expect to arrive if it will be late in the day. If you see you're not going to make it to your reserved accommodation, call and tell them. If you don't call and you arrive the next day expecting a place, they may not have one for you.

CAMPING

Carrying camping and cooking gear means more weight in your panniers, but it's worth the effort: it makes you more self-sufficient on your bike living in the outdoors.

The tours in this book generally have a good selection of campgrounds in national or provincial parks. Start your day early, so you can arrive at a campground early. It's much more pleasant to set up in daylight. With your site set up and your bike unloaded, you're free to explore the area.

A guide to each province's campgrounds, including those in national parks, provincial parks and private campgrounds, is available free from each provincial tourist information department.

BED-AND-BREAKFASTS

Bed-and-breakfasts are popular with

all manner of travelers, and cyclists are no exception. One of the joys of cycling is experiencing the country and getting to know its people. Staying at bed-and-breakfasts can be part of this experience. Bed-and-breakfasts generally cost less than hotels and are operated in private homes, so you can get to know your hosts and the other guests. You can find bed-and-breakfasts in rural towns, villages and cities.

Registries: In some areas, a central registry takes reservations for the bed-and-breakfasts in the area. This is a good way to plan and reserve accommodation for a multi-day tour in which you can stay at a different bed-and-breakfast each night. Information on bed-and-breakfast places is available from provincial tourist departments.

HOSTELS

Canadian hostels offer not only inexpensive accommodation but also an opportunity to meet people of all ages from around the world, many of them cyclists. Hostels are not limited to young people.

Along the Icefields Parkway through the Canadian Rockies is a chain of hostels within a day's ride of each other. As well, hostels are available in cities and national and provincial parks.

Membership: If you intend to use hostels regularly, get a membership in the Canadian Hostelling Association or, if you're traveling to Canada, get a membership in the hosteling federation of your country to use

here. Non-members pay a slightly higher fee to stay at a hostel. Advance reservations are recommended during the summer season. The address and telephone number of each provincial hostel association is given at the beginning of each chapter of this book. The national office of the Canadian Hostelling Association is 1600 James Naismith Drive, Gloucester, Ontario K1B 5N4, (613) 748-5638.

MOTELS AND HOTELS

If you want more comfort and privacy at night, and can afford it, you may want to stay at motels or hotels. Economical motels offering comfortable rooms are widely available. The safest place to keep your bike is in your room with you. Just make sure your bike isn't dripping with mud.

The accommodation guides available from the provincial tourism offices give details on prices and facilities.

BACKCOUNTRY TOURING ON AN ALL-TERRAIN BIKE

Using an all-terrain bike on backcountry trails combines some of the best of cycling and hiking. You're free of having to deal with cars and trucks and can get closer to nature— which is the joy of hiking. But on your bike you can cover greater distances. Some people use an all-terrain bike to cover the distance to a secluded hiking area.

When you're touring the backcountry, you need to carry all your food. If you want to camp overnight, you'll need camping equipment and lightweight foods.

TRANSPORTING YOUR BICYCLE

Many people take their bikes with them on vacation. That way, they can cycle some of these tours for a day, a weekend, a week or longer. Other people want to bicycle outside their own city and aren't excited about riding half a day just to get out of the city and past the suburbs. Whatever your plans, you're faced with the question: how do you transport your bicycle?

CARS

More and more people are loading their bicycles onto their cars to do some cycling for all or part of their vacation. They drive themselves and their bikes to the tour's starting point, park the car, and ride the tour before returning to the car.

Vans and Station Wagons: The easiest way to transport your bike by car is to have a van or station wagon that has space to put bicycles inside, although you may have to remove one or both bike wheels. However, even if you do have a van or station wagon, you may need the space inside for passengers and luggage.

Bike Carriers: To transport bicycles on the outside of your vehicle, you need a bicycle carrier. Three designs are available: bumper-mounted, trunk-mounted and car-top.

When shopping for a bike carrier, make sure the carrier fits the design of your vehicle. For example, some car-top carriers only fit cars that

have rain gutters. Also, consider the number of bicycles you want to transport. The bumper-mounted carriers can carry two or three bikes. The trunk-mounted carriers and the car-top carriers can hold up to four bicycles.

Make sure that the parts of the carrier that come in contact with your bicycle are coated with vinyl or another material that protects the bicycle's paint. A rack with rust-resistant galvanized and plasticized steel will last longer.

Loading Tips:
• Before loading bikes on a carrier, remove items that can fall off, such as pumps, panniers and handlebar bags.
• When using bumper-mounted or trunk-mounted carriers, be careful that the wheels are not so low that they'll hit the ground when you drive over a dip or up a steep road.
• The car's exhaust can melt bicycle tires. Position the bike so that the exhaust pipe is not aimed at a tire.
• Always keep in mind the car's extra bulk, especially when reversing and parking.

TRAINS

The easiest way to transport your bike overland in Canada by public transport is by train. Trains with a baggage car will take your bike without being boxed or disassembled. You can just give it to the baggage attendant, and there is no extra charge for bicycles.

Most train routes in Canada have

at least one train per day with a baggage car. VIA Rail operates most of the railway services throughout Canada and provides access to many of the bicycle tours described in this book. Check a current schedule or call VIA Rail. The telephone numbers in each province are given at the beginning of each chapter of this book.

VIA Rail recommends that you disassemble your bike and put it in a box. It sells bike boxes for a few dollars. If you have the tools you can remove the front wheels and pedals, turn the handlebars sideways and pack it into the box. Bring your own tools to do it, as VIA doesn't provide them. VIA Rail accepts bicycles at your own risk. Boxed or not, VIA Rail doesn't accept responsibility for damage.

BUSES

Check with bus companies in advance. Some take bikes but require them to be disassembled and boxed. Bicycle boxes can be obtained from a local bike shop; bus companies don't supply them. Dismantling a bike so that it fits in a box usually involves removing the front wheel and the pedals and turning the handlebars sideways. Put the pedals and any loose bolts in a sturdy bag and store them in your panniers.

If the bus company will transport your bike, it may be a good idea to ship your bike a few days ahead to make sure it's there when you arrive. Some bus companies won't guaran-

tee that the bike will travel on the same bus as you or even on the same day. On a long weekend or in high travel season your bike may get bumped to a later bus. Also, some bus companies may say the bus you want to take will transport your bike, but the bus used that day may have a small or full baggage compartment that won't accommodate your bike.

AIRLINES

Regulations vary with each airline. Some allow a bicycle as your first piece of checked luggage. Others consider it excess baggage and charge a flat fee. Call a few airlines and compare.

On some airlines you can buy extra insurance for your bike when you buy your ticket. Some sell bicycle bags for a few dollars in which you can pack a disassembled bike. If you plan to transport your bike regularly on public carriers, you can buy a good quality bicycle bag of heavy nylon.

Keep all the parts you have removed from your bike together in a sturdy bag and put them in your panniers. Remove the panniers from the bike and check them separately or take them as carry-on luggage. They will fit in a large lightweight duffel bag.

One tip: Your bicycle wrenches may trigger the airport's metal detectors; mine did. For security reasons, tools are not permitted on board aircraft. Keep them in a separate case that you can check with your bike.

FERRIES

You can walk on ferries with your bike. Almost all ferries charge for bicycles. The address and telephone number of major ferry services are given at the beginning of each chapter in this book. Information on ferry services that are part of a tour is given in the tour's description.

Safe Cycling

Defensive cycling skills are vital. Knowing how to safely handle potentially dangerous cycling situations can prevent falls and collisions.

Cycling is safest when both cyclists and drivers are aware of and respect each other's place on the road. Fortunately, drivers are becoming more accustomed to bicycles. However, there are still some drivers who aren't used to thinking of cyclists. Though they may seem to look right at you, they'll drive as if they had not seen you at all.

The most common causes of car-bike collisions in which motorists are at fault are failing to yield the right of way, making turns into cyclists and opening car doors in front of them. On the other hand, cycling on the wrong side of the road, turning without looking behind, and failing to yield the right-of-way are the usual causes of incidents in which the cyclist is at fault.

The tours described in this book generally follow roads that have light traffic, and offer pleasant cycling. Wherever you ride, proper precautions by both cyclists and drivers can help prevent conflict and increase enjoyment.

RULES AND REGULATIONS

Obey All Rules and Regulations of the Road: In the eyes of the law, bicycles are vehicles and must observe the same laws as car drivers. Ride as far to the right of the road as possible. Groups should bicycle in single file. Obey stop signs and traffic lights, even if it means losing momentum. And though you think it's perfectly safe to go through a red light or ignore other traffic regulations, you're giving all cyclists a bad name when you do.

When you stop to check your map or for any other reason, move your bike and yourself completely off the road. Don't block any part of the road for cyclists or car traffic.

Ride Defensively: Be aware of the road directly in front of you, as well as a long distance ahead. Defensive bicycling lets you plan what to do in each situation so you won't be caught by surprise by a merging road, or by obstacles such as a pothole, broken glass or a storm sewer that can cause you to fall.

Potholes: If there is a pothole or similar hazard in your path, check for approaching traffic to see if you can safely move around it. If you are going to ride over it, slow down and lift yourself out of your seat to prevent your spine from absorbing the bumps.

Road Shoulders: Roads with wide, paved shoulders generally make the best touring routes. Riding well onto the right side of a paved shoulder should keep you a good distance away from the main flow of traffic.

On a narrow road without a paved shoulder, ride where you will be visible. This may mean you are claiming the lane.

Riding a touring bike on a gravel shoulder is slow going. If you're going to tour roads with unpaved shoulders, consider using an all-terrain bike with wider tires to better handle the gravel. It's slower than a touring bike on paved road, but you're farther from the traffic.

Cars: When you're riding, put yourself in the motorist's shoes. If you're a driver, think about the occasions when you've had to pass cyclists. When I'm driving I get nervous about getting too close to bicycles, so I move left—and then worry about the car being too close to the oncoming lane. Experience teaches that sharing the road requires courtesy and effort from both cyclists and drivers. Some tips for motorists are at the end of this chapter.

CITY BICYCLING

When you're riding in a city, try to choose a route on side streets that parallel the heavily traveled main streets. City traffic can be frightening when you're looking for street names. When choosing a route from one point to another, we often think of the city's main arteries, but that's thinking like a car driver. It's usually easy to avoid these streets. Take out a map and plan a route through quieter residential streets. They have less car exhaust to inhale and are usually more scenic.

SIDEWALKS

The safest place to ride your bike is on the road, not on sidewalks. In fact, in many places biking on the sidewalk is illegal. When you're biking in a town or a city, stay off on the sidewalks and be courteous to pedestrians. Bicycles are vehicles and belong on the road.

Riding on the sidewalk, or riding on the wrong side of the road and surprising a pedestrian when they step off the curb, can make pedestrians hostile to cyclists and can even cause injury. If the street has heavy traffic, don't ride on the sidewalk. Take a less traveled road.

It's easy to think that riding on the sidewalk is safer, but it can actually be more dangerous than riding on the road. Consider this: pedestrians average 5 kilometers (3 miles) per hour while a cyclist travels about four or five times that speed. Bicycles are not as maneuverable as your own two feet and take more time and distance to stop or turn. As well, accidents can occur when a car backs out of a driveway and hits a cyclist on the sidewalk who was hidden by hedges, fences or other obstructions.

The problem of cyclists riding on sidewalks is not new. During the bicycling boom of the nineteenth century—often called bicycling's golden era—cyclists on high-wheelers shared the roads with horse-drawn carriages. An 1898 issue of the Toronto Bicycle Club newsletter observed: "The fact is that bicyclists are out of their proper place and are trespassing when they use the sidewalk. . . . As the bicycle has evidently come to stay, the sooner those using the machines know their position in reference to the use of sidewalks the better, not only for themselves but the public generally."

SIGNALS

Use hand signals when turning, changing lanes or stopping at least 30 meters (100 feet) in advance.

Left Turn: Extend your left arm to indicate a left turn.

Right Turn: For a right turn, extend your right arm. This is the way this signal is usually done today. Extending your left forearm upward while the upper arm is straight is a holdover from the days when car drivers used hand signals.

Stopping: To indicate that you're slowing down to stop, point your left forearm down perpendicular to the upper arm.

TRAIN TRACKS

Be careful when approaching railway tracks. Cross railway tracks as close as possible to a perpendicular angle. Otherwise, the tracks can catch your front wheel, which can throw you onto the road.

INTERSECTIONS

Most accidents between cars and bicycles occur at intersections, often because the bicycle is in the driver's blind spot.

Cars Turning Right: Here's a common situation. At a red light, you're be-

side a car that is in the right lane. You plan to ride straight ahead—but since you're beside the car, you cannot see if the driver is signaling to turn right or not. And the driver cannot see you between the car and the sidewalk. The traffic light turns green. You proceed straight, but the car turns right into your path.

Be Behind or In Front of Cars: Don't position yourself beside a car. Be behind the car so you can see its signals in front of you and the driver can see you. Even if there are signal lights on the side of the car, the driver may neglect to signal or wait until the last second.

Making a Left Turn: A left turn can sometimes be difficult. The safest way is to walk your bicycle across the pedestrian crosswalk, or ride through the intersection on the right, stop and turn the bike and then proceed through the intersection again.

MERGES AND TURN-OFFS

Check Traffic Behind You: Be especially careful when you're on a highway and approaching a turn-off or a merge. Cars can turn into your path if you're going straight along the right side of the road. Look behind you and check for cars signaling that they're merging or turning off.

PARKED CARS

Look Ahead for Car Occupants: When you're passing a row of parked cars look ahead into the cars to see if there's a driver or passenger who might open the car door into your path. To avoid this, cycle well out into the road away from parked cars.

If a car is emitting exhaust it may be about to pull out onto the road.

BRAKES

Use both front and rear brakes to stop. Most cyclists are aware that if you brake too hard on the front brake or use the front brake only—especially when going downhill—you'll go flying over the front handlebars. As a result there is sometimes a tendency to rely more on the rear brake.

On a bicycle equipped with front and rear hand brakes, the front brake does 80 per cent of the braking. Using the back brake helps keep the bicycle under control. To stop effectively, you must use both brakes.

For better control when braking hard in a sudden stop, shift your weight back on the bicycle as you brake. This helps prevent you from being thrown forward.

WET ROADS

Rain makes roads slippery. The water brings oil to the surface of the road, making things even more slippery. The bicycle wheel rims get wet and the brakes work poorly on them.

Sitting Out the Rain: When it rains, I usually stop at a restaurant or other sheltered place to sit it out. Not only can riding in the rain be more hazardous, but the rain is cold and stings your face when you ride into it.

If You Have to Ride When it's Wet:
When you're riding in wet conditions, including right after a rain, ride slowly and look ahead so you can begin braking gently in advance. Dragging your brakes slightly will help remove water from your rims. Avoid those slippery oil slicks on the road.

PANNIERS

Baggage should be in panniers attached securely to your bicycle, not in a knapsack on your back. Keep the load as low as possible for better handling of the bike on the road. Loose panniers can slip into the spokes.

VISIBILITY

Make sure you are seen. Wear bright, multi-colored clothing that has some dark colors and some light colors. Red and yellow show up best. Your body is the largest object on your bike, and wearing clothing that makes you visible to motorists is more effective than attaching a flag to your bike.

Reflectors: Your bicycle should have large reflectors both front and back, (white and red respectively). You can also put reflective tape on the bicycle frame. The reflectors should be visible for at least 90 meters (300 feet) at night. Pedals with built-in reflectors are a good safety device.

If you ride at night, wear light-colored clothing that can be easily reflected in car headlights. Retroreflective safety vests are also an excellent idea.

Bicycle Lights: These are not so much intended to light up the road ahead, which they do only minimally, as to ensure that drivers can see you on the road. A bicycle headlight should be visible from at least 150 meters (500 feet) at night.

Battery versus Generator: There are two main types of bicycle lights: battery powered and generator-driven lights. The generator-driven light has a wheel that revolves against the tire to produce current that powers the lights. They don't require batteries so you won't be caught with dead batteries and no light, but an older model or cheap generator increases your pedaling resistance, although the newer models less than the older ones, and the light shines only when you are moving. As soon as you stop, the light goes out.

Leglights: Lights that attach with a strap to your leg are effective in attracting motorists' attention because the light beam goes up and down as you pedal.

Extra Caution at Night: Night riding is different from day time cycling. At night, tired car-drivers might not be able to see you, and their headlights can blind you for a few seconds. If you have to ride at night, try to choose a route on lighted roadways.

Flags: Available in most bicycle shops are the 2-meter (6-foot) bicycle flags. As they extend above the height of traffic and have brightly colored flags, they make you stand out on the highway and help motorists spot you.

Hearing: Make sure you can hear traffic and pedestrians. Never wear stereo headsets when cycling. You have to be able to hear cars and trucks approaching, pedestrians calling out and emergency vehicles demanding the right of way.

HELMETS

Get the best helmet you can find and wear it, always. If you think helmets are an expensive accessory, consider how much your head is worth. In an accident, a helmet could easily save your life. Most deaths from bicycle accidents are from head injuries.

Helmet Standards: There are three standards for bicycle helmets: the Canadian Standards Association's, the American National Standards Institute (ANSI) Z90.4, and the Snell Memorial Foundation standard. The standards a helmet has met are indicated inside the helmet. Buy a helmet that has passed at least two standards. You have only one head, so get the best helmet and add some reflective strips on both the front and back.

A cycling helmet that meets these standards has a shell to distribute the effect of a blow to the head over as large an area as possible, shield the head from sharp objects, and provide an abrasion-resistant surface between your head and the road.

Helmet Liners: These should be made of expanded polystyrene (similar to a Styrofoam) which will absorb a shock by crushing and not bounce back at the head. The liner should be at least 1.2 centimeters (0.5 inch) thick and if it crushes, it stays crushed and the helmet cannot be re used. Springy foam is added only for comfort and to ensure a snug fit to best protect your head. To keep the helmet on your head if you fall, it must have a good strap with a strong fastener.

DOGS

If a dog looks like it's going to run after you, the best thing to do is speed up. You can probably outrace the dog.

Discouraging Dogs: If you can't ride fast enough to get away, yell "Stop" or "No" and threateningly shake your pump at the dog. Another way is to talk soothingly to calm the dog. Or, try crossing to the other side of the road. This may be enough to remove your threat to the dog's territory.

Other Techniques: Use the chemical repellent carried by letter carriers; put lemon juice or diluted ammonia in a squeeze bottle or a water pistol; or just use your water bottle to squirt the dog, preferably in the eye area. A more peaceful way: throw the dog some food and take off while the dog is distracted.

TRUCKS

Large trucks can be frightening for cyclists. When a truck is passing you, move as far as you can to the right. The suction that trucks create can knock you down if you're too close. Keep both hands on the handlebars and keep going as the truck passes.

Before moving back onto the road, wait until you see the entire truck in front of you. The trucks may have two trailers.

The tours in this book generally follow roads with light traffic, but you may encounter heavy trucks, particularly logging trucks on the mountain roads of western Canada. If you're on a narrow road with little or no shoulder and hear a logging truck or other heavy vehicle coming, the safest thing to do may be to get off the road completely and let the truck pass.

HEALTH

The golden rule of cycling is: drink before you're thirsty and eat before you're hungry.

Be careful to avoid sunstroke. Make sure you always carry with you fluids without sugar or caffeine. Wear a shirt with a brightly colored back to reflect the sun.

Bad Weather: Always be prepared for the worst weather that can be encountered in the area at that time of year. Carry clothing that will provide adequate warmth and dryness. Beware of hypothermia. Don't be afraid to stop and seek shelter if you begin to shiver or your body goes numb, or if you feel drowsy.

Keep in touch with your body. Stop when you get very tired. When you're tired your intellectual functions decrease and your chances of having an accident increase.

BICYCLE SAFETY CHECK

Do a safety check on your bike before starting out. Your safety and enjoyment depend on a good working bicycle. Do a thorough check of your bicycle regularly. Examine the following components:

Brakes: You should be able to apply your brakes with full force without the levers going closer than 1/8" to the handlebars. Check the brake shoes to make sure they aren't worn, loose or rubbing against the wheel.

Cables: Examine the brake and gear cables to make sure they aren't frayed where they attach to the brake or gear levers and to the brakes and derailleurs. If they are frayed, replace them now before they break. New brake cables stretch, so you have to adjust the brakes to take in that slack.

Gears: Check the operation of both derailleurs. Keep the chain clean and oiled. Grease all bearings once a year.

Tires and Wheels: Frequently check air pressure in both tires (the correct pressure is usually indicated on the tire) and look for cuts and wear. Make sure the wheels are tight in their mounts. Rims should be free from dents as this affects braking. Replace broken spokes.

If the wheel wobbles it can be straightened—called trueing the wheel—by adjusting the spokes. If the wheel is badly dented, get a new one.

Looseness: Many parts gradually become loose over time. Check your bike's pedals, cranks and headset. Also check nuts holding fenders, carrier racks, lights, water bottle cages, bells and other accessories. If anything is loose, tighten it.

BACKCOUNTRY BICYCLING

Riding an all-terrain bike through the backcountry involves some special rules to safeguard cyclists and the environment. Ride only on trails that have been designated for the use of all-terrain bikes.

Stay on the Trails: Going off the path, especially in meadows, can damage vegetation and leave unsightly tire tracks. Don't ride on muddy trails. It damages them. Don't litter. Pack out what you pack in, more if you can.

Don't Get Stranded: An all-terrain bicycle can take you farther into the backcountry than you can walk out in a day. Be equipped to repair flats and mechanical problems, so you can ride out. Carrying a tool kit, spare inner tube, patch kit and pump is essential on all backcountry rides.

Hikers and Horses: Don't startle hikers. Slow down and use a bell or call out to let them know you're coming. When cycling downhill or approaching blind corners, ride in anticipation of meeting hikers and horses.

When approaching a horse, get off the bicycle and if possible stand on the downhill side of the trail.

Wildlife: If you see wildlife on the

trail, slow down and let it move off the trail before approaching and passing.

BEARS

As cycling is a quiet means of transportation, cyclists have a better chance of seeing wildlife on a road or trail. But it also means you can surprise a bear, which may feel threatened. Bears will generally leave you alone if they're aware that you're approaching. If you're traveling with the wind, the bear may be warned by your scent. But if you're riding into the wind, the bear may not get your scent and won't be aware of your approach. Warn bears of your presence by riding in a group and talking, and using a bell or other noisemaker.

Watch for bear tracks and fresh bear droppings. Never approach a bear cub. A female bear will attack if she thinks her cub is in danger.

If you see a bear, make a wide detour or leave the area immediately. If you cannot detour or retreat, wait until the bear moves away from the path. Always leave the animal an escape route.

CYCLISTS AS DRIVERS

When you drive, be kind to cyclists. Set an example to other drivers on how to safely share the road with cyclists.

When you plan to turn right and a cyclist wants to ride straight through the intersection, slow down and let the bicycle go, then make your turn. This is safer than trying to get ahead and turning in front of the cyclist.

Before opening your car door after you've parked, or before pulling out of a parking space, turn around and look for bicycles. Looking in the rearview mirror isn't sufficient, a bicycle may be in your blind spot.

If you see a cyclist riding toward an obstacle such as a pothole or sewer grate that the rider may have to swerve around, slow down or move over so the cyclist has more room.

Dempster Highway
(Yukon government photo)

The Yukon

The Yukon offers cycling enthusiasts not only spectacular wilderness scenery and challenging routes, but also a glance of one of Canadian history's most fascinating periods—the Klondike Gold Rush. What better way to explore the haunts of infamous gold-seekers like Soapy Smith and Tagish Charlie than through two-wheel touring?

The meandering creek beds of Dawson City's past and present mining operations are ideal for the cyclist and surprisingly undiscovered. The Yukon was also home to one of the largest silver mines in the world and the original "Silver Trail" used by wagon teams is today a highway offering a fascinating cycling tour. For those who prefer longer road rides, the trips from Skagway, Alaska to Whitehorse and along the Dempster Highway offer unparalleled scenery.

The tours in this chapter explore the Yukon's less-traveled routes, away from the territory's two main highways—the Alaska Highway which runs from Dawson Creek, British Columbia through the Yukon to Alaska, and the Klondike Highway linking Whitehorse and Dawson City.

It's recommended that cyclists always carry a tent and at least a day's supply of food. There are lodges along several of the routes, but in the Yukon it's always a good idea to be well prepared. Carrying a bear-bell and a generous supply of mosquito repellent is also helpful.

Landmarks are not as frequent along highways in the Yukon as in southern Canada. You may want to use a bicycle computer to determine how far you've gone.

Terrain: Mount Logan at 5,951 meters (19,524 feet) is the Yukon and Canada's highest peak.

The Yukon Plateau is a basin-like area of rolling hills, deep valleys and isolated mountain ranges, drained by the Yukon River and its tributaries. West of the plateau are the St. Elias and Coast Mountain Ranges, to the north is the Ogilvie Range and the Mackenzie Mountains are to the east.

Area: 482,515 square km (186,250 square miles)

Weather: Cycling trips should be planned for the summer months— June through mid-September. It starts to get pretty chilly after that.

Temperatures in the Yukon are usually more extreme than those in southern Canada. Summers are dry, warm and sunny. Winters are dry, cold and dark. The dryness is caused by the Yukon's location in the rain shadow of the coastal mountain ranges. Prevailing southeast winds dump up to 350 centimeters (138 inches) of precipitation on the Alaska coast annually. But inland, only about 25 centimeters (10 inches) fall.

Annual temperatures range from winter lows of minus 50 degrees Celsius (minus 58 degrees Fahrenheit) to summer highs of 32 degrees Celsius (90 degrees Fahrenheit). July is generally the warmest month with a mean of about 13 degrees Celsius (55 degrees Fahrenheit) in lower interior valleys.

Tourist Information: General tourist information, including road maps and an accommodation guide that includes campgrounds is available through the Yukon Tourism Department, P.O. Box 2703, Whitehorse, Yukon Y1A 2C3, telephone (403) 667-5340. Information can also be obtained through the Yukon Conservation Society, Box 4163, Whitehorse, Yukon Y1A 3T3, telephone (403) 667-6786.

Accommodations: The Yukon offers accommodation ranging from expensive, moderate to inexpensive. If you want to stay in a hotel, it's recommended that you reserve as far in advance as possible. Prices for accommodation and food are slightly higher in the Yukon than in southern Canada.

Hostels: Fourth Avenue Residence in Whitehorse is not a member of the Canadian Hostelling Association, but does give discounts to hostel members. The residence can also recommend inexpensive accommodation in the Yukon's other communities. For information, contact Fourth Avenue Residence, 4051-4th Avenue, Whitehorse, Yukon Y1A 1H1, telephone (403) 667-4471.

Airports: Whitehorse Airport is served by major airlines. Connector airlines serve the smaller Yukon communities.

Ferries: The Inside Passage along the Pacific Coast is a spectacular way to get to the Yukon. Ferries leave from Bellingham, Washington, and Prince Rupert and Port Hardy, British Columbia. For schedule information, contact the Alaska Marine Highway, telephone toll-free 1-800-423-0568.

Buses: Whitehorse is served by Greyhound Lines of Canada. Motorcoach service to Whitehorse is available six times a week from Edmonton and Vancouver. Bicycles are welcome. Local coach lines also serve the communities.

Capital: Whitehorse has a population of 15,000 and is the Yukon's largest city.

Population: 28,000

History: The magical four-letter word GOLD took the Yukon from being a sleepy corner of Canadian wilderness to the home of some of the most exciting times in world history. In 1897 a steamer loaded with a glittering cargo landed at Seattle. It carried the first cache of the Klondike goldfields—nearly three tons of gold dust and nuggets.

A year later, the gold rush had begun in earnest. Gold seekers from Canada, the United States and Europe flocked to the Yukon. More than 100,000 tried their luck in the Klondike gold fields. They battled the treacherous terrain and freezing temperatures of the North. For some, the arduous journey paid off. But many others were not so lucky.

During the gold rush, many of the stampeders depended on the knowledge of the territory's Native population to help them survive. The contribution of the Yukon's Native people is still very apparent in the territory.

Archaeologists calculate the first human habitation of the Yukon occurred more than 10,000 years ago. The first people are believed to have entered what is now Alaska and the Yukon across a land bridge from northeast Asia during the last Ice Age. Today, the majority of First Nations belong to eight groups in the Athapaskan and Tlingit language families.

Roads: The Yukon's road system radiates from Whitehorse and connects with all Yukon communities except the territory's most northerly community, Old Crow. These roads have paved or well-maintained gravel surfaces. Cyclists should keep in mind that during the summer months, some stretches of Yukon roads are under construction. Roads can be quite dusty or muddy, depending on weather conditions. Routes tend to be less-travelled and the distances between services a little farther than in southern Canada. For a Yukon road report, call (403) 667-5644.

Cycling Organization: The Cycling Association of the Yukon, Box 5345, Whitehorse, Yukon Y1A 4Z2, telephone (403) 667-8213 or (403) 668-4019.

THE SILVER TRAIL: STEWART CROSSING TO KENO CITY

Length: 112 km (70 miles) one-way; 215 km (134 miles) return trip via secondary roads
Time: Two days
Rating: Easy-intermediate
Terrain: Gently rolling route with gradual ascents and descents to Elsa; secondary roads on the way back are similar.
Roads: Route is a combination of highway and secondary roads; paved road gives way to hard-packed gravel after about 50 km (31 miles); road is wide but does not have shoulders; secondary roads are well-packed gravel and quite narrow.
Traffic: Road up to Elsa has little traffic—even in summer months when a spattering of recreational vehicles may be seen; secondary roads are also sparsely traveled.
Start: Stewart Crossing on the Klon-

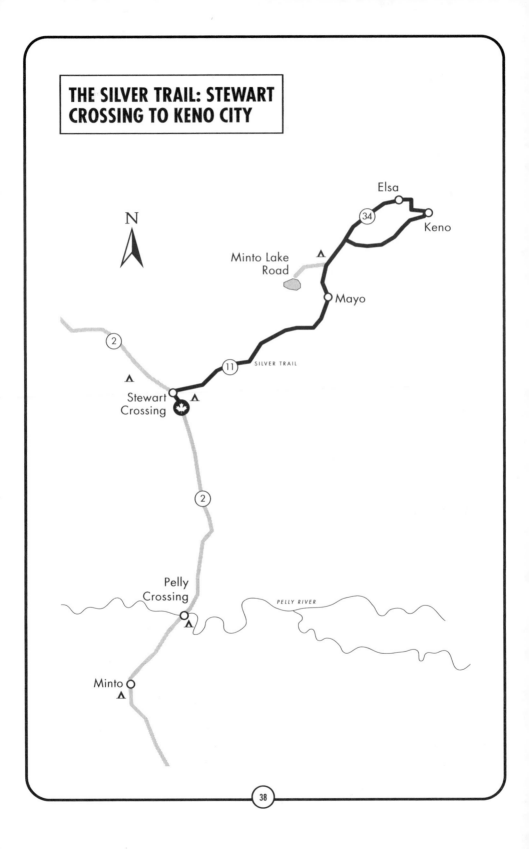

THE SILVER TRAIL: STEWART CROSSING TO KENO CITY

N

Elsa

34

Keno

Minto Lake
Road

Mayo

2

11

SILVER TRAIL

Stewart
Crossing

2

Pelly
Crossing

PELLY RIVER

Minto

dike Highway—Highway 2, 180 km (113 miles) south of Dawson City.

Overview: The spring of 1898 saw thousands of gold-hungry prospectors descend on the Yukon. Hundreds of those prospectors made their way up the Stewart River, where the Yukon's first small gold rush occurred in 1883. The gold they found in this area didn't compare to the massive claims of Dawson City, but it was the silver-lead crystals the miners found in their pans that put the Silver Trail on the map.

A couple days in this area is recommended. There are several well-maintained campsites along the route. Before beginning this trip, a guidebook to the *Surface Geology and Environmental History of the Silver Trail* can be picked up at the Stewart Crossing Information Booth (open June through August) at km 537.6 (mile 334.1) on the Klondike Highway.

THE ROUTE:

0 km (0 miles) Stewart Crossing on the Klondike Highway

Head east on the Silver Trail—Highway 11—up the Stewart River Valley. As you ride north, white spruce grove forests are abundant along the roadside. In the 1920s and 1930s this was a rich agricultural area that fed both miners and livestock.

38.3 km (23.8 miles) Conservative Trail

A back road leading to mining properties, the Conservative Trail is an easy half-hour of exploring.

51 km (31.6 miles) junction

At the junction at kilometer 51 (mile 31.6), turn left to Elsa and Keno City.

53 km (33 miles) Mayo

Situated on the bank of the Stewart River, Mayo was a supply center and shipping depot. Before the road was opened in the 1950s, river steamers moved supplies up the Stewart River to Mayo and returned carrying sacks of silver-lead ore. There are grocery stores, motels and a cafe.

64 km (39.7 miles) Minto Bridge

Minto Bridge was once a small settlement, but was flooded out with the advent of the power dam. Some of the old cabin sites can still be seen on the higher ground upstream.

76 km (47 miles) Halfway Lakes

Good fishing for northern pike is found in the Halfway Lakes.

93 km (57.7 miles) Silver King claim

Keep riding to the Silver King claim, first staked in 1903. The old mine shaft can be seen on your right at the base of the cabin.

98 km (61 miles) Elsa

Another 5 km (3 miles) down the road is Elsa. One of Canada's oldest silver mines was operated here by United Keno Hill until it closed in 1989 due to low silver prices. Elsa is now a tiny village of less than 100 people with a fascinating mining museum.

112 km (70 miles) Keno City

The 14 km (11 miles) to Keno

City provides an insightful glimpse into an important part of Yukon history. Once a flourishing silver mine camp, Keno City is now a tiny village with less than 100 people. You have a scenic view of the surrounding area. There is a small hotel here.

Option: Return by original Silver Trail from Keno City

On the way back, you can take the original Silver Trail from Keno City. Take the junction for the Duncan Creek Road to Mayo

Lake. Along the way are spectacular scenic views, and several rest stops used by the wagon teams that hauled massive loads of silver ore.

This route heads back to Mayo along the Mayo River where there is the opportunity for fabulous grayling fishing.

215 km (134 miles) Stewart Crossing on the Klondike Highway

From Mayo, take the traditional route to the Klondike Highway. There are several campsites in the area.

DEMPSTER HIGHWAY: DEMPSTER CORNER TO TOMBSTONE RECREATIONAL PARK

Length: 80 km (50 miles) each way
Time: One or two days
Rating: Easy
Terrain: Undulating through mountain valleys with gradual grades; this route has few sharp ascents or descents; there is a steep climb to North Fork Pass.
Roads: Well-maintained, hard-packed gravel; there aren't any shoulders although the road is wide with plenty of room for cyclists; road is fairly well traveled by cyclists in the summer months.
Traffic: Light to moderate in summer; traffic is generally sporadic but when recreational vehicles pass, the road can become quite dusty.
Start: Dempster Corner, near Klondike River Lodge, 38 km (24 miles)

south of Dawson on the Klondike Highway.
Overview: Canada's most northerly highway, the Dempster Highway cuts through spectacular mountainscapes and tundra.

This tour explores the Dempster's southernmost 75 km (47 miles). This section follows the valley of the North Klondike River to the treeline, and then starts a sharp ascent to North Fork Pass on the Continental Divide.

The North Klondike River begins in the southern Ogilvie Mountains at the foot of the Tombstone Range, and joins the main branch of the Klondike River near the Klondike gold fields.

Along the highway, animal life is

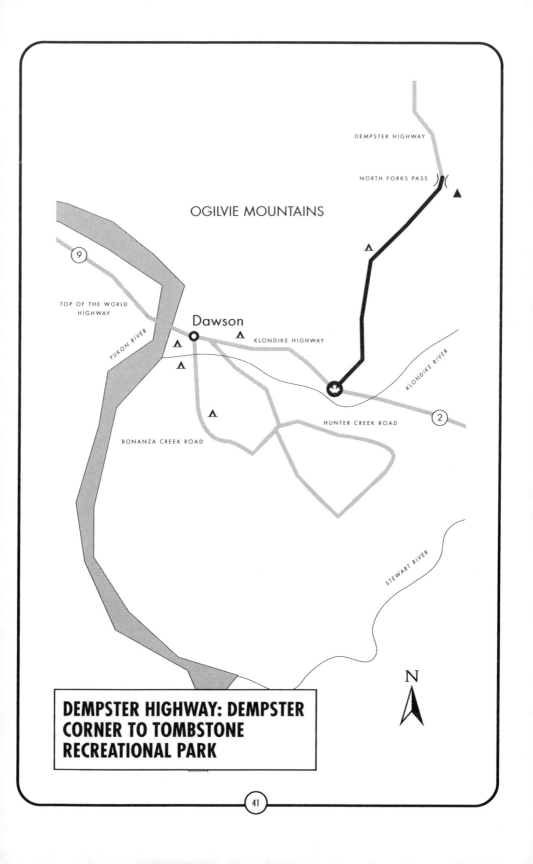

OGILVIE MOUNTAINS

DEMPSTER HIGHWAY

NORTH FORKS PASS

9

TOP OF THE WORLD
HIGHWAY

YUKON RIVER

Dawson

KLONDIKE HIGHWAY

KLONDIKE RIVER

2

HUNTER CREEK ROAD

BONANZA CREEK ROAD

STEWART RIVER

N

**DEMPSTER HIGHWAY: DEMPSTER
CORNER TO TOMBSTONE
RECREATIONAL PARK**

abundant. There are moose, wolf, wolverine, lynx, beaver, fox and both black and grizzly bears. A bear bell is recommended.

The entire 726-km (451-mile) Dempster Highway links the southern Yukon with Inuvik in the Northwest Territories. The highway is named after Royal Canadian Mounted Police Inspector W.J.D. Dempster who searched for and discovered the famous Lost Patrol, four Mounties who froze to death near Fort McPherson in the winter of 1911.

THE ROUTE:

0 km (0 miles) Dempster Corner

Head north on the Dempster Highway along the North Klondike River.

6.5 km (4 miles) North Fork Power Plant

You may want to look at the North Fork Power Plant, which opened in 1911 to supply electricity for the growing number of gold dredges operating in the Klondike area. The intake can be reached by turning east off the highway. The 3.5 km (2.2 miles) road is accessible to cars and in good condition.

73 km (45 miles) Tombstone Campground

The drama of the Tombstone Range highlights the geology of the southern portion of the Dempster. This range was formed by the solidification of molten rock resulting in highly unique geological formations

that tower above the floor of the Tombstone Valley.

The vegetation of the North Klondike River area is similar to that of central Yukon. The forest of spruce, aspen, cottonwood and birch gradually shrinks as the highway climbs the valley toward the Continental Divide.

Tombstone Campground is situated at the treeline. Above the treeline, brush and alpine tundra extend into higher elevations. The campground offers camping, a cooking shelter and firewood as well as maps and information for cyclists who may want to continue their journey. There are also opportunities for several day hikes and day rides from the park.

75 km (47 miles) Tombstone Mountain

Use the campground as a base and ride 2.5 km (1.6 miles) north. From here you can see the wedge-shaped peak of the 2,193-meter high Tombstone Mountain. The highest peak in the Tombstone Range, the mountain is at the head of the North Klondike River Valley.

For years, the distinctive mountain was a landmark for prospectors, trappers and RCMP finding their way through the wilderness.

80 km (50 miles) North Fork Pass

The highway then climbs to the 1,289-meter (4,229-foot) North Fork Pass.

NORTH CANOL ROAD: ROSS RIVER TO DRAGON LAKE CAMPGROUND

Length: 101 km (63 miles) each way

Time: One or two days

Rating: Intermediate to difficult

Terrain: A lot of variety—sections of the road are quite mountainous with several steady climbs; there are also flat sections and gently rolling terrain.

Roads: Fairly well-packed gravel, although in some sections it's fairly rough; the narrow, winding road has no shoulders.

Traffic: Extremely light.

Start: Ross River at junction of Robert Campbell Highway and Canol Road.

Overview: During the height of the Second World War, the Canol Road was built by the U.S. Army as a service road for an 1,000-km (600-mile) oil pipeline linking Norman Wells in the Northwest Territories with a refinery in Whitehorse. The oil flowed through the pipeline for 13 months. When the war ended, the pipeline was abandoned.

The North Canol Road stretches 220 km (137 miles) from Ross River to near the border with the Northwest Territories, through some of the Yukon's best scenery. This tour explores the first 101 km (68 miles)

of the North Canol Road from Ross River.

There are no services along the highway north of Ross River. The wild land along the Canol is a mountain bicyclist's untamed dream. You can see abundant wildlife including caribou, moose, bears and several species of birds including peregrine falcons.

THE ROUTE:

0 km (0 miles) Ross River

At Ross River, take the ferry across the Pelly River. The ferry operates from 8:00 a.m. to 5:00 p.m.

As you ride the Canol Road, you'll see relics of the past. Dotted along the road are abandoned army vehicles, remnants of pipeline, telegraph poles and prefabricated Quonset huts. The scenery ranges from lush growth along the southern part of the road to the drumlins, dramatic ridges and spectacular views of the Selwyn Mountains farther north.

101 km (63 miles) Dragon Lake campground

From Ross River, ride 101 km (63 miles) to the Dragon Lake campground, at kilometer 333.7 (mile 203) of the Canol Road.

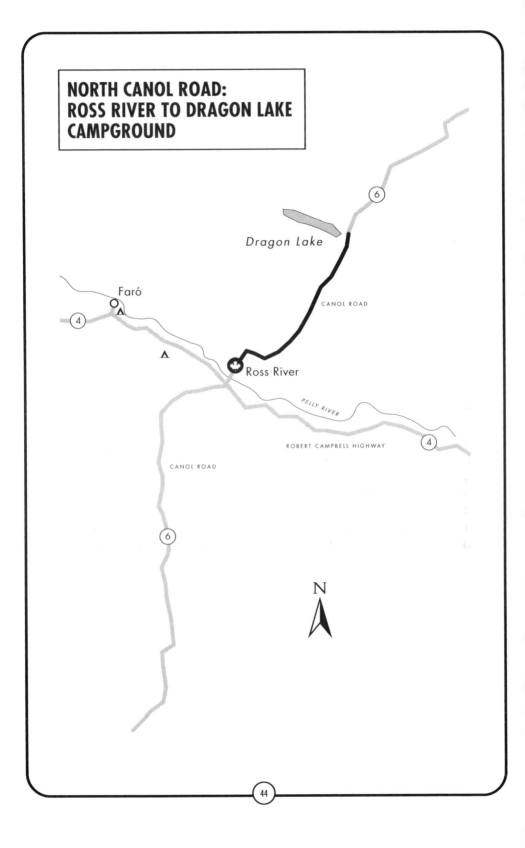

NORTH CANOL ROAD: ROSS RIVER TO DRAGON LAKE CAMPGROUND

6

Dragon Lake

Faró

4

CANOL ROAD

Ross River

PELLY RIVER

4

ROBERT CAMPBELL HIGHWAY

CANOL ROAD

6

N

BONANZA CREEK: BONANZA CREEK ROAD TO KING SOLOMON'S DOME

Length: 125 km (78 miles)
Time: One or two days
Rating: Intermediate
Roads: Packed gravel that is a little loose in some sections; there are no shoulders but the road is wide enough to accommodate both vehicles and bicycles.
Traffic: generally light on the Lower Bonanza Road since there are tourist attractions such as the Dredge in this area; there is very little traffic on the Upper Bonanza Road.
Start: Bonanza Creek Road junction near the GuggieVille campground, 2 km (1.2 miles) south of Dawson City.
Overview: The well-traveled lower Bonanza Creek Road takes travelers into the heart of Dawson City's mining operations—both past and present. Immediately apparent is the effect on the landscape of man's quest for gold. Hillsides are gouged and vegetation is minimal in the lower creek area.

THE ROUTE:

0 km (0 miles) GuggieVille campground

Turn off the Klondike Highway onto the Bonanza Creek Road. Parks Canada has marked historical sites along the way. The first of these is the White Channel Gravels where there was a gold-rich river bed.

10 km (6 miles) Dredge #4

About 10 km (6 miles) farther along the road is the massive Dredge #4. Built in 1902, it's the largest wooden-hulled dredge in the world. The dredge's net was dragged along the bottom of Bonanza Creek to gather gold.

The first claim ever staked in the Yukon is just past the dredge. It was at Discovery Claim that Tagish Charlie and his friend George Carmack found gold and struck it rich.

Just past this point, the road forks to the left and joins the Upper Bonanza Road. If you want to try panning for gold, you can continue along the lower road to the free claim area.

Once on Upper Bonanza Road, the route begins a gradual ascent for about 50 km (31 miles).

Watch for the remnants of old cabins about 20 km (12 miles) up the road. This was the site of Grand Forks, the major community in this area that once had a thriving population of about 5,000 people. Present-day mining operations can also be seen along the way.

A forest reserve begins in this area. Rarely are trees of such size seen in the Dawson region.

Once above the treeline, the views are spectacular. Box Car Dome is reached first. It was

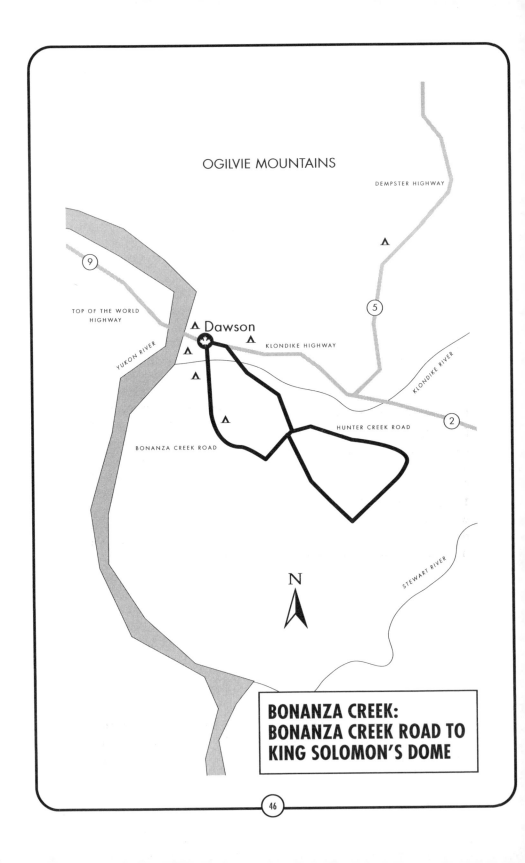

OGILVIE MOUNTAINS

DEMPSTER HIGHWAY

⑨

TOP OF THE WORLD
HIGHWAY

YUKON RIVER

⑤

Dawson

KLONDIKE HIGHWAY

KLONDIKE RIVER

②

HUNTER CREEK ROAD

BONANZA CREEK ROAD

N

STEWART RIVER

**BONANZA CREEK:
BONANZA CREEK ROAD TO
KING SOLOMON'S DOME**

here that the old Klondike Mines Railroad ran.

King Solomon's Dome looms ahead about 10 km (6 miles). The panoramic view of the creek beds and the Tombstone Mountain Range are spectacular.

To return you can retrace your route—an exhilarating and long descent.

Option: Return via Hunker Creek Road

Continue down the other side of the dome via the Hunker Creek Road, and see how extensive the mining creek system is in this area.

SKAGWAY TO WHITEHORSE

Length: 176 km (109 miles)

Time: Two days—overnight in Carcross recommended

Rating: Intermediate

Terrain: Mountainous; the ascent to the summit of White Pass is one of the steepest in the Yukon.

Roads: Highway is well-paved with paved adequate shoulders; in several sections it's winding and fairly narrow.

Traffic: Moderate; the highway is well-used by recreational vehicles in the summer months, but is lightly traveled compared to highways in southern Canada.

Start: Skagway, Alaska, terminus for the ferry up the Inside Passage

Overview: For those traveling by ferry up the Inside Passage, the ride to Whitehorse offers both spectacular scenery and a fascinating introduction to the Klondike Gold Rush. The route follows much of the trail taken by the stampeders of 1898.

As the tour crosses the United States–Canada border, be sure you have proper documentation with you.

THE ROUTE:

0 km (0 miles) Skagway, Alaska

Once off the ferry, you're met with the charm of Skagway, Alaska, which was once the bustling gateway to the Klondike Gold Rush. Meander around the historic buildings of the tiny downtown area before taking the South Klondike Highway for Whitehorse.

9.7 km (5.7 miles) United States custom house

First the route passes through the Skagway Valley and crosses the Skagway River. The original White Pass Railway route is still visible on the other side of the river. Tall cottonwood trees thrive along the river and the northern coastal mountain range provides a stunning backdrop.

22.7 km (14 miles) White Pass summit

As you climb toward West White Pass, the coastal forest gives way to scrub. The high-

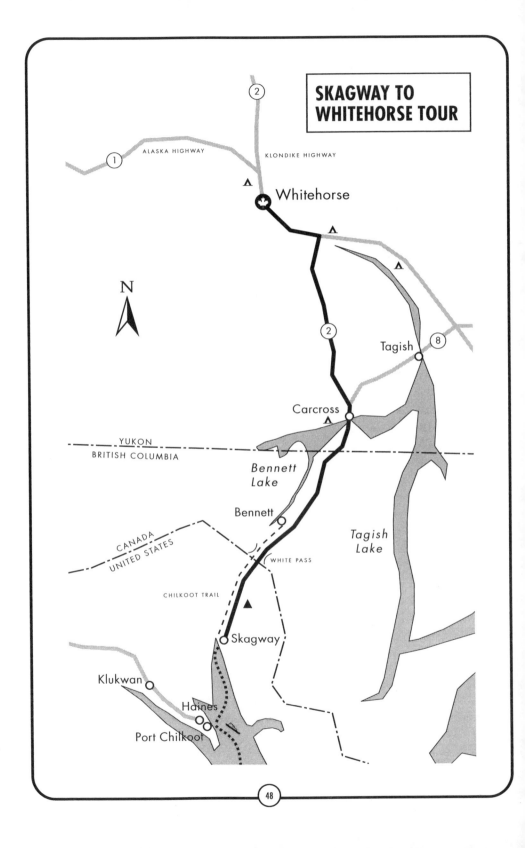

SKAGWAY TO
WHITEHORSE TOUR

② ①
ALASKA HIGHWAY   KLONDIKE HIGHWAY

Whitehorse

N

② ⑧
Tagish

Carcross

YUKON
BRITISH COLUMBIA

Bennett
Lake

Bennett

Tagish
Lake

CANADA
UNITED STATES

WHITE PASS

CHILKOOT TRAIL

Skagway

Klukwan

Haines

Port Chilkoot

way crosses the summit at 1,004 meters (3,290 feet) above sea level. Over the hills to the east, the railway line slips through White Pass.

The White Pass was often used as an alternate to the arduous Chilkoot Trail by those gold-seekers who could afford pack animals. Few drivers carried enough food and water for their burdened beasts and the White Pass route was soon known as the Dead Horse Trail.

35.6 km (22.1 miles) Canada customs

Just past the summit and around the bend is Canada customs.

From here, a rocky platform matted with heather and dotted with ragged lakes stretches away from the road for miles. The glacially gouged landscape is unlike that of virtually any other in the world.

Continue along the highway through the southern lakes area, which provides a transition from the stark summit to the dry interior valleys.

Where the highway crosses the railway, there was once a town of more than 20 buildings known as Log Cabin, which included the log quarters of the North West Mounted Police. A few weathered sheds and stumps of trees cut more than 80 years ago, are all that remain.

81.1 km (50.1 miles) British Columbia-Yukon border

Watch for the wild blueberries in this area. The long narrow Tutshi River stretches along the highway. Ride past Windy Arm where several promising claims were staked at the turn of the century.

106 km (66 miles) Carcross

The road then passes through the Carcross Indian reserve and bridges the narrows between Bennett Lake and Tagish Lake at the village of Carcross.

120 km (74.6 miles) Emerald Lake

Between Carcross and Whitehorse, the road follows the valleys of the Watson and Yukon rivers. Just north of Carcross is Emerald Lake, which reflects unforgettable brilliant hues.

You then pass the Carcross Desert, hailed as the smallest desert in the world.

About 20 km (12 miles) outside Whitehorse is the Wolf Creek Campground, a well-maintained territorial campsite with some pleasant walking and biking trails.

176 km (109 miles) Whitehorse

For a more interesting approach to the city, take the turn off the highway for Miles Canyon. It was here that hundreds of reckless gold seekers smashed their crude boats in the once treacherous White Horse Rapids of the Yukon River.

The gently hilly road follows the narrow canyon, which opens to Schwatka Lake and Whitehorse's downtown core.

(Leanna Rathkelly)

British Columbia

An immense diversity of spectacular scenery makes British Columbia—Canada's western-most province—an ideal bicycle touring destination. You can ride to wilderness Pacific coast beaches backed by rainforest, explore the picturesque and tranquil islands in the Strait of Georgia by ferry and by bike, cycle through northwestern British Columbia and board a ferry through the fjords of the Inside Passage, or ride from open ranchland in the Interior to snow-capped mountains.

Weather: British Columbia has many different climates because of its location between the Pacific Ocean and the high mountain ranges. The warm Japanese current gives the coastal region a very moderate climate of mild, wet and foggy winters and moderate dry summers.

The west coast of Vancouver Island is the wettest part of Canada, with an average annual rainfall of 305 to 483 centimeters (120 to 190 inches). Victoria's summer temperatures average from 10 degrees Celsius at night to 20 degrees Celsius in the day (50 to 68 degrees Fahrenheit).

The Coast Mountains also receive a heavy rainfall from the moisture-laden winds from the Pacific. Vancouver's summer temperatures average from a high of 23 degrees Celsius to a low of 11 degrees Celsius (74 to 52 degrees Fahrenheit).

East of the Coast Mountains, the Interior is dry. The higher air currents travel on to the lofty Selkirk Mountains, where it rains frequently. The Rocky Mountains are protected by the Selkirks and receive much less precipitation.

Tourist Information: General tourist information, including a road map and an accommodations guide with provincial and national parks campgrounds, as well as private campgrounds listings, is available from Tourism British Columbia, Parliament Buildings, Victoria, British Columbia V8V 1X4, or call toll-free from Canada or the United States 1-800-663-6000, overseas or local calls to (604) 387-1642.

Roads: Recorded reports on road conditions in main corridors are available. From Abbotsford call (604) 855-4997; Kamloops (604) 371-4994; Kelowna (604) 860-4997; Greater Vancouver (604) 525-4997; Victoria (604) 380-4997; Whistler (604) 938-4997; from all other parts of British Columbia call toll-free 1-800-663-4997.

Hostels: Canadian Hostelling Association, Pacific Region, 1515 Discovery Street, Vancouver, British Columbia V6R 4K5, (604) 224-7177.

Ferries: British Columbia Ferry Corporation operates ferries on 25 routes on the province's coastline, including:

• from Horseshoe Bay in West Vancouver to Nanaimo, the Sunshine Coast and Bowen Island in Howe Sound;
• from Tsawwassen near Delta to Swartz Bay near Victoria, the southern Gulf Islands and Nanaimo;
• from Swartz Bay to the southern Gulf Islands, and between the southern Gulf Islands;
• from Crofton on Vancouver Island to Vesuvius on Saltspring Island;
• from Vancouver Island to the northern Gulf Islands;
• from Little River near Comox and Westview near Powell River on the Sunshine Coast; and
• from northern Vancouver Island to Prince Rupert and from Prince Rupert to the Queen Charlotte Islands.

For information, call in Vancouver (604) 669-1211; in Victoria (604) 386-3431; or write BC Ferry Corp., 1112 Fort Street, Victoria, British Columbia V8V 4V2. For 24-hour recorded schedule information for mainland to Vancouver Island ferries, call in Vancouver (604) 685-1021; in Victoria (604) 656-0757; in Nanaimo (604) 753-6626.

Port Angeles, Washington, to Victoria, British Columbia: ferry operated by Black Ball Transport, 430 Belleville Street, Victoria, British Columbia V8V 1W9, (604) 386-2202; in Port Angeles (206) 457-4491.

Anacortes, Washington, to Sidney, British Columbia: Washington State Ferries, Blaney Terminals Limited, Port Agents, 2499 Ocean Avenue, Sidney, British Columbia V8L 1T3, (604) 656-1531 or 381-1551; Seattle (206) 464-6400.

Inland Ferries Crossing Rivers on the Mainland: operated by the Ministry of Transportation and Highways Marine Services, 3D-940 Blanshard Street, Victoria, British Columbia V8W 3E6, (604) 387-6931.

Trains: For information on VIA Rail in British Columbia, contact your local VIA Rail agent or call toll-free 1-800-561-8630. British Columbia Railway runs along the Howe Sound and through the Interior (passing Squamish, Whistler, Pemberton and Lillooet) to Prince George. Contact British Columbia Railway, 1311 West First Street, North Vancouver, British Columbia V6B 4X6; (604) 631-3500, or for recorded information (604) 631-3501.

Airports: The international airports at Vancouver and Victoria are served by Air Canada, Canadian Airlines International and other major airlines, with connections to smaller centers in British Columbia.

Buses: Mainland British Columbia is served by Greyhound Lines, telephone (604) 662-3222. Maverick Coach Lines runs from Vancouver to Vancouver Island (via Nanaimo) and to Squamish, Whistler, Pemberton and the Sunshine Coast; telephone (604) 662-8051. Pacific Coach Lines runs from Vancouver to Victoria; telephone (604) 662-8074.

Bicycling: Bicycling Association of British Columbia, 322-1367 West Broadway, Vancouver, British Columbia V6H 4A9, (604) 737-3034, Hotline (604) 731-RIDE.

Capital: Victoria, situated at the south tip of Vancouver Island, is known for its British flavor. The city is popular with retired seniors; it has a higher proportion of seniors than other large cities in Canada.

Population: 3,282,061 (1991 census), third-largest population of Canada's ten provinces. More than half the province's population lives in the metropolitan Vancouver area.

History: Native people, who have lived here since after the last Ice Age, developed a rich culture, which included totem poles and the potlatch. The first European to land in British Columbia was James Cook of Britain who went ashore at Nootka Sound on Vancouver Island's west coast. British fur traders developed a flourishing trade with the coastal Indians.

Settlement by Europeans began in the early nineteenth century. Gold rushes, beginning in 1857 on the Lower Fraser River and the Cariboo Mountains attracted thousands of fortune seekers.

In 1871, British Columbia joined Canada on the condition that a railway be built linking it with central Canada. The Canadian Pacific Railway was completed in 1885.

The province's economy is based on tourism, mining, forestry, fishing and agriculture.

Area: 947,800 square km (365,850 square miles)

Terrain: In the west are the Coast Mountains, averaging 130 km (80 miles) wide and extending to the deeply indented coast. The highest peak in the lush rain-forest and glacier-covered Coast Mountains is 3,978-meter (13,260-foot) Mount Waddington.

On the eastern side of the province are the Rocky Mountains, which average 80 km (50 miles) wide and form an almost continuous succession of ridges and peaks reaching 3,892 meters (12,972 feet) at Mount Robson, the highest peak in the Canadian Rockies. West of the Rockies are the Columbia Mountains consisting of the Purcell, Selkirk, Monashee and Cariboo ranges.

In the south central part of the province is the Interior Plateau. To the north are the Hazelton, Skeena, Omineca and Cassiar mountains.

British Columbia's highest point is 4,663-meter (15,298-foot) Mount Fairweather, at the south end of the St. Elias Range on the British Columbia–Alaska border; the lowest is sea level along the coast.

VANCOUVER BICYCLE ROUTES

British Columbia's largest city, Vancouver, lies on a peninsula surrounded by the Burrard Inlet, the Strait of Georgia and the Fraser River. The Coast Mountains provide a backdrop.

Cyclists can enjoy Vancouver's scenery by riding quiet streets of some of its neighborhoods. There are also multi-use paths along the Stanley Park Seawall, False Creek and at the University of British Columbia. The 7-Eleven Trail follows the route of a 1891 tram line that linked Vancouver and New Westminster.

Other good cycling is available at Pacific Spirit Regional Park (its trails are particularly suited to mountain biking) and along the shoreline of West Vancouver.

GULF ISLANDS

Overview: One of the West Coast's most spectacular and popular cycling areas, the Gulf Islands comprise approximately one hundred peaceful enchanting islands on the west side of the Straight of Georgia. In the distance are the snow-capped peaks on the mainland and Vancouver Island. Beaches abound in marine life. Bring a local tide table and guidebook to explore the tidepools and mudflats at low tide.

Ferries: Many islands are linked by ferry, so you can explore them at your leisure. To ensure your cycling trip fits with the island ferry schedule, don't plan on covering more than one island in a day. Best bets are Pender Island and Saltspring Island, both with regular ferries from Swartz Bay and Tsawwassen.

Roads: The roads on the Gulf Islands are quiet, but they are narrow, often winding, and tend to have some very steep (12 to 16 per cent grade) hills. Traffic can be heavy near ferry sailing times. These islands can be a delight, but exercise caution at all times.

Camping: Provincial park campgrounds are located on only three islands: Pender, Galiano and Saltspring. Private campgrounds are also available on several islands. Campsites are limited, and drinking water can be hard to find throughout the islands, so some advance planning is necessary. Saltspring also has a hostel operated by the Canadian Hostelling Association.

Weather: Best cycling is found from May to mid-June and late August to early October. During July and August the roads can be busy. Winter cycling can be enjoyed on the Gulf

Islands and the Saanich Peninsula, but be prepared for rain.

Following are the best tours of this very scenic region.

SALTSPRING ISLAND AND VANCOUVER ISLAND

Length: 70 km (45 miles)
Time: 2 days
Rating: Easy
Terrain: Saltspring has farms, tall trees and some steep hills.
Roads: Saltspring's roads are narrow, so keep well to the right.
Traffic: Can get heavy when ferries are loading or unloading.
Start: Long Harbour on Saltspring Island. Take the ferry from Tsawwassen, south of Vancouver. Reservations are required for motor vehicles traveling from Tsawwassen to the Gulf Islands (see beginning of chapter for BC Ferry Corporation telephone numbers).

From Swartz Bay, near Victoria, there is a ferry to Fulford Harbour on Saltspring Island. You can also reach Vesuvius Bay on Saltspring Island from Crofton on Vancouver Island.

Overview: Saltspring Island is the largest Gulf Island. It also has the best variety of accommodation in the Gulf Islands. This tour uses ferries for a circuit route visiting Saltspring Island and Vancouver Island.

THE ROUTE:
0 km (0 miles) Long Harbour

Along Saltspring Island roads are farms and Douglas fir trees. There is a long steep hill just south of Ganges and another

long hill near Fulford Harbour. There is camping at Ruckle Provincial Park at Beaver Point, where campsites overlook the straits and the ferry run to Vancouver, as well as at Mouat Provincial Park at Ganges.

Take Long Harbour Road to Robinson Road.

Option: Ruckle Provincial Park, 17km (11 miles)

Go left on Robinson Road and right on Fulford-Gonges Road to Beddis Road. Turn left onto Beddis Road. Go right on Cusheon Lake Road and then left on Stewart Road to Beaver Point Road. Go left on Beaver Point Road to Ruckle Provincial Park.

Main tour

25 km (15 miles) Vesuvius Bay

From the junction of Long Harbour Road and Robinson Road, turn right on Robinson Road. Go right on Stark Road and then left onto Walker's Hook Road. Ride Walker's Hook Road which links with North Beach Road along the water.

Go right on North End Road and follow it to Sunset Drive. Go left onto Sunset Drive to Vesuvius Bay and the ferry terminal.

Ferry: Crofton on Vancouver Island (crossing time: 20 minutes)

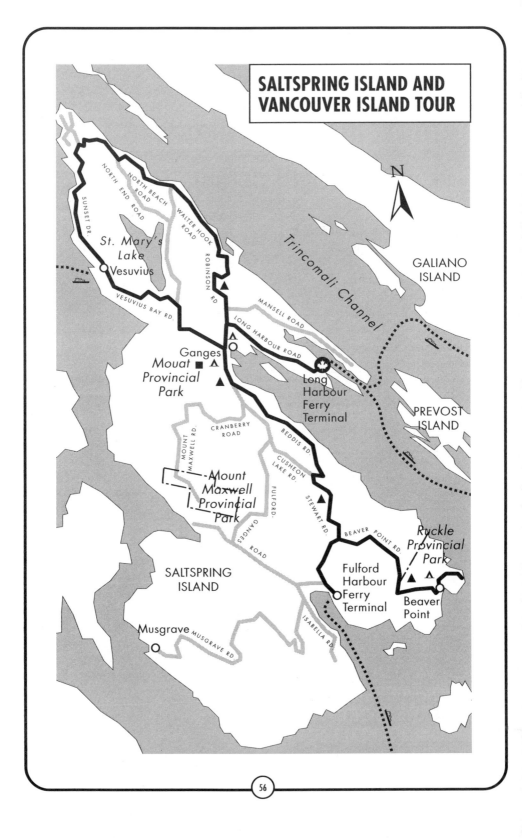

SALTSPRING ISLAND AND VANCOUVER ISLAND TOUR

N

Trincomali Channel

GALIANO ISLAND

NORTH BEACH ROAD

NORTH END ROAD

SUNSET DR.

WALTER HOOK ROAD

ROBINSON RD.

St. Mary's Lake

Vesuvius

VESUVIUS BAY RD.

MANSELL ROAD

LONG HARBOUR ROAD

Long Harbour Ferry Terminal

PREVOST ISLAND

Ganges

Mouat Provincial Park

CRANBERRY ROAD

MOUNT MAXWELL RD.

BEDDIS RD.

CUSHEON LAKE RD.

FULFORD-

Mount Maxwell Provincial Park

STEWART RD.

GANGES ROAD

Ruckle Provincial Park

BEAVER POINT RD.

SALTSPRING ISLAND

Fulford Harbour Ferry Terminal

Beaver Point

Musgrave

MUSGRAVE RD

ISABELLA RD.

Take the ferry to Crofton on Vancouver Island.

64 km (40 miles) Nanaimo

To head toward Nanaimo, 39 km (24 miles) away, ride north on Highway 1A through Chemainus to Highway 1. If it's a hot day the Chemainus River is a good spot for a swim. Continue north through the town of Ladysmith, and past rolling hills and farm country around Yellow Point. From Ladysmith to Nanaimo, Highway 1 has a well-paved shoulder.

Ferry: Nanaimo to Horseshoe Bay (crossing time: 1 hour 35 minutes); Nanaimo to Tsawwassen (crossing time: 2 hours)

At Nanaimo, the ferry takes you to Horseshoe Bay and the city of Vancouver, or to Tsawwassen south of Vancouver.

More Information: For local ferry information when you're on Saltspring Island call (604) 537-9921; in the Nanaimo area call (604) 753-6626.

SATURNA ISLAND, PENDER ISLANDS, GALIANO ISLAND AND MAYNE ISLAND

Time: Explore one island per day.
Rating: Easy
Terrain: Hilly
Roads: Generally well paved, but do not have paved shoulders.
Traffic: Quiet, with very little traffic; weekends during the peak summer season, and at the end of the workday on North Pender, can be busy.
Overview: These very scenic islands are accessible by ferries from Tsawwassen near Vancouver, Swartz Bay near Victoria, and Long Harbour on Saltspring Island. Reservations are required for motor vehicles traveling from Tsawwassen to the Gulf Islands (see beginning of chapter for BC Ferry Corporation telephone numbers).

There are provincial parks with camping on Pender Island and Galiano Islands.

SATURNA ISLAND

Length: 34 km (21 miles)
Start: Saturna Island ferry terminal
THE ROUTE:
0 km (0 miles) Saturna Island ferry terminal
15 km (9 miles) East Point

East Point Road is an enjoyable ride with little traffic. It goes along the water and is bordered by tall trees. At many places there is access to the beach. There is a steep climb en route.

From the ferry terminal, go

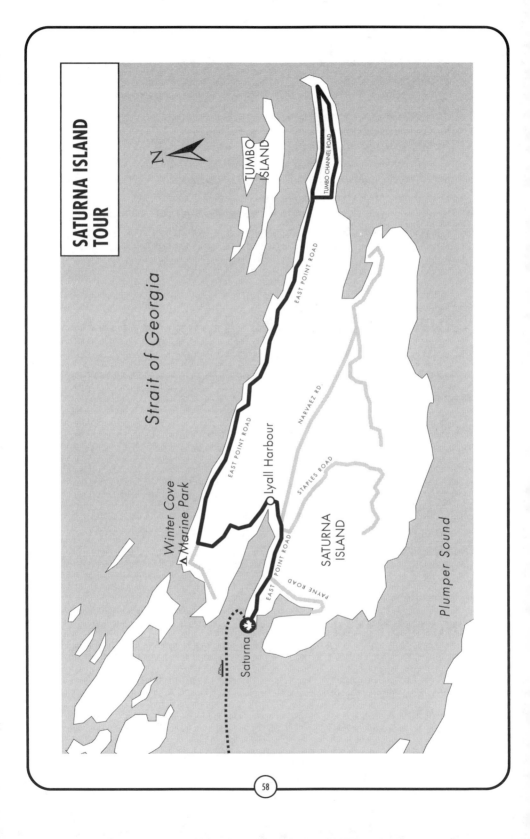

SATURNA ISLAND
TOUR

N

Strait of Georgia

TUMBO
ISLAND

TUMBO CHANNEL ROAD

EAST POINT ROAD

NARVAEZ RD.

Winter Cove
▲ Marine Park

EAST POINT ROAD

○ Lyall Harbour

STAPLES ROAD

SATURNA
ISLAND

EAST POINT ROAD

PAYNE ROAD

Saturna

Plumper Sound

up the hill and follow East Point Road which has little traffic to Tumbo Channel Road. Ride Tumbo Channel Road to East Point, 15 km (9 miles) from the ferry terminal.

At East Point is a lighthouse and a good public beach. On a clear day you can see the outline of the Tsawwassen ferry terminal.

30 km (18 miles) Saturna Island ferry terminal

From East Point, take Cliffside Road, turn right on Fiddler Road and then left on East Point Road. Ride East Point Road back to the Saturna Island ferry terminal. There are no campgrounds on Saturna Island.

NORTH PENDER ISLAND AND SOUTH PENDER ISLAND

Length: 24 km (15 miles) each way
Start: Otter Bay ferry terminal on Pender Island.
THE ROUTE:
0 km (0 miles) Otter Bay ferry terminal
24 km (15 miles) Gowlland Point

Explore the island's roads while passing many scenic bays. The island has a quiet lifestyle with many hobby farms. From the Otter Bay ferry terminal on North Pender Island, ride up to MacKinnon Road and take it to Otter Bay Road.

Go left on Otter Bay Road. Turn right on Port Washington Road, and then right on Corbett Road. Go left on Amies Road and then right onto Bedwell Harbour Road.

Turn left onto Canal Road and cross the bridge to South Pender Island. Ride Canal Road to Spalding Road. Turn right on Spalding Road and left on Gowlland Point Road to Gowlland Point.

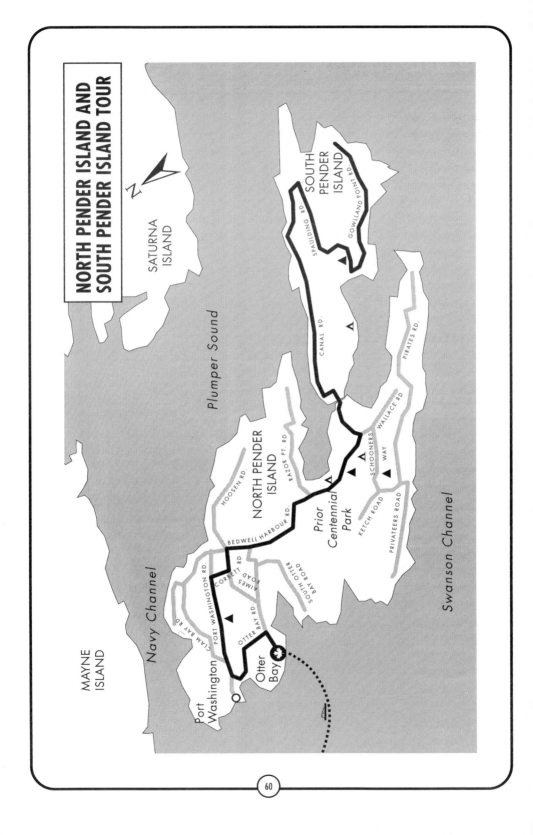

MAYNE
ISLAND

SATURNA
ISLAND

Navy Channel

Plumper Sound

Swanson Channel

NORTH PENDER
ISLAND

SOUTH
PENDER
ISLAND

Port
Washington

Otter
Bay

CLAM BAY RD.

PORT WASHINGTON RD.

CORBETT RD.

AIMES ROAD

OTTER BAY RD.

SOUTH OTTER BAY ROAD

HOOSEN RD.

RAZOR PT. RD.

BEDWELL HARBOUR RD.

Prior
Centennial
Park

KETCH ROAD

SCHOONERS WAY

WALLACE RD.

PRIVATEERS ROAD

PIRATES RD.

CANAL RD.

SPAULDING RD.

GOWLLAND POINT RD.

GALIANO ISLAND

Length: 28 km (17 miles) each way
Start: Sturdies Bay ferry terminal on Galiano Island
THE ROUTE:
0 km (0 miles) Sturdies Bay ferry terminal
28 km (17 miles) Porlier Pass

From Sturdies Bay, take Sturdies Bay Road to Georgeson Bay Road. Turn left on Georgeson Bay Road and follow it to Montague Road. Turn right onto Montague Road.

Ride Montague Road and go right onto Clanton Road and then left onto Porlier Pass Road. Ride Porlier Pass Road to Porlier Pass at the north end of the island.

At Porlier Pass you'll see fishing boats. From here you can retrace your route to Sturdies Bay.

There is camping at Montague Harbour Provincial Park and Dionisio Point Provincial Park.

MAYNE ISLAND

Length: 22 km (14 mile) loop

Start: Village Bay ferry terminal on Mayne Island

THE ROUTE:
Ride the island's quiet roads past picturesque farms. Hotel accommodations are available.

Many American miners stopped at Miner's Bay on their way to the Cariboo gold rush, and a museum describes the area's history. Mayne Island was the first place apples were grown in British Columbia.
0 km (0 miles) Village Bay ferry terminal
13 km (8 miles) Bennett Bay beach

To do a loop from the Village Bay ferry terminal: Turn left onto Village Bay road. Go left on Fernhill Road and then right onto Georgina Point Road. Then go right on Waugh Road and right again on Campbell Bay Road to Fernhill Road.

Turn left onto Fernhill Road and ride it to Bennett Bay Beach.
22 km (14 miles) Village Bay ferry terminal

From Bennett Beach ride back to the junction of Fernhill Road and Horton Bay Road. Go left onto Horton Bay Road and then right on Gallagher Road.

Turn right on Marine Drive and go right on Mariner's Way. Take another right on Dalton Drive to Village Bay Road. Turn

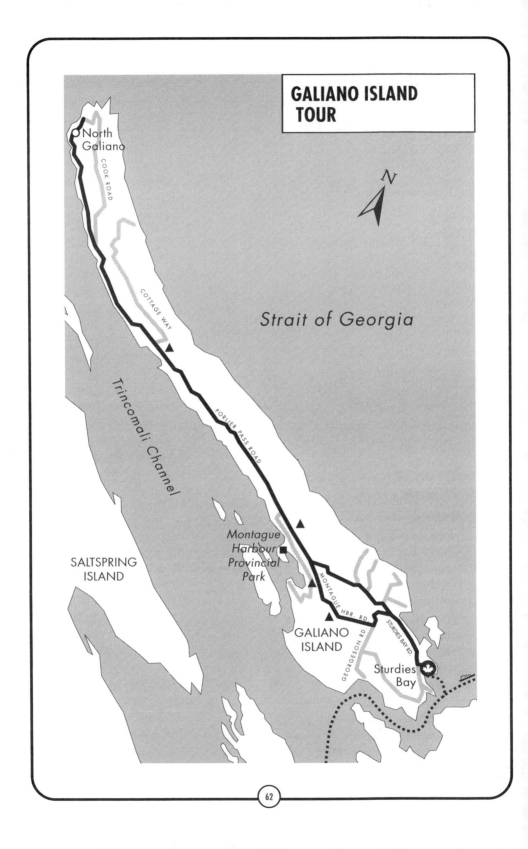

GALIANO ISLAND
TOUR

N

Strait of Georgia

North
Galiano

COOK ROAD

COTTAGE WAY

Trincomali Channel

PORLIER PASS ROAD

Montague
Harbour
Provincial
Park

SALTSPRING
ISLAND

GALIANO
ISLAND

MONTAGUE HBR. RD.

GEORGESON RD.

STURDIES BAY RD.

Sturdies
Bay

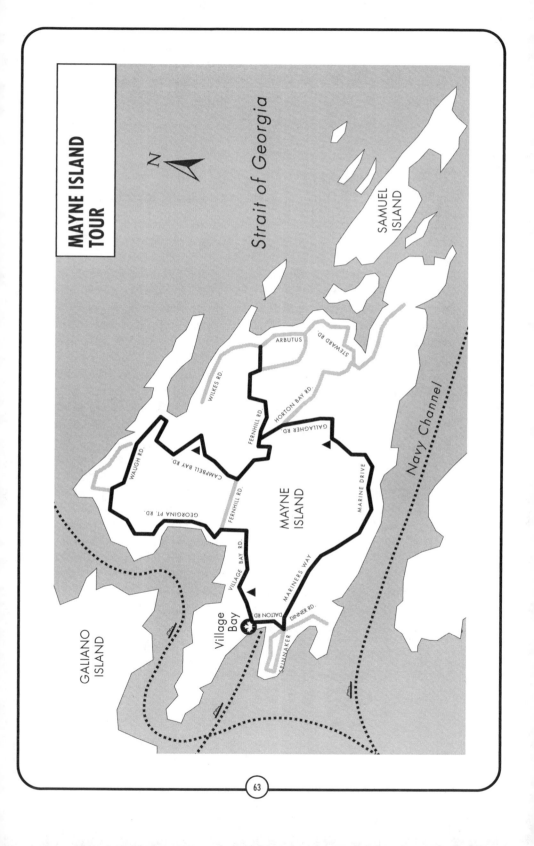

right on Village Bay Road and ride to the Village Bay ferry terminal.

More Information: For ferry information while on the southern Gulf Islands, call (604) 629-3215.

GABRIOLA ISLAND

Length: 35 km (22 miles)
Time: One or two days
Rating: Easy
Terrain: Forest, farm and residential
Roads: Mostly good, paved.
Traffic: Mostly light, except for commuting traffic to Nanaimo.
Start: Gabriola Island ferry terminal, reached by ferry from Nanaimo. Crossing time is 20 minutes.
Overview: There are many scenic farms on the island. There are no provincial park campgrounds, but there are two private campgrounds and several lodges offering accommodation.

THE ROUTE:

0 km (0 miles) Gabriola Island ferry terminal

15 km (9 miles) Silva Bay

From the ferry terminal, ride up the hill and go right on South Road. Follow South Road, which has many nice views of the water, to Silva Bay where there are several marinas.

32 km (20 miles) Orlebar Point

From Silva bay, continue on South Road to North Road. Ride North Road the length of the island. North Road links again with South Road near the ferry terminal.

Turn right on Taylor Bay Road. Along the way are sandstone formations, known as Malaspina Galleries. Turn right onto Berry Point Road. You ride past Twin Beaches in Gabriola Sands Provincial Park to Orlebar Point, a 17 km (11 mile) ride from Silva Bay and the highlight of this scenic island.

More Information: For ferry information while on the southern Gulf Islands, call (604) 629-3215.

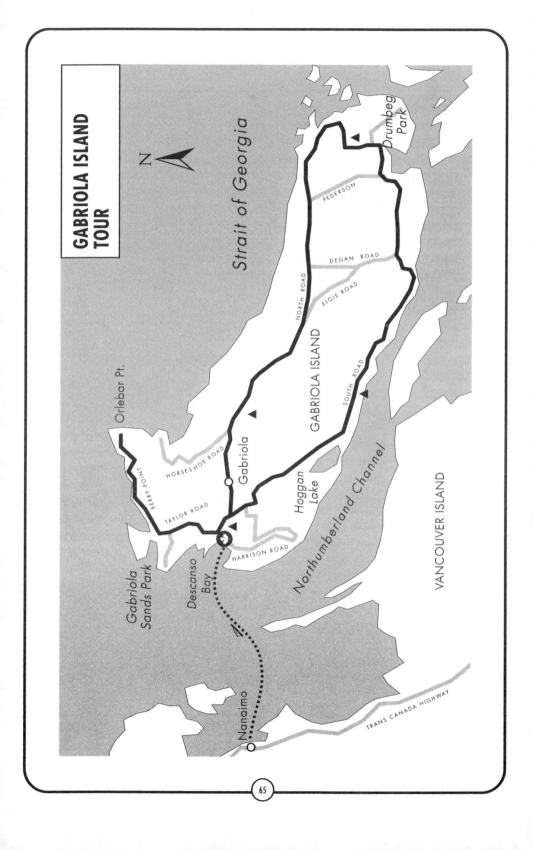

GABRIOLA ISLAND
TOUR

N

Strait of Georgia

Orlebar Pt.

Drumbeg
Park

PEDERSON

DEGAN ROAD

ELGIE ROAD

NORTH ROAD

GABRIOLA ISLAND

SOUTH ROAD

Gabriola

HORSES HOE ROAD

BERRY POINT

TAYLOR ROAD

Hoggan Lake

Northumberland Channel

HARRISON ROAD

Gabriola
Sands Park

Descanso
Bay

VANCOUVER ISLAND

Nanaimo

TRANS CANADA HIGHWAY

DENMAN ISLAND AND HORNBY ISLAND

Length: 150 km (93 miles) return
Time: Two days
Rating: Easy
Terrain: Flat, hilly
Roads: Highway 19 has a wide paved shoulder.
Traffic: Fairly light on the islands; sometimes heavy on Island Highway 19.
Start: Nanaimo, which can be reached by ferry from Horseshoe Bay or Tsawwassen both near Vancouver.
Overview: Denman and Hornby Islands, south of Courtenay, are probably the easiest islands to tour since road distances are short. There are several campgrounds on Hornby Island, and bed-and-breakfasts are available on both islands.

THE ROUTE:

0 km (0 miles) Nanaimo
90 km (56 miles) Buckley Bay

From Nanaimo, head north on Highway 19. The scenic highway is well paved and has a wide paved shoulder. Along the way, you have good views at Nanoose Bay, Parksville, Qualicum Beach, Qualicum Bay, Bowser and Fanny Bay. The beaches along the highway are good stops. Campgrounds are available near Qualicum Bay and Fanny Bay.

Ride to Buckley Bay, a distance of 90 km (56 miles) from Nanaimo.

Ferry: Buckley Bay to Denman Island (crossing time: 10 minutes)

Take the ferry from Buckley Bay to Denman Island.

90 km (56 miles) Denman Island ferry terminal

From the Denman Island ferry terminal you have a steep climb for 0.5 km (0.3 miles).

101 km (63 miles) Gravelly Bay ferry terminal

Explore Denman Island. Fillongley Provincial Park with camping facilities is on the east side of the island.

Ride along Denman Road and turn right onto East Road for 11 km (7 miles) to Gravelly Bay ferry terminal.

Ferry: Hornby Island (crossing time: 10 minutes)

101 km (63 miles) Hornby Island ferry terminal

When you're ready, take the ferry from the Gravelly Bay terminal to Hornby Island. There are several campgrounds on Hornby Island.

114 km (71 miles) Helliwell Park

From the ferry terminal, take Shingle Spit Road up the hill to Central Road. Go right onto Central Road and ride to the intersection with St. John Road. Ride up the hill to Helliwell Park, 13 km (8 miles) from

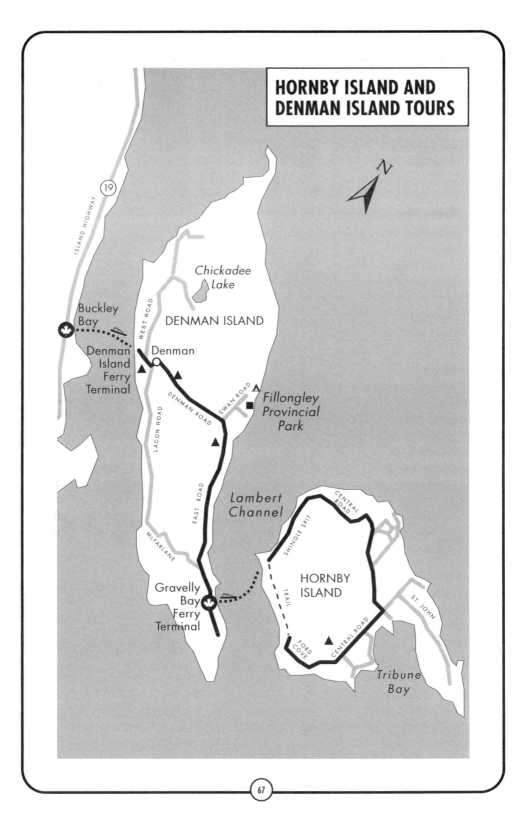

HORNBY ISLAND AND
DENMAN ISLAND TOURS

N

Island Highway (19)

Chickadee
Lake

DENMAN ISLAND

Buckley
Bay

WEST ROAD

Denman
Island
Ferry
Terminal

Denman

SWAN ROAD

Fillongley
Provincial
Park

DENMAN ROAD

LACON ROAD

EAST ROAD

McFARLANE

Lambert
Channel

CENTRAL ROAD

SHINGLE SPIT

HORNBY
ISLAND

TRAIL

Gravelly
Bay
Ferry
Terminal

FORD COVE

ST. JOHN

CENTRAL ROAD

Tribune
Bay

the Hornby Island ferry terminal.

At Helliwell Park are grassy cliffs dropping into the ocean. You can see eagles, other birds and whales during their migratory season.

More Information: For ferry information while in Buckley Bay, call (604) 335-0323.

VANCOUVER ISLAND SUNSHINE COAST LOOP

Length: 250 km (155 miles) loop; you can ride this tour in a clockwise (as described here) or counter-clockwise direction.

Time: Three to four days for the complete loop; a 2-day trip is pretty tiring; it can be a one-week trip if you add several side trips.

Rating: Challenging

Terrain: Mountainous

Roads: Paved, narrow in some areas.

Traffic: Can get a little frantic close to ferry departure time.

Connects with: Denman Island and Hornby Island

Start: Nanaimo, reached by ferry from Horseshoe Bay near Vancouver, ferry from Tsawwassen south of Vancouver, or by road from Victoria.

Overview: This challenging circuit goes north along the Strait of Georgia to the ferry at Little River. You then cross the strait to Westview and go south along the fjord-indented Sunshine Coast. This part involves two ferry rides. You eventually reach Horseshoe Bay near Vancouver, where you can take the ferry back to Vancouver Island or continue into the city of Vancouver.

Even though it's called the Sunshine Coast, the area can get some heavy rain.

THE ROUTE:

0 km (0 miles) Nanaimo

110 km (68 miles) Courtenay

From Nanaimo, go north on Highway 19 along the Strait of Georgia for 110 km (68 miles) to Courtenay. Most of the highway is level and smooth and has a wide, paved shoulder. At Parksville the shoulder is rough.

The route has beautiful views of the Strait of Georgia and Coastal Mountains. Take time to enjoy the beaches at Parksville and Qualicum Beach.

Side trip: Buckley Bay to Denman and Hornby Islands

From Buckley Bay you could take a sidetrip to Denman and Hornby Islands (described in this chapter).

Main tour

There is a long steep hill just before Comox. There are campgrounds near Qualicum Beach, Fanny Bay and Courtenay, and numerous motels along the route.

124 km (77 miles) Little River

At Courtenay turn off Highway

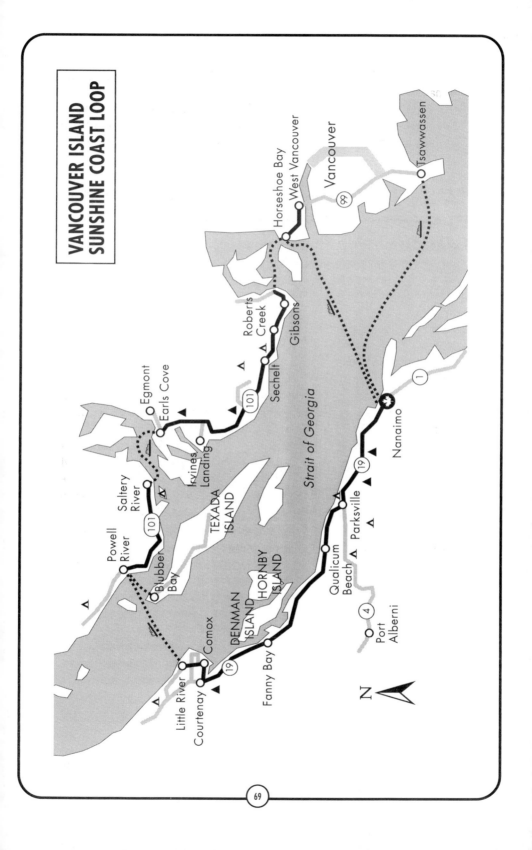

VANCOUVER ISLAND SUNSHINE COAST LOOP

Tsawwassen

Vancouver

West Vancouver

Horseshoe Bay

(99)

(1)

Gibsons

Roberts Creek

Sechelt

Strait of Georgia

(101)

Earls Cove

Egmont

Irvines Landing

Saltery River

Powell River

(101)

Blubber Bay

TEXADA ISLAND

HORNBY ISLAND

DENMAN ISLAND

Comox

Little River

Courtenay

(19)

Fanny Bay

Qualicum Beach

Parksville

Port Alberni

(4)

Nanaimo

(19)

N

19, and ride to Little River via Comox.

Ferry: Little River to Powell River/Westview (crossing time: 1 hour and 20 minutes)

Take the ferry from Little River to Powell River/Westview.

Side trip: Ferry from Powell River/Westview to Texada Island (crossing time: 35 minutes)

A side trip can be taken from Powell River/Westview by ferry to Blubber Bay on Texada Island.

Main tour
155 km (96 miles) Saltery Bay

Ride south along the Sunshine Coast from Powell River/Westview for 31 km (19 miles) on Highway 101 to Saltery Bay.

The highway is well paved, but does not have paved shoulders. It's hilly, especially near Saltery Bay where there is a long hill. The view at the top is well worth the climb.

There are nice beaches at Powell River and Saltery Bay campsites. Motels are located in Westview and Powell River.

Ferry: Saltery Bay to Earls Cove (crossing time: 50 minutes)

From Saltery Bay take the ferry to Earls Cove.

Side trip: Earls Cove to Egmont, 6 km (4 miles)

From Earls Cove, you can take a 6 km (4 mile) sidetrip to Egmont, where you can hike 3 km (1.8 miles) to the Skookumchuck Narrows to view the tidal rapids.

Main tour
238 km (148 miles) Langdale

From Earls Cove, ride south on the Sunshine Coast highway to Langdale, a distance of 83 km (52 miles). The highway is well paved and has a gravel shoulder. It's very hilly, so make sure you have a low gear range.

At Pender Harbour you have a view of the rugged coastline. At Sechelt there is a beautiful waterfront. Camping is available at Porpoise Bay just north of Sechelt and at Roberts Creek.

During peak season, car traffic from the ferry may be directed to bypass North Road— the most scenic parts of Gibsons; cyclists can, of course, ignore these signs.

Motels are available in Gibsons, Sechelt and Pender Harbour.

Ferry: Langdale to Horseshoe Bay (crossing time: 40 minutes)

Take the ferry from Langdale to Horseshoe Bay just north of Vancouver. If you want to return to the starting point, you can take the ferry from Horseshoe Bay to Nanaimo.

More Information: For local ferry information while in Little River call (604) 339-3310; in Powell River (604) 485-2943.

LONG BEACH, PACIFIC RIM NATIONAL PARK

Length: 176 km (109 miles)
Time: Two days
Rating: Challenging
Terrain: Mountainous
Roads: The road from Parksville through Port Alberni to Long Beach is narrow, winding and hilly.
Traffic: Moderate tourist traffic in summer.
Connects with: Nanaimo to Port Hardy, Sunshine Coast loop, Denman Island and Hornby Island tours.
Start: Nanaimo, reached by ferry from either Horseshoe Bay or Tsawwassen near Vancouver, or by road from Victoria.
Overview: Long Beach is 11 km (7 miles) of surf-swept sandy beaches and rocky headlands stretching along Vancouver Island's west coast. Situated between the fishing villages of Ucluelet and Tofino, Long Beach offers a beautiful sandy beach and lots of good campsites. You can take boat tours to watch Pacific gray whales breaching offshore.

Between Port Alberni and Ucluelet there are 100 km (60 miles) of wilderness, so preparation is essential. A scenic alternative to the 150 km (93 mile) hilly road from Port Alberni to Ucluelet is to take the ferry.

Be prepared for rain. Henderson Lake near Long Beach has an annual rainfall of 600 cm (236 inches).

THE ROUTE:

0 km (0 miles) Nanaimo

38 km (24 miles) Parksville

From Nanaimo go north on Highway 19 for 38 km (24 miles) to Parksville.

85 km (53 miles) Port Alberni

Go west on Highway 4 for 47 km (29 miles) to Port Alberni. The road is smooth, has a paved shoulder, and is fairly flat as far as Cameron Lake. En route at Coombs there is a farmers' market.

Cameron Lake is surrounded by towering trees. There are two picnic areas and many nature trails. Cycling from Cameron Lake to Port Alberni you climb over the Alberni Summit, also known as "the Hump".

Port Alberni is a city with hotels, supermarkets, and good salmon fishing.

To get to Long Beach from Port Alberni you have two options.

Option: Ferry from Port Alberni to Ucluelet

You and your bicycle can board the foot passenger ferry M.V. *Lady Rose* which departs from Port Alberni several times a

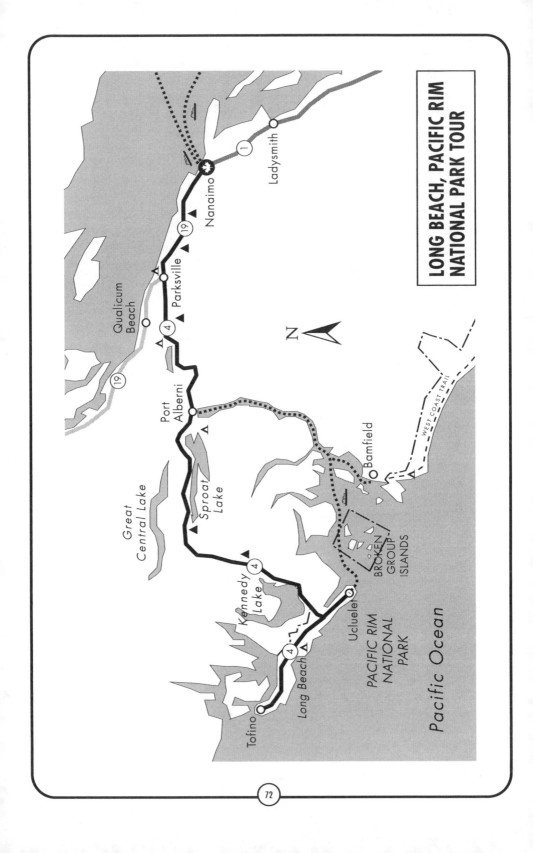

LONG BEACH, PACIFIC RIM
NATIONAL PARK TOUR

Ladysmith

Nanaimo

Qualicum Beach

Parksville

Port Alberni

Great Central Lake

Sproat Lake

Bamfield

WEST COAST TRAIL

Kennedy Lake

BROKEN GROUP ISLANDS

Ucluelet

PACIFIC RIM NATIONAL PARK

Long Beach

Tofino

Pacific Ocean

N

week to Ucluelet, situated just 8 km (5 miles) south of Long Beach. The ferry ride cruises Alberni Inlet with good views of the rugged coastline and various inlets.

Option: Port Alberni to Long Beach via Highway 4

176 km (109 miles) Long Beach

The other option is to cycle along Highway 4 for 91 km (56 miles) to Long Beach. The highway has spectacular scenery and is well paved but has steep climbs and switchbacks. Sproat Lake Provincial Park is a nice spot to stop for a meal or overnight camping. You also pass Kennedy Lake, where there are campgrounds.

There are no stores between Port Alberni and Long Beach, so stock up on food supplies at Port Alberni and be prepared to camp overnight.

Once you reach Long Beach you can get supplies at the villages of Ucluelet and Tofino. Two campgrounds are available at Long Beach, and there is accommodation in Ucluelet and Tofino.

More Informaton: The M.V. *Lady Rose* is operated by Alberni Marine Transportation Ltd., P.O. Box 188, Port Alberni, British Columbia V9Y 7M7, (604) 723-8313; toll-free 1-800-663-7192 from British Columbia, Alberta and the United States, from April to September. Pacific Rim National Park, P.O. Box 280, Ucluelet, British Columbia V0R 3A0, (604) 726-7721.

Vancouver Island

NANAIMO TO PORT HARDY

Length: 404 km (251 miles)
Time: Three to four days
Rating: Intermediate to expert
Terrain: Hilly
Roads: Rural two-lane road
Traffic: Little
Connects with: Ferries to Gulf Islands (described in this chapter)
Start: Nanaimo, which is reached by ferry (from Horseshoe Bay or Tsawwassen—both near Vancouver) or by road from Victoria.
Overview: The northern stretch of

Vancouver Island's Highway 19—the Island Highway—takes you through a scenic and relatively remote part of the island. The Island Highway is the main, north-south link on Vancouver Island. Port Hardy is the terminus for the ferry through the spectacular Inside Passage to Prince Rupert.

If you take the ferry from Port Hardy to Prince Rupert, you can connect with ferries to the Queen Charlotte Islands, Alaska, and the Yukon.

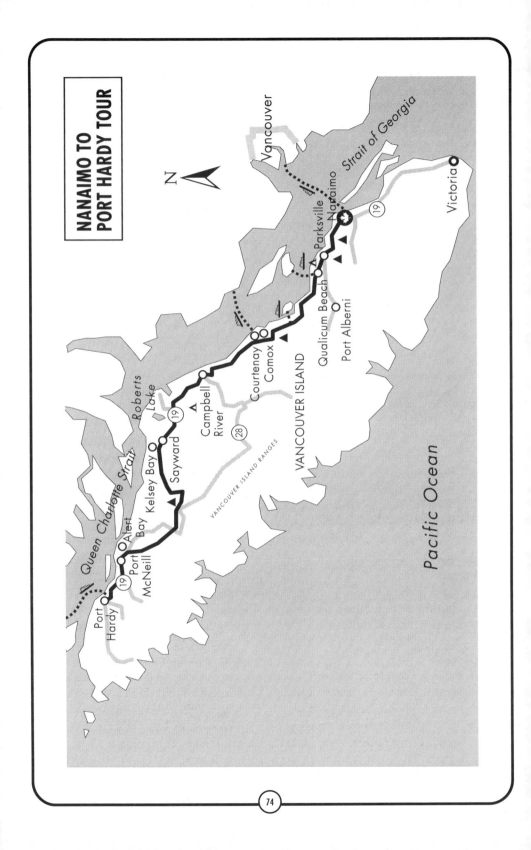

NANAIMO TO
PORT HARDY TOUR

N

Vancouver

Strait of Georgia

Nanaimo

Parksville

Victoria

19

Qualicum Beach

Port Alberni

Courtenay
Comox

VANCOUVER ISLAND

Campbell
River

28

VANCOUVER ISLAND RANGES

Roberts
Lake

19

Sayward

Kelsey Bay

Alert
Bay

Port
McNeill

19

Port
Hardy

Queen Charlotte Strait

Pacific Ocean

From Prince Rupert you can also cycle east on the Yellowhead Highway to Prince George and Jasper (these tours described in this chapter).

THE ROUTE:

0 km (0 miles) Nanaimo

38 km (24 miles) Parksville

From Nanaimo, head north on Highway 19. Generally the highway is in good condition with a good shoulder, although at Parksville the shoulder is rough. Use care on the narrow bridges.

The road follows the scenic coast of the Strait of Georgia. There are numerous beaches, campgrounds and motel accommodations.

Side trips: The Gulf Islands and the Sunshine Coast

From this part of Highway 19 you can take side trips from ferry terminal at Buckley Bay to the Gulf Islands and from the ferry terminal at Little River to Powell River on the Sushine Coast (both are described in this chapter).

Main tour

156 km (97 miles) Campbell River

Continue north along Highway 19 for 118 km (73 miles) to Campbell River, which has all facilities.

223 km (138 miles) Sayward and Kelsey Bay

From Campbell River head north on the Island Highway along a remote, mostly two-lane road with shoulder, and little traffic.

Roberts Lake, 40 km (25 miles) north of Campbell River, has a motel and campground.

At the neighboring communities of Sayward and Kelsey Bay, 67 km (42 miles) north of Campbell River, is a motel and campground.

363 km (225 miles) Port McNeil

Sayward to Port McNeil is a long 130 km (81 miles) ride through some beautiful country including the Nimpkish Valley. There are few facilities en route. Expect to see deer and elk, and possibly brown bear and cougar.

Port McNeil has motels and a campground.

Side trip: Ferry from Port McNeil to Alert Bay

From Port McNeil there is a ferry to Alert Bay, where the Kwakiutl Indian Museum is a worthwhile half-day trip. For local ferry information in Port McNeil, call (604) 956-4533.

404 km (251 miles) Port Hardy

Port Hardy, 41 km (25 miles) from Port McNeil, is at the end of the paved road. Most facilities can be found here.

Option: Ferry to Prince Rupert (cruising time: 15 hours)

Port Hardy is the southern terminus for the ferry to Prince Rupert, a 15-hour ride through the fjords and islands of the Inside Passage. From Prince Rupert you can ride in Northern British Columbia, or board other ferries to Alaska or the Queen Charlotte Islands.

KAMLOOPS TO MOUNT ROBSON

Length: 358 km (222 miles)
Time: Three days
Rating: Intermediate to expert
Terrain: Mountainous
Roads: Relatively flat; one major climb just south of Blue River
Traffic: Light; east of Kamloops there are heavy logging trucks that may use all the paved surface. It's best to pull over and let them pass.
Connects with: Columbia Icefields Parkway tour (described in Alberta chapter).
Start: Kamloops, served by VIA Rail
Overview: Kamloops, from the Indian word *Kumcloops* meaning "meeting of the waters," lies at the confluence of the North and South Thompson rivers, and the junction of the Trans Canada Highway and the Yellowhead Highway 5, about 430 km (267 miles) east of Vancouver.

This tour along Highway 5 passes a variety of scenery as it winds north from the open dry grasslands and ranches around Kamloops, through the Cariboo Mountains and rugged Wells Gray Provincial Park and to the Monarch of the Canadian Rockies at Mount Robson Provincial Park, just east of Jasper National Park.

THE ROUTE:

0 km (0 miles) Kamloops
24 km (15 miles) Heffley Creek

From Kamloops to Heffley Creek, a distance of 24 km (15 miles), Highway 5 has a poorly paved surface but wide shoulders. Exercise caution on this road since it is used by heavy logging trucks, which, at times, require the entire paved surface.

125 km (78 miles) Clearwater

Continue on Highway 5 to Clearwater, 125 km (78 miles) from Kamloops.

Side trip: Clearwater to Wells Gray Provincial Park, 40 km (25 miles)

From Clearwater, you can turn off Highway 5 to Wells Gray Provincial Park.

A vast primitive area in the Cariboo Mountains, 5,200 square-km (2,008 square-mile) Wells Gray Park encompasses glaciers, alpine meadows carpeted with colorful flowers, numerous waterfalls—including 135-meter (450-foot) Helmcken Falls—extinct volcanoes, lava beds and mineral springs. A network of 150 km (95 miles) of hiking trails takes you through the park's varied scenery. Campgrounds are available.

Main tour
190 km (118 miles) Avola

There is camping at North Thompson River Provincial Park near Clearwater and private campgrounds are available at Avola, 65 km (40 miles) from Clearwater, and at Blue River.

338 km (210 miles) Tête Jaune Cache

Ride 38 km (24 miles) north to Blue River. The 90 km (56 miles) between Blue River and Vale-

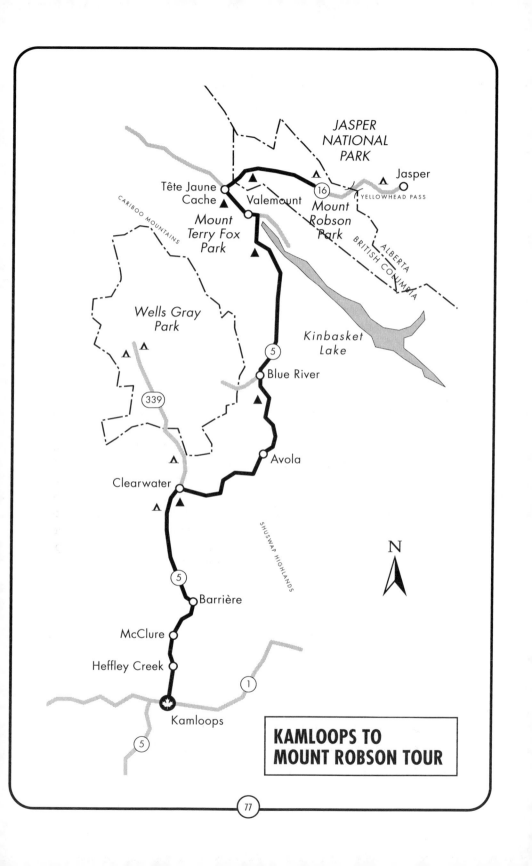

JASPER
NATIONAL
PARK

Jasper

Tête Jaune
Cache

Valemount

Mount
Robson
Park

(16)

YELLOWHEAD PASS

Mount
Terry Fox
Park

CARIBOO MOUNTAINS

ALBERTA

BRITISH COLUMBIA

Wells Gray
Park

Kinbasket
Lake

(5)

Blue River

(339)

Avola

Clearwater

SHUSWAP HIGHLANDS

N

(5)

Barrière

McClure

Heffley Creek

(1)

Kamloops

(5)

**KAMLOOPS TO
MOUNT ROBSON TOUR**

mount has no facilities, no telephones and few residences, so travel self-sufficiently.

Continue for 20 km (12 miles) on Highway 5 to Tête Jaune Cache, 148 km (92 miles) from Avola, and the junction with the Yellowhead Highway—Highway 16.

358 km (222 miles) Mount Robson Provincial Park

From Tête Jaune Cache, head east on Highway 16 for 20 km (12 miles) to Mount Robson Park, which has several campgrounds and motel accommodation.

Mount Robson, the highest peak in the Canadian Rockies, towers 3,954 meters (12,972 feet) over the western entrance to Mount Robson Provincial Park.

Bound on the east by the Continental Divide, the park is 2,172 square km (839 square miles) of rugged snow-capped mountains, broad valleys, steep canyons and glacier-fed lakes, rivers and streams.

Option: Jasper, 80 km (50 miles)

From Mount Robson Park, continue east on Highway 16 for 80 km (50 miles) to Jasper at the northern end of the Icefields Parkway (described in the Alberta chapter).

More Information: Mount Robson Provincial Park, Box 579, Valemount, British Columbia V0E 2Z0, (604) 566-4325. Also Wells Gray Provincial Park, Box 70, Clearwater, British Columbia V0E 1N0, (604) 587-6150.

JASPER TO PRINCE GEORGE

Length: 369 km (229 miles)
Time: Three days
Rating: Intermediate
Terrain: Hilly
Roads: Highway 16 is well paved and hilly; shoulders vary in areas.
Traffic: Tourist traffic during summer months.
Connects with: Icefields Parkway (described in Alberta chapter), Prince George to Prince Rupert tour (from Prince Rupert, ferries can take you to Vancouver Island, the Queen Charlotte Islands and Alaska).
Start: Jasper, Alberta, which can be reached by VIA Rail

Overview: This scenic route takes you on the Yellowhead Route—Highway 16—from Jasper at the northern end of the Icefields Parkway, past Mount Robson, the highest peak in the Canadian Rockies, and along an isolated highway to Prince George at the geographic center of British Columbia.

The Yellowhead Route was named after a French-Iroquois guide whom the French voyageurs nicknamed *Tête Jaune*, "Yellowhead," because of his blonde hair. Working for the Hudson's Bay Company, he crossed what became known as the Yellow-

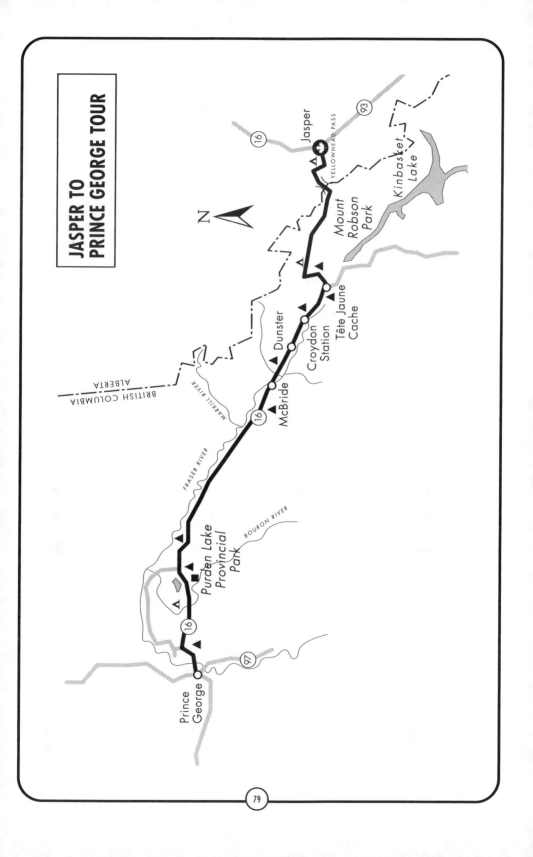

JASPER TO
PRINCE GEORGE TOUR

N

Jasper

16

93

YELLOWHEAD PASS

Kinbasket
Lake

Mount
Robson
Park

Tête Jaune
Cache

Croydon
Station

Dunster

BRITISH COLUMBIA
ALBERTA

McBride

16

McKAIL RIVER

FRASER RIVER

BOURON RIVER

Purden Lake
Provincial
Park

16

97

Prince
George

head Pass numerous times, and made a cache near what is now called Tête Jaune Cache.

THE ROUTE:

0 km (0 miles) Jasper

Jasper has camping facilities, hotel and motel accommodation, hiking trails and stores to stock up in before heading out. Leaving Jasper go west on the Yellowhead Highway 16, which has a wide shoulder.

26 km (16 miles) Yellowhead Pass at British Columbia border

Go over Yellowhead Pass, the gentlest of the five passes in the Canadian Rockies. You are now in British Columbia.

80 km (50 miles) Mount Robson Provincial Park

Mount Robson Provincial Park is 80 km (50 miles) from Jasper. Lofty and usually cloud-topped Mount Robson reaches 3,954 meters (12,972 feet), the highest peak in the Canadian Rockies. Here you will find campgrounds and motel accommodation.

The hike along the Robson River through the Valley of a Thousand Falls to Berg Lake is popular.

100 km (62 miles) Tête Jaune Cache

After Tête Jaune Cache junction, Highway 16 has narrower shoulders.

164 km (102 miles) McBride

McBride, 64 km (40 miles) from Tête Jaune Cache, is surrounded by the snow-capped peaks of the Cariboo Mountains and Rocky Mountains. McBride has private campgrounds, motel and hotel accommodation and VIA Rail service. Stock up on supplies here. There are no towns between McBride and Prince George 205 km (127 miles) to the west.

292 km (181 miles) Purden Lake Provincial Park

The isolated 128-km (80-mile) stretch of this tour from McBride to Purden Lake Provincial Park, is on a good road with wide shoulders. Purden Lake Provincial Park has camping.

369 km (229 miles) Prince George

Purden Lake Provincial Park is 77 km (48 miles) from Prince George.

The city of Prince George is situated at the geographical center of British Columbia, approximately 800 km (500 miles) from Vancouver, Prince Rupert and Edmonton. The Rocky Mountains are to the east and the Coastal Range to the west.

PRINCE GEORGE TO PRINCE RUPERT

Length: 733 km (455 miles)
Time: Five to seven days
Rating: Intermediate to expert
Terrain: Hilly, remote
Roads: Paved
Traffic: Intermediate
Connects with: At Prince Rupert are ferries south to Vancouver Island; north to Alaska and the Yukon; and west to the Queen Charlotte Islands
Start: Prince George, which can be reached by VIA Rail
Overview: At British Columbia's geographic center, Prince George is at the junction of the Yellowhead Highway—or Highway 16—which runs east to Alberta and west to Prince Rupert; and Highway 97, which runs north to the Yukon and south through the Cariboo Mountains to the Lower Mainland.

This tour follows Highway 16 from Prince George to Prince Rupert. Stock up on supplies in Prince George where there is better selection. All the major towns en route are served by VIA Rail in case you want to shorten your trip.

THE ROUTE:

0 km (0 miles) Prince George

48 km (30 miles) Bednesti Lake Resort

Head west on Highway 16. At Bednesti Lake Resort, 48 km (30 miles) west of Prince George, there are camping facilities and motel accommodations.

100 km (62 miles) Vanderhoof

Vanderhoof, 100 km (62 miles) west of Prince George, is a farm-ing and logging center. Camping facilities, motel and hotel accommodation, and VIA Rail passenger service are available here.

Near Vanderhoof is the Nechako Bird Sanctuary, where you can see migratory birds including Canada geese, ducks, trumpeter swans, seabirds, as well as great blue herons, bald eagles, cranes, and loons.

Side trip: Vanderhoof to Fort St. James National Historic Park 64 km (40 miles)

From Vanderhoof you can take a side trip north along Highway 27 for 64 km (40 miles) to Fort St. James National Historic Park. Fort St. James, the oldest town in British Columbia, lies on Stuart Lake, with camping at nearby Paarens Beach Provincial Park, as well as hotel and motel accommodation in town.

Main trip continues from Vanderhoof

Back on Highway 16, continue west from Vanderhoof to Fort Fraser, established in 1806 by explorer Simon Fraser for the Northwest Company. It became a Hudson's Bay Company post in 1821. Beaumont Provincial Park, near Lejac, 16 km (10 miles) from Fraser Lake has camping.

160 km (100 miles) Fraser Lake

Fraser Lake, a lumber and mining town 60 km (37 miles) west of Vanderhoof, is on the shores

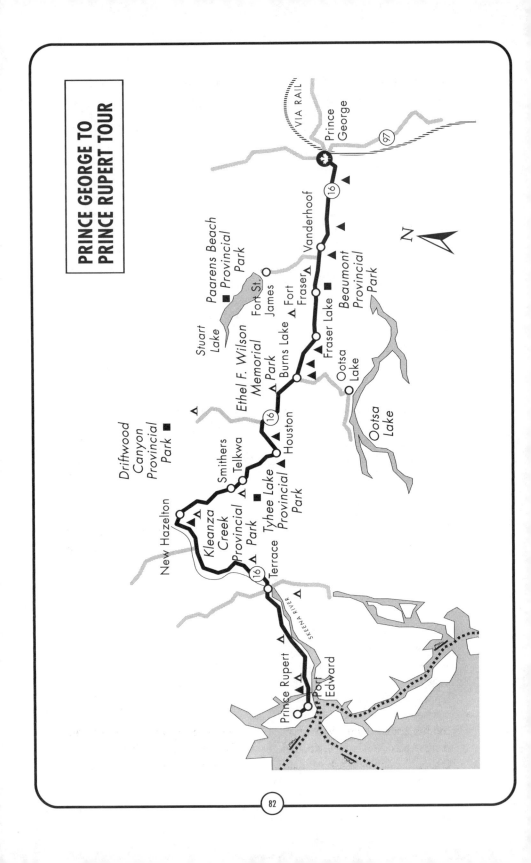

PRINCE GEORGE TO
PRINCE RUPERT TOUR

Prince George

VIA RAIL

97

16

Vanderhoof

Paarens Beach
Provincial
Park

Fort St.
James

Stuart
Lake

Fort
Fraser

Fraser Lake

Beaumont
Provincial
Park

Ethel F. Wilson
Memorial
Park

Burns Lake

Ootsa
Lake

Ootsa
Lake

N

16

Houston

Driftwood
Canyon
Provincial
Park

Smithers

Telkwa

New Hazelton

Kleanza
Creek
Provincial
Park

Tyhee Lake
Provincial
Park

16

Terrace

SKEENA RIVER

Prince Rupert

Port
Edward

of scenic Fraser Lake. Camping facilities, and hotel and motel accommodation are available here. Hiking trails at nearby Mouse Mountain include a path across the extinct volcano and lava beds of Table Top Mountain.

228 km (142 miles) Burns Lake

Burns Lake, 68 km (42 miles) from Fraser Lake, and several smaller surrounding lakes are popular with anglers.

There is camping at Ethel F. Wilson Memorial Provincial Park, 24 km (15 miles) north of Burns Lake.

300 km (186 miles) Houston

Houston, 140 km (85 miles) from Burns Lake, is also a logging and mining town where you can tour the local silver mine. Camping, hotel and motel accommodation and VIA Rail passenger service are available.

At Telkwa are a few small stores selling food. There is camping at Tyhee Lake Provincial Park.

364 km (226 miles) Smithers

Situated in fertile Bulkley Valley surrounded by mountains, rivers and lakes is Smithers, 64 km (40 miles) from Houston. It is a ranching, forestry and mining center. The Smithers Museum describes the area's history. Camping, hotel and motel accommodation, and VIA Rail service are offered. At Driftwood Canyon Provincial Park you can see fossil beds, glacial deposits and an exposed coal seam.

There is also camping at Maclure Lake Park, 18 km (11 miles) west of Smithers.

Another 7 km (4 miles) west, the Bulkley River cascades through a narrow gorge in spectacular Moricetown Canyon.

431 km (268 miles) New Hazelton

At New Hazelton, 67 km (42 miles) west of Smithers, are camping facilities, hotel and motel accommodation and VIA Rail service.

Nearby at K'san Indian Craft Village, you can see traditional Pacific Northwest Coast Indian art produced by ancient ways, six communal houses decorated with carved interior poles, and five totem pole villages including a totem pole carved in 1850. There is a campground near the village.

573 km (356 miles) Terrace

From New Hazelton, ride 142 km (88 miles) west along the banks of Skeena River to Terrace. You pass through meadows and small towns and settlements as you gradually descend to Kleanza Creek Provincial Park, which has camping facilities. The Park has a trail to an ancient Tsimshian Indian village with totem poles, and a sluice box used to find gold in the river. *Kleanza* is the Gitskan Indian word for gold.

Terrace has camping facilities, hotel and motel accommodation, and VIA Rail service.

The 153 km (95 miles) from Terrace to Prince Rupert continues along the scenic Skeena River. The road is relatively flat and has light traffic. There are few facilities on this section, so carry sufficient supplies. Prudhomme Lake Provincial Park, 16 km (10 miles) east of Prince Rupert has camping.

Prince Rupert is on Kaien Island. The largest natural ocean harbor on the Pacific Northwest coast, Prince Rupert is known for its heavy rainfall which tends to be lighter during the summer months.

Options: Ferries

Here you can board ferries for Vancouver Island, the Queen Charlotte Islands, and Alaska (providing access to the Yukon). The town offers camping facilities, hotel and motel accommodation and VIA Rail service.

More Information: The ferries from Prince Rupert to Vancouver Island and to the Queen Charlotte Islands are operated by the British Columbia Ferry Corporation. See addresses and phone numbers at the beginning of this chapter.

The ferry from Prince Rupert to Skagway, Alaska with ports of call at Ketchikan, Wrangell, Petersburg, Sitka, Haida, Stewart, Juneau and Haines, is operated by Alaska Marine Highway System, P.O. Box 458, Prince Rupert, British Columbia V9Y 7M7, telephone (604) 627-1744, or toll-free from the continental United States 1-800-642-0066. The trip is 34 to 56 hours long and reservations are required.

THE KOOTENAYS: REVELSTOKE TO CRESTON

Length: 277 km (172 miles) one way
Time: Two to three days
Rating: Intermediate to expert
Terrain: Some climbs; you may encounter strong winds off Kootenay Lake
Roads: Good condition
Traffic: Quiet
Connects with: Across British Columbia tour
Start: Revelstoke, on the Trans Canada Highway near Mount Revelstoke National Park.

Overview: Hot springs, ghost towns left over from the silver boom, fjord-like lakes, paddlewheelers, spectacular mountain scenery and fertile orchards are all found on this tour.

You pedal along a quiet highway in a valley between the Selkirk and Monashee ranges then along Upper Arrow Lake. Cross the lake on a free ferry and continue along the Slocan valley, the area of the silver boom, and then along Kootenay Lake to orchards near Creston. Roadside

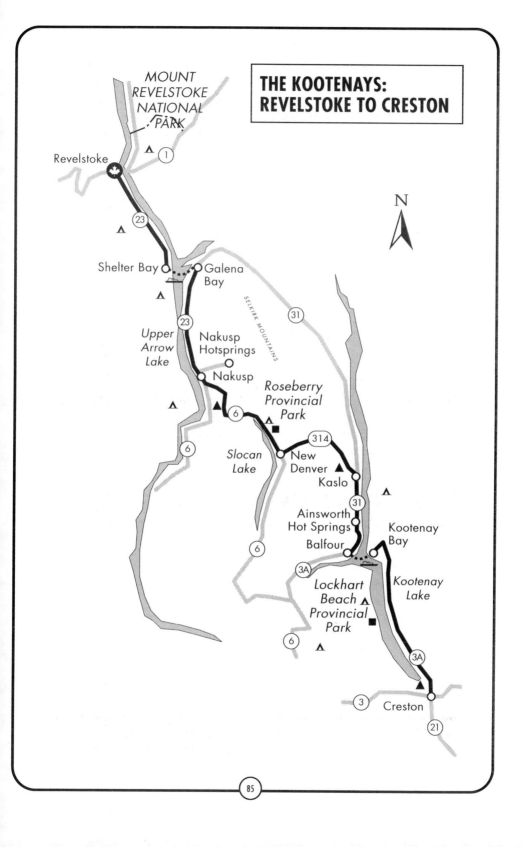

THE KOOTENAYS:
REVELSTOKE TO CRESTON

MOUNT
REVELSTOKE
NATIONAL
PARK

Revelstoke

N

Shelter Bay   Galena Bay

SELKIRK MOUNTAINS

Upper
Arrow
Lake

Nakusp
Hotsprings

Nakusp

Roseberry
Provincial
Park

Slocan
Lake

New
Denver

Kaslo

Ainsworth
Hot Springs

Balfour

Kootenay
Bay

Kootenay
Lake

Lockhart
Beach
Provincial
Park

Creston

stands sell locally grown fruit. Situated in the West Kootenay region, Creston is an important center in the Creston Valley.

Stock up on food in Revelstoke, as the tour goes through some remote territory and limited supplies are available en route.

THE ROUTE:
0 km (0 miles) Revelstoke

From Revelstoke, go south on Highway 23 along the shore of Upper Arrow Lake, a widening of the Columbia River, which is the longest river flowing into the Pacific.

50 km (31 miles) Shelter Bay

After 50 km (31 miles) is Shelter Bay.

Ferry: Shelter Bay to Galena Bay (crossing time: 30 minutes)

Take the free ferry to Galena Bay.

99 km (61 miles) Nakusp

Continue south on Highway 23, for 49 km (30 miles) to Nakusp, nestled in the Selkirk Mountains. Nearby are the hot mineral waters of Nakusp Hot Springs.

145 km (90 miles) New Denver

Take Highway 6 southeast past Summit Lake, Rosebery Provincial Park, and Slocan Lake, which resembles a fjord. After 46 km (28 miles) is New Denver. This was the center of the silver boom in this valley during the

nineteenth century. You can see artifacts of the era at the Silvery Slocan Museum.

192 km (119 miles) Kaslo

Go left onto Highway 31A for 47 km (29 miles) to Kaslo. Along the way are ghost towns left from the silver rush. A few shacks remain at Retallack and Zincton. In Kaslo you can visit the museum on board the S.S. *Moyie*, the last of the paddlewheelers that carried pioneers over the length of 120-km (75-mile) long Kootenay Lake.

228 km (142 miles) Balfour

From Kaslo, go south on Highway 31 for 36 km (22 miles) to Balfour. Along the way are the Ainsworth Hot Springs.

Ferry: Balfour to Kootenay Bay (crossing time: 45 minutes)

At Balfour take the free ferry across Kootenay Lake to Kootenay Bay.

277 km (172 miles) Creston

Head south on Highway 3A for 79 km (49 miles) to Creston. This part of the route is fairly level. En route are several beaches on Kootenay Lake, and camping at Lockhart Beach Provincial Park.

The Creston Valley's fertile green pastures are surrounded by dry hills. On the way into Creston are fruit stands selling locally grown apricots, apples, peaches and plums.

ACROSS BRITISH COLUMBIA

Length: 1,120 km (696 miles)

Time: Seven to eleven days

Rating: Moderate with some strenuous climbs

Terrain: Mountainous

Roads: Bicycles are prohibited on Highway 1 (the Trans Canada Highway) between Vancouver and Chilliwack.

Traffic: Varies from light to heavy

Connects with: Kootenays: Revelstoke to Creston tour; Across Alberta tour

Start: Vancouver, the largest city in British Columbia.

Overview: There are two highways from southwestern British Columbia to the Alberta boundary: Highway 1, which is the Trans Canada Highway, and the more southern Highway 3.

This bicycle tour combines the best of each and traverses a variety of British Columbia's spectacular terrain.

From Vancouver you ride through the lower Fraser River Valley to Hope. From Hope eastward to Rock Creek, this tour follows Highway 3 through the Cascade Mountains of Manning Provincial Park and the Okanagan Valley's orchards and vineyards.

At Osoyoos you cycle through a small desert. At Castlegar you turn north on quiet highways through the Kootenay Mountains and past lakes, hot springs and ghost towns.

Reaching the Trans Canada Highway at Revelstoke, the tour turns east and goes through the massive snow-capped Columbia Mountains and then climbs along the Kicking Horse River through the Rockies to Kicking Horse Pass on the Alberta boundary.

THE ROUTE:

0 km (0 miles) Vancouver

145 km (90 miles) Hope

From Vancouver, take Highway 7A east past Burnaby Mountain Park to Port Moody. Continue east on Highway 7 along the Fraser River valley for 145 km (90 miles) to Hope. Traffic can be heavy along Highway 7, but it has wide shoulders in some areas. Bicycles are prohibited on Highway 1—the Trans Canada Highway—between Vancouver and Chilliwack. Highway 1 is roughly parallel to Highway 7.

211 km (131 miles) Manning Park

At Hope stock up on food. Follow scenic Highway 3— the Hope–Princeton Highway— which has a wide shoulder. Ride it through the Cascade Mountains of Manning Provincial Park for 66 km (41 miles) to the village of Manning Park for a selection of campgrounds.

The route follows the Old Dewdney Trail used during the Kootenay Gold Rush and as an old stagecoach road of the 1890s.

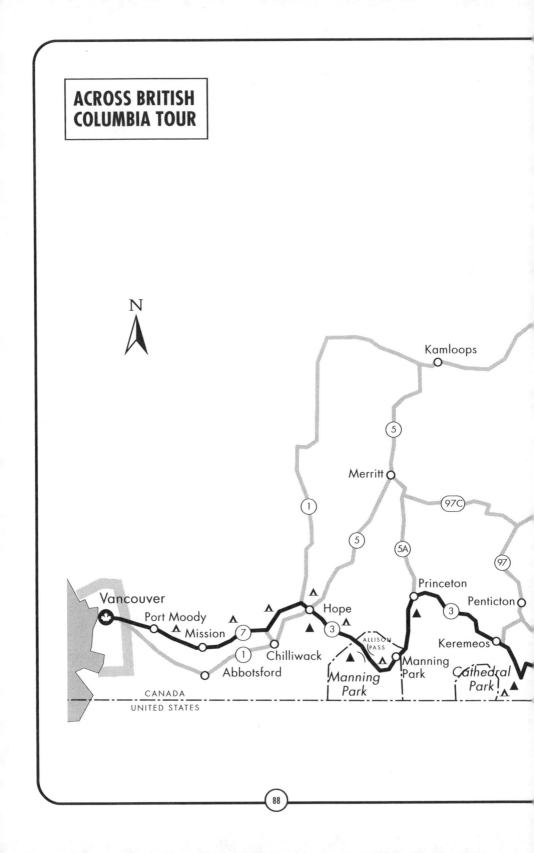

ACROSS BRITISH COLUMBIA TOUR

N

Kamloops

5

Merritt

97C

1

5

5A

97

Princeton

Penticton

Vancouver

Port Moody

Mission

Hope

7

3

ALLISON PASS

Keremeos

1

Chilliwack

3

Manning Park

Cathedral Park

Abbotsford

Manning Park

CANADA

UNITED STATES

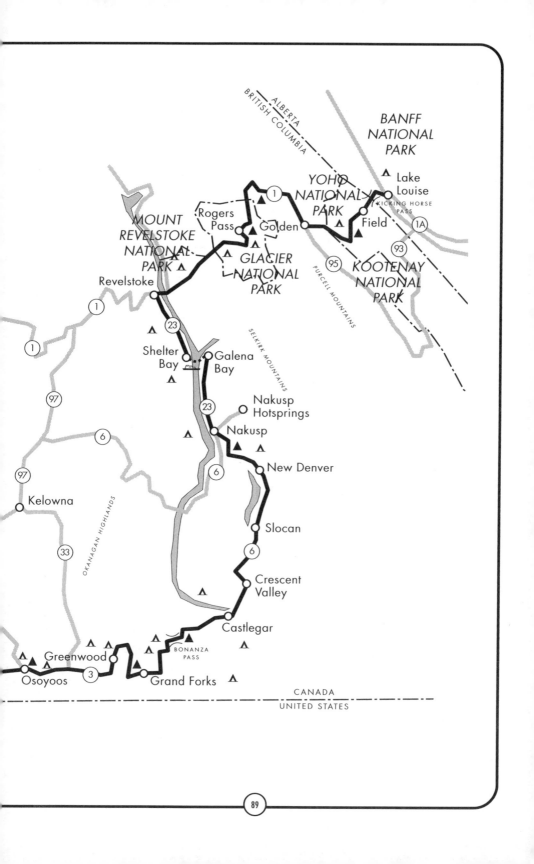

277 km (172 miles) Princeton

Continue on Highway 3 for another 66 km (41 miles) along the Sumallo River and Skagit River. Ride over 1,340-meter (4,400-foot) Allison Pass and pedal to Princeton, at the junction of five rivers that flow into Similkameen River.

315 km (196 miles) Stemwinder Provincial Park

Another 38 km (24 miles) brings you to Stemwinder Provincial Park, which offers camping.

You enter the Okanagan Valley region in the province's sunny and dry interior. The Okanagan is known for its orchards and vineyards. Roadside stands sell locally grown cherries, apples, apricots, peaches, plums, pears and grapes.

351 km (218 miles) Keremeos

Descend on Highway 3 along the Similkameen River for 36 km (20 miles) to Keremeos, a fruit-growing center.

415 km (258 miles) Richter Pass

Continue riding Highway 3 along the Similkameen River for 64 km (40 miles). The ride involves a 396-meter (1,300-foot) climb over 3 km (2 miles) to Richter Pass.

424 km (263 miles) Osoyoos

From the top of Richter Pass, descend for 9 km (5 mile) to Osoyoos, in a small desert of cactus, sagebrush and horned lizards.

445 km (276 miles) Anarchist Mountain summit

From Osoyoos, Highway 3 ascends Anarchist Mountain. At the summit, 21 km (13 miles) from Osoyoos, you have spectacular views of Mount Baldy to the north and the United States to the south. There is no water at the rest area, so be sure to bring enough with you.

476 km (296 miles) Rock Creek

Descend from Anarchist Mountain and ride through rolling country to Rock Creek, 31 km (19 miles) farther. In this area Highway 3 parallels the United States border.

551 km (342 miles) Grand Forks

Ride through the towns of Midway and Greenwood to Grand Forks, a distance of 75 km (47 miles) from Rock Creek.

647 km (402 miles) Castlegar

Continue on Highway 3 for 96 km (60 miles) over 1,535-meter (5,036-foot) Bonanza Pass to Castlegar, a Doukhobor city. Stock up on food for the ride through the Kootenay Mountains, as there are limited supplies available en route.

667 km (414 miles) Crescent Valley

Take Highway 3A north for 20 km (12 miles) to Crescent Valley.

746 km (463 miles) New Denver

Then ride Highway 6 north for 79 km (49 miles), past farms along the Slocan River, through the village of Slocan and then along the shores of glittering Slocan Lake, to New Denver. This area experienced a silver rush during the nineteenth century and you can see reminders of the era in the abandoned silver mines and ghost towns as well as artifacts in the Silvery Slocan Museum.

The tour links here with the Kootenays: Revelstoke to Creston tour (described in this chapter).

792 km (492 miles) Nakusp

Continue riding on Highway 6 for 46 km (28 miles) along Slocan Lake and past Summit Lake, taking the remote stretch of highway to Nakusp.

Nearby are the hot mineral waters of Nakusp Hot Springs, which are open year-round.

841 km (522 miles) Galena Bay

Go north on Highway 23 for 49 km (30 miles) along the shore of Upper Arrow Lake, a widening of the Columbia River to Galena Bay.

Ferry: Galena Bay to Shelter Bay, (crossing time: 30 minutes)

At Galena Bay, take the free ferry across Upper Arrow Lake to Shelter Bay.

891 km (553 miles) Revelstoke

Continue north on Highway 23 along Upper Arrow Lake for 50 km (31 miles) to Revelstoke, where food supplies can be replenished and a variety of other services are available.

912 km (567 miles) Mount Revelstoke National Park western boundary

Leaving Revelstoke, follow Highway 1—the Trans Canada Highway—east for 21 km (13 miles). You enter Mount Revelstoke National Park, which covers 260 square km (100 square miles) of the massive, snow-capped mountains and narrow valleys of the Columbia Mountains. There are no campgrounds in the park.

927 km (576 miles) Mount Revelstoke National Park eastern boundary

After 15 km (9 miles) on Highway 1, you leave Mount Revelstoke Park.

939 km (583 miles) Glacier National Park western boundary

Continue for 12 km (7 miles) to Glacier National Park. Glacier Park covers 1,350 square km (521 square miles) of the jagged Purcell and Selkirk Mountain ranges, capped with sparkling glaciers. Several campgrounds are available.

Ride Highway 1 in Glacier National Park to the summit of 1,330-meter (4,364-foot) Rogers Pass through the Selkirk Mountains. From the pass is a view of the Illecillewaet Glacier, Lookout Mountain, Glacier Crest, Feuz Peak, Asulkan Pass and Michel Peak.

This part of the route is mountainous with a good number of climbs. When you pass through tunnels and avalanche snowsheds, put on your lights and wear a reflective safety vest.

984 km (611 miles) Glacier National Park eastern boundary

It's a 45 km (28 miles) ride on Highway 1 through Glacier Park.

1,040 km (646 miles) Golden

Once you're past the park's eastern boundary, it's another 56 km (35 miles) to Golden, a major center where you can buy supplies. A variety of accommodation is available.

Highway 1 climbs intermittently for 20 km (12 miles) along the Kicking Horse River through the Rocky Mountains. The highway is narrow and used by logging trucks. If there are a lot of trucks, take a break and enjoy the spectacular views.

1,065 km (662 miles) Yoho National Park western boundary

You enter 1,313-square-km (507-square-mile) Yoho National Park 25 km (15 miles) east of Golden.

1,092 km (678 miles) Emerald Lake turn-off

The Emerald Lake turn-off, 27 km (17 miles) east of the Yoho Park gate, leads 8 km (5 miles) to Emerald Lake at the base of the President Range.

1,094.5 km (680 miles) Field

The railroad town (no passenger train service) of Field is 2.5 km (1.6 miles) past the Emerald Lake turn-off.

1,098.5 km (682 miles) Yoho Valley turn-off

Another 4 km (2.5 miles) beyond Field is the turn-off for the Yoho Valley.

Side trip: Highway 1 to Yoho Valley, 13 km (8 miles)

This worthwhile side trip leads 13 km (8 miles) to 384-meter (1,259-foot) Takakkaw Falls, the highest falls in Canada. A hostel, campgrounds and a store are located nearby.

1,110.5 km (690 miles) Kicking Horse Pass summit, Alberta border

Highway 1 climbs steeply up Kicking Horse Pass. Be sure to stop at the viewpoint of the Spiral Tunnels, where trains spiral through two mountains to climb or descend the Kicking Horse Pass.

The summit of the Kicking Horse Pass, 16 km (10 miles) east of Field, is part of the Continental Divide and the boundary with the province of Alberta.

1,120 km (696 miles) Lake Louise, Alberta

Cycle into Alberta and Banff National Park, and descend 10 km (6 miles) along Highway 1 to Lake Louise.

GUIDEBOOKS

Bicycling Fraser Valley, by Volker Bodegom. Available from: Lone Pine Publishing, Suite 206, 10426-81st Avenue, Edmonton, Alberta T6E 1X5, telephone: (403) 433-9333; $14.95.

Bicycling Vancouver, by Volker Bodegom. Available from: Lone Pine Publishing; $14.95.

Bicycling Vancouver Island and the Gulf Islands, by Simon Priest. Available from: Douglas and McIntyre, 1615 Venables Street, Vancouver, British Columbia V5L 2H1, telephone (604) 254-8218; $12.95 (for mail orders add postage of $1 plus 50 cents per book).

Bicycling Southwestern British Columbia and the Sunshine Coast, by Simon Priest. Available from: Douglas and McIntyre; $12.95.

The British Columbia Bicycling Guide, by Teri Lydiard. Available from: Gordon Soules Book Publishers Ltd., 1352-B Marine Drive, West Vancouver, British Columbia V7T 1B5; $7.95.

The Canadian Rockies Bicycling Guide, by Gail Helgason and John Dodd. Available from: Lone Pine Publishing; $9.95.

The Greater Vancouver Bicycling Guide, by Maggie Burtinshaw. Available from: Gordon Soules Book Publishers Ltd.; $9.95.

Touring the Islands: Bicycling in the San Juan, Gulf, and Vancouver Islands, by Peter Powers and Renee Travis. Available from: Terragraphics, P.O. Box 1025, Eugene, Oregon 97440, USA; $10.95.

Gulf Islands Recreation Map, by ITMB Publishing Ltd. Available from: World Wide Books and Maps, 736A Granville Street, Vancouver, British Columbia V6Z 1G3, telephone (604) 687-3320; $6.95.

Bow Lake, Banff National Park
(Alberta Tourism)

Alberta

Alberta's majestic Rocky Mountain scenery offers some of North America's most spectacular tours and attracts many cyclists every year. The Icefields Parkway, which winds through magnificent alpine scenery of glaciers, turquoise lakes, and meadows carpeted with flowers, is the best known of these tours. Less well known but offering equally breathtaking mountain scenery are tours through Kananaskis Country along Canada's highest paved road, and a loop route known as the "Golden Triangle" that crosses the Great Divide twice.

Terrain: The Rocky Mountains constitute only a part of Alberta's geography. To the east are the Foothills and the Alberta Plateau, a prairie. There is rolling prairie in the south, and forest, lake and river country in the north. Around Drumheller are the fascinating Badlands, famous for the dinosaur skeletons and unusual geological formations.

Area: 660,933 square km (255,200 square miles)

Roads: Most of the roads in Alberta have wide, paved shoulders. The Trans Canada Highway from Calgary to the British Columbia border has a lot of traffic, averaging more than 10,000 vehicles per day.

Weather: Alberta receives the most sunshine in Canada; in Banff the July average is 255 hours. Summers are hot and winters are cold, since the Rocky Mountains block the moderating influence of the Pacific Ocean. Snow is usually gone from along roads by the beginning of May.

Accommodations: Alberta has a wide selection of accommodation from luxury hotels to hostels and campgrounds. Along the Icefields Parkway, the province's most popular cycling tour, campsites and hostels are within an easy day's ride.

Tourist Information: An Alberta cycling information map, a regular road map, an accommodation guide and other tourist information is available from: Alberta Tourism, P.O. Box 2500, Edmonton, Alberta T5J 2Z4, or call toll-free within Alberta 1-800-222-6501; elsewhere in Canada and the United States 1-800-661-8888; in Edmonton (403) 427-4321.

Hostels: Information on hostels in Alberta can be obtained from the Southern Alberta Hostelling Association, 203 - 1414 Kensington Road N.W., Calgary, Alberta T2N 3P5, telephone (403) 283-5551, fax (403) 283-6503; and the Canadian Hostelling Association, Northern Alberta District, 10926-88th Avenue, Edmonton, Alberta T6G 0Z1, telephone (403) 432-7798, fax (403) 433-7781.

Airports: Calgary and Edmonton airports are served by major airlines and have connections to smaller centers.

Trains: Trains on the route through Edmonton and Jasper have baggage cars that will carry bikes. For information on VIA Rail service, call in Alberta toll-free 1-800-561-8630.

Buses: Brewster buses take bikes in boxes as one piece of luggage. They serve Banff and Jasper from Calgary airport. For more information call (403) 221-8242 or toll-free 1-800-332-1419.

Bicycling: Alberta Bicycle Association, 11759 Groat Road, Edmonton, Alberta T5M 3K6, telephone (403) 453-8518.

Capital: Edmonton, the largest city in Alberta, is situated on the North Saskatchewan River.

Population: 2,545,553 (1991 census)

History: Blackfoot, Blood and Peigan Native Indians lived in Alberta long before the European fur traders arrived. Anthony Henday, an employee of the Hudson's Bay Company was the first European to reach Alberta. In 1795 Fort Edmonton was established as a fur trading post.

The completion of the transcontinental Canadian Pacific Railway in 1885 opened western Canada to settlement. People from Great Britain, Scandinavia, Ukraine and many other countries settled on farmland throughout Alberta. They helped develop Alberta's agricultural base which remains an important part of the province's economy. In 1905 Alberta joined the Canadian confederation.

BICYCLING IN CALGARY

Calgary lies on the Bow River at the meeting point of the prairies and the foothills. The city has a network of two types of bicycle routes: 180 km (112 miles) of **pathways** are separated from roadways and shared by cyclists and pedestrians; the 140 km (87 miles) of **bikeways** are signed on-street routes. There are another 46 km (29 miles) of pathways in Fish Creek Provincial Park at the south end of the city.

Pathways go through parkland along the Bow River through the entire city and connect with trails on island parks in the river. The pathways along the Bow River lead to Fish Creek Provincial Park. They also link with pathways along the Elbow River leading to the Glenmore Reservoir, and with another pathway that parallels the Deerfoot Trail highway (bicycles are not permitted on the Deerfoot Trail highway).

The bikeways follow streets throughout the city.

Bicycles are allowed on the Light Rail Transit (LRT) trains during non-rush hour periods. There are secure bicycle lockers at the Brentwood LRT station.

More Information: A Calgary Pathways and Bikeways map is available free from: Calgary Parks and Recreation, P.O. Box 2100, Station M, Calgary, Alberta T2P 2M5, telephone (403) 268-5211.

BICYCLING IN EDMONTON

Edmonton is situated on the North Saskatchewan River. Within the river valley is a system of parks stretching from the High Level Bridge to Hermitage Park with 30 km (19 miles) of paved multi-use (pedestrians and cyclists) trails.

In other parts of the city are three types of bicycle routes: bike paths through areas where cars are prohibited; bike lanes that are separated from the main roadway; and bike routes along roadways, which are signed to inform motorists and cyclists of the cycling route.

More Information: A Cycle Edmonton map and information guide is available from Edmonton Transportation Department, 10th Floor, Century Place, 9803-102A Avenue, Edmonton, Alberta T5J 3R5, telephone (403) 428-4735.

BANFF AND JASPER NATIONAL PARKS: THE COLUMBIA ICEFIELDS PARKWAY

Length: 290 km (180 miles)
Time: Three to four days
Rating: Intermediate to advanced
Terrain: Numerous small hills and two major passes: Bow Summit at 2,069 meters (6,786 feet) is the highest point on the highway, and the 2,029-meter (6,658-foot) Sunwapta Pass is the boundary between Banff and Jasper parks, just south of the Columbia Icefields.
Roads: Wide, paved shoulders of more than 1.8 meters (6 feet) on much of the route; the shoulders disappear on steep portions where there is not enough road width to permit them—unfortunately this is where cyclists appreciate wide shoulders the most.
Traffic: A lot of tourist traffic on the Icefields Parkway
Connects with: Day tours in Banff and Jasper parks, Across Alberta tour, Golden Triangle tour.
Start: Jasper which is served by VIA Rail. The trip is much easier going south from Jasper to Banff as the grade of the climbs is gentler. The route is described here in that direction.

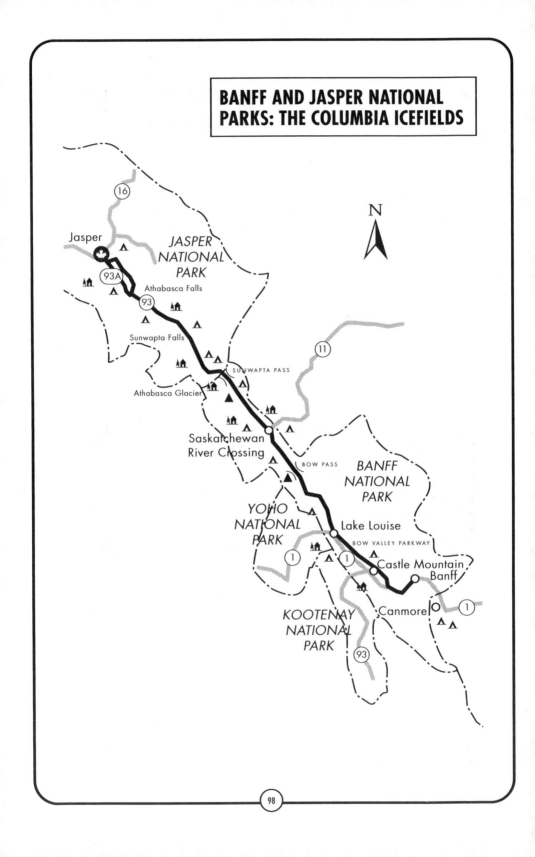

BANFF AND JASPER NATIONAL PARKS: THE COLUMBIA ICEFIELDS

N

Jasper

JASPER NATIONAL PARK

Athabasca Falls

Sunwapta Falls

SUNWAPTA PASS

Athabasca Glacier

Saskatchewan River Crossing

BOW PASS

BANFF NATIONAL PARK

YOHO NATIONAL PARK

Lake Louise

BOW VALLEY PARKWAY

Castle Mountain

Banff

KOOTENAY NATIONAL PARK

Canmore

Overview: Snow-capped peaks, glaciers, lakes and waterfalls line this highway through the grandeur of the Rocky Mountains. The spectacular mountain scenery and green valleys have made this tour one of Alberta's most popular routes.

Traversing Banff and Jasper parks, the Icefields Parkway skirts the chain of icefields lying along the Continental Divide. The icefields are the source of many rivers draining into the Pacific Ocean, the Arctic Ocean and the Atlantic Ocean via Hudson Bay. Moose, deer, elk, bear, goat, sheep and many other species of wildlife can often be seen from the road.

Within a day's ride are campsites offering washrooms with cold running water, cooking shelters, free firewood and interpretive programs. Cyclists in a small group of two or three are always accommodated in the campgrounds. While campgrounds generally cannot be reserved, larger groups may obtain a letter from the Park Superintendent reserving half a dozen campsites for them. Contact the Superintendent of Banff and Jasper parks for more details (address and telephone number at the end of the tour description).

The Canadian Hostelling Association operates a network of hostels along the route. If you want to use the hostels, plan to arrive early in the day or make reservations in advance.

There are hotels or lodges at Jasper, Sunwapta Falls, the junction with the David Thompson Highway, the Bow Glacier viewpoint, Lake Louise, Castle Mountain and Banff. Make reservations well in advance to ensure you get a place and that the hotel will be open when you expect to arrive.

Stock up on supplies in Banff or Jasper, as very limited supplies are available along the route. There are bike shops in both Banff and Jasper that rent bikes. For details contact Alberta Tourism (see details at beginning of chapter).

THE ROUTE:

0 km (0 miles) Jasper

9 km (5.5 miles) junction with Highway 93A

> From Jasper, take the Icefields Parkway—Highway 93—south for 9 km (5.5 miles) along the swift Athabasca River to the junction with Highway 93A. Along the way are the Whistlers campground and the Wapiti campground.
>
> From the junction with Highway 93A, there are two routes to Athabasca Falls.

35 km (22 miles) Athabasca Falls

Option: Athabasca Falls via Highway 93, 30 km (19 miles)

> You can continue on Highway 93 which is flat and gains only 100 meters (330 feet) in elevation.

Option: Highway 93A to Athabasca Falls, 30 km (19 miles)

> Or, you can take quieter, but narrower and more hilly Highway 93A along the west side of the Athabasca River. Route 93A rejoins Highway 93 near Athabasca Falls.

Athabasca Falls drops into a narrow canyon, and is one of the most powerful falls in the Canadian Rockies. Across the road is the Athabasca Falls youth hostel.

Main tour

56 km (35 miles) Sunwapta Falls turn-off

Continue south on the Icefields Parkway.

You pass a mineral lick where mountain goats and bighorn sheep can be seen, an Athabasca Valley viewpoint, and Honeymoon Lake campground.

Situated 24 km (15 miles) south of Athabasca Falls is the Sunwapta Falls turn-off. Take the turn-off and walk the 0.6 km (0.4 mile) trail to the falls. Nearby is the Sunwapta Falls Resort. Return to the Icefields Parkway.

87 km (54 miles) Beauty Creek Hostel

From the Sunwapta Falls turn-off, the Icefields Parkway goes past Jonas Creek campground, to Beauty Creek and the Beauty Creek Hostel. Beauty Creek is 31 km (19 miles) from the Sunwapta Falls turn-off.

104 km (65 miles) Columbia Icefield and Wilcox Creek campground

You pass Stanley Falls, the Stutfield Glacier viewpoint and the Tangle Falls viewpoint (where you may see sheep), on the way to the Columbia Icefield.

Over the next 4 km (2.5 miles) the road climbs 300 meters (1,000 feet) from the floor of the Sunwapta Valley. En route is the Sunwapta Canyon viewpoint.

Descend along the Icefields Parkway to the Columbia Icefield and the Athabasca Glacier, 19 km (12 miles) south of the Beauty Creek Hostel. Nearby is the Wilcox campground.

The largest icefield in the Rockies, the Columbia Icefield covers 325 square km (125 square miles). From here water flows to three oceans. The Athabasca River flows north to the Mackenzie River and the Arctic Ocean; the North Saskatchewan River flows east to Hudson Bay; and the Columbia River flows west to the Pacific.

At the icefields is a chalet and an information booth. Snowmobile tours of the lower part of the Athabasca Glacier are available here.

109 km (68 miles) Sunwapta Pass

The parkway ascends to the summit of 2,035-meter (6,676-foot) Sunwapta Pass, the watershed of the North Saskatchewan and Athabasca rivers, and the boundary with Jasper National Park.

113 km (70 miles) Hilda Creek hostel

Approximately 4 km (2.5 miles) farther is the Hilda Creek Youth Hostel, a 25-km (16-mile) ride south from the Beauty Creek Hostel.

114 km (71 miles) Parker's Ridge Trail

Parker's Ridge Trail, 1 km (0.6 mile) south of Hilda Creek, is a 3-km (1.8-mile) round-trip walk leading above the tree line to an alpine meadow carpeted with wildflowers and shrubs. Along the path is a view of the Saskatchewan Glacier, which is part of the Columbia Icefield and the source of the North Saskatchewan River.

143 km (89 miles) Rampart Creek campground and hostel

From Parker's Ridge Trail, the parkway descends approximately 300 meters (980 feet) over 11 km (7 miles) down the "Big Hill." As you glide down the hill you have spectacular views of the valley.

From the bottom of the "Big Hill," the parkway descends gradually along the North Saskatchewan River past the Weeping Wall viewpoint and the Cirrus Mountain campground. You also go through Graveyard Flats, where there are braided river channels.

Continue south on the Icefields Parkway along the North Saskatchewan River to Rampart Creek campground and hostel.

154 km (96 miles) Saskatchewan River Crossing

From Rampart Creek, ride south for 11 km (7 miles) to the junction with Highway 11 (the David Thompson Highway) where there is accommodation (The Crossing), a restaurant and a store with very limited food supplies (mostly snacks).

Continue along Highway 93 and ride to the viewpoint overlooking the Howse Valley, which

fur trader David Thompson traversed in 1807.

You then cross the North Saskatchewan River.

159 km (99 miles) Mistaya Canyon trail

After crossing the North Saskatchewan River, the parkway climbs for 2 km (1.2 miles) to Mistaya Canyon trail, a 0.3-km (0.2-mile) trail to the gorge of the Mistaya Canyon.

174 km (108 miles) Waterfowl Lakes campground

Continue climbing for 15 km (9 miles) to the Waterfowl Lakes campground, which offers a 4-km (2.5-mile) hiking trail leading to Cirque and Chephren Lakes.

183 km (114 miles) Snowbird Glacier viewpoint

You pass viewpoints overlooking the Waterfowl Lakes where moose can be seen, Barbette Glacier and Snowbird Glacier.

191 km (119 miles) Bow Pass

From Snowbird Glacier viewpoint, the route climbs steeply for 8 km (5 miles) to the summit of 2,069-meter (6,787-foot) Bow Pass, the route's highest point.

During the summer, the meadows here are covered with wildflowers. Near the pass is a viewpoint overlooking Peyto Lake.

Over the next 40 km (25 miles), you gradually descend 500 meters (1,640 feet).

207 km (129 miles) Mosquito Creek campground and hostel

From the summit of Bow Pass, ride 6 km (4 miles) to the Bow Lake viewpoint, where the turquoise waters reflect the surrounding glaciers and limestone cliffs. Near Bow Lake is the Num-Ti-Jah Lodge, which offers hotel accommodation and a restaurant.

Continue the descent for 10 km (6 miles) to Mosquito Creek campground and hostel.

228 km (142 miles) Herbert Lake

Along the way you skirt green Herbert Lake, and pass the Hector Lake viewpoint.

231 km (144 miles) junction with Trans Canada Highway

You gradually descend to the junction with the Trans Canada Highway—Highway 1.

233 km (145 miles) Lake Louise

Ride the Trans Canada Highway for 2 km (1.2 miles) to Lake Louise. Located 55 km (34 miles) from Banff, the Lake Louise area offers camping, hotels, motels and hostels.

259 km (161 miles) Castle Mountain Junction

From Lake Louise, turn off the busy Trans Canada Highway and cycle the quieter Bow Valley Parkway along the Bow River. The road is relatively level.

Stay on the Bow Valley Parkway, past Castle Mountain Junction, which is the link with the Banff–Windermere Parkway through Kootenay National Park in British Columbia. Hotel accommodation is offered at Castle Mountain Village chalets.

266 km (165 miles) Johnston's Canyon

At Johnston's Canyon is a 5.8 km (3.6 miles) nature trail leading past waterfalls to the Ink Pots, pools of blue-green water.

290 km (180 miles) Banff

Ride the Bow Valley Parkway into Banff, which offers a wide variety of services, supplies and accommodations.

More Information: Banff National Park, Box 900, Banff, Alberta T0L 0C0, (403) 762-3324. Jasper National Park, Box 10, Jasper, Alberta T0E 1E0, (403) 852-4401.

BANFF-RADIUM HOT SPRINGS-GOLDEN LOOP

Length: 354 km (220 miles) loop
Time: Four days
Rating: Difficult
Terrain: Mountainous
Roads: The roads through the national parks generally have paved wide shoulders. The parts of this route outside the parks have narrower shoulders.

The shoulder disappears completely in several places as the highway winds tightly along mountain edges between Golden and the Yoho Park boundary. Barricades along the edge of the road edge have gaps every so often so you can pull off and look down on the raging Kicking Horse River—much to the envy of passing

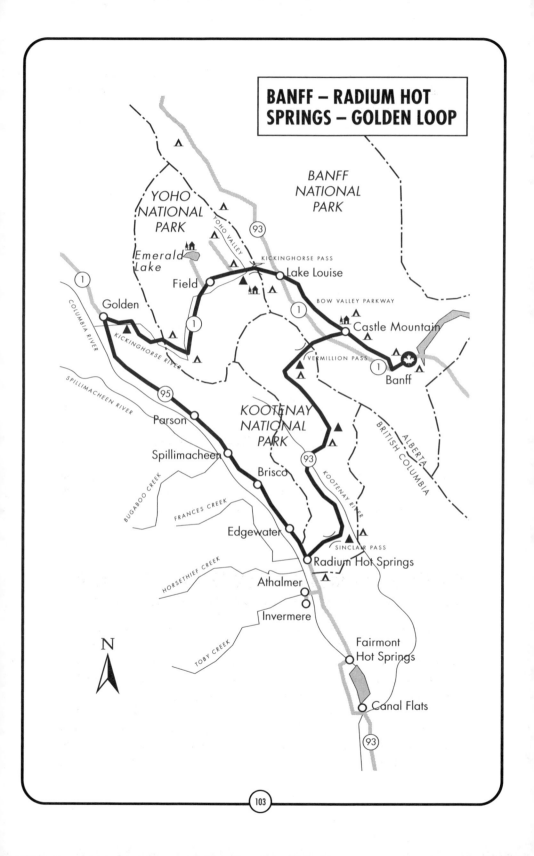

BANFF – RADIUM HOT SPRINGS – GOLDEN LOOP

BANFF NATIONAL PARK

YOHO NATIONAL PARK

Emerald Lake

Field

Golden

COLUMBIA RIVER

KICKINGHORSE RIVER

SPILLIMACHEEN RIVER

BUGABOO CREEK

Parson

Spillimacheen

Brisco

FRANCES CREEK

Edgewater

HORSETHIEF CREEK

Athalmer

Invermere

TOBY CREEK

KOOTENAY NATIONAL PARK

KICKINGHORSE PASS

Lake Louise

BOW VALLEY PARKWAY

Castle Mountain

VERMILLION PASS

Banff

ALBERTA

BRITISH COLUMBIA

KOOTENAY RIVER

SINCLAIR PASS

Radium Hot Springs

Fairmont Hot Springs

Canal Flats

YOHO VALLEY

N

motorists who have nowhere to pull off and enjoy this view.

The asphalt on the shoulders heading downhill from Vermilion Pass, and eastbound near Yoho Park's west gate is badly cracked. These 10 to 15 cm (4 to 6 inches) deep "crevasses" can grab tires and throw riders, so watch out!

Traffic: Tourist traffic in the national parks; heavy logging trucks on the roads outside the parks.

Plan to get an early start on the stretch from Golden to the Yoho Park gate, so you can get to Yoho Park before the industrial-strength traffic picks up—exhaust and burning brake pad fumes get pretty thick through this stretch.

Connects with: Icefields Parkway tour, Across Alberta tour, Across British Columbia tour.

Start: Banff

Overview: This spectacular loop tour, known as the "Golden Triangle," crosses the Continental Divide twice and takes in mountain scenery of peaks, forests and waterfalls. You go through Banff and Kootenay national parks, along the Columbia River and then through Yoho National Park back to Banff. Limited accommodation on parts of the route requires that you plan ahead.

THE ROUTE:

0 km (0 miles) Banff

30 km (19 miles) Castle Mountain Junction

From Banff, ride the Bow Valley Parkway for 30 km (19 miles) to Castle Mountain Junction, where there is a hostel.

41 km (25 miles) Vermilion Pass, Kootenay National Park

Go west on the wide-shouldered Highway 93, Banff–Windermere Highway (also known as the Banff–Radium Highway).

The road winds past Vermilion Pass Fire viewpoint and the Vista Lake viewpoint and climbs to 1,640-meter Vermilion Pass.

Vermilion Pass is on the Continental Divide, which is the boundary of Banff and Kootenay national parks and between the provinces of Alberta and British Columbia.

At the summit of the Vermilion Pass is the Fireweed Trail through an area burned in July 1968 in a forest fire started by lightning. The forest is now regenerating.

At Vermilion Pass is also the watershed for waters flowing west via the Columbia River to the Pacific; and waters going east into the Bow River and the Saskatchewan and Nelson rivers to Hudson Bay.

48 km (30 miles) Marble Canyon Campground

Continue cycling on the Banff–Windermere Highway. The Marble Canyon Campground, 7 km (4.5 miles) from Vermilion Pass, offers camping. Nearby is a 2-km (1.2-mile) nature trail along the rim of Marble Canyon.

51 km (32 miles) Paint Pots Nature Trail

The Paint Pots nature trail, 3 km (2 miles) past Marble Canyon Campground, leads through ochre-colored meadows to three Paint Pot pools. Native Indians used the colors for body paint.

72 km (45 miles) Mount Assiniboine viewpoint

Thirteen kilometers from the Paint Pots, at the Mount Assiniboine viewpoint, is a view of the 3,618-meter (11,870-foot) pyramid-shaped mountain known as the "Matterhorn of the Rockies."

79 km (49 miles) Simpson Valley viewpoint

The Simpson Valley viewpoint, 7 km (4 miles) farther, has a monument to George Simpson, a governor of the Hudson's Bay Company who explored the area searching for a more southerly route for fur traders crossing the Rockies.

Just 1 km (0.6 mile) past the monument is an animal lick, where moose, elk and deer lick the mud for salt and minerals.

89 km (55 miles) Hector Gorge viewpoint

Continue up the short climb to Hector Gorge viewpoint overlooking the Vermilion River. You can get food at Kootenay Crossing, just south of Hector Gorge.

108 km (67 miles) McLeod Meadows campground

Then descend to the McLeod Meadows campground, 60 km (37 miles) from the Marble Canyon campground.

123 km (76 miles) Sinclair Pass

From McLeod Meadows, you start climbing towards Sinclair Pass.

Along the way is the Kootenay River picnic area offering a view of the Mitchell Range and the Vermilion Range, and the Kootenay Valley viewpoint with a view of the Banff–Windermere Parkway.

The Cobb Lake trail leads 2.7 km (1.6 mile) to a small lake.

Near the top of Sinclair Pass is a small picnic area and shelter at Olive Lake.

From the summit of 1,486-meter (4,875-foot) Sinclair Pass you descend along scenic Sinclair Creek, which drops 50 meters per km (250 feet per mile) through the narrow canyon, and passes red cliffs known as the Iron Gates.

138 km (86 miles) Radium Hot Springs

Ride 10 km (6 miles) from Sinclair Pass to Radium Hot Springs.

Take a dip in the natural hot springs at the Aquacourt. Water temperature ranges from 35 to 47 degrees Celsius (95 to 116 degrees Fahrenheit). There is also a swimming pool nearby.

141 km (88 miles) Radium Hot Springs town

Descend through the narrow gap at Sinclair Canyon and then exit from Kootenay National Park to the town of Radium Hot Springs.

Radium Hot Springs has many motels and hotels, stores and restaurants. Stock up on supplies here for the trip to Golden.

Although there are several campgrounds, only the Redstreak campground allows tents. A walking trail leads there from the Aquacourt, eliminating the steep hill on the road to Redstreak.

From Radium Hot Springs, take Highway 95 north through the scenic Columbia River Valley in the Rocky Mountain Trench. To the west are the Purcell and Bugaboo ranges of the Columbia Mountains.

It's 105 km (65 miles) from Radium Hot Springs to Golden. The road's shoulder is narrower here than through the parks.

The towns on this section of the tour have limited accommodation and campgrounds. If you're camping, you may have to find a secluded spot and camp out.

151 km (94 miles) Edgewater

At Edgewater, 10 km (6 miles) north of Radium Hot Springs, are stores, an inn and a campground.

160 km (99 miles) Spur Valley

Spur Valley, 9 km (5.5 miles) north of Edgewater, has a campground and motel.

203 km (126 miles) Taliesin

At Taliesin, 43 km (27 miles) north of Spur Valley, is a guest house.

246 km (153 miles) Golden

Golden has complete services and all types of accommodations. There is a municipal campground near the curling rink.

Turn east on Highway 1 (the Trans Canada Highway). The road climbs intermittently for 20 km (12 miles) overlooking the Kicking Horse River.

The Trans Canada Highway here is narrow and is used by logging trucks. If traffic gets hectic, and even if it doesn't, take a break and enjoy the spectacular views.

271 km (168 miles) Yoho National Park

You enter Yoho National Park 25 km (15 miles) east of Golden.

Numerous viewpoints along the road offer views of the Kicking Horse Valley and the President Range.

You pass the 2.4-km (1.5-mile) Wapta Falls trail where the Kicking Horse River plummets over a wide ledge.

The 3.5-km (2.2-mile) Mount Hunter trail leads to a ridge with a panoramic view, and the 1-km (0.6-mile) Avalanche nature trail goes to the toe of an avalanche slope.

298 km (185 miles) Emerald Lake turn-off

The Emerald Lake turn-off, 27 km (17 miles) east of the Yoho Park gate, leads 8 km (5 miles) to Emerald Lake at the base of the President Range. At Emerald Lake, a highlight of Yoho Park, is a lodge.

301 km (187 miles) Field

Continue on Highway 1 for 3 km (2 miles) through the railroad town (no passenger train service) of Field.

305 km (190 miles) Yoho Valley turn-off

Approximately 4 km (2.5 miles) past Field is the turn-off for the Yoho Valley. This challenging and worthwhile side trip leads 13 km (8 miles) to 384-meter (1,259-foot) Takakkaw Falls, the highest falls in Canada. A hostel, campgrounds and a store are located nearby.

317 km (197 miles) Kicking Horse Pass

The Trans Canada Highway climbs steeply up to Kicking Horse Pass. Along the way you have a view of the Spiral Tunnels, built in 1909, where the railway spirals through two mountains to reduce the grade.

At the summit of Kicking Horse Pass, which is on the Continental Divide, 16 km (10 miles) from Field, you are back in Alberta and Banff National Park.

326 km (203 miles) Lake Louise

Descend on Highway 1 to Lake Louise.

354 km (220 miles) Castle Mountain Junction

At Castle Mountain Junction, 28 km (17 miles) past Lake Louise, ride the Bow Valley Parkway back to Banff.

DAY TOURS STARTING IN BANFF TOWNSITE

Banff Park has a number of scenic roads suitable for day outings from Banff and Lake Louise.

Mount Norquay Drive, 6 km (4 miles)

Mount Norquay Drive climbs to a viewpoint 300 meters (1,000 feet) overlooking the Bow Valley.

Vermilion Lakes Drive, 5 km (3 miles) each way

Branching off Mount Norquay Drive, is 5-km (3-mile) Vermilion Lakes Drive to the picturesque Vermilion Lakes.

Lake Minnewanka Loop, 25 km (15 miles)

The Lake Minnewanka loop takes you along the lower slopes of Cascade Mountain and climbs steadily to Lake Minnewanka, Banff Park's largest lake. Along the way are starting points of the 4-km (2.5 miles) Bankhead Trail and the Stewart Canyon and Aylmer viewpoint.

Bow Valley Parkway from Banff to Lake Louise, 55 km (34 miles)

Following along the Bow River, the Bow Valley Parkway offers a quieter route than the busy Trans Canada Highway. The road is relatively level.

At Johnston's Canyon, 24 km (15 miles) from Banff, a 5.8-km (3.6-mile) nature trail leads past waterfalls to the colorful Ink Pots pools.

Castle Junction, 6 km (4 miles) farther, is the link with the

Banff–Windermere Parkway through Kootenay National Park. (The route is described in the Icefields Parkway tour in this chapter.)

DAY TOURS STARTING IN LAKE LOUISE TOWNSITE

Moraine Lake Road, 14 km (9 miles)

The climb up Moraine Lake Road to the Valley of the Ten Peaks is a steep ascent but leads to spectacular scenery.

Icefields Parkway

For a day tour, you can ride part-way up the Icefields Parkway and return to Lake Louise. (A multi-day tour on the entire Icefields Parkway is also described in this chapter.)

From Lake Louise, go north for 3 km (2 miles) on the Trans Canada Highway to the Icefields Parkway. From here, depending on how energetic you are, you can gradually climb 500 meters (1,640 feet) over the next 40 km (25 miles) toward Bow Pass, the route's highest point.

Along the way you pass Her-bert Lake, the Hector Lake viewpoint, and the Bow Lake viewpoint. You climb steeply on the last 4 km (2.5 miles) to the 2,069-meter (6,787-foot) summit of Bow Pass.

The meadows here are covered with wildflowers during summer. From Bow Pass, you can turn around and glide back to Lake Louise.

Emerald Lake in Yoho Park, 34 km (21 miles) each way

The Emerald Lake turn-off, 28 km (17 miles) west of Lake Louise, leads 8 km (5 miles) to Emerald Lake at the base of the President Range. Emerald Lake is a highlight of Yoho Park. The route is described in the Banff–Radium Hot Springs – Golden loop in this chapter.

BACKCOUNTRY BICYCLING IN BANFF NATIONAL PARK

Overview: Banff Park has 330 km (205 miles) of trails designated for all-terrain bicycling. They range from short trails near Banff and Lake Louise townsites suitable for day tours, to longer trails that can be combined for overnight or longer tours. In the immediate vicinity of Banff and Lake Louise townsites are 50 km (31 miles) of trails for use by all-terrain cyclists.

All-terrain cyclists are not permitted to ride off the trails and should not disturb wildlife. If you are camping overnight in the backcountry, get a park use permit.

Sundance Trail, 3.7 km (2.3 miles)

The Sundance Trail goes from the Cave and Basin in Banff townsite to Sundance Canyon Trailhead.

Healy Creek Road, 4.8 km (3 miles)

Healy Creek Road goes from Sundance Trail junction to Sunshine Road.

Brewster Creek, 48 km (30 miles)

The route along Brewster Creek goes from Healy Creek Road to Bryant Creek via Allenby Pass.

Spray Fireroad, 43.3 km (27 miles)

From the Banff Springs Hotel, the Spray Fireroad leads to the Trail Center.

Goat Creek Trail, 8.4 km (5.2 miles)

The Goat Creek Trail goes 8.4 km (5.2 miles) from the Spray Fireroad to the park boundary and Canmore Road.

Bryant Creek, 10.7 km (6.6 miles)

The Bryant Creek route goes from the trail center to the junction with Allenby Pass Trail.

Redearth Trail, 11.9 km (7.4 miles)

The Redearth Trail leads from a parking lot on Highway 1 to Redearth Warden cabin.

Lake Minnewanka Trail, 36.3 km (22.5 miles)

The 36.3-km (22.5-mile) Lake Minnewanka Trail goes from the lake to Devil's Gap.

Cascade Fireroad, 9 km (5.6 miles)

The Cascade Fireroad is a 9-km (5.6-mile) route from Upper Bankhead Parking lot to Stoney Creek.

Temple Road, 4 km (2.5 miles)

The Temple Road goes from the Fish Creek parking lot to Temple Lodge.

Rundle Riverside Trail, 8.3 km (5.1 miles)

The Rundle Riverside Trail goes 8.3 km (5.1 miles) from the far end of the golf course to the park boundary.

Johnson Lake Loop Trail, 11.7 (7.2 miles)

This tail loops 11.7 km (7.2 miles) around Johnson Lake. It's reached via Lake Minnewanka Road.

More Information: Topographical maps are available at the park office in Banff. See also the guides listed at the end of the chapter.

DAY TOURS IN JASPER NATIONAL PARK

Jasper to Edith Lake, 10 km (6 miles)

For a pleasant short outing, ride the level 10-km (6-mile) route past Beauvert Lake, Jasper Park Lodge and Annette Lake to Edith Lake. There are beaches on Annette and Edith lakes.

Maligne Lake Road, 48 km (30 miles) each way

One of the most scenic routes in Jasper Park, the Maligne Lake

Road is a challenging day-long cycling tour. Some of the route's highlights are also good objectives for a shorter tour.

From Jasper, go east on Highway 16 for 4 km (2.5 miles). Turn left onto the Maligne Lake Road. The road climbs steeply for most of its route 44-km (27-mile) route to Maligne Lake. Elevation gain is over 600 meters (2,000 feet).

Maligne Canyon, 6 km (4 miles) from Highway 16, is a spectacular gorge through the limestone rock. Medicine Lake, 15 km (9 miles) farther, is a 6-km (4-mile) long lake.

Athabasca Falls, 30 km (20 miles)

From Jasper you can head south on the Icefields Parkway to thundering Athabasca Falls, 30 km (20 miles) away. Make it a loop tour by cycling Highway 93A one way and Highway 93 the other. (See the Icefields Parkway description.)

BACKCOUNTRY BICYCLING IN JASPER NATIONAL PARK

Overview: Jasper National Park allows all-terrain bicycles on many of its 1,000-km (600-mile) network of trails which wind through the mountains. Cyclists should stay on the trail and not disturb wildlife. Overnight camping requires a camp use permit.

The trails where all-terrain bicycling are not permitted are the Skyline Trail, Tonquin Trail, Lake Annette Trail, Maligne Canyon from first to sixth Bridge and Mount Edith Cavell day-use trails.

Old Fort Point and Valley of the Five Lakes, 11.2 km (6.9 miles)

A popular route, Valley of the Five Lakes trail begins on the Icefields Parkway 10 km (6 miles) south of Jasper and goes to five picturesque lakes.

• Palisade Fire Road, 10.8 km (6.7 miles)
• Whirlpool Fire Road to Tie Camp, 8.5 km (5.2 miles)
• Fortress Lake Trail, 24 km (15 miles)
• Saturday Night Lake, 24.6 km (15.2 miles)
• Geraldine Fire Road, 5.5 km (3.4 miles)
• Fryatt Trail to lower Fryatt campsite, 11.4 km (7 miles)
• Athabasca River, 22 km (13.6 miles)
• Overlander trail, 15.6 km (9.7 miles)
• Jacques Lake Trail and South Boundary Trail, 12.2 km (7.5 miles) and 56.5 km (35.1 miles)
• Merlin Pass Trail, 30 km (18.6 miles)

- North Boundary Trail, 48 km (29.8 miles)

More Information: Topographic maps are available at the park headquarters. For trail details see the trail guides listed at the end of the chapter.

JASPER TO MOUNT ROBSON

Length: 83 km (51 miles)
Time: One to two days
Rating: Easy
Terrain: No difficult climbs to Yellowhead Pass—one of the lowest passes on the Continental Divide.
Roads: Highway 16 has wide, paved shoulders
Traffic: A lot
Connects with: Icefields Parkway, Jasper to Prince George tour (described in British Columbia chapter).
Start: Jasper townsite, served by VIA Rail.
Overview: Lofty 3,954-meter (12,972-foot) Mount Robson is the highest peak in the Canadian Rockies. En route from Jasper to Mount Robson Provincial Park are rugged snow-capped peaks, lakes, rivers and wildflowers. Mount Robson is usually cloud-topped, but if the weather is good you might catch a glimpse of the peak.

THE ROUTE:

0 km (0 miles) Jasper

Leave Jasper on Highway 16, the Yellowhead Highway, which has a wide paved shoulder.

25 km (15 miles) Yellowhead Pass

The road has no difficult climbs as you ascend to Yellowhead Pass, 25 km (15 miles) west of Jasper.

At 1,131 meters (3,710 feet) Yellowhead Pass is one of the lowest passes in the Continental Divide. This is the watershed dividing waters that go east via the Miette, Athabasca and Mackenzie rivers to the Arctic Ocean; and the waters that go west into the Fraser River to the Pacific.

The divide is also the boundary between Jasper National Park and Mount Robson Provincial Park and between Alberta and British Columbia.

83 km (52 miles) Mount Robson viewpoint

Highway 16 skirts the shores of Yellowhead Lake, the Fraser River and Moose Lake. You then descend to the Mount Robson viewpoint.

Here are campgrounds and the start of a 22-km (14-mile) hike up through the Valley of a Thousand Falls. It leads to Berg Lake from which Mount Robson rises 2,400 meters (7,872 feet).

Option: Mount Robson to Kamloops

From Mount Robson you can continue farther into British Co-

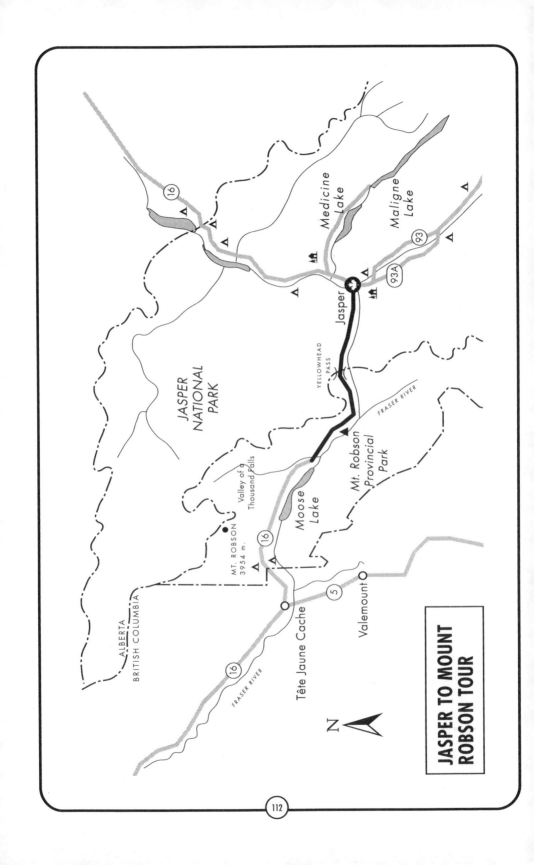

Medicine Lake

Maligne Lake

16

93

93A

Jasper

JASPER NATIONAL PARK

YELLOWHEAD PASS

FRASER RIVER

Mt. Robson Provincial Park

Valley of a Thousand Falls

Moose Lake

MT. ROBSON 3954 m.

16

ALBERTA
BRITISH COLUMBIA

16

FRASER RIVER

Tête Jaune Cache

5

Valemount

N

JASPER TO MOUNT ROBSON TOUR

lumbia. From Tête Jaune Cache you can tour on Highway 5 to Kamloops (described in the British Columbia chapter).

Option: Mount Robson to Prince George and Prince Rupert

You can continue on Highway 16 to Prince George and Prince Rupert (these tours are de-scribed in the British Columbia chapter).

More Information: Jasper National Park, P.O. Box 10, Jasper, Alberta T0E 1E0, (403) 852-4401. Mount Robson Provincial Park, Box 579, Valemount, British Columbia V0E 2Z0, (604) 566-4325.

KANANASKIS COUNTRY

Kananaskis Country is a magnificent mountain recreation area along the eastern border of Banff National Park, only 100 km (60 miles) west of Calgary.

Within its 4,000 square km (1,600 square miles) of wilderness are 17 peaks over 3,000 meters (10,000 feet), including 3,400-meter (11,300-foot) Mount Joffre, the most southerly glacier in Alberta's Rocky Mountains.

You will also encounter alpine meadows and blue lakes. Sheep, wa-piti, moose, weasel, coyote, hares, pikas (also called rock rabbits though they resemble guinea pigs), marmots, warblers, chickadees, spruce grouse and Canada jay are among the wildlife that can be seen here.

Kananaskis Country encompasses several provincial parks: Bragg Creek, Bow Valley and Peter Lougheed provincial parks. Peter Lougheed Park is the heart of Kananaskis Country.

KANANASKIS TRAIL OVER HIGHWOOD PASS TO CALGARY

Length: 50 km (31 miles) one way to Peter Lougheed Park; 210 km (130 miles) for the whole loop.
Time: One to three days
Rating: Intermediate to expert
Terrain: Mountainous
Roads: Highway 40 is well graded with wide, paved shoulders
Traffic: Light

Connects with: Off-road bicycle trails in Peter Lougheed Provincial Park; Across Alberta tour
Start: Seebe, at the junction of Highway 40 and the Trans Canada Highway, 61 km (38 miles) west of Calgary, and 47 km (29 miles) east of Banff.

To get to Seebe from Calgary, take

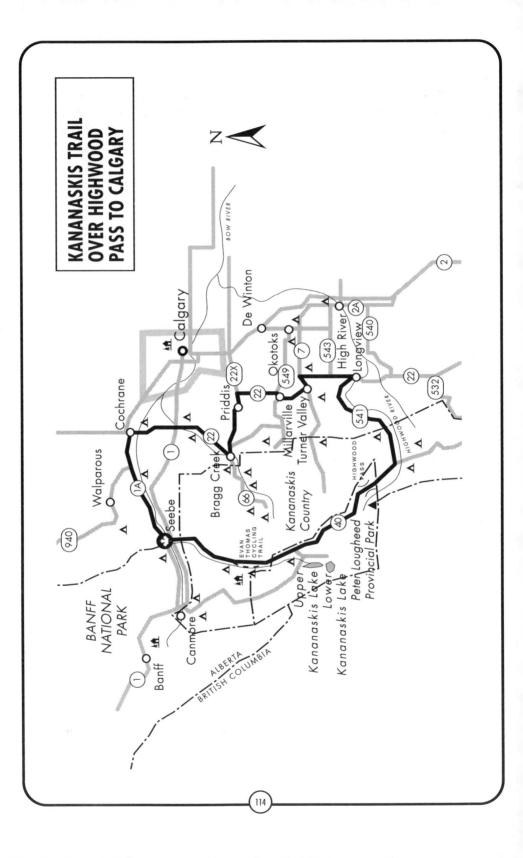

KANANASKIS TRAIL OVER HIGHWOOD PASS TO CALGARY

N

Calgary

De Winton

BOW RIVER

Cochrane

Priddis

(22X)

Okotoks

(22)

(549)

(7)

High River

(543)

(2A)

Longview

(540)

(2)

Millarville

Turner Valley

(22)

(532)

Walparous

(22)

Seebe

Bragg Creek

(1)

(1A)

(66)

Kananaskis Country

HIGHWOOD RIVER

(541)

(940)

EVAN THOMAS CYCLING TRAIL

HIGHWOOD PASS

(40)

Banff

(1)

Canmore

BANFF NATIONAL PARK

ALBERTA

BRITISH COLUMBIA

Upper Kananaskis Lake

Lower Kananaskis Lake

Peter Lougheed Provincial Park

Highway 8 west and then go north on Highway 22 through Cochrane to Highway 1A. Ride Highway 1A to Seebe.

Overview: This very scenic route takes you through the Kananaskis Valley, with spectacular mountain vistas of several ranges of snow-covered peaks and the Continental Divide to the west.

Along Highway 40, known as the Kananaskis Trail, are many picnic areas and campgrounds in scenic surroundings. You can ride to Peter Lougheed Park, use it as a base to explore the area, including the park's paved off-road bicycle trails.

Return via the same route. Or, you can do a loop by continuing south on Highway 40 over 2,227-meter (7,306-foot) Highwood Pass, Canada's highest road, and turning east through foothills to Longview and then north through ranchland to Calgary.

The road over Highwood Pass, 68 km (42 miles) south of the Trans Canada Highway, is usually open to cars June 15 to November 30, but can be used by cyclists during the off-season as well. If you're cycling over Highwood Pass, carry all your food.

THE ROUTE:

0 km (0 miles) Seebe

6 km (4 miles) Barrier Lake Information Center

Head south on Highway 40. The Barrier Lake Information Center is 6 km (4 miles) south of the Trans Canada Highway.

The road is level as you pass man-made Barrier Lake and dam, and the University of Calgary's 6,070-hectare (15,000-acre) Kananaskis Forest Experimental Station. Here are 2.3 km (1.4 miles) of interpretive trails on forest management, and a lookout tower.

14 km (9 miles) O'Shaughnessy Falls

Continue south past O'Shaughnessy Falls, a man-made waterfall, 14 km (9 miles) south of Seebe.

Follow the fast-flowing Kananaskis River past Wasootch Creek and the Mount Lorette Ponds, which are stocked with trout and are popular for fishing.

23 km (14 miles) Ribbon Creek

Ribbon Creek, 23 km (14 miles) south of Seebe, is a recreation area offering a youth hostel, 60 km (37 miles) of hiking trails and the paved Evan Thomas cycling path.

The Evan Thomas path leads 8 km (5 miles) over a flat route parallel to Highway 40 to Wedge Pond where it links with Highway 40.

26.5 km (16 miles) Kananaskis Golf Course

The Kananaskis Golf Course is 3.5 km (2 miles) farther along Highway 40. You pass the Mount Kidd Recreational Vehicle Park, the Eau Claire campground, and the Fortress Mountain ski area.

44.5 km (28 miles) Peter Lougheed Provincial Park

Enter Peter Lougheed Provincial Park 18 km (11 miles) after the golf course.

50.5 km (31 miles) turn-off to Kananaskis Visitor Center, and Upper and Lower Kananaskis Lakes bicycle paths

Take the turn-off for the Kananaskis Visitor Center, 6 km (3.7 miles) past the Peter Lougheed Park entrance. The road leads to the Upper and Lower Kananaskis Lakes and several campgrounds—including the Interlakes campground, which is for tents only.

This is the area to use as a base to explore the recreational pathways (described separately in this chapter) and the surrounding area, including Highwood Pass. If you choose, you can then return to the Trans Canada via the same route, or continue south on Highway 40.

Main tour continues on Highway 40
67.5 km (42 miles) Highwood Pass

To continue on the loop route, ride south on Highway 40. The road climbs over 17 km (10.5 miles) gradually at first and then steeply through sub-alpine meadows and past spectacular mountain scenery to the summit of Highwood Pass, Canada's highest paved road.

At Elbow Pass Junction is a picnic area that is a good resting spot 2 km (1.2 miles) before Highwood Pass. Nearby is the 0.4-km (0.2-mile) Rock Glacier interpretive trail.

At the summit of Highwood Pass is sub-alpine Highwood Meadows, with two interpretive trails: the 1-km (0.6-mile) High-wood Meadows trail and the 5-km (3-mile) Ptarmigan Cirque Trail.

69.1 km (43 miles) Peter Lougheed Provincial Park boundary

After exploring the meadows, continue south on Highway 40, descending gradually. After 1.6 km (1 mile) you pass the Peter Lougheed Park boundary, although you're still in Kananaskis Country.

As you ride along the Highwood River you gradually emerge from the mountains to the foothills and ranching country.

You pass a good selection of picnic areas including Trout Ponds, which as its name suggests offer well-stocked ponds for fishing. There is also good fishing at many of the picnic areas on the Highwood River.

104.5 km (65 miles) Highwood Junction

Turn east at Highwood Junction, 37 km (23 miles) from Highwood Pass, onto Secondary Road 541. At Highwood Junction is a store for food and limited supplies.

147.5 km (92 miles) Longview

Ride Secondary Road 541—leaving Kananaskis Country—to Longview, 43 km (26 miles) from Highwood Junction.

Option: Longview to Calgary, 66 km (41 miles)
213.5 km (133 miles) Calgary

From Longview, to head to Calgary, ride north on Highway 22, which has narrow shoulders, and then east on Highway 22X to Calgary, a distance of 66 km (41 miles). If you want to go to Calgary, turn east onto Highway 22 and ride 10 km (6 miles) into the south end of the city.

Options: Longview to Highway 1, 90 km (56 miles); or Longview to Highway 1A, 103 km (64 miles); or Longview to Highway 40, 153 km (95 miles)

237.5 km (148 miles) Highway 1

From Longview, to head back to Highway 1—the Trans Canada Highway—or quieter Highway 1A, both of which go west to Banff or east to Calgary, continue north on Highway 22 to Highway 66 near Priddis. Go west on Highway 66 and turn north on Highway 22 through Bragg Creek to Highway 1, a distance of 90 km (56 miles) from Longview.

250.5 km (156 miles) Highway 1A

Or, from Highway 1 go another 13 km (8 miles) on Highway 22 to Highway 1A just west of Cochrane.

300.5 km (187 miles) Highway 40

From Cochrane, it's approximately 50 km (30 miles) west on Highway 1A to this tour's starting point at Highway 40. There is no shoulder on Highway 1A for 20 km (12 miles) through the Stoney Indian Reserve. The route along Highway 1A is part of the Across Alberta tour (described in this chapter).

RECREATIONAL PATHS IN KANANASKIS COUNTRY

Overview: Within Peter Lougheed Provincial Park are 70 km (43 miles) of paved bicycle paths that take you through forests and along the shores of Upper and Lower Kananaskis lakes. The paths are wide and well marked. The Lodgepole, Wheeler and Lakeside trails connect to form a 20-km (12-mile) path from the Visitor Center to Elk Pass.

Lodgepole Trail, 5 km (3 miles)

The Lodgepole Trail goes from the Kananaskis Visitor Center to the Elkwood campground and picnic area, where it links with the Wheeler Trail.

Wheeler Trail, 9.4 km (5.8 miles)

From Elkwood the 9.4-km (5.8-mile) Wheeler Trail is a loop to the Boulton campground parking lot and offers scenic views. At Boulton, it links with the Lakeside Trail.

Lakeside Trail, 5 km (3 miles)

The 5-km (3-mile) Lakeside Trail from Boulton to Elk Pass parking lot has several steep hills approaching Upper Kananaskis Lake.

Evan Thomas Trail, 8 km (5 miles)

In the Ribbon Creek area, the 8-km (5-mile) Evan Thomas Trail goes from the Ribbon Creek parking area and parallels Highway 40 to the Kananaskis Golf Course.

Eau Claire recreational area
In the Eau Claire recreational area, located near Wedge Pond

on Highway 40 is a 1.5-km paved loop.

BACKCOUNTRY BICYCLING IN KANANASKIS COUNTRY

Overview: Kananaskis Country has a variety of backcountry routes for all-terrain bicycling, ranging from day routes to trips of two to five days. Topographic maps are available at the park headquarters. See the guides at the end of the chapter.

Day Tours

Skogan Pass Trail, 19 km (12 miles)
Popular day tours include the Skogan Pass trail from Dead Man's Flat to Ribbon Creek.

Moose Mountain Fire Road, 7 km (4.4 miles)
The 7-km (4.4-mile) Moose Mountain Fire Road leads north 7 km (4.4 miles) from Highway 66, just past Paddy's Flat.

Plateau Mountain traverse, 14.5 km (9 miles)
The 14.5-km (9-mile) Plateau Mountain traverse goes from Wilkinson Summit to Livingstone River and returns by the Forestry Trunk Road 940.

Carnarvon Lake trail, 10 km (6 miles)
On the 10-km (6-mile) Carnar-

von Lake trail, you can ride your mountain bikes along the stretch of trail that is a logging road, lock the bike to a tree, and hike up to the lake.

Two Days or Longer

Sheep River Trail circuit
A popular two-day trip is a circuit along parts of the Sheep River Trail, Forgetmenot Ridge and the Big Elbow Trail.

Highwood and Upper Oldman areas
For trips of two to five days, explore trails in the extensive network of logging and exploration roads in the West Highwood, East Highwood, Upper Oldman, Livingstone, West Elbow and West Sheep areas.

More Information: Kananaskis Country, 1011 Glenmore Trail S.W., Suite 412, Calgary, Alberta T2V 4R6, (403) 297-3362.

DRUMHELLER DINOSAURS AND BADLANDS: CALGARY TO DRUMHELLER

Length: 138 km (85 miles) each way
Time: Two to four days
Rating: Easy to intermediate
Terrain: Flat until abrupt descent to Badlands
Roads: Narrow, paved shoulders
Traffic: Relatively light
Connects with: Across Alberta tour
Start: Calgary, which has an international airport.
Overview: The Alberta Badlands near Drumheller are known for the rich deposits of dinosaur skeletons and prehistoric fossils that have been found here. Mushroom-shaped hoodoos, eroded from hills, give an eerie atmosphere to the arid Red Deer Valley. You can also explore remains of pioneering settlers and mines.

This tour goes from Calgary to Drumheller and then guides you to the area's attractions. During the summer the Red Deer Valley can be very warm, so always carry sufficient water. The area can also experiences strong winds from the west.

THE ROUTE:

0 km (0 miles) Calgary

20 km (12 miles) Highway 9

Go east on Highway 1—the Trans Canada Highway—for 20 km (12 miles) to the junction with Highway 9.

65 km (40 miles) Beiseker

Cycle north on Highway 9 through prairie farmland and the town of Irricana, to Beiseker 45 km (28 miles) from the Trans Canada Highway. There are municipal campgrounds at Irricana and Beiseker.

109 km (68 miles) Drumheller

At Beiseker, Highway 9 turns east. You descend 120 meters (394 feet) from the prairie level into the Badlands of the Red Deer River Valley and the town of Drumheller, 44 km (27 miles) from Beiseker.

Use Drumheller as a base to explore the area. A good selection of accommodations and campgrounds are available. Nearby Midland Provincial Park is a day-use park, which does not allow camping.

The Drumheller Dinosaur Museum at 385 First Street East, has exhibits on the prehistoric life and geological phenomena in this area, which is known as the "Valley of the Dinosaurs."

Side trip: Drumheller to Midland Provincial Park, 6 km (3.7 miles)

0 km (0 miles) Drumheller

6 km (3.7 miles) Midland Provincial Park

Just 6 km (3.7 miles) west of Drumheller on a route called the "Dinosaur Trail," Midland Provincial Park is in the midst of the Badlands. Interpretive trails

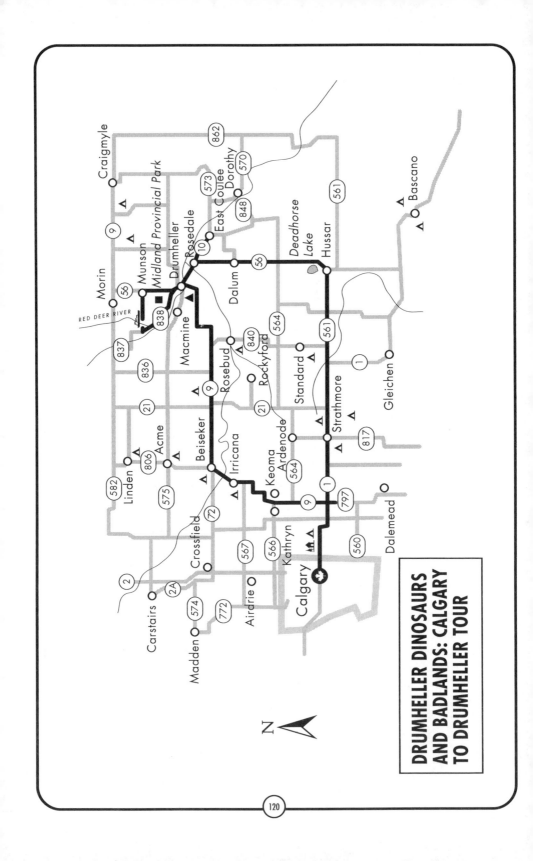

DRUMHELLER DINOSAURS AND BADLANDS: CALGARY TO DRUMHELLER TOUR

explore the geological formations, and hiking trails go through an old mine site and surrounding Badlands.

Here also is the Tyrrell Museum of Palaeontology, featuring a variety of fossils that trace the evolution of life, and an extensive display of dinosaurs. The interactive displays use computers and videos.

Side trip: Drumheller to East Coulee, 20 km (12 miles)

0 km (0 miles) Drumheller

8.5 km (5 miles) Rosedale Swinging Bridge

Take Highway 10 southeast of Drumheller toward East Coulee. The Rosedale Swinging Bridge, at 8.5 km (5 miles) from Drumheller, leads to trails through the old mining area. The bridge was built by the men of the Old Star Mine.

18 km (11 miles) Hoodoos

You see Hoodoo formations (flat rock on top of sandstone pillars), 18 km (11 miles) from Drumheller. Hoodoos are the result of years of wind and water erosion. There are picnic facilities here.

20 km (12 miles) East Coulee

East Coulee, 20 km (12 miles) southeast of Drumheller on Highway 10, was an important coal mining camp.

Side trip: Drumheller to Bleriot Ferry, 48 km (30 miles) loop

0 km (0 miles) Drumheller

24 km (15 miles) Bleriot Ferry

Another worthwhile route to explore from Drumheller is on Secondary Highway 837 along the Red Deer River to the free Bleriot Ferry. Built in 1913, it's the last cable ferry operating on the Red Deer River.

48 km (30 miles) Drumheller

Ride the ferry and cycle back to Drumheller on Secondary Highway 838. You pass Horsethief Canyon Viewpoint overlooking variations of sedimentary strata in the canyon. Paths lead down to petrified oyster beds.

Main tour continues: return from Drumheller to Calgary

To return to Calgary, you can retrace your route back from Drumheller. Or, you can take the following route.

Option: return from Drumheller to Calgary via Routes 10, 56, 561 and 1.

Take Route 10 to the junction with Route 56 and cycle south on Route 56 to Deadhorse Lake. Turn west at Hussar and follow Route 561 to Highway 1—the Trans Canada Highway—which goes through Strathmore and back to Calgary.

ACROSS ALBERTA

Length: 523 km (324 miles)
Time: Three to six days
Rating: Intermediate
Terrain: A slice of Alberta: Rocky Mountains, foothills, ranchland and prairie.
Roads: Highway 1A—the Bow Valley Parkway—has paved shoulders less than 1.2 meters (4 feet) wide; Highway 1—the Trans Canada Highway has paved shoulders more than 1.8 meters (6 feet) wide; Highway 9 from Calgary to the Drumheller area has shoulders less than 1.2 meters (4 feet) wide, west of Drumheller its shoulders are between 1.2 to 1.8 meters (4 to 6 feet) wide.
Traffic: Highways 1A and 9 have light traffic; Highway 1 has heavy traffic.
Connects with: Across British Columbia and Across Saskatchewan tours, Icefields Parkway tour, Kananaskis Country tour, Banff through Radium Hot Springs to Golden tour, Drumheller Dinosaurs and Badlands tour, and day tours in Banff Park.
Start: Lake Louise, Alberta, just east of the Kicking Horse Pass on the British Columbia border.
Overview: Crossing Alberta from west to east takes you from the heights of the Kicking Horse Pass on the British Columbia border, through the Rocky Mountain grandeur of Banff National Park. From

Banff you descend through Rocky Mountains Foothills, flat ranchland and prairie wheatfields.

The route described below goes from west to east, and if you have a choice, that direction is recommended. Strong winds often come down off the mountains helping cyclists riding east, and adding wind resistance for those cycling west. There is generally a good selection of campgrounds and accommodations across Alberta. Between Banff and Calgary there are only a few campgrounds, so if you're camping, plan in advance.

The water available along the Highway 9 part of this tour is heavy with minerals, making it undrinkable. Buy drinks in the stores along the way.

THE ROUTE:

0 km (0 miles) Lake Louise
60 km (37 miles) Banff

From Lake Louise, follow Highway 1A, the Bow Valley Parkway, which has less traffic than the Trans Canada Highway, to Banff.

82 km (51 miles) Canmore

From Banff, take Highway 1—the Trans Canada Highway—east.

Near Canmore, just outside the Banff National Park gates, turn back onto Highway 1A, which winds along the north side of the Bow River. Highway

1A is quieter than the Trans Canada Highway.

107 km (66 miles) Seebe

The turn-off for Seebe, 47 km (29 miles) east of Banff, leads to Highway 40, known as the Kananaskis Trail. (A tour on the Kananaskis Trail is described in this chapter.)

Bow Valley Provincial Park has camping.

157 km (98 miles) Cochrane

Continuing east on Highway 1A you cycle along scenic Ghost Lake as you gradually traverse the Rocky Mountain Foothills to the prairie. You climb a steep hill for several km near Cochrane, 50 km (31 miles), east of the turn-off for Seebe.

195 km (121 miles) Calgary

Ride Highway 1A to Calgary, 20 km (13 miles) farther, which has a wide selection of stores and accommodation.

215 km (134 miles) Highway 9

From Calgary, go east on Highway 1—the Trans Canada Highway—for 20 km (12 miles) to the junction with Highway 9. (The route from Calgary to Drumheller is described in the Drumheller Dinosaurs and Badlands tour.)

304 km (189 miles) Drumheller

Cycle north on Highway 9 through prairie farmland to Beiseker 45 km (28 miles) from the Trans Canada Highway. Highway 9 has paved shoulders, which are less than 1.2 meters (4 feet) wide.

At Beiseker, Highway 9 turns east. You descend 120 meters (394 feet) from the prairie level into the Red Deer River Valley and the town of Drumheller, 44 km (27 miles) from Beiseker.

Continue riding east on Highway 9. This stretch of Highway 9 has paved shoulders 1.2 to 1.8 meters (4 to 6 feet) wide.

Stay on Highway 9 for another 136 km (84 miles) to Alsask on the Saskatchewan-Alberta border.

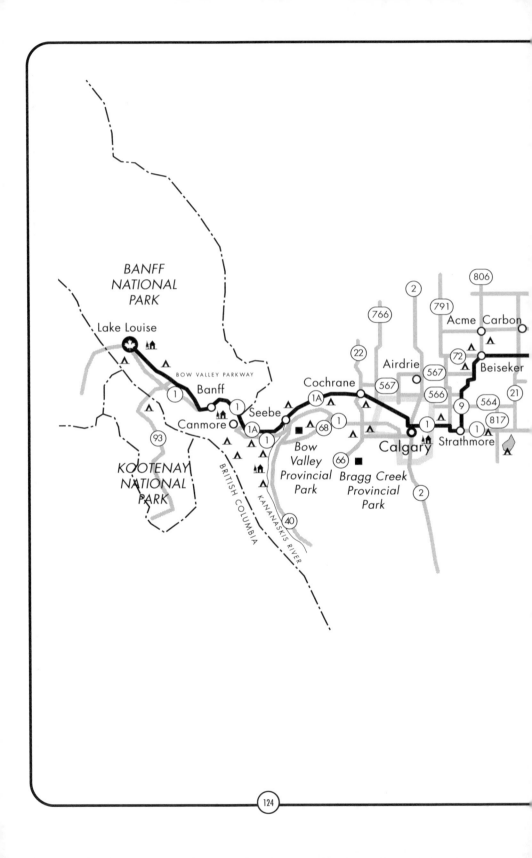

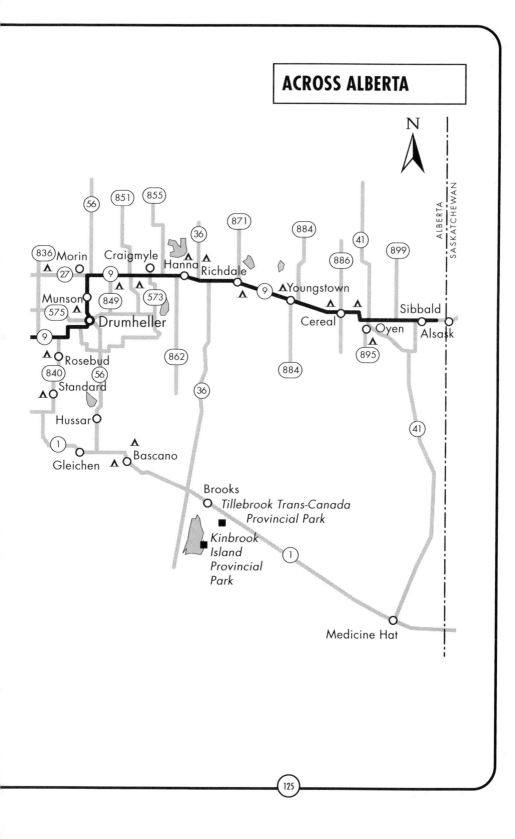

N

ALBERTA
SASKATCHEWAN

836 Morin
27
56
851 855
Craigmyle
36
871
884
41 899
886
9
Hanna Richdale
9 Youngstown
Munson
849 573
Cereal
Sibbald
575
Drumheller
Oyen Alsask
895
862
Rosebud
840 56
Standard
884
36
Hussar
1
Bascano
41
Gleichen
Brooks
Tillebrook Trans-Canada
Provincial Park
Kinbrook
Island
Provincial
Park
1
Medicine Hat

GUIDEBOOKS

A Cyclist's Guidebook to the Canadian Rockies, by Larry Barnes, details the Columbia Icefields Parkway route. Available from: Rocky Mountain Cycle Tours, Box 1978, Canmore, Alberta T0L 0M0, telephone (403) 678-6770; $6.95 (add $1 for GST and shipping).

Backcountry Biking in the Canadian Rockies, by Gerhardt Lepp. Available from: Rocky Mountain Books, #4 Spruce Centre S.W., Calgary, Alberta T3C 3B3, telephone (403) 249-9490; $15.95.

Calgary Parks and Pathways, by Terry Bullick. Available from Rocky Mountain Books; $9.95.

The Canadian Rockies Bicycling Guide, by Gail Helgason and John Dodd. Available from: Lone Pine Publishing, 206, 10426-81st Avenue, Edmonton, Alberta T6E 1X5, telephone (403) 433-9333; $9.95 (add $1.50 for GST and shipping).

The Canadian Rockies Trail Guide, by Brian Patton and Bart Robinson. Available from: Book and Art Den, P.O. Box 1420, Banff, Alberta T0L 0C0, telephone (403) 762-4126; $14.95 (plus postage and handling of $1 in Canada, $2 in the United States, $8 international).

Parkways of the Canadian Rockies, by Brian Patton. Available from: Book and Art Den; $14.95.

(Tourism Saskatchewan)

Saskatchewan

There's far more to Saskatchewan than the stereotyped image of treeless prairie. Saskatchewan has exciting tours for cyclists, who can discover glacier-carved valleys, lakes, forests, wildlife and important historic sites.

Cutting across Saskatchewan are valleys with lakes and forests that are preserved in provincial parks. Northern Saskatchewan is covered by a coniferous forest with many lakes and rivers.

These tours explore the diverse scenery in Saskatchewan's national park and provincial parks and their surrounding areas. You can use the parks as a base from which to tour. The small towns let you discover more about Saskatchewan.

Tourist Information: For general tourist information, including a map and a Saskatchewan Accommodation and Campground Guide, contact Tourism Saskatchewan, 1919 Saskatchewan Drive, Regina, Saskatchewan S4P 3V7. Or, in Canada and the United States call toll free 1-800-667-7191, in Saskatchewan toll-free 1-800-667-7538, in Regina or from overseas (306) 787-2300, Fax (306) 787-3872.

Roads: Most of Saskatchewan's highways have wide paved shoulders, which makes cycling safe and enjoyable.

Weather: Saskatchewan has a continental climate with short, hot summers and long, cold winters. During the summer, average temperature varies from 10 degrees Celsius (50 degrees Fahrenheit) at sunrise to 24 degrees Celsius (75 degrees Fahrenheit) in the afternoon. Average annual precipitation is 28 to 51 cm (11 to 20 inches), with half occurring during June, July and August.

Shifting winds can be a concern, it's a good idea to start early in the day before the wind picks up.

Hostels: Hostels in Saskatchewan are operated by the Canadian Hostelling Association/Saskatchewan Region, 628 Henderson Drive, Regina, Saskatchewan S4N 5X3, telephone (306) 721-2990, fax (306) 721-2667. The Turgeon International Hostel is at 2310 McIntyre Street, Regina, telephone (306) 791-8165.

Bicycling: Saskatchewan Cycling Association, 2205 Victoria Avenue, Regina, Saskatchewan S4P 0S4, (306) 780-9289.

Trains: For information on VIA Rail train service while in Saskatchewan, call toll-free 1-800-561-8630.

Airports: Major airports are located in Regina, Saskatoon and Prince Albert.

Buses: Saskatchewan Transportation Company (STC) bus lines, 2041 Hamilton Street, Regina, Saskatchewan S7P 2E2, (306) 787-3340.

Capital: Regina, which is situated 160 km (100 miles) north of the United States border.

Area: 651,900 square km (251,700 square miles)

Population: 988,928 in 1991. Although Saskatchewan still depends on agriculture—the province produces more than 60 per cent of the wheat grown in Canada—over 60 per cent of the people now live in cities and towns.

History: Aboriginal peoples have lived here for at least 10,000 years. In the late seventeenth century, European fur traders explored this territory seeking beaver pelts.

With the building of the Canadian Pacific Railway in the 1880s, many thousands of homesteaders—attracted by promises of free land—settled the territory. In 1885, the Métis (people of mixed North American Indian and French descent), under the leadership of Louis Riel, rebeled over rights to possession of land. The rebellion was put down by the Northwest Mounted Police. (The Battle Tour visits historic sites from these events.)

In 1905 Saskatchewan was created from part of what was then the Northwest Territories.

Terrain: The Precambrian Shield of rugged hills, forests and lakes covers the northern part of Saskatchewan. To the south, the prairie grain belt is one of the world's great wheat producers. Southwestern Saskatchewan's Cypress Hills, which reach 1,392 meters (4,566 feet) is the highest point not only in the province but in Canada between the Rocky Mountains and Labrador.

REGINA BICYCLE ROUTES

Regina's natural areas, such as the Wascana Center, are all man-made from a featureless prairie. All the city's trees were planted.

Bicycle and pedestrian paths wind through the Wascana Center and along Wascana Creek. Wascana Center, a 930-hectare (2,300-acre) park near the city center, has a man-made lake, a waterfowl park and historic points of interest. Also here are the Saskatchewan Museum of Natural History, the Saskatchewan Science Center and the MacKenzie Art Gallery.

Regina's tree-lined streets, which are laid out in a grid pattern, also offer enjoyable cycling.

More Information: Tourism Regina, Box 3355, Regina, Saskatchewan S4P 3H1, telephone (306) 789-5099

SASKATOON BICYCLE ROUTES

Saskatoon is known as the "City of Bridges" from its seven bridges spanning the South Saskatchewan River. Cyclists can enjoy riding the city's quiet tree-lined streets and riverbank trails known as the Meewasin Valley Trail System. The trails are shared with pedestrians.

More Information: You can obtain a city map from City Hall or Tourism Saskatoon, Box 369, Saskatoon, Saskatchewan S7K 3L3, telephone (306) 242-1206

SWIFT CURRENT TO SASKATCHEWAN LANDING PROVINCIAL PARK

Length: 50 km (31 miles)
Time: One to two days
Rating: Easy
Terrain: Level to rolling, occasional valleys
Roads: 1- to 2-meter- (3- to 6.5-foot-) wide shoulders
Traffic: Light
Connects with: Across Saskatchewan tour
Start: Swift Current
Overview: Saskatchewan Landing Park is one of three provincial parks on Lake Diefenbaker. The center of this 57-square-km (22-square-mile) park is at the west end of the lake, in a steeply sloped and wooded valley marking the intersection between the South Saskatchewan River and Lake Diefenbaker. The lake has sandy beaches and is popular for boating.

Attractions in Swift Current include the Prairie Wildlife Center and Wright Historical Museum.

THE ROUTE:
0 km (0 miles)
50 km (31 miles) Saskatchewan Landing Provincial Park

From Swift Current go north on Highway 4 for 50 km (31 miles) to Saskatchewan Landing Provincial Park. Highway 4 has a paved 1-meter (3-foot) wide shoulder. Gently rolling fields and a few trees line the road. You then descend the valley's slope. Return is by the same route.

More Information: Saskatchewan Landing Provincial Park, 350 Cheadle Street West, Swift Current, Saskatchewan S9H 4G3, telephone (306) 375-2434

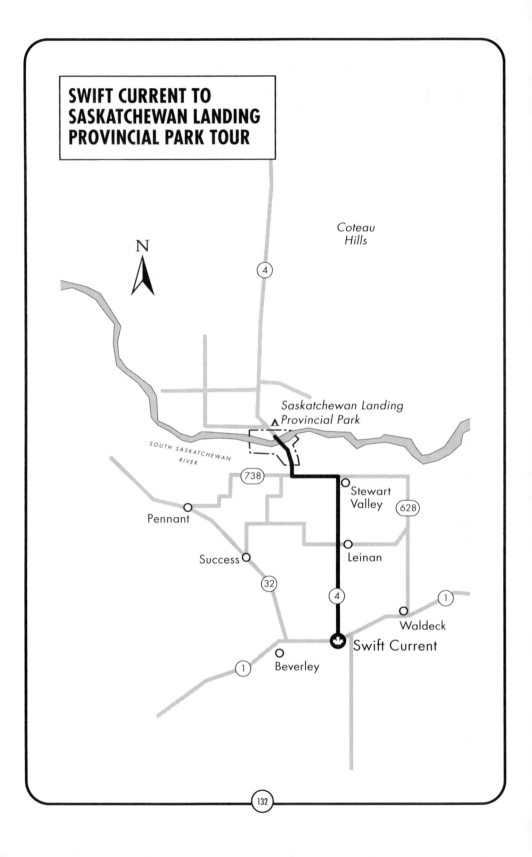

SWIFT CURRENT TO
SASKATCHEWAN LANDING
PROVINCIAL PARK TOUR

N

Coteau
Hills

4

Saskatchewan Landing
Provincial Park

SOUTH SASKATCHEWAN
RIVER

738

Stewart
Valley

628

Pennant

Success

Leinan

32

4

1

Waldeck

Swift Current

1

Beverley

MOOSE JAW TO BUFFALO POUND PROVINCIAL PARK LOOP

Length: 57 km (35 miles) round trip
Time: One to two days
Rating: Easy
Terrain: Mostly flat; some climbing and descents in the Moose Jaw Valley
Roads: Highways 1 and 2 have 1- to 2-meter- (3- to 6.5-foot-) wide paved shoulders
Traffic: Light
Connects with: Across Saskatchewan tour
Start: Moose Jaw
Overview: Southern Saskatchewan's flat featureless prairie is the picture most people have of the province. The flatness is broken by the Qu'Appelle Valley, which dips 120 meters (400 feet) below the level of the prairie. Here abound prairie wildflowers, many varieties of trees, lush meadows, and sparkling waters.

Carved by glaciers thousands of years ago, the Qu'Appelle Valley crosses two thirds of Saskatchewan. Buffalo Pound Provincial Park, 30 km (19 miles) north of Moose Jaw lies in the valley. The park's name recalls the days when Natives herded and slaughtered buffalo here. At the Bison Range you can see a herd of bison in their natural prairie habitat. At Nicolle Flats, another of the park's features, is a marshland nature walk where many species of birds can be seen.

Explore the park, and then use it as a base to visit the neighboring countryside.

Moose Jaw's attractions include the Moose Jaw Museum, a wild animal park and Bushell Park at the Canadian Forces Base, which is the home of the Saskatchewan Air Show. Camping facilities are located in southeast Moose Jaw.

The Moose Jaw River bends in the shape of a moose's jaw, hence the name of the town.

THE ROUTE:

0 km (0 miles) Moose Jaw
18 km (11 miles) Highway 202

Head north for 18 km (11 miles) on Highway 2 which has a wide, paved shoulder to Highway 202. Just outside Moose Jaw the road climbs up from Moose Jaw Creek.

29 km (18 miles) Buffalo Pound Provincial Park

Go east on Highway 202 across flat, open fields for 11 km (7 miles) to Buffalo Pound Provincial Park.

52 km (32 miles) Highway 1 the Trans Canada Highway

When you're ready to return to Moose Jaw, ride south on Highway 301 for 23 km (14 miles) over flat terrain and then down the Moose Jaw Valley to Highway 1 (the Trans Canada Highway), which has wide paved shoulders.

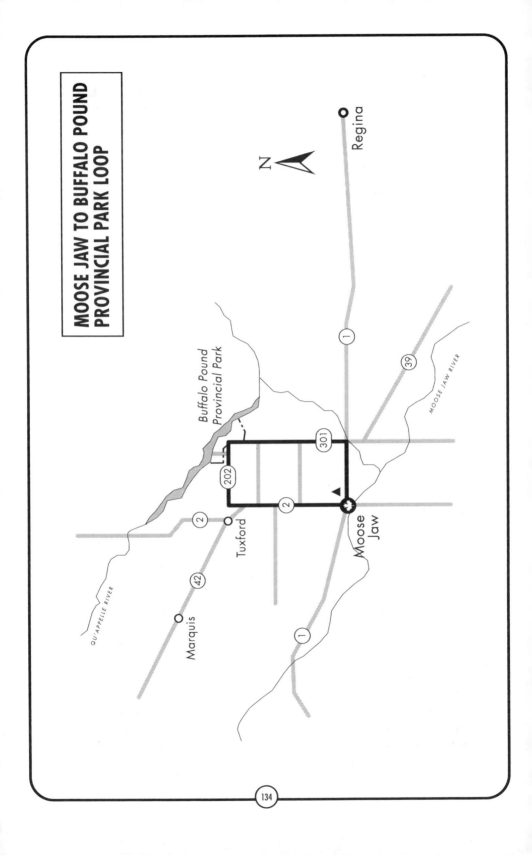

MOOSE JAW TO BUFFALO POUND PROVINCIAL PARK LOOP

N

Regina

Buffalo Pound Provincial Park

MOOSE JAW RIVER

1

39

301

202

2

Moose Jaw

Tuxford

2

42

Marquis

QU'APPELLE RIVER

1

57 km (35 miles) Moose Jaw

Go west on Highway 1 for 5 km (3 miles) to Moose Jaw.

More Information: Buffalo Pound Provincial Park, 206-110 Ominica Street West, Moose Jaw, Saskatchewan S6H 6V2, telephone (306) 694-3659.

REGINA TO ROWAN'S RAVINE PROVINCIAL PARK LOOP

Length: 191 km (119 miles)

Time: Two to four days

Rating: Easy to intermediate

Terrain: Gently rolling hills with some steep climbs

Road: Highway 20 has 1- to 2-meter- (3- to 6.5-foot-) wide paved shoulders; Highway 220 has a narrow, rough, but rideable shoulder

Traffic: Light

Connects with: Across Saskatchewan tour

Start: Regina, the provincial capital of Saskatchewan, is served by an airport and buses.

Overview: Rowan's Ravine Provincial Park, known for its beach, lies on the east shore of Last Mountain Lake in the Qu'Appelle Valley. Close by is North America's oldest bird sanctuary, Last Mountain Lake, which was founded in 1887.

The floor of the Qu'Appelle Valley is mostly grazing land with some marshy areas. The Qu'Appelle River meanders through the valley, framed by the rolling hills.

THE ROUTE:

0 km (0 miles) Regina

26 km (16 miles) Lumsden

From Regina, take Highway 11 for 26 km (16 miles) to Lumsden.

34 km (21 miles) Craven

Take Highway 99 for 8 km (5 miles) to Craven, on the floor of the Qu'Appelle Valley. Turn left onto Highway 20 which has wide, paved shoulders.

39 km (24 miles) Highway 322, Last Mountain House Historic Park

Highway 20 climbs out of the valley for some 3 km (1.8 miles), with a picnic site about halfway up. At the top of the valley is a spectacular view of the Qu'Appelle Valley.

Continue north on Highway 20 to the junction with Highway 322, 5 km (3 miles) from Craven. Here is Last Mountain House Historic Park, where reconstructed buildings show life in an 1870s fur trading outpost.

44 km (27 miles) Silton

Take Highway 322 for 5 km (3 miles) to Silton.

45 km (28 miles) Saskatchewan Beach Regional Park

About 1 km (0.6 miles) from Silton along Highway 322 is Saskatchewan Beach Regional Park.

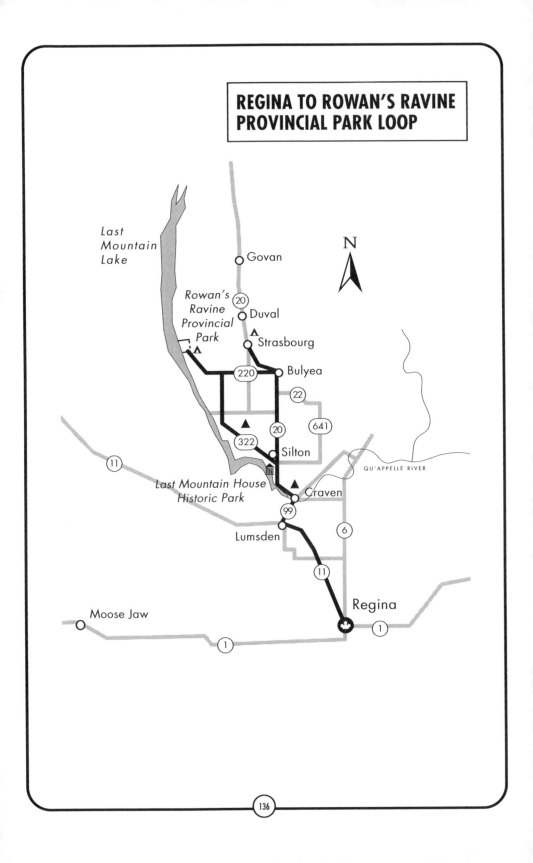

REGINA TO ROWAN'S RAVINE PROVINCIAL PARK LOOP

Last Mountain Lake

Govan

Rowan's Ravine Provincial Park

⑳

Duval

Strasbourg

⑳

Bulyea

㉒

⑳

㊽

Silton

Craven

QU'APPELLE RIVER

⑪

Last Mountain House Historic Park

㊾

Lumsden

⑥

⑪

Regina

Moose Jaw

①

①

①

Continue on Highway 322 for 23 km (14 miles) to Highway 220. The terrain is mostly gently rolling hills, but there are several steep rises. The road surface is rough pavement with a narrow but rideable shoulder.

76 km (47 miles) Rowan's Ravine Provincial Park

Go left on Highway 220 and ride 8 km (5 miles) to Rowan's Ravine Provincial Park.

99 km (61 miles) Bulyea

After visiting the park, turn back east on Highway 220. The road is roughly paved, but has a rideable shoulder. Ride through the gently rolling terrain for 23 km (14 miles) to Bulyea, at the junction with Highway 20.

112 km (69 miles) Strasbourg

Turn north on Highway 20, which has a paved shoulder, for 13 km (8 miles) through farm country to Strasbourg. A campground is situated here. The local museum in the old Canadian Pacific Railway station displays Indian and pioneer artifacts.

157 km (97 miles) Craven

To return to Regina, go south for 45 km (28 miles) on Highway 20 through Bulyea to Craven.

165 km (102 miles) Lumsden

Turn right on Highway 99 and ride 8 km (5 miles) to Lumsden.

191 km (119 miles) Regina

Then turn left on Highway 11 for 26 km (16 miles) to Regina.

More Information: Rowan's Ravine Provincial Park, Box 370, Strasbourg, Saskatchewan S0G 4V0, telephone (306) 725-4423.

INDIAN HEAD TO ECHO VALLEY AND KATEPWA POINT PROVINCIAL PARKS LOOP

Length: 101 km (63 miles) main tour; plus side trips of 2 km (1.2 miles) and 88 km (55 miles)

Time: Two to four days

Rating: Easy to intermediate

Terrain: Hilly, including some hills in the Qu'Appelle Valley

Roads: Highway 56 has a wide gravel shoulder

Traffic: Light

Connects with: Across Saskatchewan tour

Start: Indian Head

Overview: Echo Valley and Katepwa Point provincial parks are cradled in the scenic Qu'Appelle Valley. Echo Valley Park covers 6.5 square km (2.5 square miles) along the shorelines of Echo and Pasqua Lakes. Katepwa Point Park covers 8 hectares (20 acres) along Katepwa Lake.

This tour winds along hilly lake edge roads from the town of Indian Head to Echo Valley Park with a side trip to Motherwell Homestead National Historic Park.

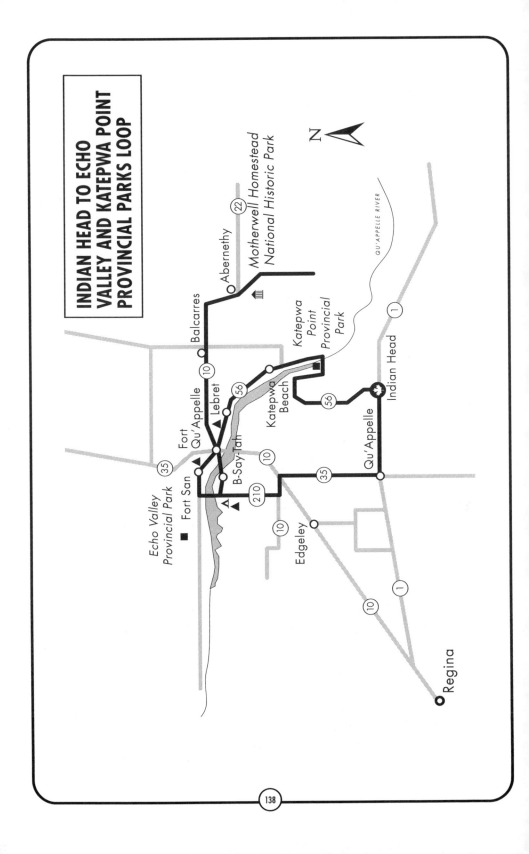

INDIAN HEAD TO ECHO VALLEY AND KATEPWA POINT PROVINCIAL PARKS LOOP

N

Motherwell Homestead National Historic Park

Abernethy
22

Qu'Appelle River

Balcarres

1

Indian Head

10

Katepwa Point Provincial Park

Lebret
56

Fort Qu'Appelle
35

Katepwa Beach

Fort San

B-Say-Tah
10

Qu'Appelle

56

Echo Valley Provincial Park

210

35

Edgeley
10

1

10

Regina

138

THE ROUTE:

0 km (0 miles) Indian Head

In Indian Head, opposite the local information center is a gravel road leading 2 km (1.2 miles) to the PFRA Tree Nursery featuring nature trails, picnic area and a campground.

Leave Indian Head by going north on Highway 56, which has 1.5 meter (5 feet) wide gravel shoulders.

16 km (10 miles) Qu'Appelle Valley

You ride through tree-dotted farmland for 16 km (10 miles), and then descend into the Qu'Appelle Valley. The slope down to the valley floor is a 6 per cent grade and about 1 km (0.6 mile) long.

26 km (16 miles) Katepwa Point Provincial Park

Katepwa Point Provincial Park, on the valley floor, is 26 km (16 miles) from Indian Head, and has campgrounds, beaches and many services.

36 km (22 miles) Lebret

Continuing north along Highway 56, 10 km (6 miles) from Katepwa Beach is Lebret.

42 km (25.7 miles) Fort Qu'Appelle

Another 6 km (3.7 miles) along the lake edge highway is Fort Qu'Appelle, the site of the Hudson's Bay Company trading post built in 1864. Here are stores, a museum and a nearby campground.

54 km (33 miles) Echo Valley Provincial Park

When leaving Fort Qu'Appelle, go west on Broadway Street, which becomes B-Say-Tah Road, 12 km (7 miles) to Echo Valley Provincial Park. Its camping facilities are a good place to set up camp from which you can explore the area.

Side tour: Echo Valley Provincial Park to Motherwell Homestead National Historic Park, 88 km (55 miles)

0 km (0 miles) Echo Valley Park

From Echo Valley Park take an interesting 88 km (55 miles) return side trip to the Motherwell Homestead National Historic Park.

7 km (4 miles) Fort San

Go north on Highway 210 from the Echo Valley Park entrance for 1 km (0.6 mile).

Then go east on hilly and winding Highway 56 to Fort San 6 km (4 miles) away. Fort San was a sanitorium from 1913 to 1972.

27 km (17 miles) Balcarres

From Fort San, continue east on Highway 56 for 4 km (2 miles).

At the junction, near Fort Qu'Appelle, take Highway 10, which has paved 2-meter (6-foot) wide shoulders, east towards Balcarres, 16 km (10 miles) away. After 1 km (0.6 mile) you approach a steep hill. Balcarres has services including groceries and a hotel.

35 km (22 miles) Highway 22

Continue east on Highway 10 for 8 km (5 miles), then turn south on Highway 22, which has gravel shoulders.

41 km (25 miles) Abernethy

Ride through low rolling hills

for 6 km (3.7 miles) to Abernethy. Here are retail stores, but no hotel accommodation or camping facilities.

44 km (27 miles) Motherwell Homestead National Historic Park

From Abernethy take the gravel road for 3 km (2 miles) to Motherwell Homestead National Historic Park. Here is the gracious, Italian-style field stone house of William Motherwell, a farmer and politician who worked to promote the causes of the western farmers.

Main tour: Return from Echo Valley Park to Indian Head

54 km (33 miles) Echo Valley Provincial Park

87 km (54 miles) Qu'Appelle

From Echo Valley Provincial Park take Highway 210 south. It has gravel shoulders 1-meter (3-feet) wide, and climbs the steep edge of the valley to the flat prairie.

After 12 km (7 miles), turn left onto Highway 10 and go 2 km (1.2 miles).

Then turn south on Highway 35, and ride 19 km (12 miles) to the town of Qu'Appelle. Picnic and camping facilities are available here.

101 km (63 miles) Indian Head

When leaving Qu'Appelle, take Highway 1 (the Trans Canada Highway), which has 1.5-meter (5-foot) wide paved shoulders. Go east for 14 km (9 miles) through rolling prairie to Indian Head, the tour's starting point.

More Information: Echo Valley and Katepwa Point Provincial Parks, Box 790, Fort Qu'Appelle, Saskatchewan S0G 1S0, telephone (306) 332-3215 and (306) 332-5615. Motherwell Homestead National Historic Park, Abernethy, Saskatchewan S0A 0A0, telephone (306) 333-2116, or (306) 333-2128.

BROADVIEW TO MOOSE MOUNTAIN PROVINCIAL PARK

Length: 158 km (98 miles) return; plus 68-km (42-mile) and 52-km (32-mile) side trips

Time: Two to four days

Rating: Easy

Terrain: Level to rolling

Roads: Highways 1, 9, 48, and 13 have wide, paved shoulders; Grid Road 603 and the Christopher Trail are gravel.

Traffic: Light

Connects with: Across Saskatchewan tour

Start: Broadview, situated on the Trans Canada Highway 154 km (96 miles) east of Regina.

Overview: Moose Mountain Park's thick forest of white birch and aspen poplar on an elevated plateau contrasts with the surrounding grass-

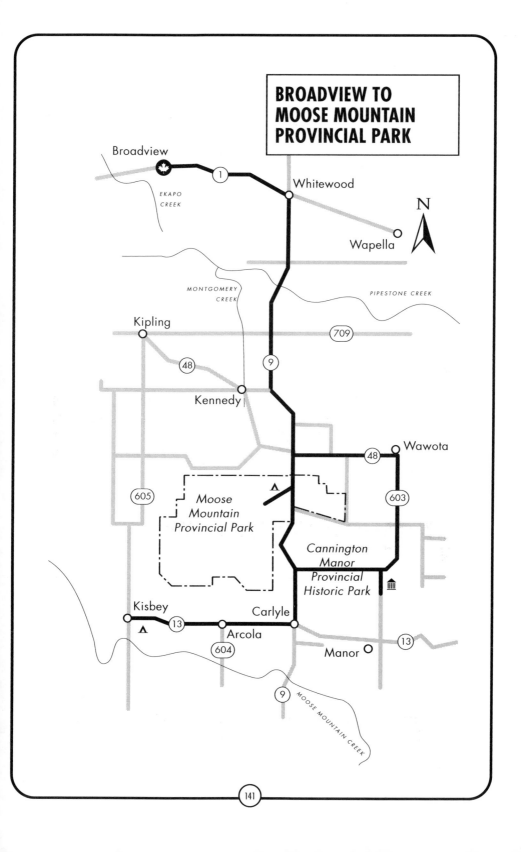

BROADVIEW TO
MOOSE MOUNTAIN
PROVINCIAL PARK

Broadview

1

EKAPO
CREEK

Whitewood

Wapella

N

MONTGOMERY
CREEK

PIPESTONE CREEK

Kipling

709

48

9

Kennedy

Wawota

48

605

603

Moose
Mountain
Provincial Park

Cannington
Manor
Provincial
Historic Park

Kisbey

13

Carlyle

Arcola

604

Manor

13

9

MOOSE MOUNTAIN CREEK

land region of southeastern Saskatchewan.

Covering 388 square km (150 square miles), the park's knob and kettle terrain (rounded mounds and small lakes) has a topographic relief of 90 to 120 meters (300 to 400 feet). There are more than 1,200 small lakes in the depressions, many offering good fishing. Kenosee Lake and its beaches are the park's focal point.

This tour goes from Broadview 80 km (50 miles) to Moose Mountain Park. Then, using the park as a base, it follows two side tours: a 68-km (42-mile) loop to Cannington Manor Historic Park, and a 52-km (32-mile) ride to Arcola.

THE ROUTE:

0 km (0 miles) Broadview

21 km (13 miles) Whitewood

From Broadview, ride east on Highway 1 (the Trans Canada Highway) for 21 km (13 miles) to Whitewood.

79 km (49 miles) Moose Mountain Park

Go south on Highway 9, which has wide, paved shoulders, for 58 km (36 miles) to Moose Mountain Park.

Side trip: Moose Mountain Park to Cannington Manor Provincial Historic Park, 68 km (42 miles)

0 km (0 miles) Moose Mountain Park

Using Moose Mountain Park as a base, you can ride a 68-km (42-mile) loop to Cannington Manor Historic Park.

26 km (16 miles) Wawota

Ride north on Highway 9 for 8 km (5 miles) through a wooded area. Go east on Highway 48 for 18 km (11 miles) through farmland towards Wawota.

Highways 9 and 48 both have wide, paved shoulders, but Highway 48's shoulders are unmarked. Along Highway 48 are several vacation farms offering horseback riding and meals on short notice.

41 km (25 miles) Cannington Manor Historic Park

From Wawota, go south on Grid Road 603 for 12 km (7 miles). The road is gravel and recommended for all-terrain bikes.

Go west for 2 km (1 mile), and then turn north for 1 km (0.6 mile) to Cannington Manor Historic Park.

Established in 1882, Cannington Manor was a colony where wealthy English families tried to bring English country life. The restored buildings and museums have exhibits from that era.

68 km (42 miles) Moose Mountain Park

From Cannington Manor, take the same gravel road south for 1 km (0.6 mile) and then go west for 5 km (3 miles).

At the intersection, take the road heading north. After approximately 9 km (6 miles), take the Christopher Trail, which is lightly graveled and easy to ride.

Go 12 km (7 miles) west along the Christopher Trail to Highway 9.

At Highway 9 turn north to Moose Mountain Park entrance.

Side trip: Moose Mountain Park to Arcola, 52 km (32 miles)

Another trip from Moose Mountain Park is the 52-km (32-mile) one-way trip to Arcola.

0 km (0 miles) Moose Mountain Park

22 km (14 miles) Carlyle

From the park, go south along the flat, tree-lined Highway 9 for 22 (14 miles) to Carlyle. Named for Scottish author Thomas Carlyle, the town has a Rusty Relic Museum in the old Canadian National Railway station.

38 km (24 miles) Arcola

Go west for 16 km (10 miles) on Highway 13, which has a paved shoulder, through flat countryside with few trees to Arcola. The feature film based on W.O. Mitchell's novel *Who Has Seen the Wind?* was filmed at Arcola. The Arcola Museum features pioneer artifacts.

51 km (32 miles) Kisbey

From Arcola take Highway 13 west for 13 km (8 miles) towards Kisbey. A picnic area and campground are located 4 km (2.4 miles) before Kisbey. The main attraction in Kisbey is its museum.

Main tour: Return from Moose Mountain Park to Broadview

79 km (49 miles) Moose Mountain Park

137 km (85 miles) Whitewood

From Moose Mountain Provincial Park, retrace your route north on Highway 9 for 58 km (36 miles) to Whitewood.

158 km (98 miles) Broadview

Go west for 21 km (13 miles) on Highway 1 to Broadview.

More Information: Moose Mountain Provincial Park, Box 100, Carlyle, Saskatchewan S0C 0R0, telephone (306) 577-2131.

YORKTON, GOOD SPIRIT LAKE PROVINCIAL PARK, AND THE DOUGHNUT RUN

Length: 165 km (103 miles)
Time: Two days
Rating: Easy
Terrain: Farmland with some thickets
Roads: Most have 1- to 2-meter- (3- to 6.5-foot wide shoulders)
Traffic: Light
Start: Yorkton. The nearest VIA Rail station is in Melville, 43 km (26 miles) on Highway 10 from Yorkton.

Overview: Sandy beaches, sand dunes and nature trails make Good Spirit Lake Provincial Park, 20 square km (7.8 square miles), an enjoyable base to explore this part of southeastern Saskatchewan.

In Yorkton is the Western Devel-

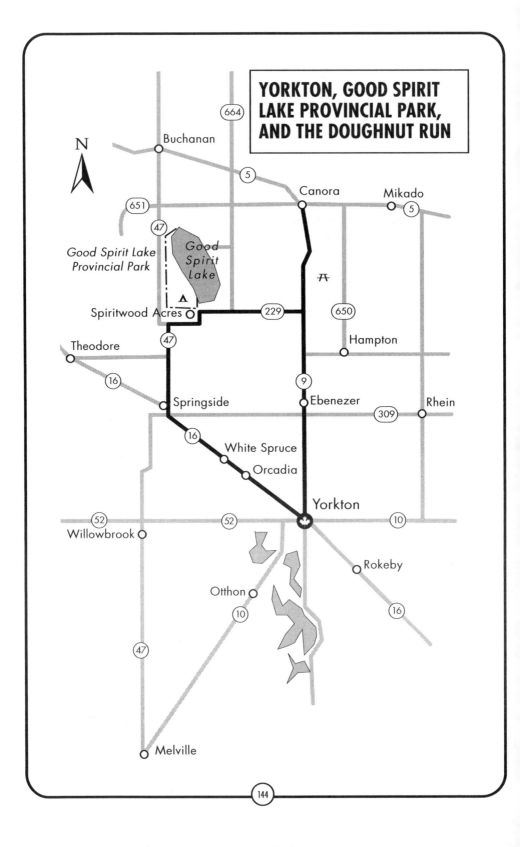

N

664

Buchanan

5

Canora

Mikado

5

651

47

Good Spirit Lake
Provincial Park

Good
Spirit
Lake

Spiritwood Acres

229

650

47

Hampton

Theodore

16

9

Springside

Ebenezer

Rhein

309

16

White Spruce

Orcadia

Yorkton

52

52

10

Willowbrook

Rokeby

Otthon

16

10

47

Melville

opment Museum and the Godfrey Dean Cultural Center as well as accommodations and campgrounds.

THE ROUTE:

0 km (0 miles) Yorkton

14 km (8.6 miles) Canadian Forces Station Yorkton at White Spruce

26 km (16 miles) Springside

From Yorkton take Highway 16, which has a shoulder, for 26 km (16 miles) through flat terrain to Springside. Along the way you pass the Canadian Forces Station Yorkton at White Spruce.

33 km (20 miles) Good Spirit Lake Provincial Park

From Springside, go north on Highway 47 to Highway 229, a flat road that has no shoulder and a rough edge, for 7 km (4 miles) to Good Spirit Lake Provincial Park.

65 km (40 miles) Canora

From the park go east on Highway 229 for 16 km (10 miles) to Highway 9.

Turn north on Highway 9. The road has a wide, paved shoulder. Head for Canora 16 km (10 miles) away through flat fields and grazing land. At the White Sand River is a pleasant picnic area.

At the entrance to Canora is the Lesia Welcoming Statue to offer you bread and salt, a traditional form of Ukrainian greeting. The town of Canora is home to bakeries known for their doughnuts, hence the name of this tour. A campground is located nearby.

115 km (71 miles) Yorkton

To return to Yorkton, ride south on Highway 9 for 50 km (31 miles).

More Information: Good Spirit Lake Provincial Park, 120 Smith Street East, Yorkton, Saskatchewan S3N 3V3, telephone (306) 792-2110.

KAMSACK TO DUCK MOUNTAIN PROVINCIAL PARK LOOP

Length: 117 km (73 miles), plus 26-km (15-mile) side trip

Time: Two to three days

Rating: Intermediate

Terrain: Manitoba Escarpment, long low hills, rolling hills—some covered with forests, others with grain fields.

Roads: Mostly paved shoulders, some gravel shoulders

Traffic: Light

Connects with: Northern Parks tour in Manitoba

Start: Kamsack, served by VIA Rail's Winnipeg-Churchill route. Kamsack is northeast of Yorkton, near the Manitoba border.

Overview: This 240-square-km (93-square-mile) park lies on the Duck Mountain Upland of the Manitoba Escarpment, the edge between the

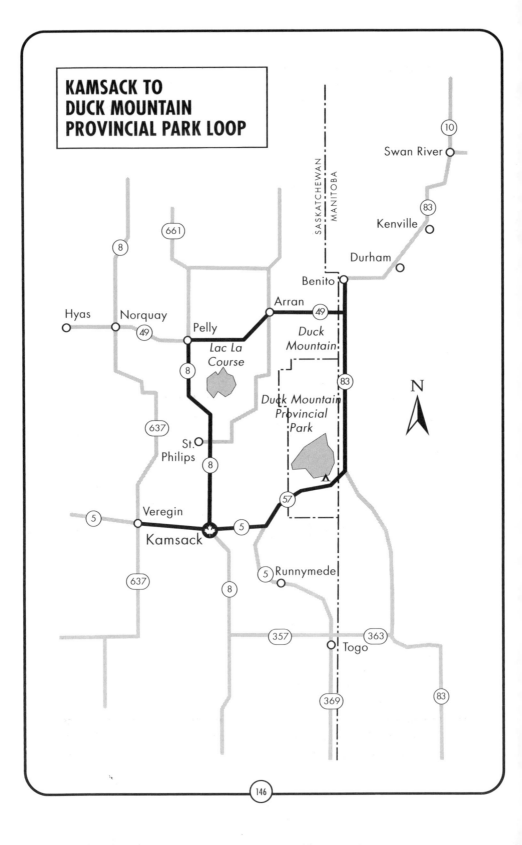

KAMSACK TO DUCK MOUNTAIN PROVINCIAL PARK LOOP

Swan River ⑩

⑧

⑥⑥①

Hyas Norquay Pelly Arran Benito
⑧ ④⑨ ④⑨ Kenville
  Lac La Course Durham

SASKATCHEWAN | MANITOBA

Duck Mountain

⑧ ⑥③⑦

⑧③

N

Duck Mountain Provincial Park

St. Philips ⑧

⑤ Veregin ⑤ ⑤⑦

Kamsack

⑥③⑦ ⑧ ⑤ Runnymede

③⑤⑦ ③⑥③

Togo

③⑥⑨ ⑧③

⑧③

146

Manitoba Plain, the first prairie steppe, and the Saskatchewan Plain which is the second prairie steppe. Duck Mountain Park is the most southerly park in Saskatchewan's forest and lake belt and is adjacent to the Manitoba border. At the heart of the park is Madge Lake with beaches and good fishing.

This route is a loop from Kamsack through Duck Mountain Park north through Manitoba, west through Pelly and south to Kamsack. Duck Mountain Park has camping.

THE ROUTE:

0 km (0 miles) Kamsack

8 km (5 miles) Highway 57

From Kamsack, go east on Highway 5, for 8 km (5 miles) to Highway 57. The trees give way to fields but the long low hills remain. The shoulders on this stretch of highway are 1.2 meters (4 feet) wide and paved.

27 km (17 miles) Madge Lake in Duck Mountain Park

Go northeast on Highway 57, over long low hills on a tree-lined route for 19 km (12 miles) to Madge Lake in Duck Mountain Provincial Park. The shoulders of the road are paved but narrow.

31 km (19.4 miles) Highway 83 just past Manitoba border

From Duck Mountain Park, ride northeast on Highway 57 for 4 km (2 miles) to Highway 83 just over the Manitoba border.

57 km (35 miles) Highway 49

Go north on Highway 83, which has gravel shoulders, for 29 km (18 miles) through rolling tree-covered hills, to Highway 49.

Side trip: Benito 6 km (3.7 miles) round trip

If you wish, you can go into Benito where there are restaurants and a hotel, or you can save the 6 km (3.7 miles) round trip. From Benito, it's 37 km (23 miles) on Highway 83 to Swan River, Manitoba on the Northern Parks tour (described in the Manitoba chapter).

Main tour: Junction of Highways 83 and 49

59 km (37 miles) Saskatchewan border

Go west on Highway 49, which has wide gravel shoulders, for the 2 km (1.2 miles) to the Saskatchewan border. Once you're back in Saskatchewan, the shoulders are paved and wide.

85 km (53 miles) Pelly

The 26 km (16 miles) trip into Pelly is through rolling hills covered with grain fields.

In Pelly is a campground, hotel and the Fort Pelly-Livingstone Museum featuring Indian artifacts and local history. Nearby are the sites of Fort Pelly, a trading post built by the Hudson Bay Company in 1824, and Fort Livingstone, built in 1874 as a post for the Northwest Mounted Police, and used in 1877 for the first session of the North West Territorial Council.

117 km (73 miles) Kamsack

Take Highway 8 south for 32 km (20 miles) to Kamsack. The road is through rolling hill country dotted with homesteads. In

Kamsack there is a campground and hotels.

Side trip: Kamsack to Veregin 26 km (15 miles) return

0 km (0 miles) Kamsack

For an interesting side trip from Kamsack, continue west on Highway 5 through fairly flat farmland. The road has 1.2-meter (4-foot) wide paved shoulders that are rough in spots. Cycle 13 km (8 miles) to Veregin.

Here is the National Doukhobor Heritage Village and Museum and a recreated early 1900s Doukhobor village that tell the story of the Doukhobor's immigration to Canada and their struggle to remain a people.

More Information: Duck Mountain Provincial Park, Box 39, Kamsack, Saskatchewan S0A 1S0, telephone (306) 542-3482.

PRINCE ALBERT TO PRINCE ALBERT NATIONAL PARK LOOP

Length: 182 km (113 miles)
Time: Two to three days
Rating: Easy
Terrain: Level to rolling
Roads: Most have paved shoulders; Highway 263 is shoulderless
Traffic: Light
Connects with: Day tours and back-country biking in Prince Albert National Park; the Battle tour.
Start: The city of Prince Albert, which can be reached by Saskatchewan Transportation Company bus.
Overview: The rugged country of the Canadian Shield is the setting for this cycling tour. Prince Albert National Park, 200 km (120 miles) north of the city of Saskatoon, is in the transition zone between the northern forest, which covers half the park, and aspen parkland and prairie grasslands. The park's roads lead to lakes and points of interest.

The park may be reached via the Saskatchewan Transportation Company bus line, which will take boxed bicycles on a space-available basis; don't depend on it during high season.

THE ROUTE:

0 km (0 miles) Prince Albert

77 km (49 miles) Highway 264

From Prince Albert go north on Highway 2 for 77 km (49 miles) to Highway 264.

90 km (57 miles) Waskesiu Lake in Prince Albert National Park

Turn left at Highway 264 and ride 13 km (8 miles) to the Waskesiu Lake townsite in Prince Albert National Park.

Explore the park. See day tour and backcountry biking information that follow this tour description.

131 km (82 miles) South gate of Prince Albert National Park

When you're ready to head back,

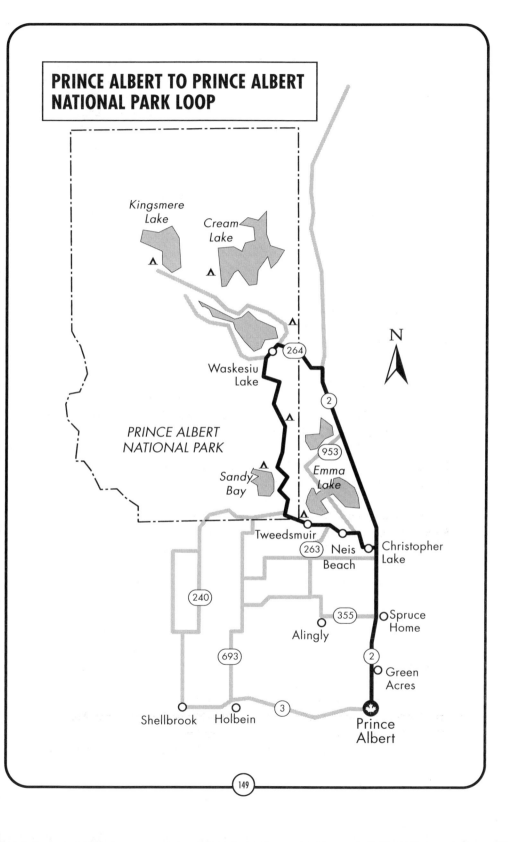

PRINCE ALBERT TO PRINCE ALBERT NATIONAL PARK LOOP

Kingsmere
Lake

Cream
Lake

264

2

Waskesiu
Lake

PRINCE ALBERT
NATIONAL PARK

953

Sandy
Bay

Emma
Lake

Tweedsmuir

263 Neis
Beach

Christopher
Lake

240

355 Spruce
Home

Alingly

693

2 Green
Acres

3

Shellbrook Holbein

Prince
Albert

N

go south on Highway 263 to the park's south gate, 41 km (25 miles) from Waskesiu Lake.

148 km (92 miles) Highway 2

Continue for 15 km (9 miles) on shoulderless Highway 263 past Emma Lake, which has seven beaches, to the hamlet of Christopher Lake. Just 2 km (1.2 miles) past Christopher Lake is Highway 2.

182 km (113 miles) city of Prince Albert

Go south on Highway 2 for 34 km (21 miles) to the city of Prince Albert.

More Information: Prince Albert National Park, P.O. Box 100, Waskesiu Lake, Saskatchewan S0J 2Y0, telephone (306) 663-5322.

DAY TOURING AND BACKCOUNTRY BICYCLING

Prince Albert Park Narrows Tour, 25 km (15 miles) each way

Parts of Narrows Road are hilly and rough.

0 km (0 miles) Waskesiu Lake beach

From the beach at Waskesiu Lake, go south along Lake View Drive, following Highway 263 for 5 km (3 miles). Turn left where the road is sign-posted for the Narrows Campground.

The Narrows Road is fairly hilly and rough in places, but the scenery makes up for it. Along the way are Paignton and Tree Beard's nature trails and the South Bay and Trippe's beaches.

25 km (15 miles) Narrows Campground

At the end of the trip is the Narrows Campground.

50 km (30 miles) Waskesiu Lake

Return along the same route to Waskesiu Lake.

Prince Albert National Park Backcountry Trails

Prince Albert National Park's 250-km (155-mile) network of backcountry trails takes cyclists with all-terrain bicycles into the seldom-visited southwestern area of the park. Trails range from graveled roadways to overgrown pathways.

Elk Trail, 13.5 km (8 miles)

Formerly used for hauling freight from Prince Albert to La Ronge, the Elk Trail traverses rolling hills with grades that may require you to push your bike.

Westside Boundary Road, 63 km (39 miles); Fifty-Seven Trail, 44 km (27 miles)

A gravel roadway through the Sturgeon River Valley and Fox/Rabbit Creek Basins (there is camping at Nesslin Lake), the Westside Boundary Road can be combined with the 44-km (27 miles) Fifty-Seven Trail to form a good overnight circuit.

More Information: Guides to some of the backcountry trails and topographic maps are available from the park office: Prince Albert National Park, P.O. Box 100, Waskesiu Lake, Saskatchewan S0J 2Y0, telephone (306) 663-5322.

THE BATTLE TOUR

Length: 160 km (100 miles), plus 26-km (16-mile) and 30-km (18-mile) side trips.

Time: Two to four days

Rating: Easy

Terrain: Level to rolling

Roads: Paved shoulders; some gravel roads on side trips

Traffic: Light

Connects with: Prince Albert to Prince Albert National Park tour

Start: Prince Albert, served by an airport and Saskatchewan Transportation Company bus lines.

Overview: In 1885 the Métis of the Northwest Territories (as the provinces of Saskatchewan and Alberta were then known) proclaimed their own government at Batoche under the leadership of Louis Riel and Gabriel Dumont. An armed rebellion ensued.

These tours in the South Saskatchewan River Valley and Prince Albert area explore historic sites of the Riel Rebellion, including three battle grounds.

THE ROUTE:

0 km (0 miles) Prince Albert

Prince Albert's attractions include the Heritage Museum, Lund's Wildlife Museum and the former home of Prime Minister John Diefenbaker.

32 km (20 miles) St. Louis

Take Highway 2 south from Prince Albert for 32 km (20 miles) through hilly countryside, to St. Louis on the South Saskatchewan River. Here are picnic sites.

48 km (30 miles) Highway 225

Continue south on Highway 2 for 16 km (10 miles) to Highway 225.

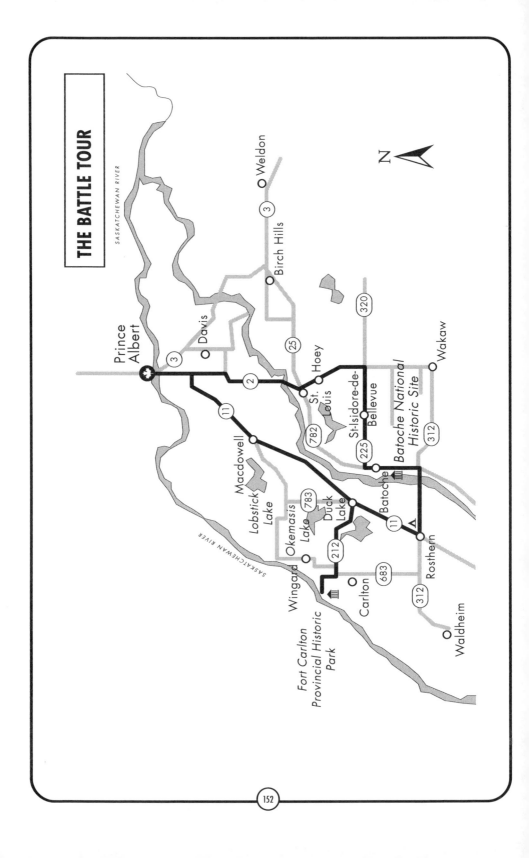

THE BATTLE TOUR

SASKATCHEWAN RIVER

N

Prince Albert

Weldon

Birch Hills

Davis

Hoey

St. Louis

St-Isidore-de-Bellevue

Wakaw

Batoche National Historic Site

Macdowell

Lobstick Lake

Okemasis Lake

Duck Lake

Batoche

Wingard

SASKATCHEWAN RIVER

Rosthern

Carlton

Waldheim

Fort Carlton Provincial Historic Park

3

2

11

25

320

782

225

312

783

212

683

312

11

65 km (47 miles) Batoche

Go west on Highway 225 for 27 km (17 miles) into Batoche.

Established by the Métis in the 1870s, Batoche was the heart of the rebellion. It was the site of the final battle between the Métis and the North West Field Force, who reasserted government sovereignty. Here you can see the NWFF encampment, bulwarks and foxholes, as well as a museum.

75 km (53 miles) Highway 312

Leave Batoche by Highway 225 and travel south for 10 km (6 miles) to Highway 312.

Side trip: Fish Creek 30-km (18-mile) return

If you're riding an all-terrain bike, or don't mind riding a gravel road, you can go south from this junction to Fish Creek.

At Fish Creek are several historic sites, including an abandoned church. The site of the Battle of Fish Creek where the Métis surprised the NWFF is marked by a cairn. General Middleton's encampment site used after the Battle of Fish Creek is reached by a dirt road through Fish Creek valley.

Retrace your route.

Main tour continues: Junction of Highways 225 and 312

80 km (56 miles) Rosthern

Go west on Highway 312 for 15 km (9 miles) across the South Saskatchewan River into Rosthern. Here is camping, as well as the Rosthern Cultural Museum, which depicts the history of the local Mennonite and other ethnic communities.

98 km (67 miles) Duck Lake

From Rosthern go north on Highway 11 for 18 km (11 miles) to Duck Lake.

Just outside Duck Lake is a cairn marking the site of the first battle of the North West Rebellion. In town, the Duck Lake Historical Museum presents the history of the rebellion and includes an old North West Mounted Police jail on its grounds. Three km (1.8 miles) south of town is a replica of Duck Lake as it looked in 1895.

Side trip: Duck Lake to Fort Carlton Historic Park, 52 km (32 miles) return

From Duck Lake, it's a 52 km (32 miles) side trip on lightly traveled Highway 212 (which has no shoulder) to Fort Carlton Historic Park.

At Fort Carlton is a replica of the fort when it was a Hudson's Bay post and North West Mounted Police station. Take the road leaving the fort to see the cairn marking the signing of the treaty.

Main tour continues:

98 km (67 miles) Duck Lake

160 km (100 miles) Prince Albert

From Duck Lake continue north on Highway 11 for 55 km (34 miles) to Highway 2, and then go 7 km (4 miles) to return to Prince Albert.

ACROSS SASKATCHEWAN

Length: 801 km (497 miles)
Time: Five to eight days
Rating: Intermediate
Terrain: Generally flat, some hills
Roads: Highway 1 has paved shoulders 3- to 3.6-meters (10-to-12 feet) wide; Highway 4 has a 1-meter (3-foot) wide paved shoulder.
Traffic: Since the Trans Canada Highway is the main thoroughfare across Saskatchewan, traffic can be heavy; secondary roads have less traffic.
Connects with: Swift Current to Saskatchewan Landing Provincial Park tour; Moose Jaw to Buffalo Pound Provincial Park tour; Broadview to Moose Mountain Provincial Park tour; Regina to Rowan's Ravine Provincial Park tour; and Indian Head to Echo Valley and Katepwa provincial parks loop tour.
Start: Alsask on Highway 44 at the Alberta–Saskatchewan boundary. The route is described going west to east.
Overview: If you're going across Saskatchewan, Highway 1 (the Trans Canada Highway), is most popular with cyclists. Numerous campgrounds and a good variety of accommodations are available.

THE ROUTE:

0 km (0 miles) Alsask
115 km (71 miles) Eston

From Alsask, go south and then east on Highway 44 for 115 km (71 miles) through agricultural land to Eston.

221 km (137 miles) Saskatchewan Landing Provincial Park

Continue east on Highway 44 for 21 km (13 miles) to Route 342 near the community of Plato.

Ride south and then east on Route 342 for 61 km (38 miles) to Highway 4.

Turn south on Highway 4. Ride for 24 km (15 miles) and descend to Saskatchewan Landing Provincial Park on Lake Diefenbaker. (A tour from Swift Current to Saskatchewan Landing Park is decribed in this chapter.)

327 km (203 miles) Swift Current

Ascending from the valley, continue south on Highway 4 for 50 km (31 miles) to Swift Current. In this area are some of Saskatchewan's oil and gas wells.

501 km (311 miles) Moose Jaw

From Swift Current go west on Highway 1—the Trans Canada Highway for 174 km (108 miles) to Moose Jaw. On the way you descend the Missouri Coteau, the long narrow escarpment extending from south-central Saskatchewan into northeastern Alberta and separating the Saskatchewan Plain and the Alberta Plateau.

At Moose Jaw you can take the tour to Buffalo Pound Provincial Park (described in this chapter).

572 km (355 miles) Regina

Continue on the Trans Canada Highway for 71 km (44 miles) to Regina, Saskatchewan's capital.

Regina had its beginnings as a tiny settlement near what was known as Pile of Bones Creek. It was later named Regina in honor of Queen Victoria.

In the heart of the city is Wascana Lake, set in a 930-hectare (2,300-acre) park that has bicycle paths (see Regina bicycle routes at beginning of chapter). Here also are the Legislative Buildings, the Saskatchewan Museum of Natural History, the Wild Bird Sanctuary, the Diefenbaker Homestead and the Science Center.

From Regina, you can link with the tour to Rowan's Ravine Provincial Park (described in this chapter).

641 km (398 miles) Indian Head

Leaving Regina, ride east on the Trans Canada Highway for 69 km (43 miles) to Indian Head, named after the westerly peak of a range of hills southeast of the community. Here you can take a side tour to the Echo Valley and Katepwa Provincial Parks (described in this chapter).

719 km (447 miles) Broadview

Continue east on the Trans Canada Highway. At Broadview, 78 km (48 miles) from Indian Head, you can join with the Moose Mountain Provincial Park tour (described in this chapter).

787 km (489 miles) Moosomin

Keep riding east for 68 km (42 miles) to Moosomim, the last town before the Manitoba border.

801 km (497 miles) Manitoba border

Manitoba is 14 km (8 miles) past Moosomin.

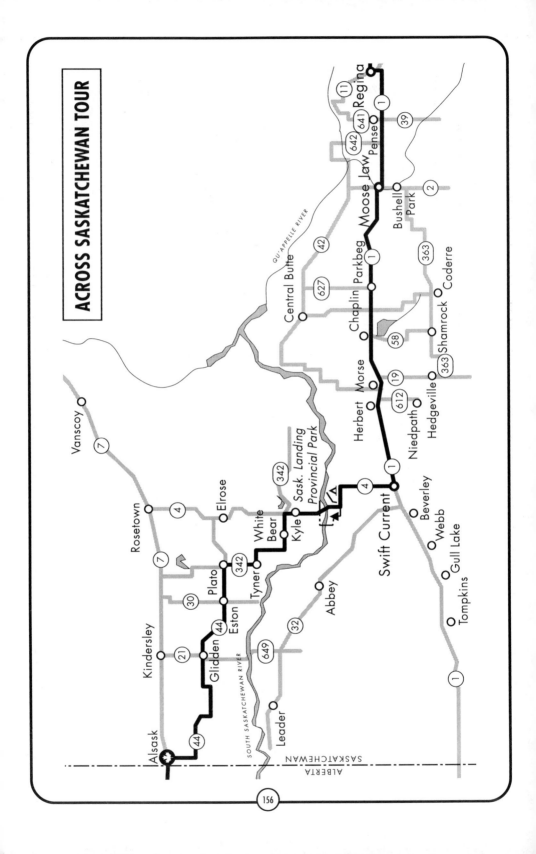

ACROSS SASKATCHEWAN TOUR

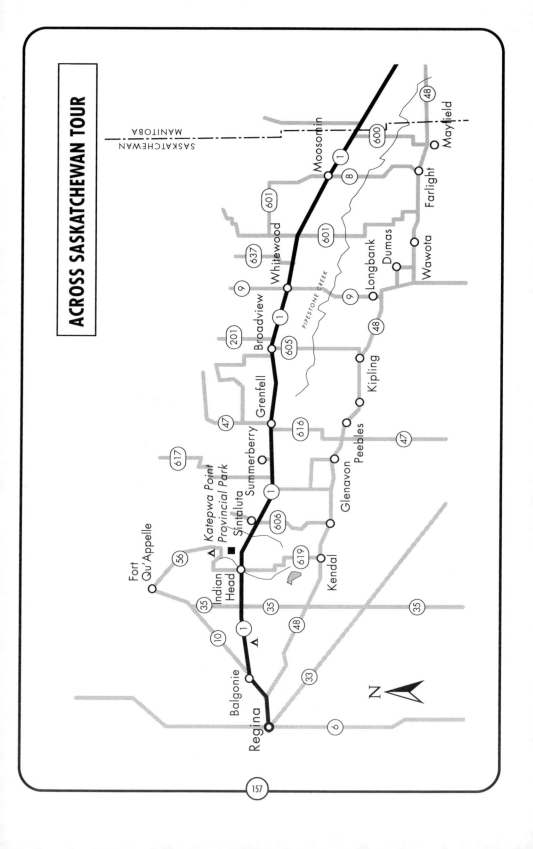

ACROSS SASKATCHEWAN TOUR

(Vivian Schultz)

Manitoba

Manitoba offers cyclists much more than its settled image of flat wheatfields might suggest. You can tour in the rugged forests and lakes of the Precambrian Shield, which covers eastern and northern Manitoba. Or you can ride along wooded hills and valleys of the Manitoba Escarpment that rises above the prairie in the west. Cycling the prairie of southern Manitoba also makes for enjoyable touring.

These tours explore the variety that Manitoba offers: white sand beaches, wilderness, pioneering towns and rivers once traveled by fur traders. Many towns have historical museums about the area's pioneer past.

Tourist Information: For general tourist information, including a road map and vacation guide describing campgrounds, hotels, motels and bed and breakfasts, contact: Travel Manitoba, 155 Carlton Street, 7th Floor, Winnipeg, Manitoba R3C 3H8, call toll-free 1-800-665-0040, in Winnipeg call (204) 945-3777.

Roads: Most Manitoba roads do not have paved shoulders. Distances given for tours starting in Winnipeg are from the Perimeter Highway at the city's edge.

Weather: Manitoba has the most temperate climate of the three prairie provinces. Average annual precipitation varies from 41 to 53 cm (16 to 21 inches), and most falls during the summer.

Southern Manitoba: Summer daytime temperatures are usually between 21 and 28 degrees Celsius (70 and 80 Fahrenheit), but during hot weather can top 40 degrees Celsius (104 Fahrenheit). Nights are cool, ranging between 12 and 15 degrees Celsius (55 and 60 Fahrenheit), and during May and September can dip below freezing.

Northern Manitoba: At The Pas, average daytime summer temperature is 17 degrees Celsius (62 Fahrenheit).

Hostels: Manitoba Hostelling Association, 194-A Sherbrook St., Winnipeg, Manitoba R3C 4M2, (204) 784-1131, operates hostels in Winnipeg, Brandon and a farm hostel near Glenboro, 160 km (100 miles) west of Winnipeg.

Trains: Within Manitoba, for information on VIA Rail service, call in Winnipeg (204) 944-8780; elsewhere in Manitoba call toll-free 1-800-561-8630.

Airports: Winnipeg International Airport is served by major airlines, and offers connections to smaller centers.

Buses: Inter-city bus service in Manitoba is provided by: Greyhound Bus Lines, 487 Portage Ave, Winnipeg, Manitoba R3B 2E3, telephone toll-free in Manitoba 1-800-661-8747, or (204) 783-8857; and by Grey Goose Bus Lines, 301 Burnell Street, Winnipeg, Manitoba R3G 3M6, telephone (204) 786-8891.

Bicycling: Manitoba Cycling Association, 200 Main Street, Winnipeg, Manitoba R3C 2B6, (204) 985-4055.

Capital: Winnipeg, the provincial capital and Manitoba's largest city, is located at the confluence of the Red River and Assiniboine River, approximately 100 km (62 miles) north of the Minnesota border. Known as the "Gateway to the West," Winnipeg is situated near the transition from rugged forests of the Canadian Shield to the prairie.

Area: Manitoba's 650,087 square km (251,135 square miles), comprises 6.5 per cent of Canada

Terrain: Several tours explore the Manitoba Escarpment, which is a highland plateau that rises 450 meters (1,500 feet) above the surrounding prairie. The escarpment forms the edge between the Manitoba Plain, the first prairie steppe and the Saskatchewan Plain which is the second prairie steppe.

The highest point is 832-meter (2,730-foot) Baldy Mountain on the Manitoba Escarpment; the lowest point is the Hudson Bay shore.

Population: 1,091,942 (1991 census), fifth of Canada's 10 provinces

History: Manitoba's early history is tied to the fur trade. In 1670, King Charles II of England established the Hudson's Bay Company and granted it Rupert's Land, a territory that included Manitoba, as well as northern Québec, northern Ontario, most of Saskatchewan and southern Alberta. The Hudson's Bay Company established fur trading posts throughout northern Manitoba.

In 1812 settlers began to farm here. In 1870 Manitoba—then a small colony at the Red and Assiniboine rivers—entered into Confederation with Canada. The provincial boundaries were extended in 1881, 1884 and reached their current size in 1912.

WINNIPEG BICYCLE ROUTES

The *Cyclist's Map of Winnipeg* indicates on-street routes throughout the city preferred by local cyclists who commute regularly. There are also several on-street cycle routes—signposted with a white bicycle on a green background—along stretches of the banks the Red and Assiniboine rivers. A few recreational cycle paths run through riverbank parks such as St. Vital Park, Kings Park, Assiniboine Park and Kildonan Park.

More Information: Maps can be obtained from the Manitoba Cycling Association, 200 Main Street, Winnipeg, Manitoba R3C 2B6, telephone (204) 985-4055; or Winnipeg Cycle-touring Club, Box 2068, Winnipeg, Manitoba R3C 3R4, telephone (204) 772-4034.

WINNIPEG TO BIRDS HILL PROVINCIAL PARK LOOP

Length: 35 km (22 miles)
Time: One day or less
Rating: Easy
Terrain: Route 213 has some hills in and around Birds Hill Park; otherwise, flat.
Roads: Highway 59 has paved shoulders; the rest have gravel shoulders.
Traffic: Sunday is the best day to ride on Route 213 because of the gravel truck traffic on other days.
Start: Winnipeg
Overview: The closest provincial park to Winnipeg, Birds Hill Park is an enjoyable destination for a day tour or an overnight camping trip. The park covers 31 square km (12 square miles) of hills, ridges and valleys formed as a result of sediment deposits from ancient glacial lakes and rivers.

A large population of white-tailed deer inhabit the forest and within the park are hiking trails, campgrounds, and a 32-hectare (80-acre) man-made lake. The park's 7.2-km (4.5-mile) Pine Ridge Bicycle Trail winds through pine groves and aspen stands and circles the lake.

THE ROUTE:

0 km (0 miles) Winnipeg

18 km (11 miles) Birds Hill Provincial Park east gate
Ride north on Lagimodiere Boulevard, which is Highway 59. Take Highway 59, which has a wide, paved shoulder, to Route 213 which is also called Garven Road.

Go east on Route 213 to Route 206. Turn north on Route 206 to the east gate of Birds Hill Park.

Once you're there, explore the Pine Ridge Bicycle Trail.

24 km (15 miles) Birds Hill Provincial Park, west gate
When you're ready to leave, ride through the Birds Hill Park to the west gate, a 8-km (5-mile) ride from the park's east gate.

35 km (22 miles) Winnipeg
From Birds Hill Park's west gate, take Highway 59, which has paved, wide shoulders, for 11 km (7 miles) back into Winnipeg.

More Information: For information

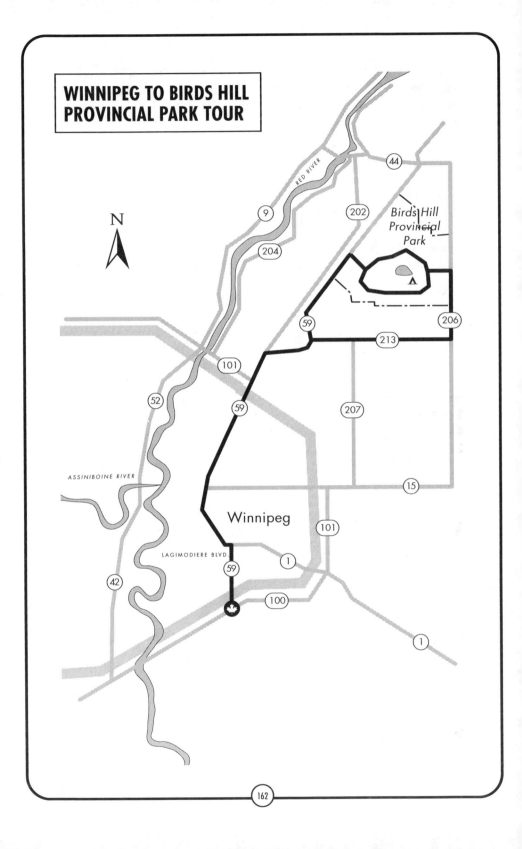

WINNIPEG TO BIRDS HILL PROVINCIAL PARK TOUR

N

RED RIVER

Birds Hill Provincial Park

ASSINIBOINE RIVER

Winnipeg

LAGIMODIERE BLVD.

on Birds Hill Park, contact Travel Manitoba, 155 Carlton Street, 7th Floor, Winnipeg, Manitoba R3C 3H8, telephone (204) 945-3777, or toll-free 1-800-665-0040.

WINNIPEG TO ST. MALO

Length: 82 km (51 miles)
Time: One to two days
Rating: Easy
Terrain: Flat
Roads: All have gravel shoulders
Traffic: Light
Start: Winnipeg
Overview: St. Malo Recreation Park offers camping, a beach, fishing and three short trails. Also in St. Malo is Le Pionnier Museum, where the pioneer life of the early settlers is depicted.
THE ROUTE:
0 km (0 miles) Winnipeg
23 km (14 miles) Route 311

Go south from Winnipeg on Route 200 for 16 km (10 miles) to St. Adolphe and Route 311, 7 km (4 miles) farther.

42 km (26 miles) Route 216

Go east on Route 311 for 19 km (12 miles) through Niverville to Route 216.

73 km (45 miles) Route 403

Go south on Route 216 through New Bothwell (home of the cheese factory), Kleefeld and Grunthal to Route 403.

80 km (50 miles) Highway 59

Then go west on Route 403 to Highway 59.

82 km (51 miles) St. Malo Recreation Park

Follow Highway 59 south for 2 km (1 mile) into St. Malo Recreation Park.

WINNIPEG TO STEPHENFIELD PROVINCIAL RECREATION PARK LOOP

Length: 168 km (104 miles)
Time: Two days
Rating: Easy
Terrain: Flat
Roads: All have gravel shoulders.
Traffic: Highway 2 and 3 have a lot of traffic including large trucks.
Start: Winnipeg

Overview: This pleasant tour takes you to Stephenfield Park which has campgrounds, fishing and a beach.
THE ROUTE:
0 km (0 miles) Winnipeg
53 km (33 miles) Elm Creek

From Winnipeg, take Highway 2 for 53 km (33 miles) to Elm Creek.

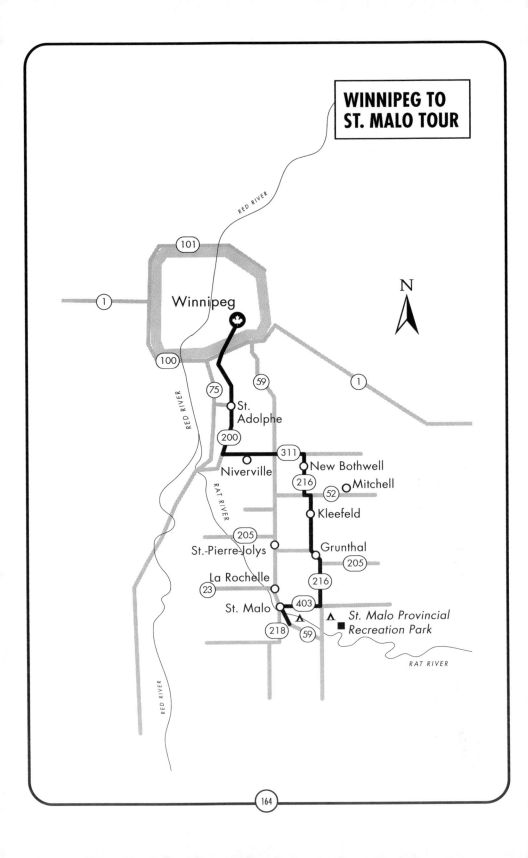

N

101

1 Winnipeg

100

75

59

1

St. Adolphe

200

311

Niverville

New Bothwell

216

52 Mitchell

Kleefeld

205

St.-Pierre-Jolys

Grunthal

205

216

La Rochelle

23

St. Malo

403

218 59

St. Malo Provincial Recreation Park

RED RIVER

RAT RIVER

RED RIVER

RAT RIVER

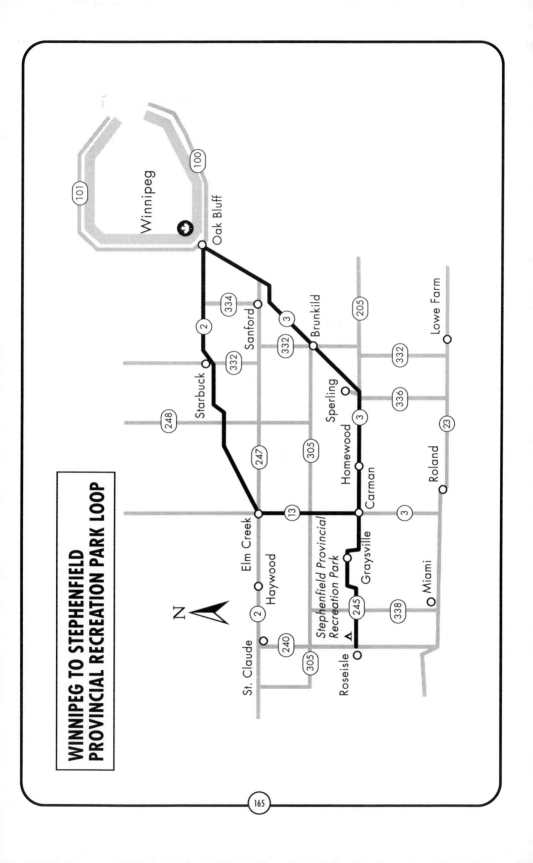

WINNIPEG TO STEPHENFIELD PROVINCIAL RECREATION PARK LOOP

N

Winnipeg

101

100

Oak Bluff

2

334

Sanford

332

Brunkild

3

205

332

Lowe Farm

Starbuck

332

Sperling

336

332

248

247

305

Homewood

3

23

Elm Creek

13

Carman

Roland

3

Haywood

2

Graysville

Miami

St. Claude

240

245

338

305

Stephenfield Provincial Recreation Park

Roseisle

72 km (45 miles) Carman

Go south on Highway 13 for 19 km (12 miles) to Carman. At Carman is Dufferin Historical Museum, with displays depicting pioneer life, and Friendship Field, home of restored Second World War aircraft.

88 km (55 miles) Stephenfield Provincial Recreation Park

From Carman, go west on Route 245 for approximately 16 km (10 miles) to Stephenfield Provincial Recreation Park near Roseisle.

104 km (65 miles) Carman

After exploring Stephenfield Park, head back east on Route 245 for 16 km (10 miles) to Carman.

168 km (104 miles) Winnipeg

At Carman, continue east on Highway 3 for 64 km (40 miles) back to Winnipeg.

More Information: For information on Stephenfield Park, contact Travel Manitoba, 155 Carlton Street, 7th Floor, Winnipeg, Manitoba R3C 3H8, telephone (204) 945-3777, or toll-free 1-800-665-0040.

LAKE WINNIPEG BEACHES LOOP

Length: 282 km (175 miles)
Time: Three to four days
Rating: Intermediate
Terrain: Mostly flat with some hills in Grand Beach Provincial Park and Belair Provincial Forest areas.
Roads: Route 500 is a gravel road; Route 204 has 1.5-meter (5-foot) wide paved shoulder; Highway 59 has full-width paved shoulders between Patricia Beach and Victoria Beach; all other roads have gravel shoulders.
Traffic: Busy during summer.
Connects with: Whiteshell Provincial Park tour and Across Manitoba tour.
Start: Winnipeg
Overview: Here's a good tour for the warm days of summer. Grand Beach is known for its white beaches and shifting sand dunes that reach 8 meters (30 feet) in height. Behind the dunes is a lagoon that's home to orioles, finches, pelicans and cranes.

Grand Beach Provincial Park, 34 square km (13 square miles) in area, also features interpretive nature trails and campgrounds. From Victoria Beach, you can explore the white sands and see the bank swallows of Elk Island Heritage Park.

THE ROUTE:

0 km (0 miles) Winnipeg

From Winnipeg, take Henderson Highway—Route 42 within the city, and Route 204 outside the city—along the banks of the Red River. Along the way you pass Lockport.

30 km (19 miles) Lower Fort Garry

Continue on Route 204 to Lower Fort Garry National Historic Park, situated 30 km (19 miles)

166

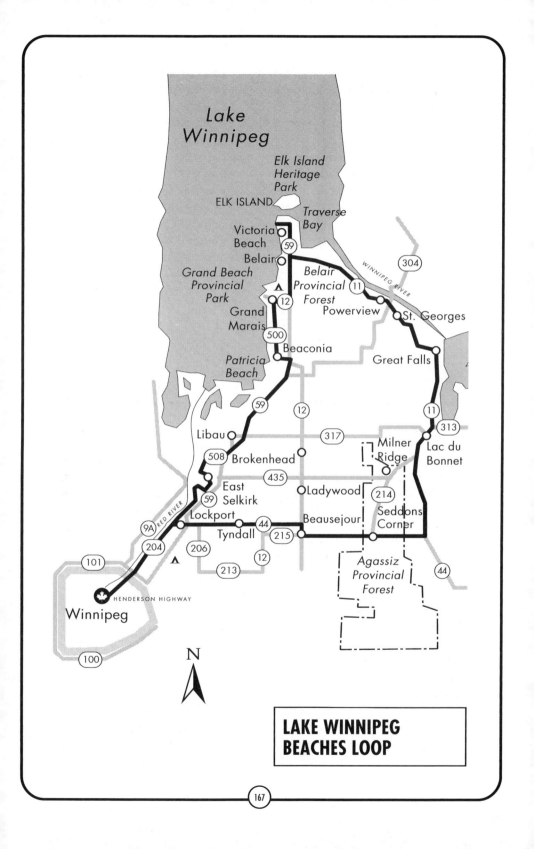

Lake Winnipeg

Elk Island Heritage Park

ELK ISLAND

Traverse Bay

Victoria Beach

Belair

Grand Beach Provincial Park

Belair Provincial Forest

Powerview

St. Georges

Grand Marais

Beaconia

Great Falls

Patricia Beach

Libau

Milner Ridge

Lac du Bonnet

Brokenhead

East Selkirk

Ladywood

Seddons Corner

Lockport

Tyndall

Beausejour

Agassiz Provincial Forest

RED RIVER

HENDERSON HIGHWAY

Winnipeg

WINNIPEG RIVER

N

**LAKE WINNIPEG
BEACHES LOOP**

north of Winnipeg. Lower Fort Garry is a Hudson's Bay Company fur-trading post dating from the 1830s.

72 km (45 miles) Lake Winnipeg

Continue on Route 204 to Route 212. Take Route 212 to East Selkirk. Continue north on Route 508 past Highway 4 to Highway 59. Route 508 intersects with Highway 59 some 8 km (5 miles) south of the village of Libau.

Ride Highway 59 and turn off onto unpaved Route 500 along the shore of Lake Winnipeg. At Route 12 turn left to Grand Beach Provincial Park, which has camping.

101 km (63 miles) Victoria Beach

From Grand Beach Park, go 6 km (4 miles) east along Route 12 to Route 59, which can be very busy in summer.

Go north along Route 59 for 23 km (14 miles) to Victoria Beach.

From here, depending on how high the water is, you can walk, wade, or boat to Elk Island Heritage Park. It is separated from the mainland by a narrow strait.

111 km (69 miles) Highway 11

To continue the loop tour, go south from Victoria Beach for 10 km (6 miles) to Highway 11. Ride Highway 11 alongside Traverse Bay and the Winnipeg River, a former fur trade route of the voyageurs between Lake Superior and Lake Athabasca.

181 km (112 miles) Lac du Bonnet

Continue riding along Highway 11 to Great Falls, 50 km (31 miles) away, and Lac du Bonnet, 20 km (12 miles) farther.

207 km (129 miles) Highway 44

Another 26 km (16 miles) from Lac du Bonnet brings you to Highway 44.

From here you can link with the Whiteshell Provincial Park Tour, or go 19 km (12 miles) southeast along Highway 44 and connect with the Across Manitoba Tour (both tours are described separately in this chapter).

270 km (168 miles) Lockport

To complete the loop tour, go west on Highway 44 for 63 km (39 miles) to Lockport.

282 km (175 miles) Winnipeg

Take Route 204 back into Winnipeg.

More Information: Grand Beach Provincial Park, Grand Beach, Manitoba R0E 0S0, telephone (204) 754-2212.

WHITESHELL PROVINCIAL PARK LOOP

Length: 113 km (70 miles) one way from Winnipeg to Whiteshell Park; 288 km (179 miles) loop tour

Time: One to two days one way from Winnipeg to Whiteshell Park; three to four days loop tour.

Rating: Intermediate

Terrain: Transition from flat prairie to Precambrian Shield forest and lake; short and steep hills in Whiteshell Park, otherwise flat.

Roads: Some road sections, including a 14-km- (9-mile-) section of Highway 44 between Highway 11 and Rennie, are in poor condition; Route 204 has 1.5-meter- (5-foot-) wide shoulders; there are no shoulders whatsoever on Route 307 or on Highway 44 in Whiteshell Park; all other road sections have gravel shoulders only.

Traffic: Most roads have light traffic.

Connects with: The route from Winnipeg to the park is part of the Across Manitoba tour.

Start: Winnipeg

Overview: Whiteshell Park, Manitoba's oldest and largest provincial park, covers 2,734 square km (1,056 square miles) of thick Precambrian Shield forest dotted with more than 200 lakes. Situated along the Manitoba–Ontario boundary, the park is popular for canoeing and hiking.

Accommodation and campgrounds are available in Whiteshell Park and along the route.

THE ROUTE:

0 km (0 miles) Winnipeg

90 km (55 miles) Elma

From Winnipeg, take Lagimodiere Boulevard—Highway 59 —north to Route 213. Go east on Route 213 to Highway 12. Turn south on Highway 12 to Anola on Highway 15.

Cycle east on Highway 15 along flat terrain. Watch out for farm dogs between Anola and the Brokenhead River.

Ride through Vivian, and Ste. Rita to Agassiz Provincial Forest, which has picnic sites but does not offer camping.

At Elma, 90 km (56 miles) from Winnipeg, turn north on Highway 11 for 8 km (5 miles).

Then go east on Highway 44 over rolling country.

128 km (80 miles) Rennie at Whiteshell Provincial Park

At Rennie, 30 km (19 miles) farther, you enter Whiteshell Provincial Park.

Explore Whiteshell Park on routes 307 and 309. The park's hiking trails include the 60-km (37-mile) Mantario Hiking Trail, 16-km (10-mile) Hunt Lake Hiking Trail and several short interpretive trails. Streams contain northern pike, perch, smallmouth bass, walleye and lake trout. Wildlife includes

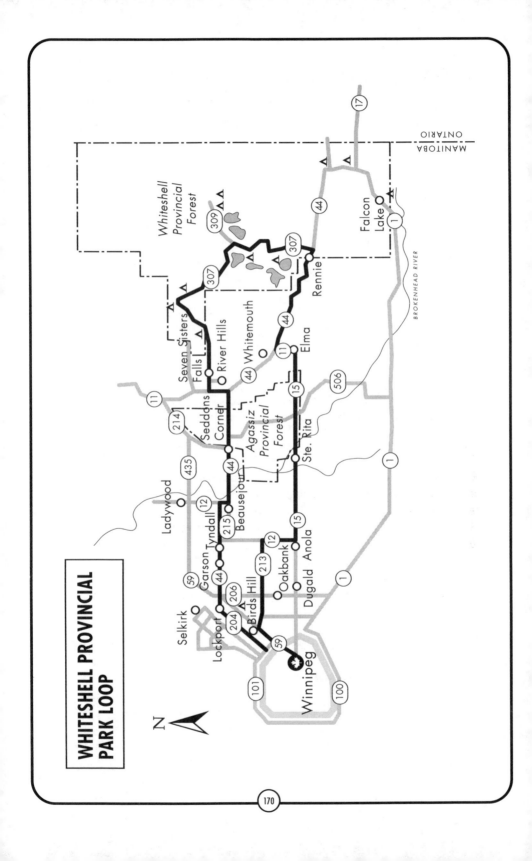

WHITESHELL PROVINCIAL
PARK LOOP

N

Whiteshell
Provincial
Forest

Agassiz
Provincial
Forest

MANITOBA
ONTARIO

BROKENHEAD RIVER

17

44

Falcon
Lake

1

309

307

Rennie

Seven Sisters
Falls

River Hills

307

44

Whitemouth

44

11

Elma

506

11

214

Seddons
Corner

15

Ste. Rita

435

Ladywood

12

215

Beausejour

44

59

Garson
Tyndall

44

206

Birds Hill

204

12

213

Oakbank

15

Dugald
Anola

1

Lockport

Selkirk

101

59

Winnipeg

100

1

moose, fox, coyote, lynx, deer, black bear, beaver, bald eagle, turkey, vultures, spruce grouse and ruffed grouse.

207 km (129 miles) Highway 11

When you're ready to continue on the loop tour, take Route 307 north and west through the park past Seven Sisters Falls to Highway 11. It's 79 km (49 miles) along Route 307 from Rennie northwest through Whiteshell Park to Highway 11.

212 km (131 miles) Highway 44

Go south for 5 km (3 miles) to Highway 44, and then west on Highway 44 for 63 km (39 miles), through Beausejour and Garson.

284 km (176 miles) Lockport

Ride to Lockport on the Red River. Lockport has a number of historic buildings dating back to the Red River Settlement of the mid-nineteenth century.

288 km (179 miles) Winnipeg

Take Route 204 back into Winnipeg.

More Information: Whiteshell Provincial Park, Park Headquarters, Rennie, Manitoba R0E 1R0. Telephone (204) 369-5232.

RIDING MOUNTAIN NATIONAL PARK LOOP

Length: 271 km (168 miles)
Time: Three days
Rating: Intermediate
Terrain: Flat on Highway 5; rolling terrain on Highway 16; hilly on Highway 10.
Roads: Highway 10 has 1-meter (3-foot-) wide paved shoulder only in Riding Mountain National Park; Highway 16 has 1-meter- (3-foot-) wide paved shoulder; otherwise all roads have gravel shoulders.
Traffic: Tourist traffic during summer
Start: Neepawa, Manitoba, which is along the Across Manitoba tour. Towns on this tour that can be reached by VIA Rail are McCreary and Ochre River. Dauphin, 10 km (6 miles) from the northwestern-most

point of this tour, is also served by VIA Rail.
Connects with: Across Manitoba tour, Northern Parks tour.
Overview: This tour takes you on a loop through Riding Mountain Park and along the edge of the Manitoba Escarpment. Located 265 km (165 miles) northwest of Winnipeg, the Riding Mountain Park lies on the Manitoba Escarpment, a rolling highland plateau that dramatically rises 450 meters (1,500 feet) above the flat prairie.

The park's 2,978 square km (1,150 square miles) of lush forest wilderness contrasts with the surrounding wheatfields. Within the park is 750-meter (2,460-foot) Riding Mountain, Manitoba's third highest point.

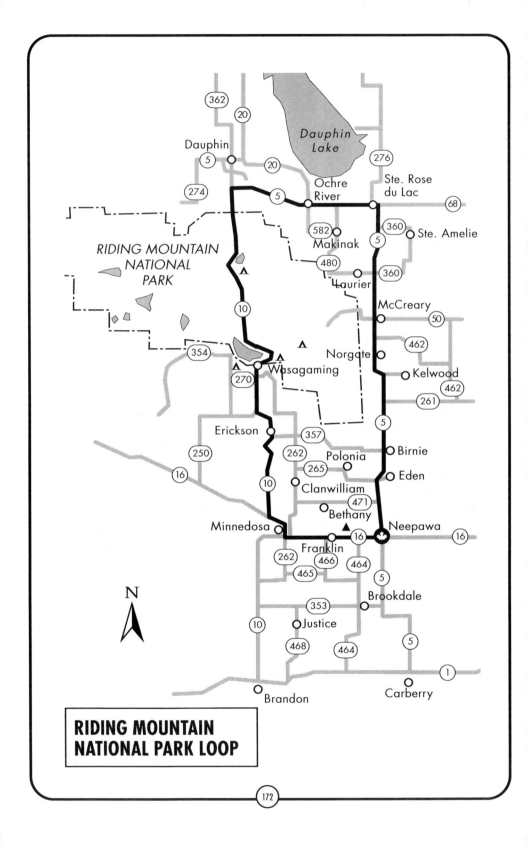

RIDING MOUNTAIN NATIONAL PARK LOOP

Campgrounds and accommodations are available at the park, as well as along the route outside the park.

Black bear, wapiti, moose and white-tailed deer are among the larger mammals in the park. Beaver can be seen in almost every pond. Northern pike, walleye, whitefish, lake trout and brook trout can be found in the park's lakes. Riding Mountain Park's 320-km (200-mile) network consists of 17 day-use trails, and 14 overnight trails.

THE ROUTE:

0 km (0 miles) Neepawa

In Neepawa a historical plaque marks the Saskatchewan Trail, once a major route for settlers traveling west.

35 km (22 miles) Minnedosa

From Neepawa, go west and climb the Manitoba Escarpment for 35 km (22 miles) on Highway 16—the Yellowhead Highway—which has a 1-meter- (3-foot-) wide shoulder, to Minnedosa.

61 km (38 miles) Erickson

At Minnedosa turn north on Highway 10 for 26 km (16 miles), past a campground, and through Erickson.

79 km (49 miles) Wasagaming, Riding Mountain National Park

Another 18 km (11 miles) brings you to Wasagaming, the entrance to Riding Mountain National Park.

139 km (86 miles) Highway 5

When you're ready to leave Riding Mountain Park, ride north on Highway 10 to Highway 5, 60 km (37 miles) north of Wasagaming.

Option: 10 km (6 miles) to Dauphin and link with Northern Parks tour

From this junction you can go 10 km (6 miles) north on Highway 10 to Dauphin and link with the Northern Parks Tour (described separately in this chapter).

Main tour continues: Highway 5

Turn east on Highway 5.

179 km (111 miles) Ste. Rose du Lac

You leave the Manitoba Escarpment near Ochre River, and travel to Ste. Rose du Lac, 40 km (25 miles) away.

211 km (131 miles) McCreary

Stay on Highway 5 as it turns south to McCreary, 32 km (20 miles) south of Ste. Rose du Lac.

271 km (168 miles) Neepawa

For the next 60 km (37 miles) you go through or near several small towns before riding into Neepawa, this tour's starting point.

More Information: Riding Mountain National Park, Wasagaming, Manitoba R0J 2H0, telephone (204) 848-2811.

NORTHERN PARKS TOUR

Length: 593 km (368 miles) one way
Time: Five to seven days
Rating: Intermediate
Terrain: Flat to rolling
Roads: All roads have gravel shoulders only.
Traffic: Light
Connects with: Riding Mountain National Park loop
Start: Dauphin, Manitoba, which is served by VIA Rail's Winnipeg to Churchill service. This tour can be a continuation of the Riding Mountain National Park loop tour.
Overview: Ride north through or near provincial parks and forests on the Manitoba Escarpment, and in wilderness from Dauphin to Flin Flon. Summer evenings in this northern region have long hours of daylight. The parks offer abundant wildlife, lakes and rivers. From Cranberry Portage or The Pas you can take the VIA Rail train to return south to Dauphin or Winnipeg.

Few services are available between towns. Be sure to stock up on food and other supplies at the major towns en route.

THE ROUTE:

0 km (0 miles) Dauphin

60 km (37 miles) Ethelbert

From Dauphin, the site of the Ukrainian Folk Arts Center, go west on Highway 5 for 16 km (10 miles). Go north on Highway 10 toward Ashville, where there is a game farm featuring lions, tigers and monkeys. There is a campground to the north of Ashville, on the way to Ethelbert 60 km (37 miles) from Dauphin.

78 km (48 miles) Duck Mountain Park turn-off

The turn-off for Duck Mountain Provincial Park is 18 km (11 miles) north of Ethelbert. It's a 29-km (18-mile) side trip to the center of the park.

Duck Mountain Park's broad valleys are dominated by 831-meter (2,727-foot) Mount Baldy, Manitoba's highest point. Great blue herons, double-crested cormorants, pelicans, great horned owls, elk and mule deer can be seen.

157 km (97 miles) Minitonas

Continue north on Highway 10 to Minitonas, 97 km (60 miles) from Ethelbert, where there is another game farm.

173 km (107 miles) Swan River

Swan River, 16 km (10 miles) farther, is the largest community in the area. Stock up on food here. There are two local history museums.

213 km (132 miles) turn-off for Porcupine Provincial Forest

Approximately 40 km (23 miles) north of Swan River, and just north of Birch River, Route 365 leads off Highway 10 into Porcupine Provincial Forest. There are several campgrounds in the area.

The lakes and rivers in the 2,089-square-km (807-square-mile) Porcupine Provincial Forest contain northern pike, walleye, rainbow trout, whitefish, lake trout, perch and goldeye. A road leads to the base of 823-meter (2,700-foot) Hart Mountain, Manitoba's second highest point.

243 km (151 miles) Mafeking

Continuing north on Highway 10 from Mafeking, you leave the Manitoba Escarpment and ride near the shores of Dawson Bay and Overflow Bay of Lake Winnipegosis.

398 km (247 miles) The Pas

The next 155 km (96 miles) of Highway 10 to The Pas is isolated, passing through the small settlements of Overflowing River, Westray and Freshford. Be sure you have sufficient food supplies. There are campgrounds along the route.

The Pas is a major center in northern Manitoba offering accommodation, campgrounds and other services. Here is the Little Northern Museum featuring natural history specimens, local history and Native artifacts. A cairn honors Henry Kelsey, the Hudson Bay Company fur trader and explorer who traveled inland from York Factory to the Saskatchewan River via The Pas.

417 km (259 miles) Clearwater Lake Provincial Park

Clearwater Lake Provincial Park is 19 km (12 miles) north of The Pas on Highway 10.

You can see through the Clearwater Lake's blue water to a depth of 11 meters (35 feet). The water's constant motion on the southern shore's dolomite cliffs created caves. Trophy-sized lake trout, northern pike and whitefish inhabit the waters. There are accommodations and campgrounds in the 595-square-km (230-square-mile) park.

472 km (293 miles) Simonhouse turn-off for Grass River Provincial Park

Continue on Highway 10 to Simonhouse, 74 km (46 miles) north of The Pas. At Simonhouse, Route 391 branches off to Grass River Provincial Park.

A 2,288-square-km (885-square-mile) wilderness of lakes and evergreen forest, Grass River Park straddles the Precambrian Shield country and limestone flatbeds. The park is home to woodland caribou, timber wolves and bald eagles. The river system includes the 130-km (80-mile) Grass River canoe route. The more than 150 lakes have northern pike, trout, walleye and whitefish. Campgrounds are available.

539 km (335 miles) Flin Flon

Continue north on Highway 10 through Cranberry Portage to Flin Flon, 67 km (42 miles) northwest of Simonhouse. Supplies and accommodation are available in Flin Flon.

Flin Flon, the tour's endpoint, acquired its unusual name in

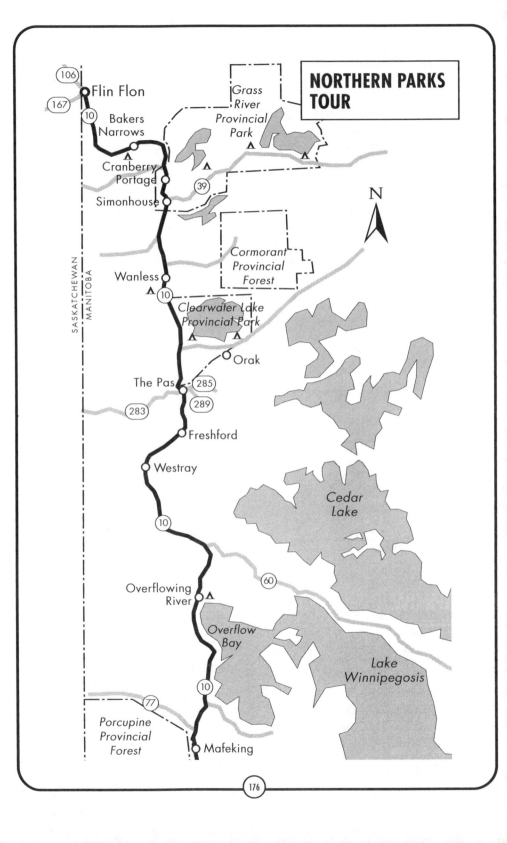

NORTHERN PARKS TOUR

N

Flin Flon
106
167
10
Bakers
Narrows
Cranberry
Portage
Simonhouse
39

Grass
River
Provincial
Park

Cormorant
Provincial
Forest

Wanless
10

Clearwater Lake
Provincial Park

Orak
The Pas
285
289
283

Freshford

Westray

10

Cedar
Lake

Overflowing
River

Overflow
Bay

60

Lake
Winnipegosis

10

77

Porcupine
Provincial
Forest

Mafeking

SASKATCHEWAN
MANITOBA

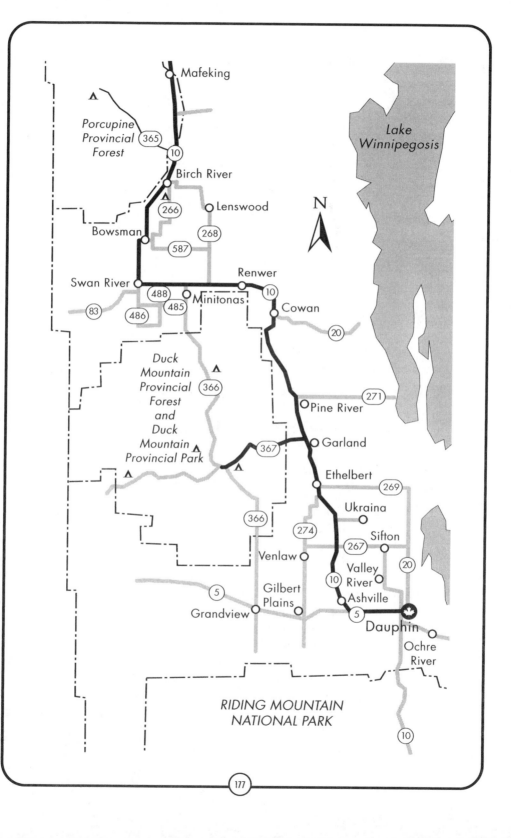

1915 when prospectors found a copy of the novel *The Sunless City* on a portage near the Churchill River. The town's name is an abbreviation for Professor Josiah Flintabbetey Flonatin, the novel's hero who discovers a city of gold in the center of the earth. In Flin Flon is a statue designed by cartoonist Al Capp, representing Josiah Flintabbetey Flonatin.

593 km (368 miles) Cranberry Portage and VIA Rail train

To return, ride south of Highway 10 for 54 km (33 miles) to Cranberry Portage and board the VIA Rail train, which goes to The Pas. There you can catch another train south to Dauphin and Winnipeg.

More Information: For details on the provincial parks contact: Parks Branch, P.O. Box 239, Swan River, Manitoba R0L 1Z0, telephone (204) 734-2321.

ACROSS MANITOBA

Length: 529 km (317 miles). Though a bit longer than taking the Trans Canada Highway straight across Manitoba, this route is more scenic.

Time: Five to six days

Rating: Intermediate

Terrain: Hilly sections between the Saskatchewan border and Neepawa; flat between Neepawa and Whiteshell Provincial Park; short steep hills in Whiteshell Park.

Roads: Most roads are in good condition; a 14-km (9-mile) section of Highway 44 between Highway 11 and Rennie is very rough; Highway 16 has a 1-meter- (3-foot-) wide paved shoulder; the Trans Canada Highway between West Hawk Lake and the Ontario border has a full-width paved shoulder; Highway 44 in Whiteshell Provincial Park has no shoulder; all other roads have gravel shoulders.

Traffic: This route takes you off the more heavily traveled Trans Canada Highway onto less-traveled routes that connect with some of the tours in this chapter.

Connects with: most of the tours in this chapter

Start: Begin at the Saskatchewan-Manitoba border on the Trans Canada Highway. Nearest towns are Virden, Manitoba 22 km (14 miles) east of the boundary, and Moosomin, Saskatchewan, 41 km (25 miles) west.

THE ROUTE:
0 km (0 miles) Saskatchewan–Manitoba border
35 km (22 miles) Highway 83

Starting from the Saskatchewan–Manitoba border, go east for 35 km (22 miles) on the

Trans Canada Highway to Highway 83.

62 km (38 miles) Route 24

Go north for 27 km (17 miles) on Highway 83 to Route 24.

144 km (89 miles) Highway 10

Go east on Route 24 for 82 km (51 miles) to Highway 10.

160 km (100 miles) Highway 16, the Yellowhead Highway

At Highway 10 go north for 16 km (10 miles), almost to Minnedosa, to the junction with Highway 16, known as the Yellowhead Highway.

276 km (172 miles) Highway 1, the Trans Canada Highway

Continue east on Highway 16 past Neepawa and Gladstone to Highway 1, the Trans Canada Highway just west of Portage la Prairie, 116 km (72 miles) from the junction of Highway 10 and Highway 16.

364 km (226 miles) Winnipeg

Go east on Highway 1 and take Highway 1A for 18 km (11 miles) through Portage la Prairie to Highway 26. Then ride Highway 26 for 62 km (38 miles) through Poplar Point to the Trans Canada Highway just west of Winnipeg. Take the Trans Canada Highway 13 km (8 miles) into Winnipeg.

454 km (282 miles) Highway 11 near Elma

From Winnipeg, take Lagimodiere Boulevard—Highway 59 —north to Route 213. Go east on Route 213 to Highway 12. Turn south on Highway 12 to Anola on Highway 15.

Cycle east on Highway 15 along flat terrain. Watch out for farm dogs between Anola and the Brokenhead River.

Ride through Vivian, and Ste. Rita to Agassiz Provincial Forest, which has picnic sites but does not offer camping. Stay on Highway 15 to Highway 11 near Elma, a ride of 90 km (56 km) from Winnipeg.

462 km (287 miles) Highway 44

Go 8 km (5 miles) north on Highway 11 to Highway 44.

524 km (326 miles) Trans Canada Highway in Whiteshell Provincial Park

Cycle 62 km (38 miles) east on Highway 44 through Whiteshell Provincial Park where you link with Highway 1, the Trans Canada Highway.

529 km (329 miles) Ontario boundary

From here you can continue east on the Trans Canada Highway into Ontario.

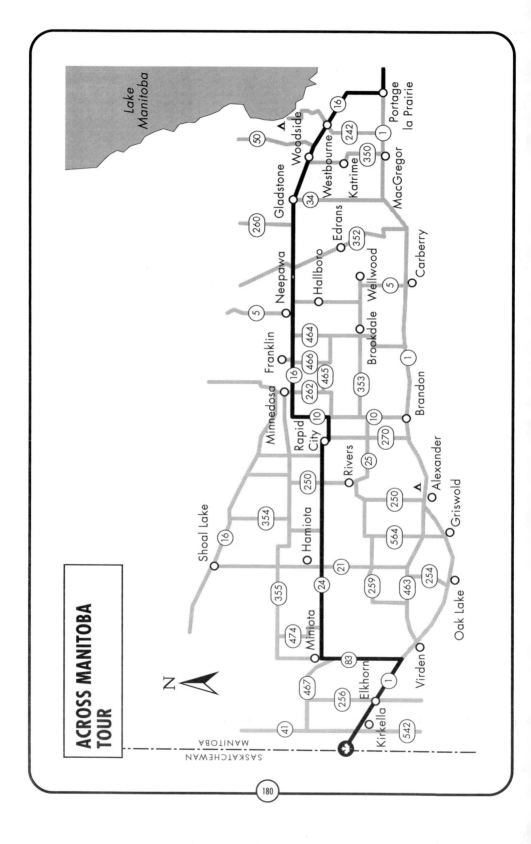

ACROSS MANITOBA TOUR

N

Lake Manitoba

SASKATCHEWAN | MANITOBA

Portage la Prairie
Woodside
Westbourne
Katrime
MacGregor
Gladstone
Edrans
Hallboro
Carberry
Neepawa
Wellwood
Franklin
Brookdale
Minnedosa
Brandon
Rapid City
Rivers
Alexander
Shoal Lake
Griswold
Hamiota
Oak Lake
Miniota
Elkhorn
Virden
Kirkella

16
50
242
1
350
34
260
352
5
5
464
466
465
262
10
353
1
10
270
25
250
250
564
354
16
21
259
463
254
355
24
474
83
467
256
1
41
542

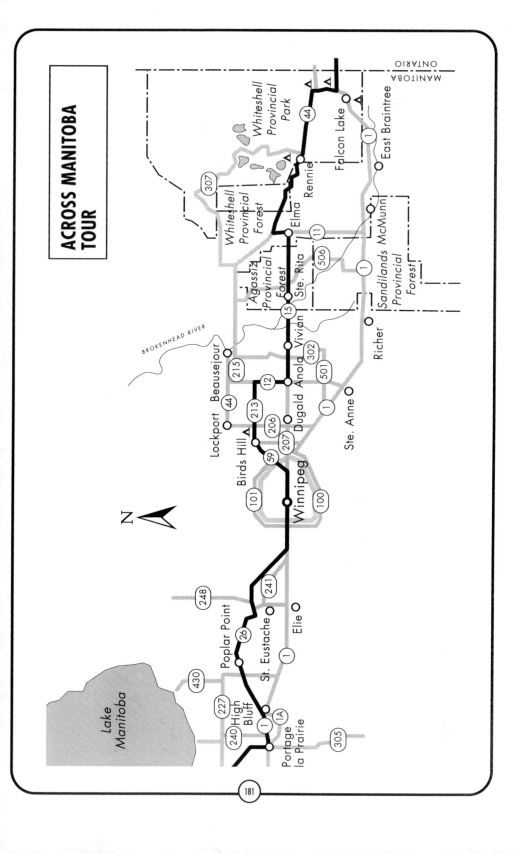

ACROSS MANITOBA TOUR

N

Lake Manitoba

BROKENHEAD RIVER

Whiteshell Provincial Park

Whiteshell Provincial Forest

Agassiz Provincial Forest

Sandilands Provincial Forest

MANITOBA
ONTARIO

Portage la Prairie
High Bluff
St. Eustache
Elie
Poplar Point
Winnipeg
Lockport
Birds Hill
Beausejour
Dugald
Anola
Vivian
Ste. Anne
Richer
Ste. Rita
Elma
Rennie
McMunn
East Braintree
Falcon Lake

240
227
305
430
248
26
241
1A
1
101
59
44
213
215
206
207
12
100
1
501
302
15
506
11
1
307
44

GUIDEBOOKS

Manitoba Outdoor Adventure Guide to Cycling, by Ruth Marr is a guide to off-road, paved-road and dirt-road cycling in Manitoba. Available from: Fifth House Publishers, 620 Duchess St., Saskatoon, Saskatchewan S7K 0R1, telephone (306) 242-4936; $12.95.

Winnipeg by Cycle, by Alex Naivey. Available from: Thunder Enlightening Press, P.O. Box 332, 905 Croydon Ave., Winnipeg, Manitoba R3M 3V3; $7.95.

(Saul Goldman, Velotique)

Ontario

Ride these tours and discover there is a lot more to Ontario than six-lane expressways and endless suburban development. These tours take you on picturesque country roads with minimal traffic through farmland, orchards and charming Victorian villages that have retained an unhurried pace. You can explore nature trails and bird sanctuaries and ride along historic canals, lakeshores, sand beaches and limestone cliffs. Absent on many routes is the overwhelming commercialism found in other scenic areas. During autumn, nature puts on a spectacular display of color.

Most of these routes involve a series of connecting county roads. The directions may appear a bit confusing to read, but once you're on your bike, the routes are not difficult to follow.

Tourist Information: For general tourist information, including a road map and guides to accommodation and provincial parks and campgrounds, contact Ontario Travel, Queen's Park, Toronto, Ontario M7A 2E5, or call (416) 314-0944; or toll-free from Canada and the United States 1-800-668-2746; TDD (for speech or hearing disabled) (416) 314-6557.

Campsite Vacancies: For a 24-hour taped campsite vacancy report for provincial parks south of Sudbury and North Bay, you can call the above Ontario Travel telephone numbers from the Victoria Day weekend (usually the third weekend in May) to Labour Day weekend (the first weekend in September).

Fall Colors and Spring Blossoms: Call the above Ontario Travel telephone numbers for seasonal reports on the colors during autumn and blossoms during the spring (and during winter for reports on cross-country skiing conditions).

Roads: Ontario's best cycling is on the county roads through rural Ontario. Bicycles are not allowed on controlled-access highways in Ontario, such as the 400 series (i.e., Highway 401) the Queen Elizabeth Way, Toronto's Don Valley Parkway and Gardiner Expressway and Ottawa's Queensway.

For details on road conditions and highway construction, call the Ontario Ministry of Transportation's road information line at (416) 235-1110, or toll-free in Ontario 1-800-268-1376.

Maps: Most routes in this chapter are marked on the provincial road map. For more detailed maps there are two sources:

• Ontario Transportation Map Series (OTMS), which have a 1:250,000 scale, are available from: Ministry of Transportation, Map Sales Unit, Room B-034 East Building, 1201 Wilson Avenue, Downsview, Ontario M3M 1J8, (416) 235-4339, in Ontario call toll-free 1-800-268-0637.

• Ontario Cycling Route Map Series, available from the Ontario Cycling Association (OCA), 1220 Sheppard Avenue East, Willowdale, Ontario M2K 2X1, telephone (416) 495-4141. See listing at the end of chapter for more details.

Many of the tour descriptions indicate which OTMS and OCA maps can be used.

Weather: During June, July and August, days are usually warm, though nights can be cool, particularly in northern Ontario. During fall (from mid-September to mid-November) and in spring (from mid-March through April), medium-weight clothing is required.

Average summer temperatures range from 14 to 16 degree Celsius (57 to 79 degrees Fahrenheit) in Ottawa, which is in eastern Ontario; 16 to 27 degrees Celsius (60 to 81 degree Fahrenheit) in Toronto in southern Ontario; and 11 to 23 degrees Celsius (52 to 73 degrees Fahrenheit) in Thunder Bay in northwestern Ontario.

Accommodations: Ontario offers a large range of accommodation from bed-and-breakfasts and inexpensive hotels to top-notch hotels and resorts. There are provincial park campgrounds throughout the province, as well as many privately-owned campgrounds. Ontario has a wide range of accommodation and campgrounds. Use the *Accommodations and Camping* guides available from Ontario Travel for details.

Hostels: For information on hostels in Ontario, contact: Canadian Hostelling Association—Ontario East, 18 Byward Market, Ottawa, Ontario K1N 7A1, telephone (613) 230-1200, fax (613) 230-6986; and Canadian Hostelling Association—Great Lakes Region, 219 Church Street, Toronto, Ontario M5B 1Y7, telephone (416) 862-2665, fax (416) 368-6499.

Airports: Toronto's Pearson Airport is the province's largest airport. It is served by numerous airlines with connections to airports in other Ontario cities including Ottawa, Hamilton, Thunder Bay and Sault Ste. Marie.

Trains: For information in Ontario on VIA Rail services contact: Toronto (416) 366-8411; Ottawa (613) 244-8289; Hamilton (416) 522-7533; Kingston (613) 544-5600; London (519) 672-5722; Windsor (519) 256-5511; elsewhere in area codes 416, 519 and 613, and all of area code 705, call toll-free 1-800-361-1235; in area code 807 call toll-free 1-800-561-8630.

Organized Bicycle Tours: For names of companies and organizations offering organized trips, contact Ontario Travel and the Ontario Cycling Association.

Bicycling: Ontario Cycling Association, 1220 Sheppard Avenue East, Willowdale, Ontario M2K 2X1, (416) 495-4141.

Area: 1,068,582 square km (412,580 square miles); Canada's second largest province in area, Ontario reaches from Lake Erie in the south to Hudson's Bay in the north, and from Manitoba in the west to the banks of the St. Lawrence River and the Ottawa River to the east.

Terrain: The geographic division between northern and southern Ontario is generally considered a line lying roughly along the Mattawa River, Lake Nipissing and the French River. Most of the 932,000 square km (360,000 square miles) of northern Ontario is covered by the forests, lakes and rocks of the rugged Precambrian Shield. About one-third of the 129,500-square-km (50,000-square-mile) area of southern Ontario is covered by a southern extension of the Precambrian Shield known as the Frontenac Axis. The remaining two-thirds of southern Ontario is largely agricultural land and forests.

The Niagara Escarpment is a steep rock face that stretches 725 km (450 miles) from the Niagara River through Hamilton, Collingwood, the Bruce Peninsula, Tobermory and Manitoulin Island. At Niagara Falls, the Niagara River plummets 54 meters (177 feet) over the escarpment.

Capital: Toronto, on the shores of Lake Ontario, is Ontario's provincial capital and Canada's largest city.

Population: 10,084,885 (1991 census); Ontario is the country's most populous province with more than one third of the nation's people. More than 80 per cent of Ontario's people live in cities. Concentrated in the Golden Horseshoe—the Toronto, Oshawa, Hamilton and St. Catharines areas at the western end of Lake Ontario—is more than 50 per cent of the province's population. Here also is the province's manufacturing industrial base.

Northern Ontario, which has almost 90 per cent of Ontario's land, has only 10 per cent of its population. Mining and forestry dominate northern Ontario's economy.

History: Algonquin and Iroquois Indians lived in Ontario when the Europeans arrived. French explorer Étienne Brûlé, who came to Québec with Samuel de Champlain in 1608, was the first European to enter what is now the province of Ontario. In 1613, he journeyed from Québec by way of the Ottawa River (a bike tour through this valley is included). In 1615, he traveled down the Humber River Valley—then an Indian portage trail (and now a recreational path in Toronto)—and was the first European to see Lake Ontario and the site of what would become the city of Toronto.

Following the American Revolution, many Loyalists settled in Ontario. At Confederation in 1867, Ontario became a province of Canada.

BICYCLING IN TORONTO

Toronto does have wilderness areas with cycling paths, but you have to know where to look. Although Toronto is relatively flat, there are wooded ravines and river valleys with a network of trails stretching across much of the city.

You can take your bike on the subway during non-rush hours (bikes are not allowed on the subway from 6:30 a.m. to 9:30 a.m. and from 3:30 p.m. to 6:30 p.m. Monday to Friday). In the central part of the city are paths for cycling through the Rosedale Valley and the Don River, which connects with a path north along Wilket Creek, and another path east along Taylor Creek. In the east are also bike trails along Highland Creek and near the Metro Zoo.

In the west, the Humber River Valley goes from Lake Ontario northwards; and High Park offers enjoyable cycling on park roads. Across Toronto's entire waterfront is the Martin Goodman Trail. For more details pick up *The Great Toronto Bicycling Guide*, or a *Cyclist's Map of Toronto*, from bike shops.

There are also bike lanes on parts of several downtown streets including College Street and Carlton Street between Manning Avenue and Church Street; Bay Street from Davenport Road to Cumberland Street; Davenport Road from Dupont Street to Bay Street; and St. George Street and Beverley Street between Dupont Street and Queen Street West.

More Information: Toronto City Cycling Committee, 81 Elizabeth Street, Toronto, Ontario M5H 2N2, telephone (416) 392-7592.

OTTAWA RECREATIONAL TRAILS

Ottawa is well known as a bicycle-friendly city. The city's scenic recreational trails along the Rideau Canal, Rideau River and Ottawa River link to offer many kilometers of enjoyable cycling for an afternoon or day-long ride. As the nation's capital, Ottawa's park system is well developed and many have trails. Also indicated on the *Cyclists' Guide* map are unsigned cycling routes on mostly residential streets throughout the city.

More Information: Canada's Capital Information Center, 14 Metcalfe Street, Ottawa, Ontario K1P 5L1, telephone (613) 239-5000.

LAKE SIMCOE AND HURONIA HIGHLANDS LOOP

Length: 297 km (185 miles), or 232 km (144 miles) shorter option

Time: Three to four days

Rating: Intermediate

Terrain: Starts out flat but becomes hilly north of Orillia.

Roads: Route is shown on Ontario road map or the more detailed Ontario Transportation Map Series map #5 or Ontario Cycling Association Route Maps #4 and #5 (see "ROADS" at beginning of chapter for information on how to obtain OTMS maps).

Traffic: Can be busy on weekends.

Connects with: Across Ontario; other tours beginning in Toronto

Start: Toronto, Ontario's largest city. Orillia and Barrie are the towns along the loop served by VIA Rail.

Overview: Huronia is a popular recreation area directly north of Toronto. It encompasses rural communities like Cookstown, includes the shores of Georgian Bay and extends east to the shores of Lake Simcoe.

The region is named for the Huron Indian tribe, which first settled in this region. Étienne Brûlé visited the Huron Indians in the area in the early seventeenth century.

This loop tour goes through Cookstown, along the beaches of Lake Simcoe, then turns west to beaches on Georgian Bay and returns through Cookstown to Toronto. Or,

from Orillia you can go east along Lake Simcoe and south to Toronto.

THE ROUTE:

0 km (0 miles) Toronto

50 km (31 miles) Highway 89

From Toronto, go north on Weston Road (County Road 56) to Highway 9. Go left on Highway 9 for a short distance and then right on Rupke Road.

Go right on Canal Road along the Holland Canal.

At County Road 54 go left to Highway 89, 50 km (31 miles) from Toronto.

72 km (45 miles) Barrie

Go east on Highway 89, which has more traffic than the country roads.

Go left on County Road 53 northward, and turn right onto Highway 27. Ride down a steep hill into Barrie to Blake Street (Highway 11 north). Situated on Lake Simcoe's Kempenfelt Bay, Barrie is a major center in the area. It's a 22-km (14-mile) ride from the junction of Highway 89 and County Road 54 to Barrie.

107 km (66 miles) Orillia

Ride through Barrie to Shanty Bay Road (County Road 20) along the quiet Lake Simcoe shoreline.

At the T-junction, go right, over tracks and left onto gravel.

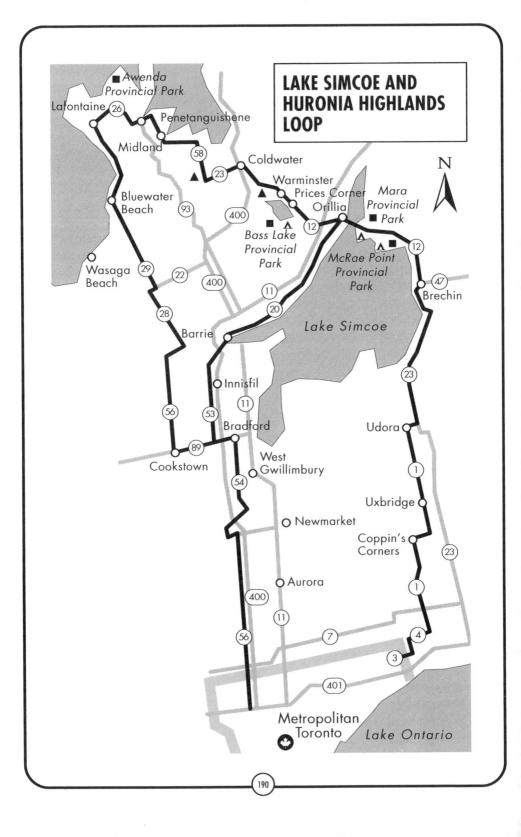

LAKE SIMCOE AND HURONIA HIGHLANDS LOOP

Awenda Provincial Park

Lafontaine (26)
Penetanguishene
Midland (58)
(23) Coldwater
Warminster
Prices Corner
Bluewater Beach
(93)
(400)
Orillia
Mara Provincial Park
(12)
N
McRae Point Provincial Park
(12)
Wasaga Beach
(29) (22) (400)
Bass Lake Provincial Park
(11)
(20)
(47)
Brechin
Lake Simcoe
(28)
Barrie
(23)
Innisfil
(11)
(56) (53)
Bradford
Udora
(1)
(89)
Cookstown
West Gwillimbury
Uxbridge
(1)
(54)
Newmarket
Coppin's Corners
(23)
Aurora
(1)
(400)
(11)
(4)
(7)
(56)
(3)
(401)
Metropolitan Toronto
Lake Ontario

At next T-junction, keep right onto pavement. Follow the lake edge past Eight Mile Point Road to Highway 12.

Turn right into Orillia, a ride of 35 km (22 miles) from Barrie.

There is a youth hostel at Borland Street and camping at Mara Provincial Park. Situated on the narrows between Lake Couchiching and Lake Simcoe, Orillia is a major link in the Trent-Severn Canal System. Among its attractions is the house of Stephen Leacock, built in 1929 on the lakeshore.

Option: East around Lake Simcoe and south to Toronto, 125 km (75 miles)

From Orillia, you have an option of going east around Lake Simcoe and south to Toronto.

To follow this 125-km (75-mile) option go east on Highway 12, past the turn-offs for Mara Provincial Park and McRae Point Provincial Park.

At Brechin, turn right on County Road 47 which joins with County Road 23. Ride County Road 23 south and go right on County Road 32 to Udora.

Then turn left on County Road 1 through Uxbridge and to County Road 21.

Go right on County Road 21 to Coppin's Corners, then left on County Road 1, and right again on Concession Road 4 to County Road 27.

Go left on County Road 27, then right on Concession Road

3, and right on Pickering Town Line.

Turn left onto Steeles Avenue, the boundary of Metropolitan Toronto, just north of the Metro Toronto Zoo.

Main tour continues

145 km (90 miles) Midland

To continue from Orillia on the Huronia loop tour, take Highway 12 for 18 km (11 miles) past the turn-off for Bass Lake Provincial Park and through Prices Corner and Warminster.

Just past the turn-off for Coldwater, turn left onto County Road 23 through forests.

Turn right at County Road 58, which rejoins Highway 12.

You can visit the reconstructed seventeenth century Jesuit mission Sainte-Marie among the Hurons, the Martyrs' Shrine and the Wye Marsh Wildlife Center on your way to Midland, 20 km (12 miles) from Coldwater.

Ride into Midland. Go along the waterfront to County Road 2. Take County Road 2 to Highway 27.

151 km (94 miles) Penetanguishene

Turn right onto Highway 27, which leads into Penetanguishene, 6 km (4 miles) farther. Here is the restored Historic Naval and Military Establishment, built after the War of 1812.

You can either stay in Penetanguishene or follow County Road 26 to the turn off for

Awenda Provincial Park, which has camping and a view of Giant's Tomb Island in Georgian Bay.

183 km (114 miles) Bluewater Beach

Take County Road 26 from Penetanguishene 12 km (7 miles) to Lafontaine, and turn left past Lafontaine onto what becomes the Lakeshore Road. Follow this road past several beaches.

After Bluewater Beach, a ride of 20 km (12 miles) from Lafontaine, take County Road 29 southward.

247 km (153 miles) Cookstown

Take County Road 29 south-ward and turn right onto County Road 22 at the T-junction, and then left onto Highway 26 east.

At Minesing, go right onto County Road 28, and right on County Road 40.

Cross Highway 90 and continue south on County Road 56.

Go left on Highway 89 to Cookstown, 64 km (40 miles) from Bluewater Beach.

297 km (184 miles) Toronto

Retrace your route from Cookstown back to Toronto, 50 km (31 miles) farther.

NIAGARA ESCARPMENT AND ORCHARDS

Length: 369 km (229 miles)
Time: Three to four days
Rating: Easy to intermediate
Terrain: Mostly flat except for some good climbs up the Niagara Escarpment.
Roads: Include the Niagara River Recreational Trail, a off-street walking and bicycle path along the Niagara River; this route is shown on the Ontario road map or the more detailed Ontario Transportation Map Series map #5, or OCA map #4 (see "ROADS" at the beginning of chapter for information on how to obtain these maps).
Traffic: Mostly light, except when your riding out of Hamilton and on Highway 20 which tends to have heavier traffic; R.R. 81 can be busy, especially during fresh fruit season where there is a lot of weekend traffic of people picking their own fruit.
Connects with: Lake Erie Edge and Tillsonburg Tobacco Plains
Start: Toronto. If you want to begin outside Toronto, you can take the VIA Rail train to Aldershot Station near Hamilton and pick up the tour from there.
Overview: On this tour you explore part of the Niagara Escarpment. On the way are orchards and vineyards where Niagara wineries offer wine tours and samples. Niagara-on-the-Lake is one of the best-preserved nineteenth century towns in North America, and is the home of the

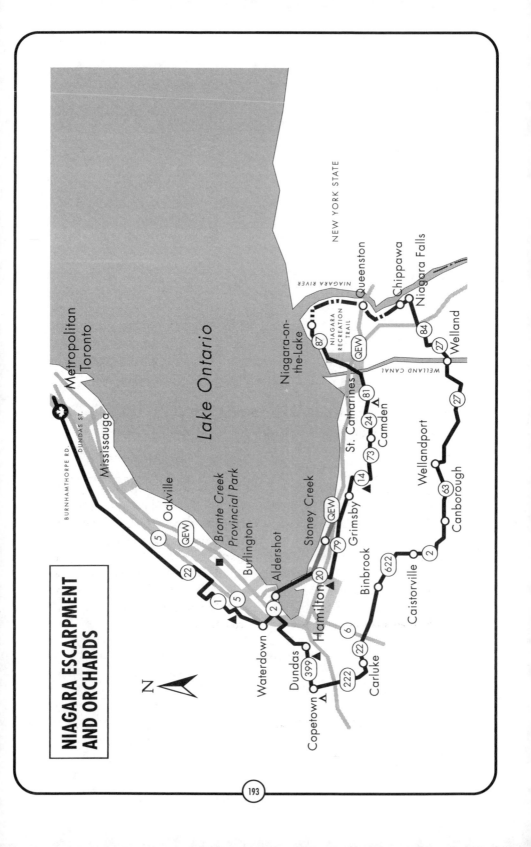

NIAGARA ESCARPMENT AND ORCHARDS

N

Metropolitan Toronto

Mississauga

Lake Ontario

Oakville

Bronte Creek Provincial Park

Burlington

Aldershot

Stoney Creek

Niagara-on-the-Lake

NEW YORK STATE

Queenston

Chippawa

Niagara Falls

NIAGARA RIVER

NIAGARA RECREATION TRAIL

87

QEW

St. Catharines

81

24

Camden

73

14

Grimsby

QEW

79

20

Hamilton

Binbrook

622

Caistorville

2

Canborough

63

Wellandport

27

27

Welland

84

WELLAND CANAL

BURNHAMTHORPE RD.

DUNDAS ST.

5

QEW

22

1

5

2

Waterdown

Dundas

399

222

Carluke

6

22

Copetown

193

Shaw Festival. You ride the Niagara Parkway past gardens and nature trails along the Niagara River to Niagara Falls, Canada's most popular tourist destination.

THE ROUTE:

0 km (0 miles) Toronto

65 km (40 miles) Waterdown

From Toronto, go west on Dundas Street and turn right on Burnhamthorpe. Follow Burnhamthorpe out through Mississauga, which has some heavy traffic.

Past Erin Mills the route is flat and has little traffic.

Go left on Fourth Line and then right on Highway 5.

Go right on Tremaine Road (County Road 22). Ride over the tracks then turn left onto No. 2 Sideroad.

At the T-junction turn left onto Appleby Line, and then right onto Burnhamthorpe Road (No. 1 Sideroad) and follow it into Waterdown, 65 km (40 miles) from Toronto.

76 km (47 miles) Stoney Creek

In Waterdown, turn left at Main Street, which runs into Snake Road.

Ride down the escarpment to Plains Road (Highway 2) in Burlington and turn left.

Turn right at Lasalle Park Road, then left on North Shore Road East, which eventually rejoins Highway 2.

Turn right onto Lakeshore, and then left at Beach Boulevard on the spit facing the steel mills of Hamilton. If you're camping, head to the Confederation Park campground near Highway 20 and the Queen Elizabeth Way.

Follow Highway 20 south through Stoney Creek, 11 km (7 miles) from Waterdown. Here is the Historic Battlefield House and Monument, a 1759 settler's home, now a museum devoted to the Battle of Stoney Creek fought during the War of 1812.

119 km (74 miles) Ball's Falls Conservation Area

Climb Highway 20 up the escarpment to Ridge Road. It's a tough climb but you're rewarded with great views.

Turn left and follow this panoramic road along the top of the escarpment. Ridge Road ends at R.R. 14 south of Grimsby.

Turn right on R.R. 14, and then left onto Fly Road (R.R. 73).

Ride through Campden to R.R. 24. Turn right and then left into the Ball's Falls Conservation Area, 43 km (27 miles) from Stoney Creek. Ball's Falls Conservation Area, which has camping, includes an old mill site on Sixteen Mile Creek.

134 km (83 miles) St. Catharines

Go north on R.R. 24 and turn right onto R.R. 81 and take it into St. Catharines, where it becomes St. Paul Street.

St. Catharines, 15 km (9 miles) from Ball's Falls Conservation Area, is in the heart of the wine country and Niagara fruit belt. You can see ships go through the locks on the nearby Welland Canal.

149 km (93 miles) Niagara-on-the-Lake

From St. Catharines, take County Road 87 for 15 km (9 miles) along the lakeshore to Niagara-on-the-Lake, situated on Lake Ontario at the mouth of the Niagara River. Along the way are wineries that offer tours and tasting.

Niagara-on-the-Lake has many well-preserved nineteenth century neoclassical and Georgian homes. It's the home of the annual Shaw Festival and Fort George National Historic Park.

169 km (105 miles) Niagara Falls

Leaving Niagara-on-the-Lake, ride south along the Niagara River Recreation Trail, a walking and bicycling path along the Niagara Parkway. At Queenston is the Brock Monument overlooking the site of the Battle of Queenston Heights, an important victory during the War of 1812.

Continue south past the floral clock to Niagara Falls, Canada's most popular tourist destination. It's a 20-km (12-mile) ride from Niagara-on-the-Lake.

After you've seen thundering Niagara Falls, there are many attractions here. There is a wide range of accommodation—hotels, bed-and-breakfasts, a hostel, and campgrounds—in the Niagara area.

194 km (120 miles) Welland

Continue along the Niagara River Recreational Trail south to Chippawa.

Turn right onto Lyons Creek Road, which becomes R.R. 47.

Turn left on R.R. 84 and then right onto R.R. 27. Ride R.R. 27 through the tunnel under the Welland Canal—watch for broken glass in the tunnel—into Welland, 25 km (15 miles) from Niagara Falls.

Ships from all over the world cruise the Welland Canal through the center of the city.

Stay on R.R. 27 through Welland and along the south side of the Welland River to Wellandport.

294 km (183 miles) Dundas

Follow R.R. 63 along Oswego Creek to Canborough.

Turn right onto R.R. 2 through Caistorville. Turn left onto R.R. 622 and go through Binbrook. Stay on R.R. 622 as it becomes R.R. 22 and then Carluke Road. Follow it to R.R. 222 and go north on R.R. 222 and then Highway 52, to Copetown.

Go right here onto R.R. 399 into the town of Dundas. Dundas is in a valley surrounded by the Niagara Escarpment, a ride of 100 km (62 miles) from Welland.

304 km (189 miles) Waterdown

Turn left at King Street and then right onto Old York Road to Highway 6. A quick right and then left will take you to Snake Road.

Turn left on Snake Road and

follow it to Waterdown, 10 km (6 miles) from Dundas. Camping and accommodation are available at Waterdown.

369 km (229 miles) Toronto

Return the 65 km (40 miles) to Toronto by the same route you left by.

Turn right onto Parkside Drive, which becomes No. 1 Sideroad.

At the T-junction, turn left and then right. At the next T-junction at Tremaine Road, turn right and go to Highway 5.

Turn left onto Highway 5, then left onto Fourth Line.

Turn right on Burnhamthorpe Road and follow it to Dundas Street and into Toronto.

LAKE ERIE EDGE AND TILLSONBURG TOBACCO PLAINS

Length: 335 km (210 miles)
Time: Three to four days
Rating: Easy
Terrain: Mostly flat
Roads: Route is shown on the Ontario road map or the more detailed Ontario Transportation Map Series maps #1 and #5, or OCA maps #4 and #1 (see "ROADS" at beginning of chapter for information on how to obtain these maps).
Traffic: Light
Connects with: Lake Erie and Thames Valley tour, Niagara Escarpment and Orchards tour.
Start: Dundas. VIA Rail serves nearby Aldershot Station. If you want to ride to Dundas from Toronto, see the first part of the Niagara Escarpment and Orchards tour.
Overview: Ride on quiet highways and country roads along the scenic shoreline of Lake Erie, passing through small port towns. You cycle the Talbot Trail, a route followed by pioneers settling the area.

Then turning inland, you go through Ontario's tobacco country. In the town of Tillsonburg are the largest auction exchanges in the tobacco belt. Many vegetables are also grown in this area.

THE ROUTE:
0 km (0 miles) Dundas
14 km (9 miles) Ancaster

From Dundas take Old Dundas Road to Wilson Street (Highway 2). Go right on Wilson Street into Ancaster, a ride of 14 km (9 miles) from Dundas.

89 km (55 miles) Port Dover

From Ancaster, continue on Wilson Street (Highway 2), go south on Fiddlers Green Road (R.R. 216), and turn right on R.R. 222. Past Carluke, go left onto R.R. 22. At Highway 54, turn right and go through Middleport. Go

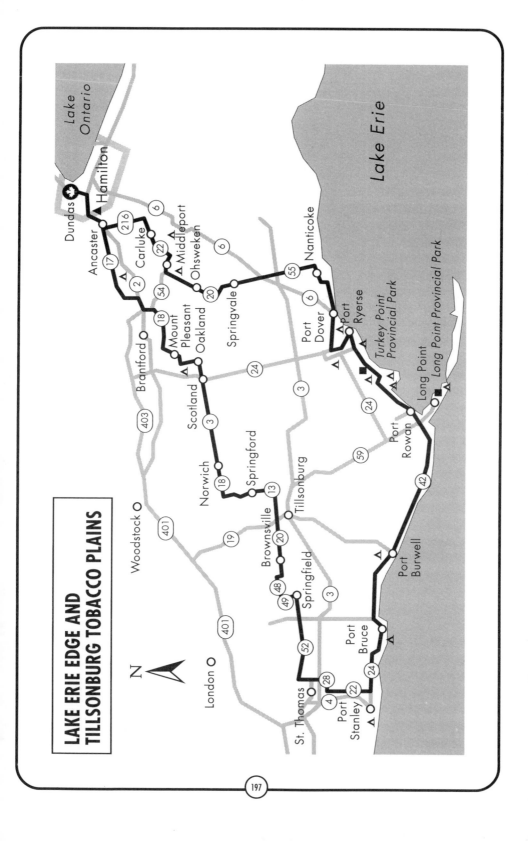

LAKE ERIE EDGE AND TILLSONBURG TOBACCO PLAINS

N

Lake Ontario

Lake Erie

Dundas

Hamilton

Ancaster

Carluke

216

17

2

Middleport

Ohsweken

6

22

54

6

Mount Pleasant

18

Brantford

Oakland

Springvale

20

Nanticoke

55

6

Port Dover

Port Ryerse

Turkey Point Provincial Park

Scotland

3

24

3

24

Long Point

Long Point Provincial Park

Norwich

18

Springford

Springford

13

Tillsonburg

Port Rowan

59

Brownsville

19

20

42

Springfield

48

49

3

Port Burwell

52

Woodstock

401

London

401

St. Thomas

28

Port Bruce

24

4

22

Port Stanley

197

left at the Pauline Johnson Homestead and cross the Grand River to Ohsweken. The Six Nations Indian Reserve here is the last tract of land grant given to Natives in the late 1700s.

Continue south and turn left on R.R 20, and then right onto R.R. 55. Ride through Springvale. Cross Highway 6 and Highway 3 to R.R. 3 and the Talbot Trail. Turn right onto the Talbot Trail and ride into Nanticoke. Just past Nanticoke, turn left and follow along the shore of Lake Erie to the picturesque town of Port Dover, a distance of 75 km (47 miles) from Ancaster.

In Port Dover, turn left down to the harbor. Go up the main street and turn left to Hay Creek Conservation Area. At Hay Creek Conservation Area, turn left and go through Port Ryerse.

119 km (74 miles) Port Rowan

Continue on the Talbot Trail along the shore road, past Turkey Point Provincial Park to Port Rowan, 30 km (19 miles) from Port Dover.

Side trip: Port Rowan to Backus Mill

At Port Rowan you can take R.R. 42 north to Backus Mill, a restored mill dating back to the early 1800s that is still producing flour by water power. Follow R.R. 42 back to Port Rowan.

Main tour

There is camping at Long Point Provincial Park—take Highway 59 south to the Long Point peninsula, which juts into Lake Erie.

149 km (92 miles) Port Burwell

Leaving Port Rowan, continue on R.R. 42 through Port Burwell, a distance of 30 km (19 miles) from Port Rowan, to Highway 73, which leads to Port Bruce.

199 km (124 miles) St. Thomas

Go right onto County Road 24 to County Road 22. Turn right on County Road 22 and ride into St. Thomas, 50 km (31 miles) from Port Burwell. The road becomes Fairview Avenue and eventually Burwell Road. Turn right on South Edgeware Road, and then left onto Centennial Avenue (County Road 30) going north.

243 km (151 miles) Tillsonburg

Turn right onto County Road 52 and head through Springfield. Turn left at County Road 49 and then right onto County Road 48. The road jogs to the right and becomes County Road 20. Go through Brownsville and Tillsonburg, 44 km (27 miles) from St. Thomas.

At County Road 13, turn left through Springford and a Mennonite farming area.

333 km (207 miles) Ancaster

Turn right onto County Road 18 and go through Norwich. The road becomes County Road 3 on the other side of Norwich and County Road 4 between Scotland and Oakland. Turn left at Oakland onto County Road 24 (not Highway 24), and stay on it when it makes a right turn 2 km (1.2 miles) farther.

North of Mount Pleasant, turn right onto County Road 18. Follow County Road 18 around Brantford onto Highway 54. At Highway 2, turn right. Go on here a short distance, then left onto Jerseyville Road (County Road 17). Follow it into Ancaster, a 90-km (56-mile) ride from Tillsonburg.

347 km (216 miles) Dundas

Take Wilson Street to Old Dundas Road. Go left onto Old Dundas Road and follow it back to Dundas.

LAKE ERIE AND THAMES VALLEY: LONDON TO WINDSOR LOOP

Length: 396 km (246 miles)
Time: Three to five days
Rating: Easy
Terrain: Mostly flat
Roads: Route is shown on the Ontario road map or the more detailed Ontario Transportation Map Series map #1, or OCA route map #1 (see "ROADS" at beginning of chapter for information on how to obtain these maps).
Traffic: Light
Connects with: This tour can be combined with the preceding Lake Erie Edge and Tillsonburg Tobacco Plains tour.
Start: London, a major center in southwestern Ontario, is served by VIA Rail.
Overview: Highlights of this tour include Lake Erie beaches and peaceful towns with charming Victorian architecture. At Point Pelee National Park, over three hundred bird species have been observed. On the return route you ride through farmland along the Thames River.

THE ROUTE:

0 km (0 miles) London

London is situated on the Thames River and many of the street names are the same as those of its British namesake. From London, go south on Wellington Road, which becomes County Road 36 after crossing over Highway 401.

30 km (18 miles) St. Thomas

Continue south on County Road 36 to Glanworth. Turn right onto County Road 35 and then left onto County Road 25 to St. Thomas, a distance of 30 km (18 miles) from London. St. Thomas has a wealth of Victorian architecture.

105 km (65 miles) Morpeth

Take County Road 16, known as the Talbot Trail, through Fingal to the shore of Lake Erie. Ride along the shore of Lake Erie. County Road 16 ends at a T-junction. Turn right and then left onto Highway 3. At

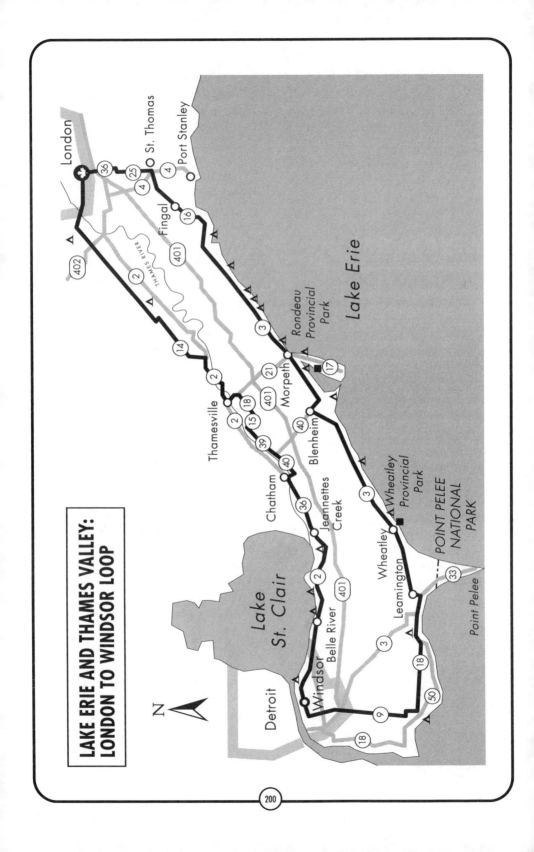

LAKE ERIE AND THAMES VALLEY: LONDON TO WINDSOR LOOP

N

London

St. Thomas

Port Stanley

36

25

4

4

Fingal

16

401

THAMES RIVER

402

2

14

2

Thamesville

18

15

401

39

2

21

Morpeth

Rondeau Provincial Park

Lake Erie

3

17

40

Blenheim

40

Chatham

36

Jeannettes Creek

Wheatley Provincial Park

3

Wheatley

Lake St. Clair

Detroit

2

Belle River

401

Leamington

POINT PELEE NATIONAL PARK

Windsor

3

33

Point Pelee

18

9

50

18

Morpeth, 75 km (47 miles) from St. Thomas, you can turn off and take Route 17 to Rondeau Provincial Park, which offers camping.

170 km (106 miles) Wheatley

Continue on Highway 3 through Blenheim and along the shores of Lake Erie. At Wheatley, 65 km (40 miles) from Morpeth, is Wheatley Provincial Park which offers camping.

183 km (114 miles) Leamington

On the way to Leamington, 13 km (8 miles) from Wheatley, there are tomato fields as far as the eye can see.

Side trip: Leamington to Point Pelee National Park, 13 km (8 miles)

At Leamington is the access via Route 33 to Point Pelee National Park, a sandspit reaching 10 km (6 miles) into Lake Erie.

Canada's southernmost point, the 1,619-hectare (4,000-acre) park is on the same latitude as northern California, and is well known for its birdwatching. Over three hundred bird species have been recorded here. A boardwalk winds through the marshes, and a 4.5-km (2.8-mile) mixed-use trail parallels the road leading to the park's sand beaches. There are no campgrounds in the park.

208 km (67 miles) Windsor

From Leamington, continue west on Highway 18 to Route 9. Turn right on Route 9 for 25 km (15 miles) into Windsor.

The southernmost city in Canada, Windsor is an important industrialized center heavily involved with the automobile industry based in Detroit across the river.

Route 9 becomes Howard Avenue which takes you through Windsor to Wyandotte Street. Turn right on Wyandotte Street, then left on Walker Street to Riverside Drive along the Detroit River. Turn right on Riverside Drive. At Puce, ride along Highway 2. Past Belle River, turn off Highway 2 onto County Road 2 along the shore of Lake St. Clair.

288 km (179 miles) Chatham

Past Jeannettes Creek, County Road 2 becomes County Road 36. Ride County Road 36 along the south side of the Thames River into Chatham, 80 km (50 miles) from Windsor.

Like its namesake in England, Chatham is situated near the mouth of the Thames River. Before the American Civil War, Chatham was a northern terminus of the "Underground Railroad," a secret route that brought slaves from the southern United States north to freedom.

In Chatham take Highway 40 south and east to County Road 39 along the Thames River. Ride Country Road 39 and turn right onto County Road 15. Then turn left onto County Road 18 and take it to Highway 21.

316 km (196 miles) Thamesville

    Turn left on Highway 21 to Thamesville, 28 km (17 miles) from Chatham, and then right onto Highway 2.

396 km (246 miles) London

    Turn left onto County Road 14, and ride County Road 14 into London, 80 km (50 miles) from Thamesville.

GRAND RIVER VALLEY TOUR

Length: 245 km (152 miles)
Time: Two to three days
Rating: Easy to intermediate
Terrain: Mostly flat but some ascents out of river valleys and gorges.
Roads: Route is shown on the Ontario road map or the more detailed Ontario Transportation Map Series #5, or OCA route maps #4 and #2 (see "ROADS" at beginning of chapter for information on how to obtain these maps).
Traffic: Light to moderate
Connects with: Grey and Bruce Counties tour
Start: Brantford, served by VIA Rail.
Overview: The historic valley of the Grand River is an area of woodlots and rolling hills. At Elora Gorge the Grand River flows swiftly through a 22-meter- (70-foot-) deep gorge.

Brantford, this tour's starting point, was named for Indian Chief Joseph Brant, who led the Six Nations Indians from their lands in upper New York state to this site on the Grand River. Brantford is also known as the place where Alexander Graham Bell invented the telephone.

On this route you go past Cambridge's stately stone buildings and through Kitchener, which is known for its annual "Oktoberfest" celebrations. Kitchener is located in Amish and Mennonite farm country, and has had a farmers' market since 1830, where a wide range of produce is sold by vendors, many of them Mennonites. West Montrose is home to Ontario's last nineteenth century covered bridge.

THE ROUTE:

0 km (0 miles) Brantford

    Take Highway 2 (called Brant Avenue, and later Paris Road) out of Brantford. Turn right onto Golf Road and when it ends, turn left onto Highway 5.

    Turn right at the edge of Paris onto County Road 53 (Green Lane). Go right again onto the East River Road (County Road 14), through to Glen Morris, then left onto County Road 28 across the Grand River.

    Turn right and follow along the West River Road, which offers scenic views of the river valley.

    Follow this road into Cambridge, where it becomes Glenmorris Street. Go right on Cedar

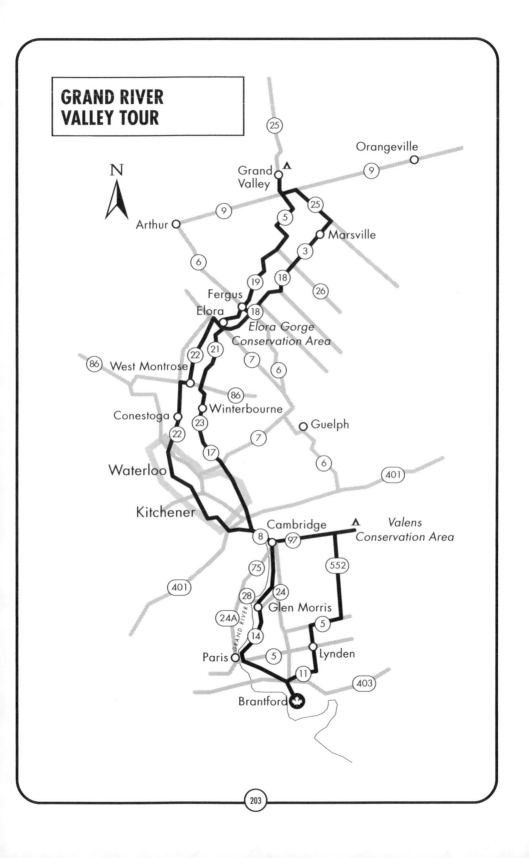

GRAND RIVER VALLEY TOUR

N

Orangeville

Grand Valley

Arthur

25

9

9

25

5

Marsville

3

6

19

18

26

Fergus

18

Elora

18

Elora Gorge Conservation Area

22

21

7

6

86 West Montrose

86

Winterbourne

Conestoga

23

7

Guelph

22

17

6

Waterloo

401

Kitchener

Cambridge

Valens Conservation Area

8

97

75

552

401

28

24

24A

Glen Morris

GRAND RIVER

14

5

5

Lynden

Paris

11

403

Brantford

Street and then turn left onto Blair Road (which becomes County Road 42). Follow Blair Road out of Cambridge to Fountain Street. Turn left onto Fountain Street and ride over Highway 401.

40 km (25 miles) Kitchener-Waterloo

The road becomes Huron Road Boulevard. Turn right onto Manitou Drive, which becomes Courtland Avenue. Follow this road into Kitchener, a ride of 40 km (25 miles) from Brantford.

Turn right onto Ottawa Street, then left onto Weber Street and follow it through neighboring Waterloo.

Turn right on Northfield Drive and head along Country Road 22 for Conestogo beside the Grand River. Continue north on County Road 22. Just before R.R. 86, turn right and follow the road leading to West Montrose where a nineteenth century covered bridge is still in use.

Continue east and turn left on R.R. 23. Follow this road to the Elora Gorge Conservation Area, a picturesque 134-hectare (330-acre) park on both banks of the 22-meter (70-foot) deep gorge. Here also are unusual rock formations, waterfalls and campgrounds.

70 km (43 miles) Town of Elora

Continue north on the same road, which becomes R.R. 21, into the town of Elora, 30 km (19 miles) from Waterloo. The houses and buildings of the old district beside the river have been restored.

Take County Road 21 to the nearby town of Fergus. Continue on County Road 18, which becomes County Road 3 through Marsville.

110 km (68 miles) Grand Valley

Go left onto Highway 25, left on Highway 9 and then right onto Highway 25 into the town of Grand Valley, a 40-km (25-mile) ride from Elora. The source of the Grand River is at Luther Marsh northwest of here. There is camping available nearby.

145 km (90 miles) Town of Elora

From Grand Valley the tour turns southward. Ride south to Highway 9. Take a quick right then left onto County Road 5, which becomes County Road 19, and ride into Fergus.

Take Route 18 to back into Elora, a 35-km (22-mile) ride from Grand Valley.

195 km (121 miles) Cambridge

Turn right onto County Road 7 and then left to follow River Road to West Montrose.

At West Montrose, turn left and go up County Road 23. Then turn right through Winterbourne to County Road 17. Turn left and follow County Road 17 to Cambridge, 50 km (31 miles) from Elora.

Go right on Highway 8 (Coronation Boulevard and then Dundas Street) east and left onto R.R. 97. This leads to Valens Reservoir Conservation Area which has camping.

245 km (152 miles) Brantford

From Valens Conservation Area, take Highway 52 southward to Highway 5. Turn right onto Highway 5 and then left onto Lynden Road. South of Lynden, turn right onto County Road 11 and ride into Brantford, 50 km (31 miles) from Cambridge. A left at West Street takes you back into downtown Brantford, this tour's starting point.

GREY AND BRUCE COUNTIES TOUR LOOP

Length: 589 km (366 miles)
Time: Four to six days
Rating: Easy to moderate
Terrain: Rolling hills
Roads: Route is shown on the Ontario road map or the more detailed Ontario Transportation Map Series maps #2 and #5, or OCA route maps #2 and #3 (see "ROADS" at beginning of chapter for information on how to obtain these maps).
Traffic: Light to moderate; some cottage traffic
Connects with: Across Ontario; Grand Valley River tour.
Start: Guelph, served by VIA Rail.
Overview: One of the most rural areas in southern Ontario is explored on this tour. Starting in Grey County, you ride through quiet villages and along roads through rolling hills to the Bruce Peninsula, which divides Lake Huron and Georgian Bay. On the Bruce Peninsula you take a road that winds beneath the limestone cliffs of the Niagara Escarpment along the shore of Georgian Bay.

Along the edge of the escarpment is the Bruce Trail, where you can see caves and rock pillars called flowerpots. At Tobermory there is scuba diving at Fathom Five Underwater Provincial Park. Riding south you go along Lake Huron's sandy beaches.

THE ROUTE:

0 km (0 miles) Guelph

From Guelph, take Highway 6, to County Road 7.

40 km (25 miles) Arthur

Ride County Road 7 to County Road 12, turn right and ride into Arthur, a distance of 40 km (25 miles) from Guelph.

110 km (68 miles) Durham

From Arthur, go north on Highway 6, then turn right onto the Conn Road (County Road 14). Follow this flat road to Conn.

Turn right onto Highway 89, and then left onto County Road 14 and ride past swampy lakes with few farms.

At Highway 4, turn left and follow the rolling hills into Dur-

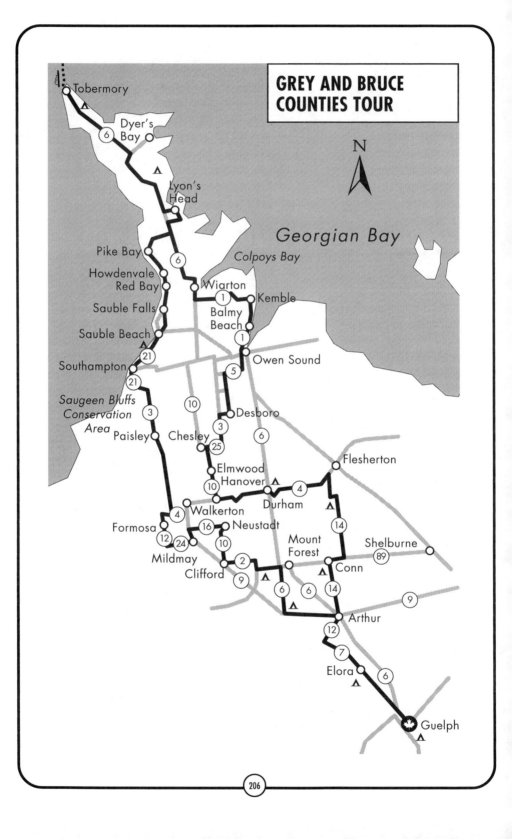

GREY AND BRUCE
COUNTIES TOUR

N

Georgian Bay

Tobermory

Dyer's
Bay

6

Lyon's
Head

Pike Bay

6

Colpoys Bay

Howdenvale
Red Bay

Wiarton

1

Kemble

Sauble Falls

Balmy
Beach

Sauble Beach

1

21

Owen Sound

Southampton

5

21

Saugeen Bluffs
Conservation
Area

3

10

Desboro

Paisley

Chesley

3

25

6

Elmwood
Hanover

Flesherton

10

4

Durham

Walkerton

Formosa

4

14

12

16

Neustadt

24

10

Mount
Forest

Shelburne

Mildmay

2

Conn

89

Clifford

9

6

6

14

9

Arthur

12

7

Elora

6

Guelph

ham, a 70-km (44-mile) ride from Arthur. Here is good swimming and overnight camping.

129 km (80 miles) Hanover

Follow Highway 4 west for 19 km (12 miles) to Hanover.

Go north on County Road 10 (signed to Elmwood), which has some cottage traffic.

Turn right onto County Road 25 and then left onto County Road 3. It's gravel at first for about 2 km (1.2 miles) and then paved.

189 km (117 miles) Owen Sound

Go north on County Road 3 and turn right on County Road 4 to Desboro. The road bends north and then east.

Turn left at the second road past the big bend north of Desboro and follow County Road 5 into Owen Sound, a 60-km (37-mile) ride from Hanover. Owen Sound is a port town on Georgian Bay, surrounded by the limestone cliffs of the Niagara Escarpment.

Take the Balmy Beach Road (County Road 1) up the scenic shore of the peninsula along the clear waters of Georgian Bay.

Follow County Road 1 through Kemble. Turn left and continue on County Road 1 to Highway 6. (Route 26 through Big Bay along the shore is a bad gravel road and not recommended for cycling.)

229 km (142 miles) Wiarton

At Highway 6 turn right and go into Wiarton, an old-world town on Colpoys Bay at the base of the Bruce Peninsula. It's a 40-km (25-mile) ride from Owen Sound to Wiarton.

304 km (189 miles) Tobermory

Go north from Wiarton on Highway 6 and turn right on County Road 9 through Lion's Head, which is situated in a sheltered harbor.

At the T-junction, go left on County Road 9A to Highway 6 and then go right on Highway 6. Along the way is the turn-off for Cyprus Lake Provincial Park, which offers camping.

Follow Highway 6 to Tobermory, a 75-km (47-mile) ride from Wiarton.

At Tobermory, at the tip of the peninsula, is Fathom Five Underwater Provincial Park offering scuba diving among wrecks in the waters of Georgian Bay. Flowerpot Island, part of Georgian Bay Islands National Park, abounds in caves and walking trails.

Tobermory is also the terminus for the ferry M.S.S. *Chi-Cheemaun* (Ojibway for "the big canoe") to South Baymouth on Manitoulin Island. Cruising time is 1 hour and 45 minutes. (A tour on Manitoulin Island is described in this chapter.)

404 km (251 miles) Southampton

From Tobermory, head south on Highway 6 and take the turn-off for Pike Bay. Ride this road along the shore of Lake Huron through Howdenvale and Red Bay.

Connect with County Road 21 and follow it through Sauble Falls and Sauble Beach to Southampton, a 100-km (62-mile) ride from Tobermory.

474 km (295 miles) Mildmay

Turn right onto Highway 21. When you're out of Southampton, turn left onto County Road 3. Take this road through Paisley and the rolling hills past the Saugeen Bluffs Conservation Area.

Continue south on County Road 3, and turn right on Highway 4.

Go left onto County Road 12 and through Formosa, the site of the old Formosa Springs Brewery.

Continue south on County Road 12, and turn left onto County Road 24 to Mildmay, a 70-km (44-mile) trip from Southampton.

Go north on Highway 9 and then turn right onto County Road 16 to Neustadt. This is the birthplace of former Prime Minister John Diefenbaker.

549 km (341 miles) Arthur

Turn right here onto County Road 10 to Clifford.

Go left onto County Road 2 to Highway 89. This area is Old Order Mennonite country and you might see a few horse-drawn buggies.

Go left and follow Highway 89 to County Road 6. Turn right onto County Road 6 and follow this scenic road to Highway 9.

Turn left onto Highway 9 and follow it into Arthur, 75 km (47 miles) from Mildmay.

589 km (366 miles) Guelph

From Arthur, retrace the 40-km (25-mile) route to Guelph, this tour's starting point.

More Information: Tobermory-South Baymouth ferry is operated by Ontario Northland Marine Services, 1155 First Avenue West, Owen Sound, Ontario N4K 4K8, (519) 376-6601, or call toll-free year-round in Canada, and from mid-April to mid-October in the United States 1-800-265-3163.

MANITOULIN ISLAND LOOP

Length: 145 km (90 miles); with one side-trip of 53 km (33 miles)
Time: One to two days
Rating: Easy
Terrain: Rolling
Roads: Route is shown on Ontario road map or the more detailed Ontario Transportation Map Series #3, or OCA route map #3 (see "ROADS" at beginning of chapter for information on how to obtain these maps).
Traffic: Light
Connects with: Across Ontario tour;

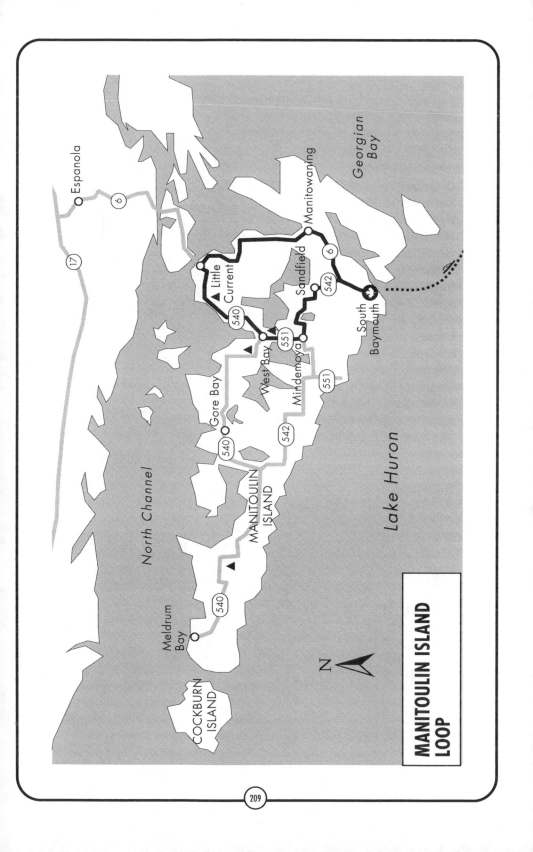

MANITOULIN ISLAND
LOOP

linked with Grey and Bruce Counties tour by ferry from Tobermory.

Start: South Baymouth, reached by road from Espanola, or by ferry from Tobermory (cruising time: 1 hour and 45 minutes.).

Overview: The world's largest freshwater island, Manitoulin has sand beaches along its picturesque shoreline, numerous lakes and bays, and quiet towns and villages.

Only 80 km (50 miles) long and ranging from 5 to 75 km (3 to 47 miles) in width, the island has more than twenty inland lakes. Along the island's north shore are cliffs and fjord-like bays.

High on the cliffs are hiking trails and picnic sites. On the south side are flat plains. At one time a Native Indian stronghold, today Manitoulin Island has six Indian reserves.

THE ROUTE:

0 km (0 miles) South Baymouth

13 km (8 miles) Route 542

From South Baymouth ride along Highway 6 for 13 km (8 miles) to the junction with Route 542.

39 km (24 miles) Mindemoya

Go left on Route 542 through Sandfield to Mindemoya, 26 km (16 miles) farther.

51 km (32 miles) West Bay

Go north on Route 551 from Mindemoya for 12 km (7.4 miles) to West Bay, a Native reserve.

81 km (50 miles) Little Current

Turn right and ride Route 540 for 30 km (18 miles) along the base of the escarpment to Little Current.

Option: Little Current to Espanola on Highway 17, 53 km (33 miles)

From Little Current you can go north for 53 km (33 miles) on Highway 6 across the white La Cloche Mountains that rise from Georgian Bay. Passing through the town of Espanola to Highway 17, you can link with the Across Ontario Tour (described in this chapter).

Main tour continues

145 km (90 miles) South Baymouth

To continue the loop tour of Manitoulin Island, ride south from Little Current on Highway 6 for 64 km (40 miles) to South Baymouth, this tour's starting point.

More Information: Tobermory-South Baymouth ferry is operated by Ontario Northland Marine Services, 1155 First Avenue West, Owen Sound, Ontario N4K 4K8, (519) 376-6601, or call toll-free year-round in Canada, and from mid-April to mid-October in the United States 1-800-265-3163.

PRINCE EDWARD COUNTY: QUINTE'S ISLE

Length: 38 km (24 miles); plus side-trips of 25 km (15 miles) and 18 km (11 miles)

Time: One to two days

Rating: Easy

Terrain: Mostly flat, with the odd hill

Roads: Route is shown on the Ontario road map or the more detailed Ontario Transportation Map Series map #7, or OCA route map #6 (see "ROADS" at beginning of chapter for information on how to obtain these maps).

Traffic: Light

Start: Belleville, which can be reached by VIA Rail.

Overview: Sand dunes and villages untouched by time characterize this rural peninsula on Lake Ontario, just south of Belleville. Prince Edward County—within easy reach by train or car from Toronto, Ottawa and Montreal—is a popular touring area for a weekend, or for a longer tour. Bed-and-breakfast places in this area are popular with cyclists.

The spectacular sand dunes of Sandbanks Provincial Park and wide beaches washed by waves of Lake Ontario are reminiscent of an ocean setting. Prince Edward County's beaches are within an easy day's ride of Belleville.

Settled by United Empire Loyalists after the American Revolution

over 200 years ago, the county has retained its unhurried pace and charming nineteenth century homes.

THE ROUTE:

0 km (0 miles) Belleville

Ride through Belleville and cross the bridge to Prince Edward County.

28 km (17 miles) Bloomfield

Follow Highway 62 which begins at the bridge, for 28 km (17 miles) to Bloomfield.

38 km (24 miles) Sandbanks Provincial Park

Then take County Road 12 for 10 km (6 miles) to Sandbanks Provincial Park. The 3-km (1.8-mile) sandbar at Sandbanks Park juts into Wellington Bay and almost touches the other side at the town of Wellington.

Explore Sandbanks Park and then use it as a base to explore the county's narrow, tree-lined country roads. You pedal past cornfields, cow barns and orchards. In addition to Sandbanks Park there are two day-use parks well worth visiting on side trips.

Side trip: Bloomfield to North Beach Provincial Park, 25 km (15 miles)

North Beach Provincial Park, similar to Sandbanks, has a 1.2-km (0.7-mile) baymouth sandbar sheltering North Bay from Lake Ontario. Take Highway 33 west

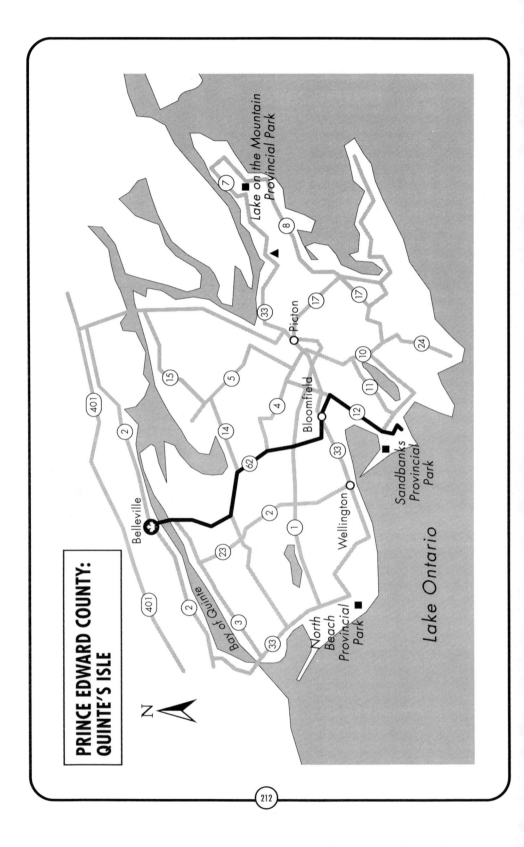

PRINCE EDWARD COUNTY:
QUINTE'S ISLE

N

Belleville

Bay of Quinte

Bloomfield

Picton

Lake on the Mountain
Provincial Park

Wellington

Sandbanks
Provincial
Park

North
Beach
Provincial
Park

Lake Ontario

401
2
62
14
23
3
33
2
1
33
15
5
4
12
33
11
10
17
17
8
7
24

for 25 km (15 miles) from Bloom-field through Wellington to North Beach Park.

Side trip: Bloomfield to Lake on the Mountain Provincial Park, 18 km (11 miles)

On the other side of the county is Lake on the Mountain Provincial Park, which borders a small lake. It is a stone's throw from the edge of the Prince Edward Escarpment, which rises nearly 62 meters (204 feet) over the Bay of Quinte. Go east for 18 km (11 miles) on Highway 33 from Bloomfield through Picton to Lake on the Mountain Park.

More Information: Sandbanks Provincial Park, RR 1, Picton, Ontario K0K 2T0, (613) 393-3319.

THOUSAND ISLANDS PARKWAY LOOP

Length: 35 km (22 miles) Thousand Islands Bikeway one-way day tour; 230 km (143 miles) for the whole loop

Time: One to two days

Rating: Easy

Terrain: Flat

Roads: The Thousand Islands Bikeway is a bicycle path; the route is shown on the Ontario road map or the more detailed Ontario Transportation Map Series map #8, or OCA route maps #6 and #7 (see "ROADS" at beginning of chapter for information on how to obtain these maps).

Traffic: Be cautious when riding on the bicycle path especially in the direction facing traffic as there are numerous private driveway intersections and there is also gravel strewn onto the path; the rest of the route has mostly light traffic.

Start: Gananoque, served by VIA Rail

Overview: The famous Thousand Islands Parkway is a 35-km (22-miles) route along the St. Lawrence River through the scenic Thousand Islands area between Gananoque and Brockville. Beside the entire length of the parkway is a two-lane 1.8-meter (6-foot-) wide paved bicycle path. En route are two provincial parks and St. Lawrence Islands National Park.

From the parkway bicycle path, this tour continues along the St. Lawrence River to Upper Canada Village. It then returns through a rural area of forests and lakes to form a loop.

THE ROUTE:

0 km (0 miles) Gananoque

From Gananoque, cycle on the bicycle path along the Thousand Islands Parkway. There are campgrounds at Ivy Lea Campsite and Brown's Bay Campsite.

Mallorytown Landing is the headquarters of St. Lawrence Islands National Park. There is a campground here, and primitive campsites on 13 of the park's 22 islands, which are accessible

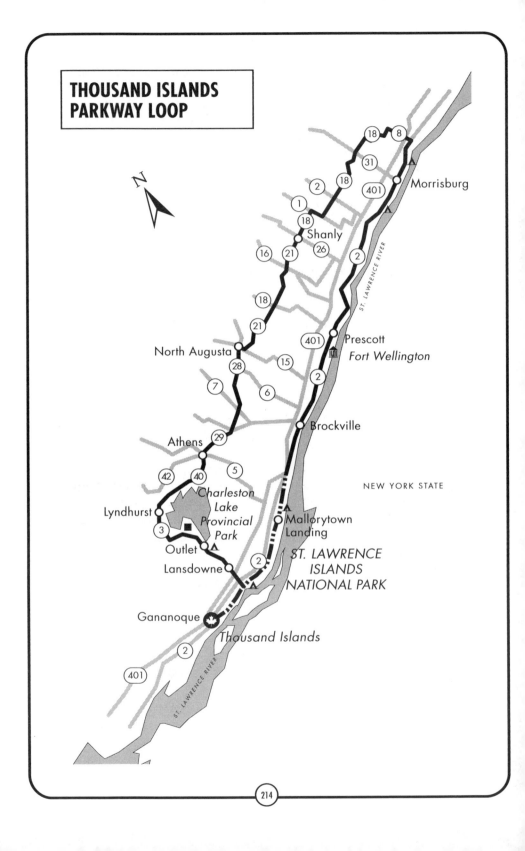

THOUSAND ISLANDS
PARKWAY LOOP

N

18 8

31

2 18 401 Morrisburg

1

18 Shanly

16 21 26 2

18

21

North Augusta 401 Prescott
28 15 Fort Wellington

7 6 2

Athens 29 Brockville

42 40 5 NEW YORK STATE

Charleston
Lake
Lyndhurst Provincial
Park

3 Mallorytown
Outlet Landing

Lansdowne 2 ST. LAWRENCE
ISLANDS
NATIONAL PARK

Gananoque Thousand Islands

2

401

ST. LAWRENCE RIVER

only by boat. Commercial water taxis operate between the mainland and the park's islands.

35 km (22 miles) Brockville

The parkway ends at Butternut Bay Road, 8 km (5 miles) west of Brockville, and a 35-km (22-mile) ride from Gananoque. Brockville is served by VIA Rail.

Day-touring option: return to Gananoque, 35 km (22 miles)

If you want to cycle just the parkway bicycle path, you can retrace your route back to Gananoque.

Loop route continues

55 km (34 miles) Prescott

To ride the loop route, continue along Highway 2 from Brockville. At Prescott, 20 km (12 miles) from Brockville, is Fort Wellington National Historic Park.

The first British fort at this strategic location on the St. Lawrence River was built during the War of 1812 and fell to ruins after the war. The second fort now standing here was built in 1838–39 in response to the Upper Canada Rebellion of 1837.

100 km (62 miles) Morrisburg and Upper Canada Village

Near Morrisburg is Upper Canada Village, a re-created nineteenth century pioneer village including a millstone, sawmill, blacksmith shop, a general store

and corduroy roads. It's a 45-km (28-mile) ride from Prescott to Upper Canada Village.

185 km (115 miles) Athens

From Upper Canada Village, go west on Highway 2 to Route 8. Go north on Route 8 to Route 18. Turn left onto Route 18. At Route 1 turn right and then turn left onto Route 18. Route 18 soon becomes Route 21. Ride Route 21 to Route 15. Turn right on Route 15 to North Augusta, and then go left on Route 28 to Highway 29.

Take Highway 29 west to Athens, an 85-km (53-mile) ride from Upper Canada Village. Then take Route 40. Along the way is Charleston Lake Provincial Park, which offers camping and hiking trails.

230 km (143 miles) Thousand Islands Parkway

Go left on County Road 2 and then left onto County Road 3 at Lyndhurst. Ride through Outlet and Lansdowne to the Thousand Island Parkway just east of Gananoque, a 45-km (28-mile) ride from Athens and this tour's starting point.

More Information: St. Lawrence Parks Commission, R.R. 1, Morrisburg, Ontario K0C 1X0, (613) 543-3704. St. Lawrence Islands National Park, Box 469, R.R. 3, Mallorytown Landing, Ontario K0E 1R0, (613) 923-5261.

ALGONQUIN PROVINCIAL PARK LOOP

Length: 476 km (295 miles)

Time: Five to seven days

Rating: Moderately hard; the toughest in the Ontario chapter

Terrain: Much of the route is rolling with a few short but good climbs.

Roads: Route is shown on Ontario road map or the more detailed Ontario Transportation Map Series map #6, or OCA route maps #5 and #7 (see "ROADS" at beginning of chapter for information on how to obtain OTMS maps).

Traffic: Light to very light

Connects with: Across Ontario tour

Start: Renfrew, situated 130 km (80 miles) west of Ottawa and 320 km (200 miles) northeast of Toronto.

Overview: The land of lakes, rivers, hills and forests east of Algonquin Provincial Park is explored on this hilly circuit.

This picturesque region is on the Frontenac Axis, a southern extension of the rocky Precambrian Shield. In this transition zone between the northern and southern forests, wildlife and flora of both forest types are found together.

At Bon Echo Provincial Park, you can hear your echo on Mazinaw Rock, a 114-meter (275-foot) cliff that drops to Mazinaw Lake. Native pictographs can be seen at canoe level.

Algonquin is Ontario's oldest provincial park and one of its best known. Its wilderness offers camping, canoeing and hiking trails, and

there are exhibits about the park's pioneer logging past.

This tour goes through some remote, sparsely populated areas, so be well prepared. Bed-and-breakfast accommodations are scarce but you can do the route staying in them with careful advance planning.

THE ROUTE:

0 km (0 miles) Renfrew

10 km (6 miles) Burnstown

From Renfrew, go southeast on Raglan Street, which becomes County Road 2. It's 10 km (6 miles) to Burnstown.

25 km (16 miles) Calabogie

Go right on to hilly County Road 508 for 15 km (9 miles) to Calabogie.

73 km (45 miles) Lanark

Turn left onto Secondary Highway 511 and ride 47 km (29 miles) to Lanark.

103 km (64 miles) Elphin

Then go right on County Road 12 for 30 km (19 miles) to Elphin.

111 km (69 miles) Snow Road Station

Go right on County Road 36 for 8 km (5 miles) to Snow Road Station.

180 km (112 miles) Highway 41

Go right on Secondary Highway 509 through Ompah, Plevna and Fernleigh, where the road becomes Secondary Highway 506. Ride Secondary Highway 506 to Highway 41, a ride of 65 km (40 miles) from Snow Road Station.

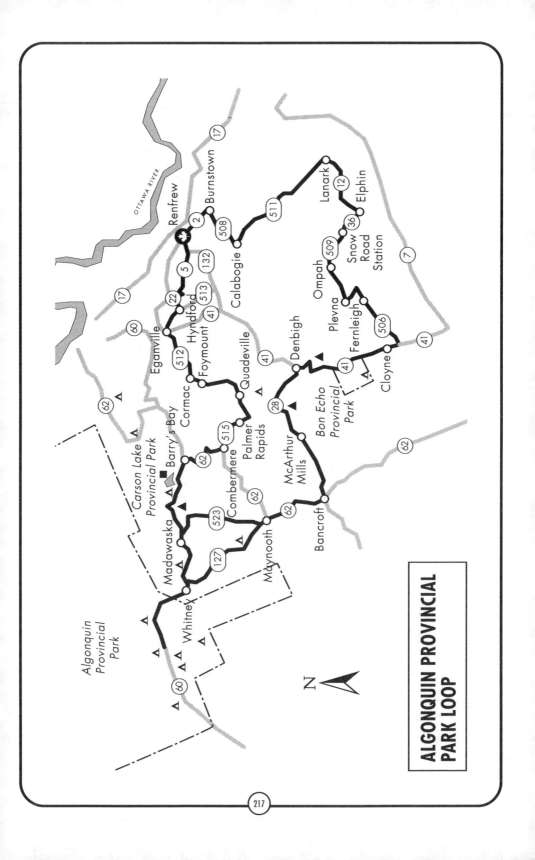

OTTAWA RIVER

17

Burnstown

Renfrew

2

508

511

Lanark

12

Elphin

5

132

36

Snow Road Station

Calabogie

509

Ompah

7

22

513

41

Foymount

Plevna

Eganville

60

17

512

Hyndford

Quadeville

Denbigh

Fernleigh

506

Cormac

41

41

Cloyne

62

515

Palmer Rapids

28

Bon Echo Provincial Park

41

Carson Lake Provincial Park

Barry's Bay

62

Combermere

McArthur Mills

62

Madawaska

523

62

62

Algonquin Provincial Park

127

Maynooth

Bancroft

Whitney

60

N

ALGONQUIN PROVINCIAL PARK LOOP

192 km (119 miles) Bon Echo Provincial Park

Turn right at Highway 41 and ride 12 km (7 miles) through Cloyne, to the entrance of Bon Echo Provincial Park which offers camping, canoeing and hiking.

The scenic highlight of this 66-square-km (25-square-mile) park is Mazinaw Rock, a 114-meter (275-foot) cliff that drops to Mazinaw Lake. The name Bon Echo refers to the rock's acoustic properties. Scattered along the rock at canoe level are scores of Native pictographs.

225 km (140 miles) Denbigh

Continue riding on Highway 41. Turn left onto Highway 28 at Denbigh situated 33 km (21 miles) from Bon Echo Provincial Park. This winding, hilly road goes through mixed forests.

285 km (177 miles) Bancroft

Continue for 60 km (38 miles) on Highway 28 through McArthur Mills and Hermon to Bancroft, the major center for the Hastings Highlands area. The region offers swimming, canoeing and fishing and is popular with rock collectors.

Stock up on food supplies at Bancroft, as there are few facilities between here and Barry's Bay (or Whitney if you're taking a side trip into Algonquin Park).

308 km (191 miles) Maynooth

From Bancroft take Highway 62 north for 23 km (14 miles) to Maynooth.

Option: Maynooth to Algonquin Provincial Park

If you want to take a side trip to Algonquin Provincial Park, continue for 39 km (24 miles) on Highway 127 from Maynooth to Highway 60 near Whitney. Turn left and ride several kilometers into Algonquin Park.

Located on the southern edge of the Precambrian Shield, Algonquin Park is 7,600 square km (2,925 square miles) of rounded hills, rocky ridges, spruce bogs, fast-flowing rivers and thousands of lakes, ponds and streams. You can camp, canoe and hike. The park's museum and a pioneer logging exhibit are worth a visit.

To leave Algonquin Park, ride east on Highway 60 and rejoin this loop tour just east of Madawaska.

Main tour continuing from Maynooth

345 km (214 miles) Highway 60 east of Madawaska

From Maynooth take Highway 127 and turn right onto Secondary Highway 523. Ride Secondary Highway 523 to Highway 60, just east of Madawaska (linking with the optional route from Algonquin Park). Distance from Maynooth to Highway 60 is 37 km (23 miles).

373 km (232 miles) Barry's Bay

Continuing the loop tour, go east on Highway 60 through the lumber town of Barry's Bay, 28 km (17 miles) from the junction of Highway 60 and Secondary

Highway 523. At Barry's Bay you can arrange river rafting trips. Highway 60 is busier than the other roads so far on this tour.

391 km (243 miles) Highway 515

From Barry's Bay, take Highway 62 south for 18 km (11 miles) to Highway 515, just east of Combermere.

434 km (270 miles) Foymount

Take Secondary Highway 515 for 43 km (27 miles) through Palmer Rapids and Quadeville to Foymount, the highest populated point in Ontario.

459 km (285 miles) Eganville

Just past Foymount, take Secondary Highway 512 to Cormac. Between Foymount and Cormac is a steep downhill run. (Make sure your baggage is secure and nothing is flapping.)

Continue on Secondary Highway 512 for 25 km (15 miles) to Eganville, which is in a deep valley bisected by the Bonnechere River. You can visit the nearby Bonnechere Caves in summer.

494 km (307 miles) Renfrew

Cross Highway 41 and follow the Hyndford Road along the Bonnechere River to Hyndford, where it links with Secondary Highway 513.

Go left on Secondary Highway 513. It soon becomes County Road 22. Then turn right on County Road 5 to Highway 132. Turn left and ride into Renfrew, 35 km (22 miles) from Eganville and this tour's starting point.

More Information: Algonquin Provincial Park, P.O. Box 219, Whitney, Ontario K0J 2M0, telephone (705) 633-5572 for information, (705) 633-5538 for campground reservations.

RIDEAU RIVER: KINGSTON TO OTTAWA LOOP

Length: 208 km (129 miles) Kingston to Ottawa one way; 173 km (108 miles) Ottawa to Kingston part; 381 km (237 miles) loop

Time: Two to five days

Rating: Medium as far as Jones Falls; then easy

Terrain: Rolling; then flat

Roads: Route is shown on the Ontario road map or the more detailed Ontario Transportation Map Series map #8, or OCA route maps #6 and #7 (see "ROADS" at beginning of chapter for information on how to obtain these maps).

Traffic: Light to very light

Connects with: Across Ontario tour; Ottawa to Montréal tour; Ottawa-Hull to Gatineau Hills (described in Québec chapter).

Start: Kingston or Ottawa, both served by VIA Rail.

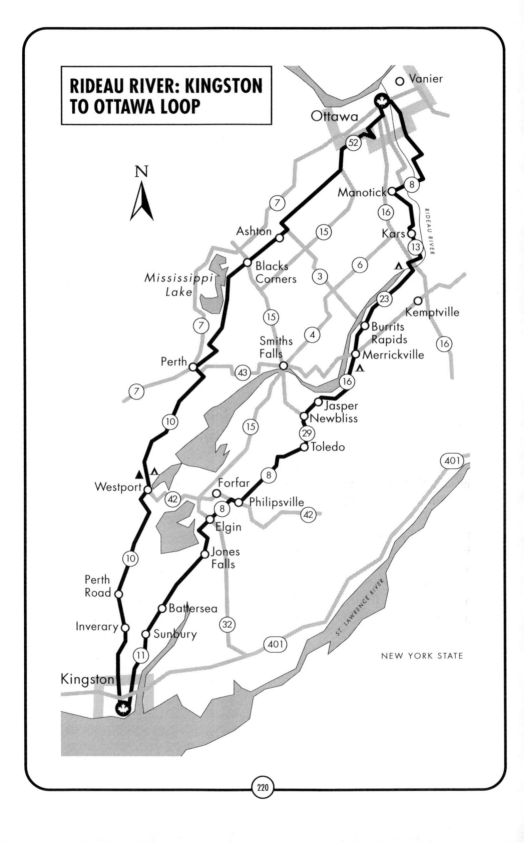

RIDEAU RIVER: KINGSTON TO OTTAWA LOOP

N

Vanier

Ottawa

52

7

Manotick

8

16

Ashton

15

Kars

13

Blacks
Corners

3

6

RIDEAU RIVER

Mississippi
Lake

23

Kemptville

7

15

Burrits
Rapids

4

16

Smiths
Falls

Merrickville

Perth

43

16

10

15

Jasper

Newbliss

29

Toledo

8

401

Westport

42

Forfar

8

Philipsville

42

Elgin

Jones
Falls

10

Perth
Road

ST. LAWRENCE RIVER

Battersea

Inverary

32

Sunbury

401

11

NEW YORK STATE

Kingston

Overview: The scenic Rideau Canal system linking Kingston and Ottawa was built after the War of 1812 to ensure that British gunboats could travel from Ottawa to Kingston without the threat of attack from American shore batteries along the St. Lawrence River. Built from 1826 to 1832, the Rideau system spans 200 km (125 miles) including forty-nine locks and 19 km (12 miles) of excavated channels. The canal was never used in a war but became an artery for immigration and commerce. Today it's popular with recreational boaters.

The country crossed by the Rideau waterway includes beautiful lakes, forests, rocky granite hills and rolling farmland. This loop tour takes you on backroads through this scenic area from Kingston to Ottawa.

Kingston, strategically located at the point where Lake Ontario flows into the St. Lawrence River, is at the southern end of the Rideau Canal. The city has an impressive concentration of nineteenth century buildings including Old Fort Henry, which was one of Canada's mightiest fortresses, and Bellevue House, once the home of Sir John A. Macdonald, Canada's first prime minister. Kingston has a campground, good Bed-and-breakfasts and hotel accommodations.

Ottawa, the capital of Canada, is situated at the junction of the Rideau River and the Ottawa River. It has many attractions worth visiting, including a variety of museums, and the Parliament Buildings, which house Canada's government.

THE ROUTE:
0 km (0 miles) Kingston
43 km (27 miles) Jones Falls

Leave Kingston on Montréal Street. Ride over Highway 401 and onto County Road 11. Take this gently rolling road through rugged woods and past rock outcrops. Ride through Sunbury and Battersea to Jones Falls to see some of the locks of the Rideau Canal.

103 km (64 miles) Merrickville

From Jones Falls, head north on County Road 8, crossing Highway 15 at Elgin.

Continue on County Road 8 to Highway 42.

Side trip: Forfar cheese, 4 km (2.5 miles) each way
Cheese lovers will not want to miss sampling Forfar cheese in the community of Forfar. To reach Forfar, turn left on Highway 42 and ride for 4 km (2.5 miles).

Main tour continues from junction of County Road 8 and Highway 42

Turn right on Highway 42 and ride to Philipsville. At Philipsville, turn left onto County Road 8. The countryside has opened up as you ride on the ancient Champlain sea bed. The road takes you through pastures and farmland.

Ride County Road 8 to Toledo, and then take Highway 29 for 8 km (5 miles) to Newbliss.

Then take County Road 16 through Jasper and into Merrickville, 60 km (37 miles) from Jones Falls.

Merrickville is a picturesque village with many nineteenth century stone buildings, and Rideau Canal locks. The Blockhouse Museum, built as a fort to protect the canal, is now a museum of the district's early days. A campground and bed-and-breakfasts are available here and make it a good half-way stopping point.

139 km (86 miles) Kars

Leave Merrickville on Highway 43. Just outside town, about 1 km (0.6 mile) past the railway overpass, go left at the fork onto County Road 23.

Ride through the ghost town of Andrewville, and watch pleasure boats go through the Rideau Canal locks.

From Burritts Rapids, where there are more canal locks, continue on scenic County Road 23 to County Road 44. Turn left over the bridge. Here is Rideau River Provincial Park.

Keep right on County Road 5 and right again onto County Road 13. Take County Road 13 to the Baxter Conservation Area and to Kars, 69 km (43 miles) from Merrickville.

208 km (129 miles) Ottawa

From Kars, continue on County Road 13 into Manotick, where you can admire century homes. Here is Dickinson Square Conservation Area which features Watson's Mill, an 1860s water-powered flour mill, and other nineteenth century buildings.

From Manotick, turn right onto County Road 8, and cross the bridges over the Rideau River. Ride past County Road 19 and turn left at Spratt Road.

Turn, right at Rideau Road and then left at Limebank Road (at the flashing light), which links with River Road—County Road 19. Continue north on River Road, which becomes Riverside Drive. The Lebreton Flats Campground in downtown Ottawa is a good campground especially for cyclists and hikers.

Ottawa has many attractions including its scenic network of recreational paths along the Rideau Canal and the Rideau River (see Ottawa bicycling paths described in this chapter).

254 km (158 miles) Ashton

Once you leave Ottawa, there are no stores or restaurants until Ashton. Leave Ottawa via Prince of Wales Drive and turn right onto Meadowlands Drive —Regional Road 51.

Turn left onto Woodroffe Avenue—Regional Road 15, and then right onto Knoxdale Road—Regional Road 52. At Regional Road 11, do a quick right and then a left to stay on Regional Road 52.

Go left on Richmond Road— Regional Road 59. At the second road you come to, turn right onto Hope Side Road—Regional Road 86.

At the junction with Eagleson Side Road—Regional Road 49, turn quickly left, then right onto Flewellen Road—Regional Road 49.

Ride through Stanley Corners into Ashton for a rest stop.

294 km (158 miles) Perth

From the general store in Ashton, turn left at the T-junction and then go right at the first junction. Ride up a low incline to Blacks Corners on Highway 15.

Cross Highway 15 and continue on the Mississippi Lake Road, a picturesque and winding old road.

About 34 km (21 miles) from Ashton, look for Hand's Road (there's a large yellow brick house on your right) and turn left onto it. It's the only gravel section on the route but it's pretty.

Turn right onto County Road 10 and into Perth, 40 km (25 miles) from Ashton. Perth has a campground and other accommodations.

One of Ontario's oldest towns, Perth is known for its restored nineteenth century stone buildings, many built by stonemasons who settled here after completing the Rideau Canal.

324 km (201 miles) Westport

Leaving Perth, go southeast on Gore Street. Turn right onto County Road 10, which goes over rolling terrain with several good climbs. You'll see the sparse farmlands give way to the bush and rock outcrops of the Canadian Shield.

Ride County Road 10 for 30 km (19 miles) to Westport, at the head of Upper Rideau Lake. Careful, there is a steep downhill run—cyclists have been clocked at 75 km/h (47 mph)—with a quick right turn at the bottom into Westport. There are campgrounds nearby and bed-and-breakfasts in Westport.

361 km (224 miles) Inverary

Leave Westport on Highway 42 and turn right onto County Road 10—the Perth Road. Climb out of the Upper Rideau Lake basin and then ride over a flat plateau. As you cross into Bedford County, you're on the section cyclists call "snake pits." The road here twists and turns over gently rolling terrain; an invigorating 20 km (12 miles) through rugged scenery.

Past the village of Perth Road, which has no services, you leave the "pits" as the scenery opens up again. A nice downhill run, which you pay for on a good climb, gets you into Inverary, 37 km (23 miles) from Westport.

381 km (237 miles) Kingston

It looks like a flat ride into Kingston, but don't be fooled! There are still a couple of climbs left. Continue riding County Road

10. Cross over Highway 401, and ride through the strip of fast-food restaurants on Division Street back to downtown Kingston.

OTTAWA-TORONTO BICYCLE BYWAY

Length: 433 km (260 miles)
Time: Three to six days
Rating: Moderate-easy
Terrain: Flat from Ottawa to Perth and from west of Highway 35 to Toronto
Roads: Mostly quiet secondary roads; two sections are rough and another two sections (a few km) each are well-packed gravel; most of the route is shown on the Ontario road map; you can also use OTMS map #8 or Ontario Cycling Association Route Maps maps 6, 7 and 4 (see "ROADS" at beginning of chapter for information on these maps).
Traffic: Light to very light, except near Toronto
Connects with: Across Ontario tour, Rideau River: Kingston to Ottawa loop tour, Ottawa to Montréal tour, tours starting in Toronto
Start: Ottawa, served by VIA Rail
Overview: This tour links two of Ontario's most important cities: Ottawa—the national capital of Canada, and Toronto — Ontario's provincial capital and the city with the largest population in Canada. Both cities have a wide range of attractions including scenic networks of multi-use recreational trails. (See sections on Toronto and Ottawa near beginning of chapter.)

From Ottawa to Westport, this tour follows the route of part of the Rideau River: Kingston to Ottawa loop.

THE ROUTE:
0 km (0 miles) Ottawa
46 km (29 miles) Ashton

Once you leave Ottawa, there are no stores or restaurants until Ashton. Leave Ottawa via Prince of Wales Drive and turn right onto Meadowlands Drive —Regional Road 51.

Turn left onto Woodroffe Avenue—Regional Road 15, and then turn right onto Knoxdale Road—Regional Road 52. At Regional Road 11, do a quick right and then a left to stay on Regional Road 52.

Go left on Richmond Road— Regional Road 59. At the second road you come to, turn right onto Hope Side Road—Regional Road 86.

At the junction with Eagleson Side Road—Regional Road 49, turn quickly left, then right onto Flewellen Road—Regional Road 49.

Ride through Stanley Corners into Ashton for a rest stop.

86 km (53 miles) Perth

From Ashton, turn left at the T-junction and then go right at the first junction. Ride up a low incline to Blacks Corners on Highway 15.

Cross Highway 15 and continue on the Mississippi Lake Road, a picturesque winding road.

About 34 km (21 miles) from Ashton, look for Hand's Road (there's a large yellow brick house on your right) and turn left on it, a short gravel road, to County Road 10.

Go right onto County Road 10 and ride into Perth, 40 km (25 miles) from Ashton.

Perth, which has a campground and other accommodations, is known for its restored nineteenth century stone buildings.

116 km (72 miles) Westport

Leaving Perth, go southeast on Gore Street. Turn right onto County Road 10, which goes over rolling terrain with several good climbs. You'll see the sparse farmlands give way to the bush and rock outcrops of the Canadian Shield.

Ride County Road 10 for 30 km (19 miles) to Westport, at the head of Upper Rideau Lake. Careful, there is a steep downhill run with a quick right turn at the bottom into Westport. There are campgrounds nearby and bed-and-breakfasts places in Westport.

221 km (137 miles) Tweed

As you enter Westport, turn right and ride straight through to County Road 12, which becomes County Road 8 in Bedford County.

Continue on County Road 8 to Godfrey on Highway 38. Follow Highway 38 for 10 km (6 miles), and then turn right onto County Road 7 to Belrock where County Road 7 becomes County Road 14.

Ride County Road 14 to Highway 41. Ride north on Highway 41 for two km, and turn left onto County Road 3 and 32 to Marlbank.

From Marlbank, take County Road 13 to Tweed, a 105-km (65-mile) ride from Westport.

289 km (180 miles) Hastings

From Tweed, take County Road 38 to Highway 62. Do a quick right and then a left back onto County Road 38.

Continue on County Road 38 along the Trent River into Campbellford. The town's old homes with verandahs and other pine trimmings are reminders of the vast pine forests that this area had.

Leave Campbellford on Highway 30, and turn left at West Corners onto County Road 35.

Ride County Road 35 and then turn right onto County

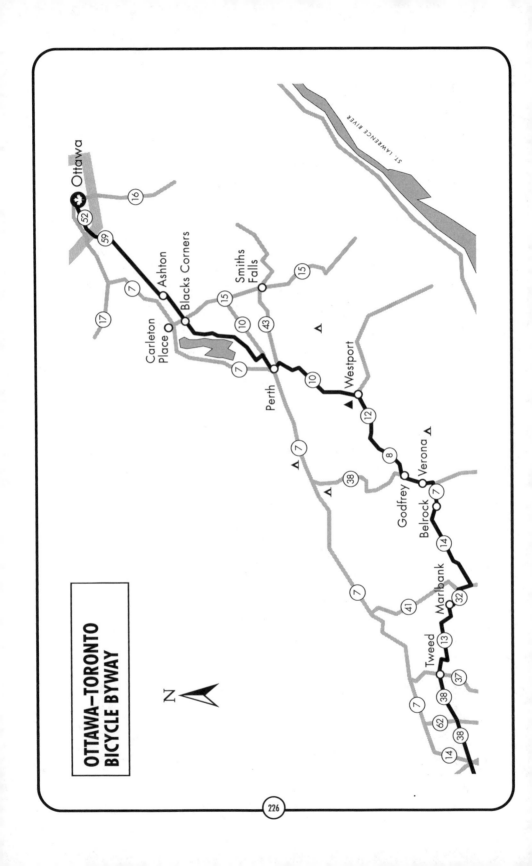

OTTAWA–TORONTO
BICYCLE BYWAY

N

ST. LAWRENCE RIVER

Ottawa

16

52

59

Ashton

Blacks Corners

7

Carleton Place

17

15

Smiths Falls

15

10

43

7

Perth

10

Westport

12

7

38

8

Verona

Godfrey

Belrock

7

14

7

41

Marlbank

32

Tweed

13

37

7

38

62

38

14

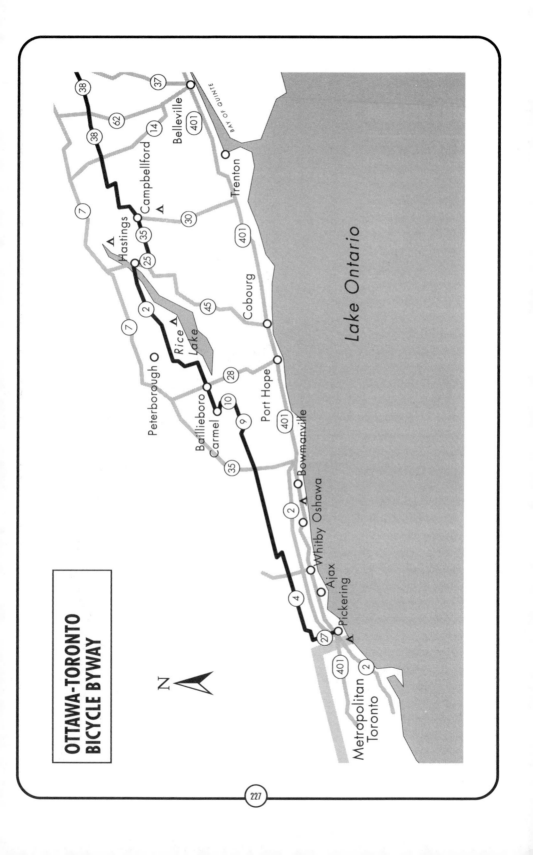

OTTAWA-TORONTO
BICYCLE BYWAY

N

Lake Ontario

BAY OF QUINTE

Belleville
Trenton
Campbellford
Hastings
Peterborough
Rice Lake
Baillieboro
Carmel
Port Hope
Cobourg
Bowmanville
Oshawa
Whitby
Ajax
Pickering
Metropolitan
Toronto

Road 25 into Hastings, 68 km (42 miles) from Tweed. There are several campgrounds and other accommodations in the area.

433 km (269 miles) outskirts of Metropolitan Toronto

From Hastings, take County Road 2 to Highway 28. Cross Highway 28 at Bailieboro and continue on the secondary road to Carmel.

From Carmel, turn left onto County Road 10 and then right onto County Road 9. After conquering your last couple of tough hills, it's flat from here into Toronto.

Ride County Road 9 to Kirby, where you cross Highway 35/115. Go straight on through Solina to County Road 2.

Turn left on County Road 2, and then right onto County Road 4, known as Taunton Road. At Clarke's Hollow, turn left onto Whites Road (County Road 38).

Follow Whites Road to Finch Avenue. Go right on Finch Avenue, which is Regional Road 37, and then left on Altona—Regional Road 27. Ride to the junction with Highway 2. There's a campground in Glen Rouge Park just west of here.

OTTAWA TO MONTRÉAL

Length: 211 km (131 miles) one way
Time: Two days
Rating: Easy-medium
Terrain: Flat and slightly rolling
Roads: Mostly quiet secondary roads; route is shown on Ontario road map or the more detailed Ontario Transportation Map Series #8, or OCA route map #7 (see "ROADS" at beginning of chapter for information on how to obtain these maps).
Traffic: A little heavy leaving Ottawa, then light to very light.
Connects with: Across Ontario tour, Rideau River: Kingston to Ottawa loop tour, Montréal to Oka tour in Québec.
Start: Ottawa, served by VIA Rail.

Overview: The Ottawa River was an important route into Canada's interior. It was traveled by explorers, fur traders and pioneering loggers and settlers. Today the river is the boundary between the provinces of Ontario and Québec.

The valley on both sides of the river is home to rustic farmhouses and barns and French-Canadian villages. From the valley are views of the mountains of Québec. This tour takes you along both sides of the river through the Ottawa River Valley.

THE ROUTE:
0 km (0 miles)
18 km (11 miles) Orleans

From Ottawa, follow Ogilvie

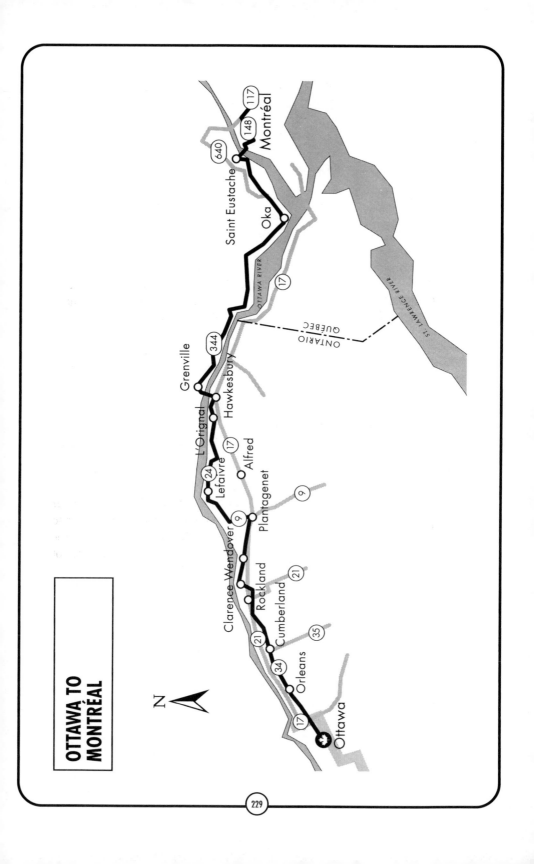

OTTAWA TO MONTRÉAL

N

Montréal
117
148
640
Saint Eustache
Oka
17
OTTAWA RIVER
ST. LAWRENCE RIVER
ONTARIO
QUEBEC
Grenville
344
L'Orignal
Hawkesbury
17
Alfred
24
Lefaivre
Plantagenet
9
9
Clarence Wendover
Rockland
21
Cumberland
21
35
34
Orleans
17
Ottawa

Road through Gloucester to St. Joseph's Boulevard—which becomes Regional Road 34—to Orleans.

45 km (28 miles) Rockland

Follow County Road 34 to St. Martin's Corners near Cumberland which is the next intersection after County Road 57. Turn right onto Frank Kenny Road, go straight up the hill and then turn left onto Wilhaven Drive.

Follow Wilhaven Drive as it meanders along—including a short section of hard-packed gravel—to County Road 21 and into Rockland, 27 km (17 miles) from Orleans.

75 km (47 miles) Plantagenet

Leaving Rockland, stay on rue Edward (the town's main street), not Highway 17, and exit town. Just past the golf course, take County Road 8 across Highway 17. Ride through the town of Clarence, and along the Ottawa River with many splendid views, and cross Highway 17 again to Plantagenet, 30 km (19 miles) from Rockland.

A good selection of motel accommodation is available along this part of the tour.

80 km (50 miles) Treadwell

From Plantagenet, turn left onto County Road 9 to Treadwell.

118 km (73 miles) Hawkesbury

Go right onto County Road 24 through Lefaivre and L'Orignal along the river.

Cycle into Hawkesbury, a 35-km (22-mile) ride from Treadwell, and cross the bridge over the Ottawa River and into the province of Québec.

171 km (106 miles) Oka

Turn right and ride Route 344 along the north side of the river. Near Oka, 53 km (33 miles) from Hawkesbury, is Oka Provincial Park which offers camping.

211 km (131 miles) Montréal

From Oka, take Route 344 to St-Eustache. Cross the Arthur Sauvé Bridge into Laval. From the bridge and take Route 148 to Route 117.

Go right on Route 117 across the Lachapelle Bridge and into Montréal, a 40-km (25-mile) ride from Oka. (The Montréal to Oka route is described in more detail in the Québec chapter.)

ACROSS ONTARIO

Length: 2,595 km (1,612 miles) if you cycle the whole route; 1,611 km (1,001 miles) if you take the bus from Thunder Bay to Espanola. The distance is divided into five parts.

Time: Seventeen to twenty-two days if you ride your bike the whole way

Rating: Intermediate with some easy sections

Terrain: Most of the route is along lightly rolling terrain through forests; the Ottawa Valley section is mostly flat farmland.

Roads: Mostly good pavement

Traffic: Most of this route follows roads with light to medium traffic and avoids heavily traveled roads as much as possible,

Connects with: Across Manitoba, Across Québec, Manitoulin Island tour

Start: Manitoba–Ontario border at Highway 17 (the Trans Canada Highway).

Overview: If you're cycling across Canada, Ontario is the longest province to cross. It is strongly recommended that cyclists do **not** ride Highway 17—the Trans Canada Highway—through northern Ontario. The route's traffic and road conditions are no longer safe enough for cyclists.

The Canadian Cycling Association suggests these alternatives:

• Take a bus from Thunder Bay to Espanola with your bike carried as baggage, and continue riding from there.

• Fly from Thunder Bay to Sault Ste. Marie with your bike carried as baggage, and continue riding from there.

• Ride south and east through the United States.

If you take the route through the United States, ensure you have proper travel documents to enter the United States and return to Canada, are carrying U.S. currency, and have travel health insurance. Also don't bring in any fruit or dairy products.

The route across Minnesota, Wisconsin and Michigan takes you through some great forests. Towns where you can buy food are close so you're not weighed down with a lot of supplies.

Take the time to stop and enjoy Ontario's magnificent scenery. Accommodation is available in the towns and cities. Stock up on supplies in the major centers. Some of the Ontario route is relatively remote so food selection may be limited and, when available, may be more expensive.

In eastern Ontario you ride along the historic Ottawa River and go through picturesque towns and cities, including Ottawa, the nation's capital.

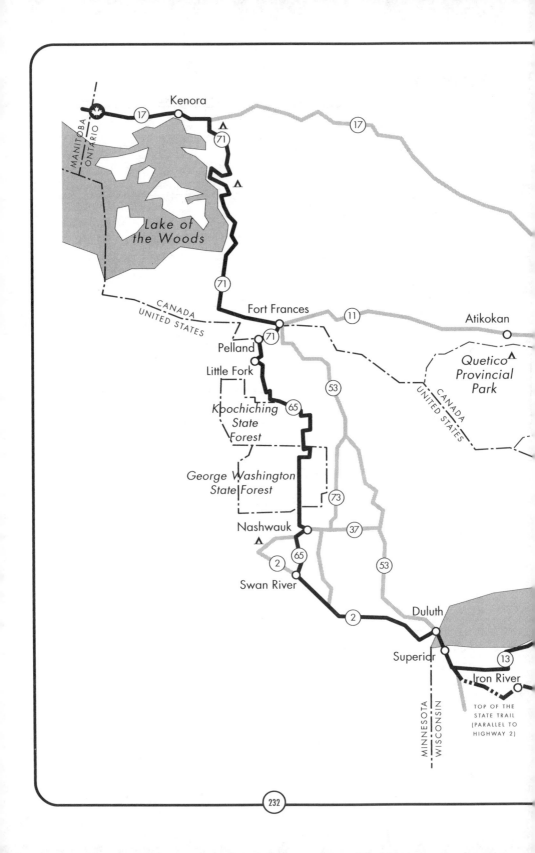

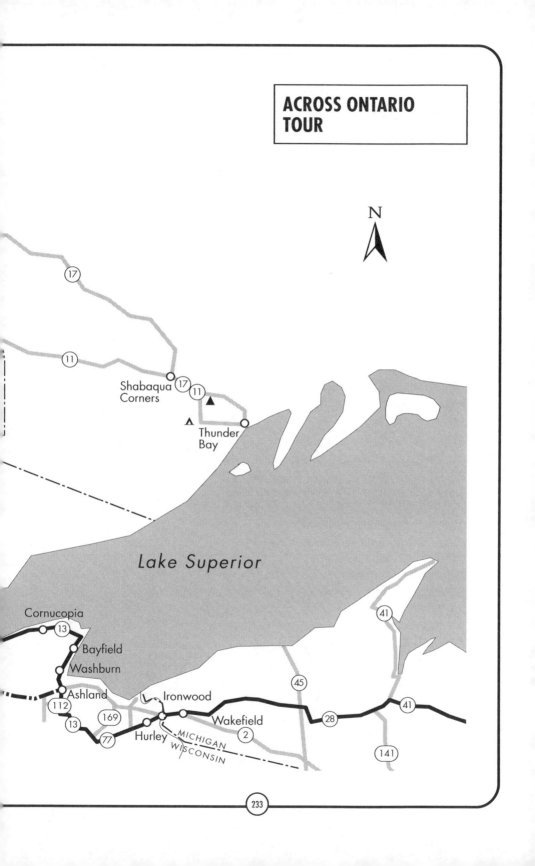

**ACROSS ONTARIO
TOUR**

N

17

11

17
11
Shabaqua
Corners

Thunder
Bay

Lake Superior

41

Cornucopia
13
Bayfield
Washburn
45
Ashland
Ironwood
112
28
41
13
169
Wakefield
77
Hurley
2
MICHIGAN
141
WISCONSIN

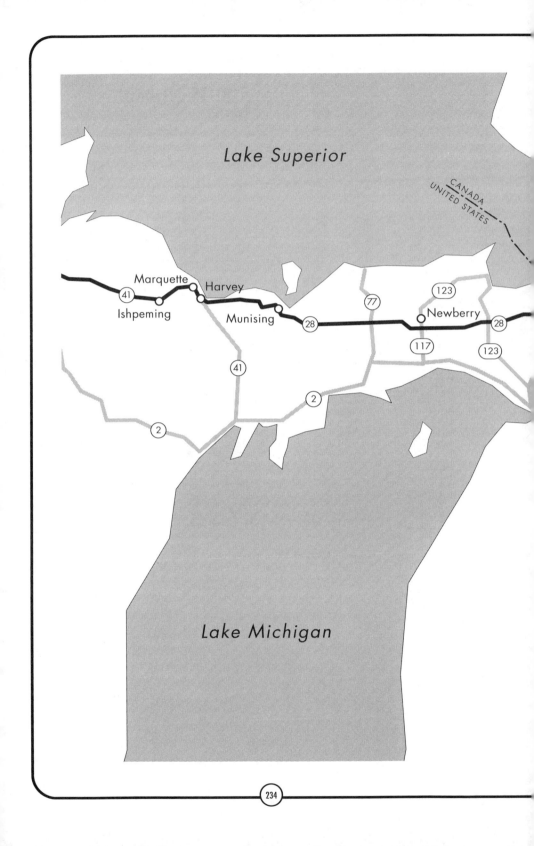

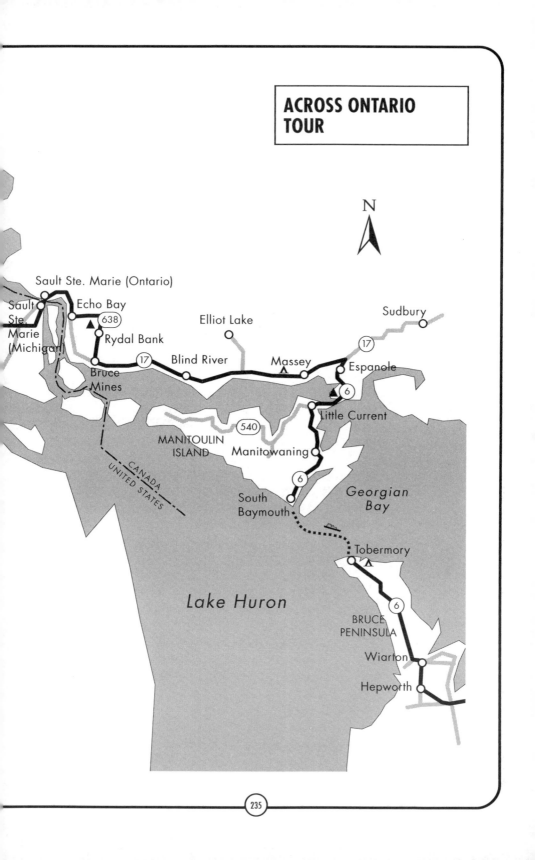

N

Sault Ste. Marie (Ontario)

Sault
Ste.
Marie
(Michigan)

Echo Bay

638

Rydal Bank

Elliot Lake

Sudbury

Blind River

Massey

17

Espanole

Bruce
Mines

17

6

Little Current

CANADA
UNITED STATES

540

MANITOULIN
ISLAND

Manitowaning

6

South
Baymouth

Georgian
Bay

Tobermory

Lake Huron

6

BRUCE
PENINSULA

Wiarton

Hepworth

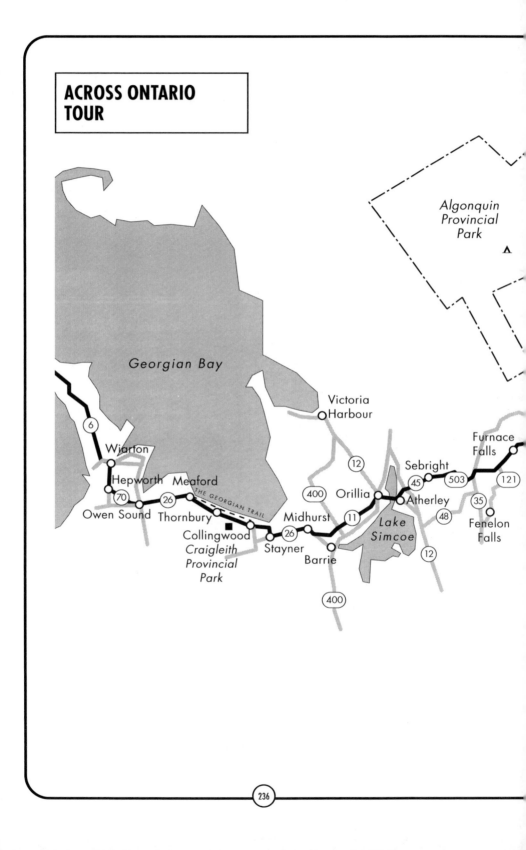

ACROSS ONTARIO
TOUR

Georgian Bay

Algonquin
Provincial
Park

Victoria
Harbour

Furnace
Falls

Wiarton

Hepworth   Meaford

Sebright

(6)

(12)

(45)   (503)   (121)

(70)   (26)   THE GEORGIAN TRAIL

(400)   Orillia   Atherley

Owen Sound   Thornbury

Midhurst   (35)

Collingwood   (11)   Lake   (48)   Fenelon
Craigleith   (26)   Simcoe   Falls
Provincial   Stayner
Park   Barrie   (12)

(400)

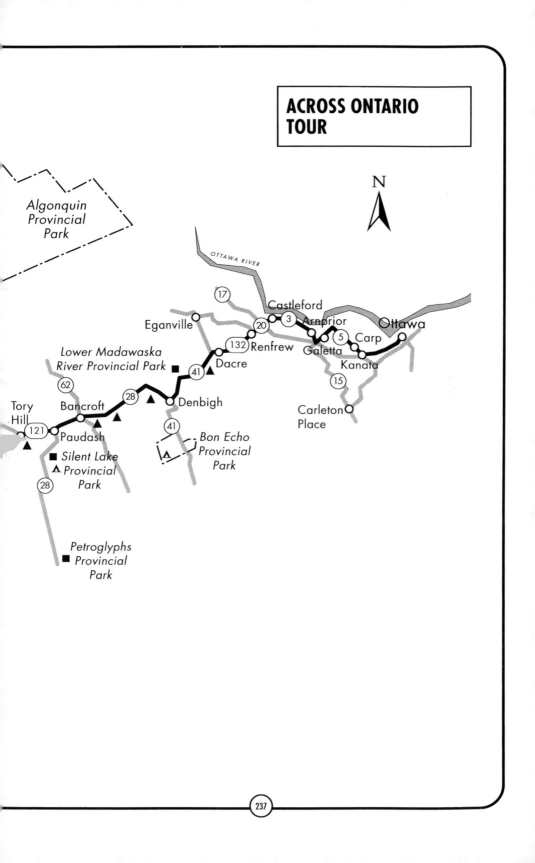

ACROSS ONTARIO TOUR

N

OTTAWA RIVER

Algonquin Provincial Park

(17)

Castleford

Eganville

(20)

(3) Arnprior

Ottawa

Lower Madawaska River Provincial Park

(132) Renfrew

(5) Carp

Galetta

Kanata

(41) Dacre

(62)

(28)

Denbigh

(15)

Tory Hill

Bancroft

(121)

Paudash

(41)

Carleton Place

Silent Lake Provincial Park

Bon Echo Provincial Park

(28)

Petroglyphs Provincial Park

THE ROUTE:

0 km (0 miles) Manitoba–Ontario border

52 km (32 miles) Kenora

From the Manitoba border, ride east on Highway 17 (the Trans Canada Highway) to Kenora.

72 km (45 miles) Highway 71

Continue 20 km (13 miles) on Highway 17 to Highway 71. Turn right onto Highway 71, which winds its way through a maze of lakes and rivers past Lake of the Woods. Along the way are Sioux Narrows Provincial Park and Caliper Lake Provincial Park. This area was a vital link for voyageurs traveling from Lake Superior to the prairies.

229 km (142 miles) Highway 11

Cycle south on Highway 71 through the farming area of the Rainy River District to Highway 11, which is 157 km (98 miles) from Highway 17.

270 km (168 miles) Fort Frances

Turn left onto Highway 11 and go 41 km (25 miles) to Fort Frances.

Option: Fort Frances to Thunder Bay, 352 km (219 miles)

Highway 17—the Trans Canada Highway—is not recommended for bicycle touring. As suggested at the beginning of this tour, you can ride to Thunder Bay and either take a bus to Espanola, fly to Sault Ste. Marie or ride from Fort Frances through the United States.

418 km (260 miles) Turn-off for Atikokan

Continue east on Highway 11 through hilly forested country for 148 km (92 miles) to the turn-off for Atikokan.

440 km (273 miles) Turn-off for Quetico Provincial Park

Located 22 km (14 miles) past Atikokan is the turn-off for Quetico Provincial Park, a 4,669-square-km (1,800-square-mile) wilderness famous for its spectacular canoeing. The park also offers camping and hiking.

558 km (347 miles) Shabaqua Corners

Continuing on Highway 11, it's 118 km (73 miles) east to the junction with Highway 17 at Shabaqua Corners.

622 km (387 miles) Thunder Bay

Another 64 km (40 miles) on Highway 11/17 takes you to Thunder Bay. Along the way is magnificent 39-meter (128-foot) Kakabeka Falls. Adjacent to the falls is Kakabeka Falls Provincial Park offering camping.

From Thunder Bay arrange to take a bus to Espanola and fly to Sault Ste. Marie to avoid Highway 17 through northern Ontario.

Main tour continues from Fort Frances

Ontario–Minnesota border

0 km (0 miles) International Falls, Minnesota, USA

From Fort Frances ride south across the bridge over the Rainy River. Cross the United States border to International Falls, Minnesota.

180 km (112 miles) Nashwauk, Minnesota

Leave International Falls on U.S. Highway 71 southwest. At

the intersection at mile 10, turn left and stay on Highway 71.

At Littlefork, take State Highway 65 through an Indian Reserve and several state forests to Nashwauk, 180 km (112 miles) from International Falls.

318 km (198 miles) Duluth, Minnesota

From Nashwauk, ride west on U.S. Highway 169. Then cycle south again on State Highway 65 to the junction with U.S. Highway 2 near Swan River. Take Highway 2 to Duluth, 138 km (86 miles) from Nashwauk.

In Duluth take Bridge Street across the St. Louis Bay to 21st Street in Superior, Wisconsin.

Minnesota–Wisconsin border

0 km (0 miles) Superior, Wisconsin

169 km (105 miles) Ashland, Wisconsin

Leave Superior on East 2nd Street which becomes U.S. Highway 2/53. Take the road parallel to the highway to State Highway 13.

(If you're riding an all-terrain bike, you may want to try the Top of the State Trail. This bike path parallels U.S. Highway 2 from Superior to near Ashland. The trail is not recommended for narrow-tired touring bikes.)

Take Highway 13 which goes along the shore of Lake Superior and Chequamegon Bay to Highway 2. Then go east on Highway 2 into Ashland.

257 km (160 miles) Ironwood, Michigan

From Ashland, go west 1.6 km (1 mile) on State Highway 137. Turn left onto State Highway

112 for 21 km (13 miles) to State Highway 13. Go right on State Highway 13 for 22 km (14 miles) to Mellen.

Then ride State Highway 77 for 43 km (27 miles) to U.S. Highway 2 and into Ironwood, Michigan, a 88-km (55-mile) ride from Ashland, Wisconsin.

Wisconsin–Michigan border

0 km (0 miles) Ironwood, Michigan

255 km (158 miles) Marquette, Michigan

Continue east on U.S. Highway 2 to Wakefield, 23 km (14 miles) from Ironwood. Turn left onto State Highway 28. Ride on State Highway 28 and U.S. Highway 41 into Ishpenning. Continue on State Highway 28 to Marquette, 255 km (158 miles) from Ironwood.

521 km (323 miles) Sault Ste. Marie, Michigan

From Marquette, take U.S. Highway 41 and turn left past Harvey back onto State Highway 28. Keep riding State Highway 28 to reach Sault Ste. Marie, Michigan, 266 km (165 miles) from Marquette.

Ontario–Michigan border

0 km (0 miles) Sault Ste. Marie, Ontario

Cross the border into Canada at Sault Ste. Marie, Ontario.

240 km (149 miles) Espanola

From Sault Ste. Marie, take Highway 17 to Echo Bay there turn onto Regional Road 638 and ride it through Leeburn, Ophir and Rydal Bank to Bruce Mines on Highway 17.

Ride east on Highway 17 through to Espanola, 240 km

(149 miles) from Sault Ste. Marie, Ontario.

344 km (214 miles) South Baymouth

From Espanola, take Highway 6 through the La Cloche Mountains to Little Current on Manitoulin Island (a tour of Manitoulin Island is described in this chapter).

Ride Highway 6 to South Baymouth, 104 km (65 miles) from Espanola. At South Baymouth, board the ferry to Tobermory. (Cruising time: 1 hour and 45 minutes). To check the ferry schedule call: Ontario Northland Marine Services (519) 376-6601, or toll free 1-800-265-3163.

454 km (282 miles) Owen Sound

Once you're off the ferry in Tobermory, let the traffic from the ferry get ahead of you. Then follow Highway 6 to Wiarton.

From Wiarton, take Highway 70 into Owen Sound, 110 km (68 miles) from Tobermory. (A tour of the Bruce Peninsula is described in this chapter.)

602 km (374 miles) Orillia

Leave Owen Sound via Highway 26 through flat farmland and ride to Meaford.

From Meaford, ride on the Georgian Trail, an off-road recreational path on an abandoned railway line. The trail goes along the shore of Nottawasaga Bay through Thornbury, past Craigleith Provincial Park to Collingwood.

From Collingwood, rejoin Highway 26 as it turns south to Stayner. Keep riding Highway 26 as it turns east to Midhurst.

At Midhurst, leave Highway 26, and follow signs toward Highway 400. Cross over Highway 400 at interchange 111.

Continue onto Regional Road 11 to Orillia, 148 km (92 miles) from Owen Sound.

765 km (475 miles) Bancroft

At Orillia, take Highway 12 across the bridge over Lake Couchiching to Atherley. Turn left onto Regional Road 44, and then right on Regional Road 45, which twists and turns through Canadian Shield landscape to Sebright and the junction with Highway 503.

Take Highway 503 east through Uphill and Furnace Falls to Highway 121 at Tory Hill.

Turn left onto Highway 121 and ride to Highway 28. Turn left on Highway 28 and ride into Bancroft, 163 km (101 miles) from Orillia.

892 km (554 miles) Renfrew

From Bancroft, continue on Highway 28 with more twists and turns through the forest.

At Denbigh, turn left onto Highway 41. After 38 km (24 miles) of gentler grades on Highway 41, turn right on Highway 132 to Dacre.

Continue on Highway 132 for another 30 km (19 miles) to Renfrew, 127 km (79 miles) from Bancroft. When you reach Renfrew—which has good accommodations—you've left the Canadian Shield and have entered the Ottawa Valley.

1,018 km (632 miles) Ottawa

From Renfrew, go northwest on Raglan Street, which becomes Stewart Street. Turn right on Bruce Avenue (watch for this one), which leads to Regional Road 20.

Take Regional Road 20 to Castleford, and go right onto Regional Road 3—also known as the Ottawa River Parkway.

Take Regional Road 3 into Arnprior, which was an important lumbering town during the nineteenth century. Regional Road 3 takes you onto Elgin Street, which becomes Madawaska Boulevard.

Ride Madawaska Boulevard through Arnprior. At the town limit, turn right and then left onto Regional Road 3. Cross Highway 17.

At the next junction turn left onto Regional Road 22 and ride through Galetta.

Turn right onto Regional Road 5 and ride to Carp. Just before the railway crossing, turn left onto the Old Ottawa Road to Southmarch.

Go right on Regional Road 48 into Kanata, and then go left onto Regional Road 19—Corkstown Road. Follow Corkstown Road until it ends at Carling Avenue.

Take Carling Avenue for a few hundred meters until a multi-use recreational trail crosses it. Turn left onto the path. Watch for it, as it's not marked. This path follows the Ottawa River right into downtown Ottawa and to Lebreton Flat campground, which is in view of the Peace Tower of Canada's Parliament Buildings. Ottawa is 126-km (78-miles) from Renfrew.

1,229 km (764 miles) Montréal, Québec

From here follow the 211-km (131-mile) Ottawa to Montréal tour (described in this chapter) and you're in Québec.

More Information: Minnesota Office of Tourism, 375 Jackson Street, 250 Skyway Level, St. Paul, MN 55101, USA, telephone toll-free from Canada 1-800-766-8687. For Minnesota county maps: Minnesota Department of Transportation, Map Sales, Room B-20, St. Paul, MN 55155, USA, telephone (612) 296-2126.
Wisconsin Division of Tourism, P.O. Box 7606, Madison, WI 53707, USA, telephone (608) 266-2161, or toll-free 1-800-432-8747.
For Wisconsin county maps: Wisconsin Department of Transportation, Document Sales, 3617 Pierstorff Street, Madison, WI 53704, USA, telephone (608) 246-3265. Michigan Travel Bureau, Department of Commerce, P.O. Box 30226, Lansing, MI 48909, USA, telephone: 1-800-5432-YES.

GUIDEBOOKS

The Great Toronto Bicycling Guide, by Elliott Katz. Available from: Great North Books, 60 Bayhampton Crescent, Thornhill, Ontario L4J 7G9; $3.95.

Ontario Cycling Route Map Series: 1. Southwestern Ontario (Windsor/London areas); 2. Western Ontario (London/Waterloo areas); 3. Bruce Peninsula/Manitoulin Island; 4. Golden Horseshoe (Niagara/Toronto areas); 5. Muskoka/Haliburton; 6. Lake Ontario/St. Lawrence (Peterborough/Kingston areas); 7. Ottawa Valley (Ottawa/Renfrew areas). Available from: Ontario Cycling Association, 1220 Sheppard Avenue East, Willowdale, Ontario M2K 2X1; $5.00 each.

The Bicycle Guide to Southwestern Ontario by Gary Horner. Available from: Lone Pine Publishing, 206, 10426-81st Avenue, Edmonton, Alberta T6E 1X5, telephone (403) 433-9333; $9.95

Bicycle Guide to Eastern Ontario by Gary Horner. Available from Lone Pine Publishing; $14.95.

MapArt Bicycle Day Trip Routes: South Central Ontario. Map available from MapArt Corporation, 72 Bloor Street East, Oshawa, Ontario L1H 3M2, telephone (416) 436-2525; $4.95.

Loyalist Roots: Cycling Tours of the Kingston Area, by Thomas Sylvester. Available from: Curbside Publishing, South Shore East, Stella, Ontario K0H 2S0, telephone (613) 389-1320; $7.00 ($9.00 postpaid).

Cycling the Sound, Available from Ginger Press, 848 Second Ave East, Owen Sound, Ontario N4K 2H3, telephone (519) 376-4233; $14.95.

Îles-de-la-Madeleine
(Tourisme Québec)

Québec

Québec's beauty, charm and *joie de vivre* are best experienced by bicycle. Ride along the St. Lawrence River through historic villages and see traditional woodcarvers at work. Enjoy the province's ambience everywhere; in the lively Laurentian Mountain villages, at Percé in the Gaspé Peninsula or on the sand beaches in the îles-de-la-Madeleine. Québec's French language and culture makes touring in Québec a bit like exploring a foreign country. Most residents do speak some English, however a French phrase-book can be helpful.

Area: 1,667,926 square km (643,820 square miles); the Canadian province with the largest area, Québec is more than twice the size of Texas, three times the size of France and seven times the area of Great Britain.

Terrain: The province's three main geological regions are the Canadian Shield stretching north of the Saint Lawrence River to Hudson Bay, the Appalachian region south of the Saint Lawrence, and the Saint Lawrence Lowlands between the Canadian Shield and the Appalachian region.

The Canadian Shield, known in southern Québec as the Laurentians, forms an immense rolling plateau with a coniferous forest and many rivers and lakes. Québec's Appalachian region is an extension of the Appalachian Mountain chain of the eastern United States. The region includes the 900-meter (3,000-foot) Chic-Chocs Mountains in the Gaspé, which are a continuation of the 600- to 900-meter (2,000- to 3,000-foot) Sutton, Stoke and Megantic ranges of the Eastern Townships region southeast of Montréal.

Roads: Québec roads generally do not have paved shoulders. The limited-access expressways have paved shoulders but do not permit bicycles.

Weather: Most of Québec experiences a temperate climate with hot summers and cold winters. Average rainfall during the summer months is around 11 cm (4 inches) per month. Summer average temperatures range from 17 to 26 degrees Celsius (62 to 79 degrees Fahrenheit) in Montréal; 15 to 25 degrees Celsius (59 to 77 degrees Fahrenheit) in Québec City; and 12 to 24 degrees Celsius (54 to 76 degrees Fahrenheit) in Gaspé. Québec's mild autumn temperatures provide comfortable cycling weather while the forests are a dazzling display of colors; this is the time of year when the country-side is at its peak of beauty and should not be missed.

Hostels: Hostels in Québec are operated by the Regroupement tourisme jeunesse, 4545 Avenue Pierre de Coubertin, Montréal, Québec H1V 3R2, telephone (514) 252-3117, fax (514) 252-3119, or toll-free 1-800-461-8585.

Tourist Information: For general tourist information, including a road map and camping and hotel directories, contact: Tourism Québec, P.O. Box 20,000, Québec City, Québec G1K 7X2, telephone from Montréal (514) 873-2015; elsewhere in Québec, Canada and the United States, call toll-free 1-800-363-7777.

Airports: Montréal and Québec are served by major airlines, and have connections to smaller centers.

Trains: For information on VIA Rail service, call in Montréal (514) 871-1331; Québec City (418) 692-3940; from elsewhere call toll-free 1-800-361-5390. Bicycles are carried at no extra charge on trains that have a baggage car.

Buses: Voyageur Bus Lines connects Ontario with Montréal. Orleans Express Coach Lines links the rest of the province. Both require that bicycles be dismantled and put in a box or a plastic bag, and both charge the bus parcel rate for the bike's weight.

Bicycling: Vélo Québec, 3575 Saint Laurent Blvd., Suite 310, Montréal H2X 2T7, telephone (514) 847-8356.

Capital: Québec City, the only walled city in North America, is known for its historic sites. UNESCO declared it a World Heritage Site.

Population: 6,895,963 (1991 census); approximately 83 per cent is French speaking, and 12 per cent English speaking. Among the 35 other languages found in Québec are Italian, Greek and Chinese.

History: Before the arrival of the Europeans, Québec was inhabited by Native Iroquois and Montagnais–Naskapi Indians in the south and by Inuit in the north. In 1534, Jacques Cartier landed in the Gaspé Peninsula and claimed the territory for France. In 1608 Samuel de Champlain landed at the site of Québec City and established the first French settlement in the territory, then called New France.

In the 1759 Battle of the Plains of Abraham, the British troops defeated the French. In the Treaty of Paris of 1763, France gave up the territory to the British. Québec was one of the four founding provinces in Canadian confederation in 1867. In the constitution—the British North America Act of 1867—Québec was given control over its language, religion and civil law.

Until the early twentieth century, Québec's economy depended mainly on farming. During this century, Québec became more urbanized as people from rural areas moved to the cities. A large influx of immigrants, at first mostly from Europe but later from all parts of the world, settled in Québec.

MONTRÉAL BICYCLING ROUTES

Situated on an island at the confluence of the St. Lawrence and Ottawa rivers, Montréal was for many years Canada's most populous city. Many of Montréal's bicycling route paths lead along waterways.

Off-street bicycling routes include the Lachine Canal bicycle path, the Aqueduct Canal, the Lachine waterfront, and the Lasalle waterfront. There are off-street paths or separated bicycle routes along most of the waterfront of the island of Montréal. A north–south separated bicycle route crosses Montréal on Avenue Christophe-Colomb, Boyer, de Brébeuf and Berri streets.

Mont-Royal Park, Parc Maisonneuve, île-Ste-Hélène and Parc Angrignon are city parks with designated cycling routes.

St. Lawrence Seaway bikeway is a path on top of a dyke in the St. Lawrence River with the river on one side and the South Shore Channel on the other. Îles-des-Bouchervilles Provincial Park has a network of bicycle trails covering four of the park's islands.

More Information: For a bicycle route map, contact: Service de la planification du territoire, 2580 Boulevard St-Joseph East, 2nd Floor, Montréal, Québec H1Y 2A2, telephone (514) 280-6700.

MONTRÉAL THROUGH ST-EUSTACHE TO OKA

Length: 43 km (27 miles)
Time: One or two days
Rating: Easy
Terrain: Mostly flat to St-Eustache, then rolling hills
Roads: Unpaved shoulders; recreational path for part of route
Traffic: Heavy while leaving, then lighter
Connects with: Ottawa to Montréal tour (described in Ontario chapter)
Start: Montréal
Overview: Winding back roads through gently rolling hills bring you to Oka, the setting of the Trappist monastery that produces the world-renowned Oka cheese. St-Eustache has many historic sites from the Battle of St-Eustache during the Rebellion of 1837.

This easy tour can be done as a day trip, or you can make it a two-day tour and camp overnight at Oka Provincial Park, which also has a beach and nature trails.

THE ROUTE:
0 km (0 miles) Montréal
21.5 km (13 miles) St-Eustache

Head to Laval by going north on Route 117 to Route 148.

Go west on Route 148 through farm country to the Arthur

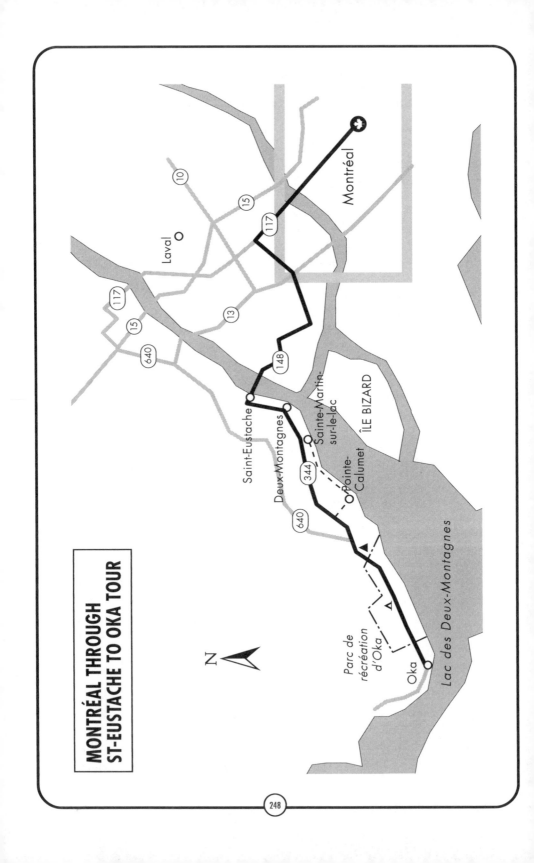

MONTRÉAL THROUGH
ST-EUSTACHE TO OKA TOUR

N

Montréal

Laval

Saint-Eustache

Deux-Montagnes

Sainte-Martin-
sur-le-lac

Pointe-
Calumet

ÎLE BIZARD

Parc de
récréation
d'Oka

Oka

Lac des Deux-Montagnes

248

Sauvé Bridge over the Rivière des Milles îles and into the town of St-Eustache, founded in 1768.

After crossing the bridge, turn left on St-Louis to the St-Eustache church.

The church, built in 1793, was damaged during the Battle of St-Eustache in 1837 between 150 patriots led by Dr. Olivier Chénier, who had taken refuge in the church, and 2,000 militia soldiers under Sir John Colborne. Chénier and 70 of his followers were killed in this last encounter of the Rebellion of 1837. Scars made by the cannon-balls can be seen on the church walls.

Turn right onto rue St-Eustache through the area called "Le Vieux St-Eustache," of old houses and a mill built in 1762.

43 km (27 miles) Oka Provincial Park and town of Oka

After exploring St-Eustache, ride southwest on Route 344 along the river.

At Ste-Marthe, take the bicycle path, which parallels Route 344 as far as Pointe-Calumet, and then rejoin Route 344. You pass the Trappist Monastery and enter Oka Provincial Park, which has campgrounds, hiking trails and a sandy beach.

Continue on Route 344 to the town of Oka, 22 km (miles) from St-Eustache.

Option: ferry from Oka to Hudson (crossing time: 10 minutes)

In the town of Oka is a ferry across Lac des Deux-Montagnes to Hudson.

More Information: Oka Provincial Park, Box 1200, Oka, Québec J0N 1E0, telephone (514) 479-8329.

LAURENTIAN MOUNTAINS LOOP

Length: 211 km (131 miles)
Time: Two or three days
Rating: Intermediate
Terrain: Mountainous, with some climbing
Roads: Narrow country roads, most with no shoulder
Traffic: Light, except for Highway 117 which can have heavy traffic
Start: St-Jérôme, 56 km (35 miles) north of Montréal.
Overview: Known as Québec's "little Switzerland," the Laurentians is

a beautiful land of wooded hills, glacier-worn mountains, lakes and valleys. Follow the winding country roads to unspoiled mountain villages, many over one hundred years old. You can swim, fish, canoe and boat.

Fall season turns the foliage into a display of blazing colors. This tour explores picturesque secondary roads east and west of Highway 117 and the Laurentian Autoroute, the main roads into the Laurentians

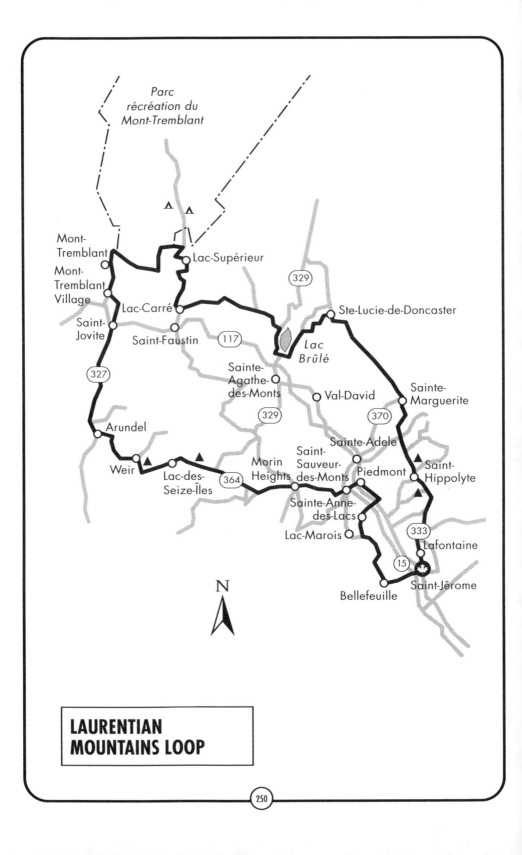

Parc
récréation du
Mont-Tremblant

Mont-
Tremblant
Lac-Supérieur
Mont-
Tremblant
Village
Lac-Carré
(329)
Saint-Jovite
Saint-Faustin
(117)
Ste-Lucie-de-Doncaster
Lac
Brûlé
(327)
Sainte-
Agathe-
des-Monts
Val-David
Sainte-
Marguerite
Arundel
(329)
(370)
Weir
Morin
Heights
Saint-
Sauveur-
des-Monts
Sainte-Adele
Saint-
Hippolyte
Lac-des-
Seize-Îles
(364)
Piedmont
Sainte-Anne-
des-Lacs
Lac-Marois
(333)
Lafontaine
(15)
Bellefeuille
Saint-Jêrome

N

**LAURENTIAN
MOUNTAINS LOOP**

from Montréal. There are motels, hotels and resorts in most of the Laurentian towns, as well as campgrounds along the route.

THE ROUTE:

0 km (0 miles) St-Jérôme
17 km (11 miles) St-Hippolyte

From St-Jérôme, known as the "Gateway to the Laurentians," take Route 333 through Lafontaine to St-Hippolyte.

31 km (19 miles) Ste-Marguerite

Then take the road to Ste-Marguerite on the shores of Lac Masson. The route is steep and climbs constantly.

47 km (29 miles) Ste-Lucie-de-Doncaster

Ride to Ste-Lucie-de-Doncaster where there is a public beach.

58 km (36 miles) Lac Brûlé near Ste-Agathe-des-Monts

From Ste-Lucie, turn southwest. You continue to climb and pass several lakes on the way to Lac Brûlé on Route 329 just north of Ste-Agathe-des-Monts, the largest city in the Laurentians.

81 km (50 miles) Lac-Carré near St-Faustin

Take Route 329 north for 6 km (4 miles). Turn left onto the secondary road leading 17 km (11 miles) to Lac-Carré located north of St-Faustin.

106 km (66 miles) village of Mont-Tremblant

From Lac-Carré head north towards Lac-Supérieur and turn west. Go through the southern edge of Mont-Tremblant Provincial Park. Mont-Tremblant Park, 2,564 square km (990 square miles), offers camping, hiking trails, swimming, canoeing and fishing.

Ride to Mont-Tremblant Village.

119 km (74 miles) St-Jovite

From the village of Mont-Tremblant, take Route 327 south for 13 km (8 miles) to St-Jovite.

Then continue south on Route 327 along the winding banks of the Rouge River and the Diable River.

137 km (85 miles) Arundel

Along the way to Arundel, 18 km (11 miles) from St-Jovite, you pass a covered bridge.

153 km (95 miles) Lac-des-Seize-îles

Go west on Route 364 through Weir to Lac-des-Seize-îles, 16 km (10 miles) from Arundel.

174 km (108 miles) Morin Heights

Another 21 km (13 miles) farther is the community of Morin Heights, where there is a campground.

185 km (115 miles) St-Sauveur

Picturesque St-Sauveur-des-Monts, 11 km (7 miles) from Morin Heights, is a charming village with boutiques and cafes in a valley surrounded by popular ski hills.

211 km (131 miles) St-Jérôme

To get from St-Sauveur back to St-Jérôme, cross Autoroute 15 on the overpass and take Highway 117 south.

Go right on Chemin de Lac Marois, and then left on Montée Filion to Chemin Rivière-des-Lacs. Take Chemin Rivière-des-

Lacs to the village of Belle-feuille, which has camping.

Return to St-Jérôme by Boulevard de la Salette, Chemin de la Montagne and Boulevard Demartiny.

More Information: Mont-Tremblant Provincial Park, Box 129, 731 Chemin de la Pisciculture, St-Faustin, Québec J0T 2G0, telephone (819) 688-2281. Laurentian Tourism Association, 14142 rue de la Chapelle, R.R. 1, St-Jérôme, Québec J7Z 5T4, telephone (514) 436-8532.

THE EASTERN TOWNSHIPS LOOP

Length: 223 km (138 miles)

Time: Two to three days

Rating: Easy to intermediate

Terrain: Mountains and farmland

Roads: Secondary roads with unpaved shoulders

Traffic: Mostly light

Start: Sherbrooke, the largest city in the Eastern Townships, is served by VIA Rail from Montréal on its service to Halifax.

Overview: Situated southeast of Montréal, the Eastern Townships, known in French as *l'Estrie*, is part of the Appalachian Mountain chain.

The region of forests, lakes and farms is a northern extension of the Green Mountains of Vermont. Both areas share the similar magnificent mountain and rural scenery, but relatively few cyclists have discovered the Eastern Townships compared to the throngs of cyclists touring in Vermont just across the border.

During summer several theaters are open, and there are concerts at the Orford Art Center. North Hatley is known for its handicrafts. There are numerous accommodations and campgrounds along the route.

THE ROUTE:

0 km (0 miles) Sherbrooke

From Sherbrooke, head south on Queen Sud to Lennoxville. Then take Route 108 to the town of North Hatley on Lake Massawippi. Here are a summer theater, antique shops, craftsmen and artists.

Continue on Route 108 to Sainte-Catherine-de-Hatley and take Chemin de la Montagne south to Route 141.

Ride northwest on Route 141 and turn left at Chemin Fitch Bay. Take this road to Fitch Bay and then take Route 247 west to Georgeville.

Cycle north on Route 247 along the shores of Lake Memphrémagog, to the town of Magog. Located at the northern tip of Lake Memphrémagog, Magog offers cruises on the lake, a beach and a summer theater.

Take Route 141 out of Magog to Mont-Orford Provincial Park where, in addition to camping on the shores of Lake Stukely, you can go hiking or

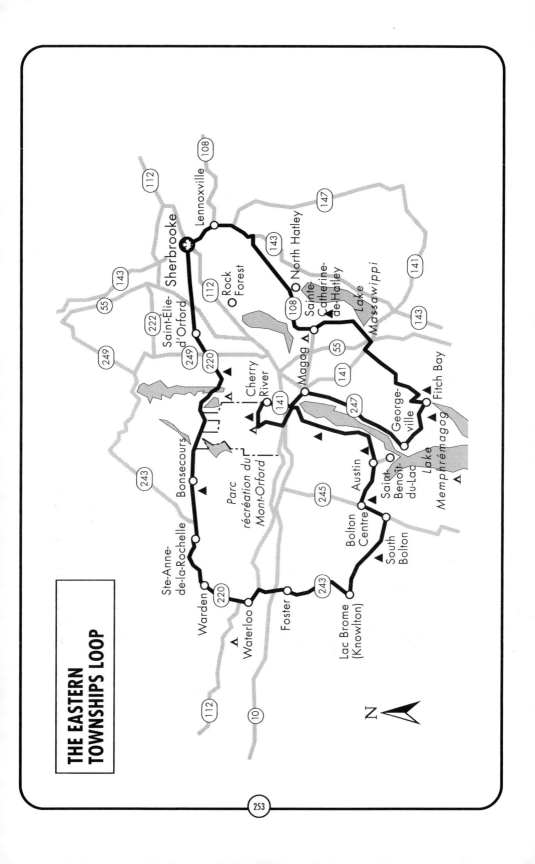

THE EASTERN
TOWNSHIPS LOOP

112
10
N

112
Sherbrooke
Lennoxville
108
112
147
143
North Hatley
Sainte-Catherine-de-Hatley
108
Lake Massawippi
141
143
55
143
222
249
249
220
Rock Forest
Saint-Élie-d'Orford
Cherry River
141
Magog
55
141
247
Fitch Bay
George-ville
Parc récréation du Mont-Orford
Lake Memphrémagog
Saint-Benoît-du-Lac
Austin
Bonsecours
243
Ste-Anne-de-la-Rochelle
Warden
220
245
Bolton Centre
South Bolton
Waterloo
Foster
243
Lac Brome (Knowlton)

take in a concert at the Orford Art Center.

Going south again from Mont-Orford Park, take Route 112 for 1 km (0.6 mile) to Chemin du Bolton-Est which goes to Austin.

Side trip: Austin to St-Benoît-du-Lac, 3 km (2 miles) each way

From Austin, take a short side-trip to the Benedictine Abbey of St-Benoît-du-Lac, known for its cheese, cider and chocolate.

Main tour continues from Austin

Head west to Bolton Centre. Go south on Route 245 for 5 km (3 miles) to the town of South Bolton and then take Route 243 for 14 km (9 miles) to Lac-Brome (Knowlton).

Continue on Route 243 through Waterloo (known for its mushrooms) and Warden to Ste-Anne-de-la-Rochelle, 29 km (18 miles) from Lac-Brome.

Head east on Route 220 for 35 km (22 miles) to the tour's starting point at Sherbrooke.

More Information: Mont-Orford Provincial Park, Box 146, Magog, Québec J1X 3N7, telephone (819) 843-6233.

Estrie Tourism Association, 25 Bocage Street, Sherbrooke, Québec J1L 2J4, telephone (819) 820-2020.

MONTRÉAL THROUGH L'ÎLE-PERROT TO COTEAU-LANDING

Length: 50 km (31 miles)
Time: One or two days
Rating: Easy
Terrain: Flat
Roads: Unpaved shoulders
Traffic: Light
Start: Ste-Anne-de-Bellevue at the western tip of the island of Montréal is reached from downtown by cycling on Lakeshore Drive along Lac St. Louis. At the town of Ste-Anne-de-Bellevue, Lakeshore Drive becomes Chemin Ste-Anne.

Overview: This day tour or leisurely overnight trip takes you through rural land and past several historic sites. As the route follows the shores of rivers and lakes, it can be windy. There are hotels and campgrounds along the way.

THE ROUTE:

0 km (0 miles) Ste-Anne-de-Bellevue

Ride on Chemin Ste-Anne to the Ste-Anne Canal, which allows boats to bypass the Ste-Anne Rapids. Here is a park and picnic area.

5 km (3 miles) L'île-Perrot

Cross the Highway 20 bridge to L'île-Perrot.

12 km (7 miles) Pointe-du-Moulin Historical Park

Turn left onto boulevard Perrot and follow it for 7 km (4 miles) to Pointe-du-Moulin Historical Park. The 12-hectare (30-acre) park encompasses a renovated

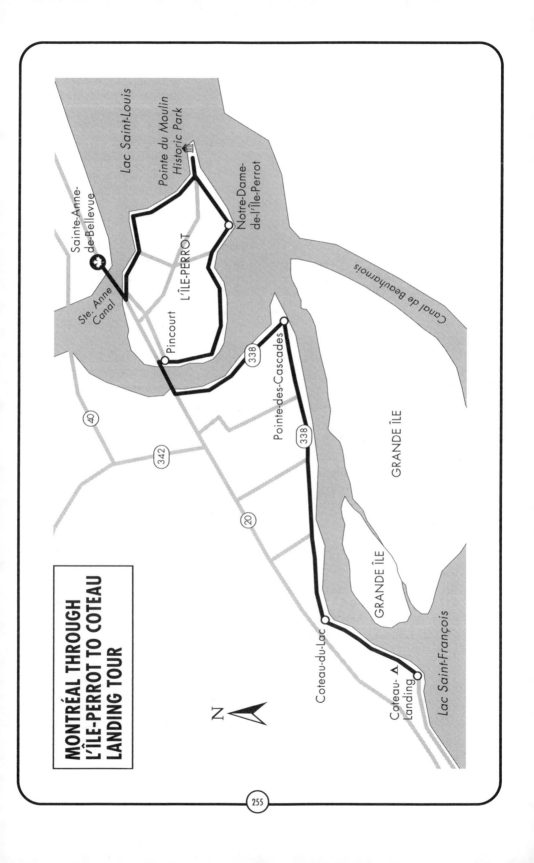

MONTRÉAL THROUGH
L'ÎLE-PERROT TO COTEAU
LANDING TOUR

N

Lac Saint-Louis

Pointe du Moulin
Historic Park

Sainte-Anne-
de-Bellevue

Notre-Dame-
de-l'île-Perrot

Ste. Anne
Canal

L'ÎLE-PERROT

Canal de Beauharnois

Pincourt

40

342

338

Pointe-des-Cascades

338

20

GRANDE ÎLE

Coteau-du-Lac

GRANDE ÎLE

Coteau-
Landing

Lac Saint-François

windmill and miller's house, as well as a heritage center with exhibits on early eighteenth century technology.

23 km (14 miles) Highway 20

From the park, turn left on Boulevard Perrot and follow it for 12 km (7 miles) along the water's edge to Highway 20.

Go west on Highway 20 across the Ottawa River.

30 km (19 miles) Pointe-des-Cascades

Turn left onto Route 338 and ride it for 7 km (4 miles) to Pointe-des-Cascades where there is a campground.

50 km (31 miles) Coteau-Landing

From Pointe-des-Cascades follow the winding road along the St. Lawrence River for 18 km (11 miles) to Coteau-Landing, where there is a campground. Coteau-du-Lac served as a port for exporting to Ontario.

At Coteau-du-Lac National Historic Park are remains of a port and canal, as well as a reconstructed octagonal blockhouse.

More Information: Pointe-du-Moulin Historic Park, 2500 boulevard Don Quichotte, L'île-Perrot, Québec J7V 7P2, telephone (514) 453-5936. Coteau-du-Lac National Historic Site, Box 550, 550 Chemin du Fleuve, Coteau-du-Lac, Québec J0P 1B0, telephone (514) 763-5631.

MONTRÉAL TO THE CHÂTEAUGUAY VALLEY

Length: 200 km (124 miles)
Time: Two days
Rating: Easy
Terrain: Relatively flat
Roads: Country roads with unpaved shoulders
Traffic: Light
Start: Côte-Ste-Catherine Provincial Park, which can be reached from Montréal by the St. Lawrence Seaway bikeway accessed from L'île-des-Soeurs (Nun's Island) near downtown Montréal.
Overview: This tour takes you through the orchards and farmlands south of Montréal towards the American border, and returns through the valley of the Châteauguay River. You can begin this tour from downtown Montréal.

THE ROUTE:

0 km (0 miles) Côte-Ste-Catherine Provincial Park

Côte-Ste-Catherine Park offers birdwatching for herons and ducks. It's one of the closest campgrounds to Montréal.

From Côte-Ste-Catherine Park, go east on Highway 132, and then south on Route 209. After several kilometers, go right at the fork in the road onto Rang St-Pierre Nord. Follow this road as it eventually merges back into Route 209.

57 km (35 miles) Hemmingford

Ride on Route 209 as far as St-

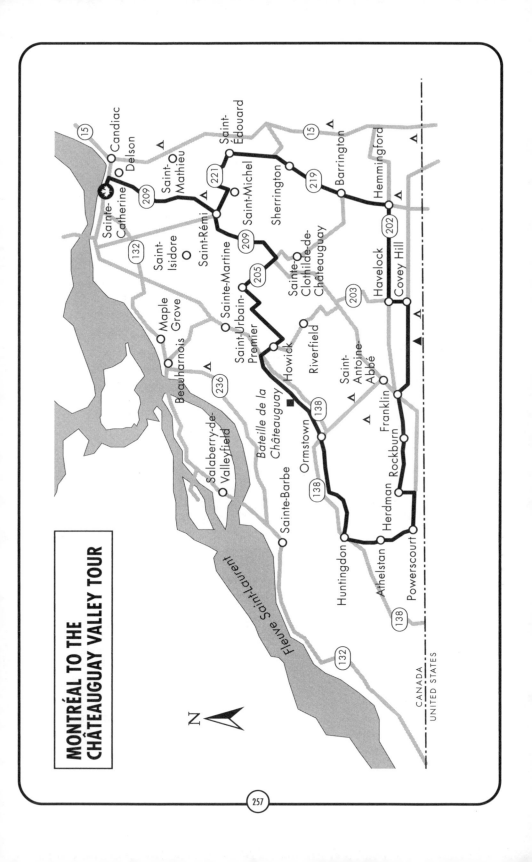

MONTRÉAL TO THE CHÂTEAUGUAY VALLEY TOUR

N

Fleuve Saint-Laurent

15 Candiac
Delson
Saint-Mathieu
Saint-Édouard
221 Saint-Michel
15 Barrington
Hemmingford
209 Saint-Catherine
Sherrington
219
202 Havelock
Covey Hill
132 Saint-Isidore
Saint-Rémi
209
Sainte-Clothilde-de-Châteauguay
203
Maple Grove
Sainte-Martine
205
Beauharnois
Saint-Urbain-Premier
Howick
Riverfield
Saint-Antoine-Abbé
236
Franklin
Salaberry-de-Valleyfield
Bateille de la Châteauguay
Ormstown
138
Herdman
Rockburn
Sainte-Barbe
138
Huntingdon
Athelstan
Powerscourt
138
132

CANADA
UNITED STATES

Rémi, and turn left onto Route 221 to Sherrington. Then take Route 219 to Hemmingford.

From Hemmingford, follow Route 202 west for 13 km (8 miles) to Havelock, then go south for 3 km (2 miles) on Route 203 to Covey Hill.

From Covey Hill ride west on a secondary road to rejoin Route 202 at Franklin.

Side trip: Franklin to St-Antoine-Abbé, 5 km (3 miles) each way

You can make a side trip to St-Antoine-Abbé, which is known for its apple cider.

Main tour continues from Franklin

100 km (62 miles) Herdman

Continue on Route 202 for 14 km (9 miles) to Herdman, 43 km (27 miles) from Hemmingford.

Go south on Route 202 and then west on a secondary road to Powerscourt, where you are 2 km (1.2 miles) from the United States border.

114 km (71 miles) Huntingdon

Head north to Huntingdon, 14 km (9 miles) from Herdman.

130 km (81 miles) Ormstown

Follow the secondary road along the south side of the Châteauguay River for 16 km (10 miles) to Ormstown.

147 km (91 miles) Howick

From Ormstown, the road follows the north side of the river for 17 km (11 miles) and take the turn-off to Howick.

158 km (98 miles) St-Urbain-Premier

From Howick head along a small country road for 11 km (6 miles) to St-Urbain-Premier. Then ride for 6 km (4 miles) on Route 205 southeast to Route 209.

176 km (110 miles) St-Rémi

Turn left and ride Route 209 to St-Rémi.

200 km (124 miles) Côte-Ste-Catherine Park

From St-Rémi go north on Route 209 to Route 132. Go west on Route 132 to Côte-Ste-Catherine Park, 24 km (15 miles) from St-Rémi.

OTTAWA-HULL TO THE GATINEAU HILLS

Length: 40 km (25 miles)
Time: Day trip
Rating: Easy
Terrain: Hilly
Roads: Park roads
Traffic: Light, heavier in summer and on weekends
Connects with: Rideau Tour; Ottawa to Montréal tour (both described in Ontario chapter)
Start: Hull, across the Ottawa River from the city of Ottawa, which is served by VIA Rail. From Ottawa, cross the Alexandra Bridge to Hull. The bridge gives you a good view of the Parliament Buildings.

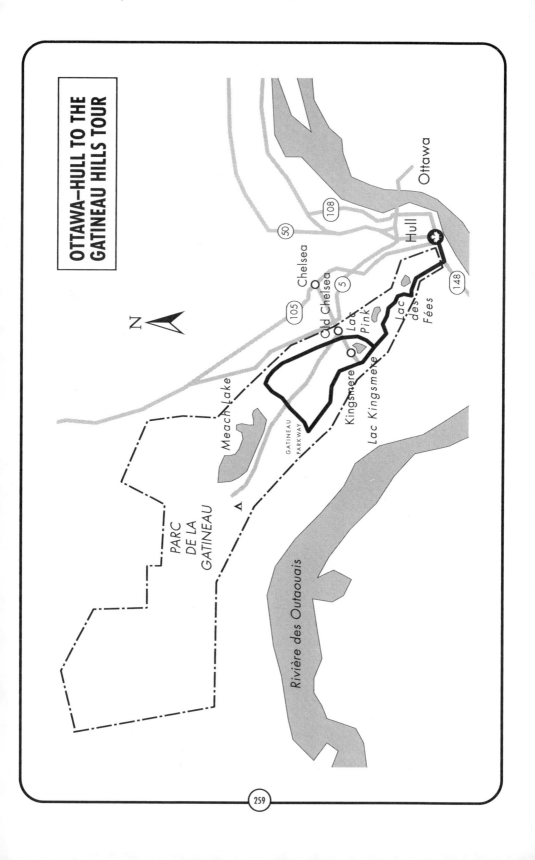

OTTAWA–HULL TO THE GATINEAU HILLS TOUR

N

Ottawa

Hull

108

50

Chelsea

105

Old Chelsea

5

148

Lac Pink

Lac des Fées

Kingsmere

Lac Kingsmere

Meach Lake

GATINEAU PARKWAY

PARC DE LA GATINEAU

Rivière des Outaouais

Overview: Gatineau Park covers 356 square km (138 square miles) of wooded Canadian Shield mountains and lakes at the confluence of the Ottawa River and the Gatineau River. This route is suitable for a day trip from Ottawa or Hull. Ottawa has an extensive network of recreational paths (see Ontario chapter).

THE ROUTE:

0 km (0 miles)

40 km (25 miles) Gatineau Park

From Hull, take Boulevard Alexandre Tache—which is also Route 148—and then go north on Promenade de La Gatineau into Gatineau Park.

Cycling routes in Gatineau Park

Lac Pink offers cyclists scenic panoramas. Tour Lac Pink, and the 30-km (19-mile) Promenade de la Gatineau loop along Kingsmere Lake, Fortune Lake and Meach Lake. In the park are picnic grounds and hiking trails.

More Information: Gatineau Park, National Capital Commission, 161 Laurier Street West, Ottawa, Ontario K1Y 6J6, telephone (613) 239-5000, or 1-800-465-1867; or call Gatineau Park at (819) 827-2020. Outaouais Tourism Association, Box 2000, rue Laurier, Hull, Québec J8X 3Z2, telephone (819) 778-2222.

QUÉBEC CITY THROUGH ÎLE D'ORLÉANS TO CAP-TOURMENTE

Length: 115 km (71 miles); plus side trips of 10 km (6 miles) and 2 km (1.2 miles)

Time: One to two days

Rating: Easy

Terrain: Flat farmland, some hills

Roads: Unpaved shoulders along the river's edge

Traffic: Tourist traffic in summer

Start: Québec City, served by VIA Rail and several airlines.

Overview: On this tour in the Québec City area you step back into the seventeenth, eighteenth and nineteenth centuries. Founded in 1608 by Samuel de Champlain, Québec City was built on high cliffs overlooking the St. Lawrence River,

and is North America's only walled city north of Mexico City.

Nearby île d'Orléans, a gem of historic Québécois homes, old farming villages, and traditional Québécois restaurants, is the most popular cycling tour in the Québec City area.

Breathtaking Montmorency Falls, east of Québec City, are higher than Niagara Falls. Farther on is Ste-Anne-de-Beaupré, a well-known Catholic shrine. Also on this tour is Mont-Ste-Anne Provincial Park, and the Cap-Tourmente Wildlife Reserve, home to thousands of migrating snow geese. There is a good selection of campgrounds and accommodations along the route.

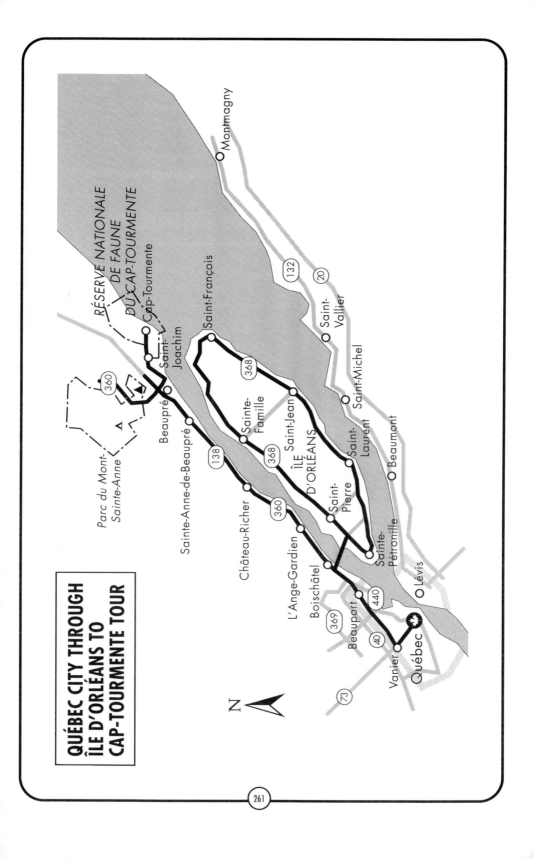

QUÉBEC CITY THROUGH ÎLE D'ORLÉANS TO CAP-TOURMENTE TOUR

N

Montmagny

RÉSERVE NATIONALE
DE FAUNE
DU CAP-TOURMENTE
Cap-Tourmente

132

20

Saint-
Vallier

Saint-François

Saint-
Joachim

368

Beaupré

360

Sainte-
Famille

Saint-Michel

Parc du Mont-
Sainte-Anne

Sainte-Anne-de-Beaupré

138

Saint-Jean

Château-Richer

368

ÎLE
D'ORLÉANS

Saint-
Laurent

Beaumont

L'Ange-Gardien

360

Saint-
Pierre

Boischâtel

Sainte-
Pétronille

369

Beauport

440

Lévis

40

Vanier

Québec

73

261

THE ROUTE:

0 km (0 miles) Québec City

6 km (4 miles) île d'Orléans Bridge

Leave Québec City via Route 138 to the île d'Orléans Bridge.

Cross the bridge to île d'Orléans, first visited by Europeans in 1542. Here you can experience the rural Québec of centuries ago.

Go right and follow Route 360 for a tour of 66 km (41 miles) around the shores of île d'Orléans through the island's tranquil and picturesque villages.

11 km (7 miles) Ste-Pétronille

Ste-Pétronille, 5 km (3 miles) from the île d'Orléans Bridge, offers a panoramic view of Québec City and Lévis.

22 km (14 miles) St-Laurent

St-Laurent, 11 km (7 miles) from Ste-Pétronille, was founded in the late seventeenth century. The old mill is now an art center.

33 km (21 miles) St-Jean

St-Jean, 11 km (7 miles) from St-Laurent, has a church dating from 1732, historic houses and a lighthouse.

44 km (27 miles) St-François

At St-François, 11 km (7 miles) from St-Jean, is a campground and a view of île Madame, île aux Ruaux and Cap-Tourmente.

58 km (36 miles) Ste-Famille

At Ste-Famille, 14 km (9 miles) from St-François, the oldest parish on the island, the church dates from 1749.

71 km (44 miles) St-Pierre

At St-Pierre, 13 km (8 miles) from Ste-Famille, the church dates from 1717.

74 km (46 miles) île d'Orléans Bridge

From St-Pierre, ride 3 km (2 miles) to the île d'Orléans Bridge and recross over.

75 km (47 miles) Montmorency Falls

Take Highway 360 for approximately 1 km (0.6 mile) to Montmorency Falls, which drop 83 meters (272 feet).

96 km (60 miles) Ste-Anne-de-Beaupré

Continue for 21 km (13 miles) to Ste-Anne-de-Beaupré, where pilgrims have come since 1658. The current neo-romanesque basilica dates from 1923.

100 km (62 miles) Cap-Tourmente Wildlife Reserve

From Ste-Anne-de-Beaupré ride the 4 km (2.5 miles) to Beaupré and take Chemin du Cap-Tourmente for 15 km (9 miles) to the Cap-Tourmente Wildlife Reserve.

The reserve was created in 1969 to protect the natural habitat of snow geese, and 250 species of wild birds have been observed. Explore the reserve from its network of nature trails.

115 km (71 miles) Beaupré

Return to Beaupré.

Side trip: Beaupré to Grand Canyon of Ste-Anne Falls, 2 km (1.2 miles)

You can take Route 138 for 2 km (1.2 miles) east to the Grand Canyon of Ste-Anne Falls, which drop 74 meters (243 feet) in a gorge.

Also from Beaupré, you can ride 10 km (6 miles) on Route 360 to Mont-Ste-Anne Provincial Park, which has a 6.5 km (4 miles) cycling path, camping, hiking trails and a gondola to the 800-meter (2,625-foot) summit of Mont-Ste-Anne.

MONTRÉAL TO QUÉBEC ALONG THE ST. LAWRENCE RIVER

Length: 260 km (162 miles)
Time: Two to three days
Rating: Easy
Terrain: Mostly flat
Roads: Unpaved shoulders
Traffic: Heavy on Highway 132 leaving Montréal, lighter traffic until you reach Québec City.
Connnects with: The Québec to Mont-Joli tour, which links with the Gaspé tour
Start: Montréal, served by VIA Rail and numerous airlines.
Overview: This tour is one of the province's most popular cycling tours. Called "Route of the Pioneers," the road along the Saint Lawrence River is one of Québec's first roads. It takes you through villages founded in the seventeenth century, farms that were feudal seigneuries of colonial New France and past many scenic and historic sites.

THE ROUTE:
0 km (0 miles) Montréal

Leave Montréal by the sidewalk, as bikes are prohibited on the roadway of the Jacques Cartier Bridge. Cross the bridge and head towards rue St-Charles

north into the city of Longueuil. It's also possible to transport your bike via the Metro to the Longueuil station (for information, call the Montréal Urban Community Transit Commission (514)-288-6287) or on the South Shore Transit Commission buses (call the South Shore Transit Commission (514)-463-0131).

Ride on Rue St-Charles north through Longueuil, passing the historic buildings of Vieux Longueuil. Rue St-Charles links with Boulevard Marie-Victorin.

Continue on Boulevard Marie-Victorin through Boucherville, founded in 1668 and one of Québec's oldest towns. Along the route is Maison Louis Hippolyte Lafontaine, the residence of a former prime minister.

Just south of Varennes, Boulevard Marie-Victorin links with Highway 132. Varennes is a farming community with many historic homes and religious buildings.

Continue on Highway 132

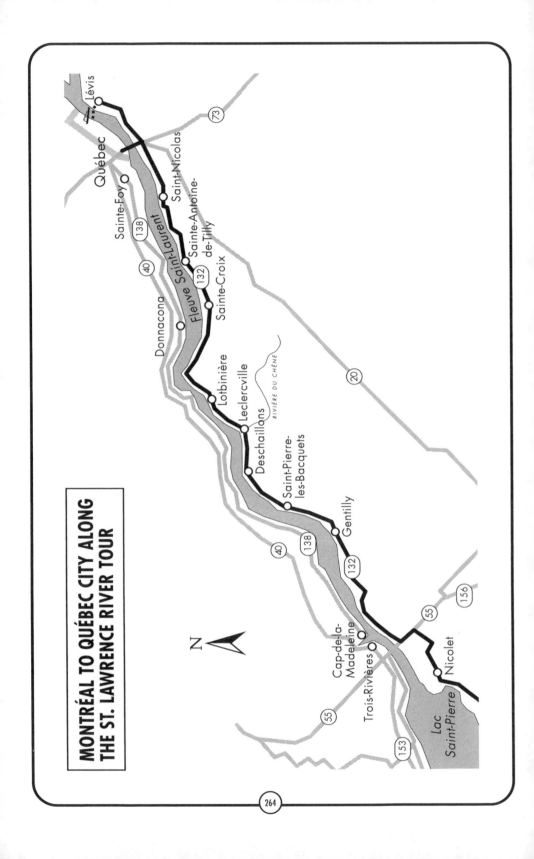

MONTRÉAL TO QUÉBEC CITY ALONG
THE ST. LAWRENCE RIVER TOUR

Lévis

73

Québec

Saint-Nicolas

Sainte-Foy

138

Sainte-Antoine-
de-Tilly

132

40

Sainte-Croix

Fleuve Saint-Laurent

Donnacona

Lotbinière

Leclercville

Deschaillons

RIVIÈRE DU CHÊNE

20

Saint-Pierre-
les-Bacquets

Gentilly

138

40

132

156

55

N

Cap-de-la-
Madeleine

Nicolet

Trois-Rivières

55

153

Lac
Saint-Pierre

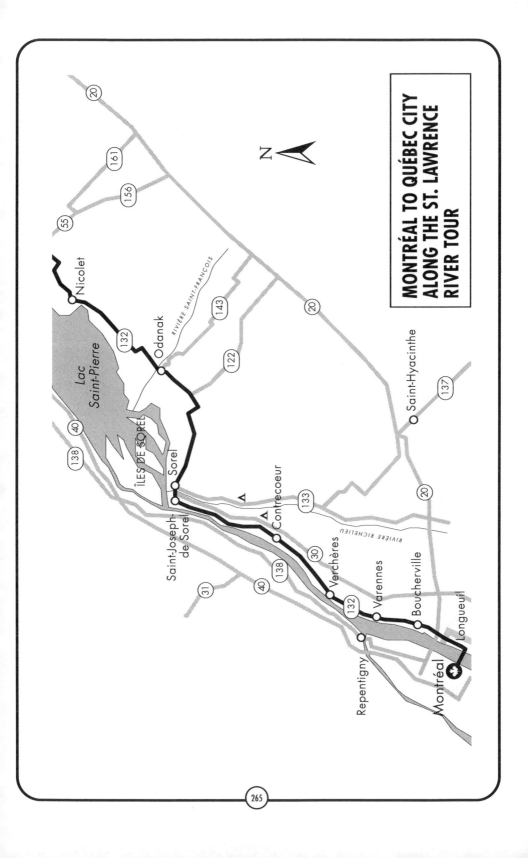

MONTRÉAL TO QUÉBEC CITY ALONG THE ST. LAWRENCE RIVER TOUR

N

Lac Saint-Pierre

ÎLES DE SOREL

RIVIÈRE SAINT-FRANÇOIS

RIVIÈRE RICHELIEU

Nicolet

Odanak

Sorel

Saint-Joseph-de-Sorel

Contrecoeur

Verchères

Varennes

Boucherville

Longueuil

Repentigny

Montréal

Saint-Hyacinthe

20

161

156

55

132

143

122

40

138

133

20

30

138

31

40

132

137

20

along the shores of the St. Lawrence River and go through Verchères, a former seigniory located where Madeleine de Verchères fought the Iroquois in 1692.

60 km (37 miles) Sorel

Go through Contrecoeur and St-Joseph-de-Sorel, and cross the Richelieu River to the port and shipbuilding city of Sorel. Founded in 1642, Sorel is Canada's fourth oldest city.

90 km (56 miles) Odanak

At Odanak, 30 km (18 miles) farther along is a Native reserve with a museum.

118 km (73 miles) Nicolet

Continue riding Highway 132 through Nicolet, 28 km (17 miles) from Odanak.

202 km (126 miles) Lotbinière

Stay on Highway 132, through Gentilly, St-Pierre-les-Becquets,
Deschaillons and Leclercville, which is on a plateau at the mouth of the Rivière du Chêne to Lotbinière, 84 km (52 miles) from Nicolet.

Lotbinière was founded in 1692, part of a seigneury granted in 1672.

260 km (162 miles) Québec City suburbs

Continue along the river for 58 km (36 miles) through Ste-Croix, St-Antoine-de-Tilly, St-Nicholas and into the suburbs of Québec City.

Option: Québec City via the Québec Bridge

You can cross the Saint Lawrence River and go into the city of Québec via the Québec bridge.

Option: Québec City via ferry from Lévis, 11 km (7 miles) (ferry crossing time: 15 minutes)

Or, continue along Highway 132 for 11 km (7 miles) to Lévis and take the ferry to Québec City.

QUÉBEC TO MONT-JOLI ALONG THE ST. LAWRENCE RIVER

Length: 321 km (199 miles); possible side trips riding ferries
Time: Two to four days
Rating: Intermediate
Terrain: Hilly
Roads: Unpaved shoulders
Traffic: Heavier as you leave Québec, a lot of tourist traffic on whole route during summer.
Connects with: This tour links the Montréal to Québec City tour and

the Gaspé Tour; St. John River Valley tour in New Brunswick.
Start: Québec City, reached by VIA Rail and several airlines.
Overview: Cycle Highway 132, "the Route of the Pioneers," through the farmland of the St. Lawrence Valley past many historic buildings open to visitors. The area has spectacular sunsets and magnificent panoramas of the St. Lawrence River. Most

of the islands in the river are bird sanctuaries. Whale watching is also possible. Highlights include St-Jean-Port-Joli, well known for its woodcarvers and artisans.

THE ROUTE:

0 km (0 miles) Québec City

Ferry: Québec City to Lévis (crossing time: 15 minutes)

From Québec City, take the ferry across the St. Lawrence River to Lévis. Lévis has many historical buildings including Pointe-Lévis Fort No. 1 National Historic Park.

Leave Lévis via Highway 132, and go through Beaumont where there is camping.

From Berthier-sur-Mer, popular for windsurfing and small sailboats, you can see the Montmagny archipelago of sixteen islands, islets and sandbanks.

54 km (33 miles) Montmagny

Ride Highway 132 to the town of Montmagny, 54 km (33 miles) from Lévis.

Side trip: Ferry from Montmagny to L'île-aux-Grues, (crossing time: 30 minutes)

On L'île-aux-Grues you may see thousands of seabirds and shorebirds.

Main tour continues from Montmagny

Leaving Montmagny, the first village you encounter is 300-year-old Cap-St-Ignace.

80 km (50 miles) St-Jean-Port-Joli

St-Jean-Port-Joli, 26 km (16 miles) farther, was founded in 1721 and is known as the woodcarving capital of Canada. You can see traditional Québec wood carvers, weavers, craftsmen, and artists at work and buy their works in the numerous handicraft shops.

Continue along the picturesque Highway 132 through Village-des-Aulnaies and La Pocatière, which has a scenic view of the river and many tourist facilities. Rivière-Ouelle has a beach.

At the village of St-Denis is the home of Jean-Charles Chapais, one of the Fathers of Confederation.

131 km (81 miles) Kamouraska

Kamouraska, 51 km (32 miles) from St-Jean-Port-Joli, reflects three centuries of Québec history. Kamouraska is an Algonquin word meaning "there are bullrushes at the water's edge." The area is known for its great beauty and magnificent views of the St. Lawrence River, and the mountains on the river's north shore.

Past St-André you have views of the Pèlerins Islands where a large number of seabirds nest.

Nôtre-Dame-du-Portage was named after the colonial road "Le Portage du Temiscouata," a portage used by the Natives and fur traders.

174 km (108 miles) Rivière-du-Loup

At the town of Rivière-du-Loup, 43 km (27 miles) from Kamouraska, the river cascades 30 meters (100 feet) into a natural basin carved in the rock. Rivière-du-Loup dates from

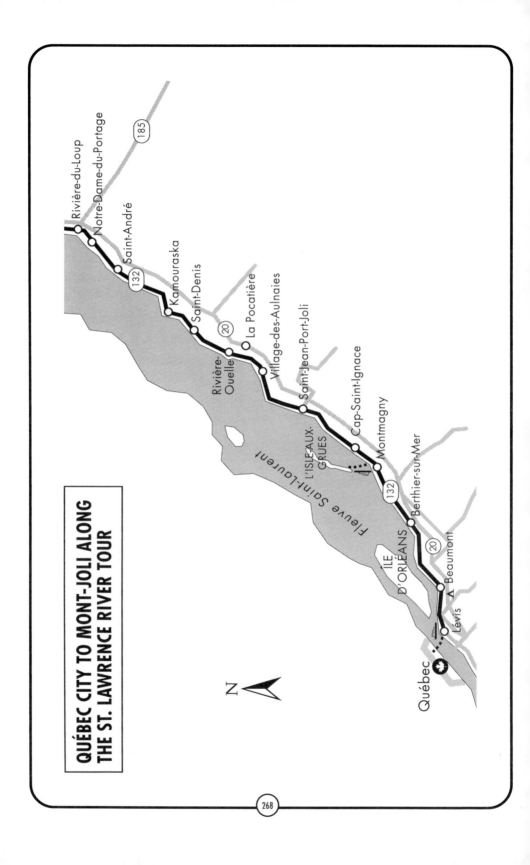

QUÉBEC CITY TO MONT-JOLI ALONG
THE ST. LAWRENCE RIVER TOUR

N

Québec

Lévis

Beaumont

20

ÎLE
D'ORLÉANS

Berthier-sur-Mer

132

Montmagny

L'ISLE-AUX-
GRUES

Cap-Saint-Ignace

Saint-Jean-Port-Joli

Village-des-Aulnaies

Fleuve Saint-Laurent

Rivière-
Ouelle

La Pocatière

20

Saint-Denis

Kamouraska

Saint-André

132

Notre-Dame-du-Portage

Rivière-du-Loup

185

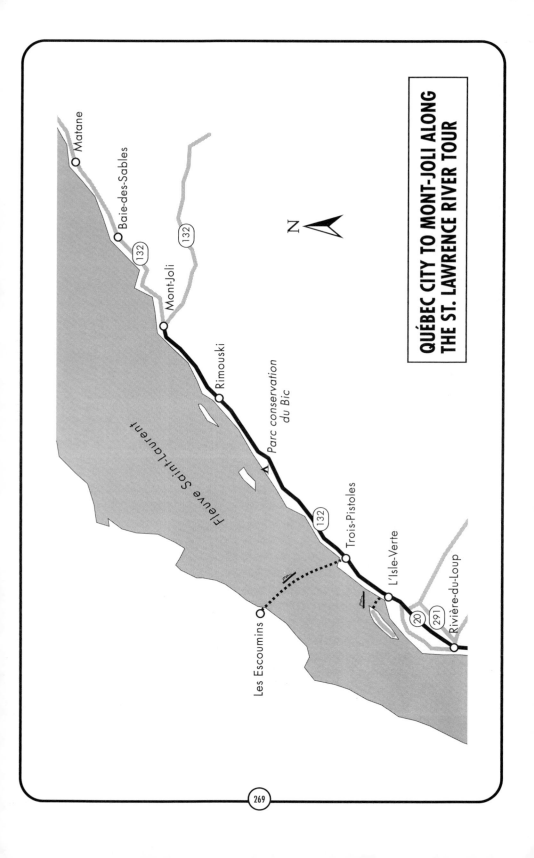

QUÉBEC CITY TO MONT-JOLI ALONG THE ST. LAWRENCE RIVER TOUR

N

Matane

Baie-des-Sables

132

Mont-Joli

132

Rimouski

Parc conservation du Bic

Fleuve Saint-Laurent

132

Trois-Pistoles

L'Isle-Verte

Les Escoumins

20

291

Rivière-du-Loup

1683. Here is the Museum of Bas-Saint-Laurent.

Option: Rivière-du-Loup to New Brunswick border, 100 km (60 miles)

If you're heading to New Brunswick, turn off Highway 132 at Rivière-du-Loup and take Highway 185—the Trans Canada Highway—for 100 km (62 miles) to the New Brunswick border.

Main tour continues from Rivière-du-Loup

Continuing along the St. Lawrence River shore from Rivière-du-Loup, avoid Highway 132 which has heavy traffic on this section, and take Route 291 to St-Arsène.

204 km (127 miles) Village of L'Isle-Verte

Then ride on the secondary road, along the Canadian National Railway line, back to Highway 132, and the farming village of l'Isle-Verte, 30 km (19 miles) from Rivière-du-Loup. At the bay is a bird sanctuary.

Option: Ferry from the village of l'Isle-Verte to île Verte, (crossing time: 15 minutes)

On the island of île Verte is the oldest lighthouse in Québec.

Main tour continues from village of l'Isle-Verte

As you travel farther east along Highway 132, the strip of farmland narrows and is cut by rocky ledges.

223 km (139 miles) Trois-Pistoles

In Trois-Pistoles, 19 km (12 miles) from l'Isle-Verte, are campgrounds, the Musée St-Laurent of antiques, the Maison du Notaire arts and crafts center. You can also take an excursion to île aux Basques, an important bird sanctuary with seagulls, eider-ducks, and blue herons.

Option: Whale watching on ferry from Trois-Pistoles to Les Escoumins, (crossing time: 1 hour, 15 minutes)

Trois-Pistoles has become known for whale-watching from the ferry boat, which cruises to Les Escoumins on the north shore of the St. Lawrence River.

Main tour continues from Trois-Pistoles

From Trois-Pistoles, ride along the coast. At Bic is a campground and hotels.

290 km (180 miles) Rimouski

Rimouski, 67 km (42 miles) from Trois-Pistoles, has a museum and a variety of accommodation including hotels, motels and campgrounds.

321 km (199 miles) Mont-Joli

Leaving Rimouski, continue on Highway 132 for 31 km (19 miles) to Mont-Joli where you can continue on the Gaspé tour (described in this chapter). There is camping at Ste-Flavie and at Mont-Joli.

More Information: For information and reservations for the ferry from Trois-Pistoles to Les Escoumins, call (418) 851-4676. Bas-St-Laurent Tourism Association, 189 rue Hôtel-de-Ville, Rivière-du-Loup, Québec G5R 3C4, telephone (418) 867-3015.

GASPÉ PENINSULA

Length: 903 km (561 miles) loop; plus a 39-km (24-mile) side trip; and a 15-km (9-mile) short-cut to save 33 km (21 miles)
Time: Six to ten days
Rating: Strenuous
Terrain: Mountainous, many climbs and descents. The route can be windy.
Roads: Mostly unpaved shoulders
Traffic: A lot of tourist traffic during summer
Connects with: Northeast Coast tour in New Brunswick
Start: Mont-Joli, served by VIA Rail which also serves the southern coast of the Gaspé Peninsula to the town of Gaspé.
Overview: Mountains plunging to the sea, panoramic ocean views and unspoiled fishing villages make the Gaspé coast one of Québec's most visited areas and a challenging, exciting bicycle tour.

Magnificent Percé Rock, L'île Bonaventure—once a pirate hideout and now one of the world's largest bird sanctuaries—spectacular Forillon and Gaspésie parks are some of the Gaspé's best-known highlights. In 1534 at the site of the town of Gaspé, Jacques Cartier first stepped shore in North America.

This tour has four parts. From Mont-Joli to Madeleine-Centre, 255 km (158 miles) along the Gulf of St. Lawrence, is the coast section. The road squeezes between the cliffs and the water in many places. At each river mouth is a cove protecting a coastal fishing village. In Gaspésie Provincial Park are the highest mountains in southern Québec.

The Land's End area at the tip of the peninsula stretches 282 km (175 miles) from Madeleine-Centre to Newport. The most popular part of the Gaspé, Land's End, encompasses Forillon National Park, the village of Gaspé and Percé Rock.

After rounding the tip of the Gaspé Peninsula, you reach the Baie des Chaleurs, named by Jacques Cartier during the hot days of July 1534. Here are red cliffs and sandbars. You can swim, sail and windsurf in the water. The villages along the 226 km (140 miles) from Newport to Matapédia were settled by Acadian refugees in 1755. Two villages were settled by United Empire Loyalists.

The last part of the tour goes inland for 149 km (92 miles) along the Matapédia River, known for its salmon fishing. You pass through the valley's farming and forestry villages to your starting point at Mont-Joli.

There are campgrounds and accommodation along its entire route. If you're going during high tourist season (mid-July to mid-August) and plan to stay in hotels or motels, make reservations in advance.

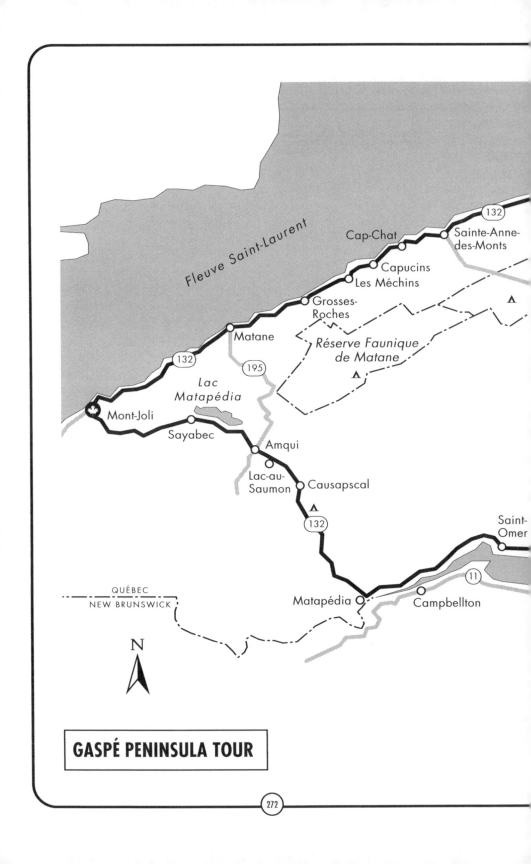

GASPÉ PENINSULA TOUR

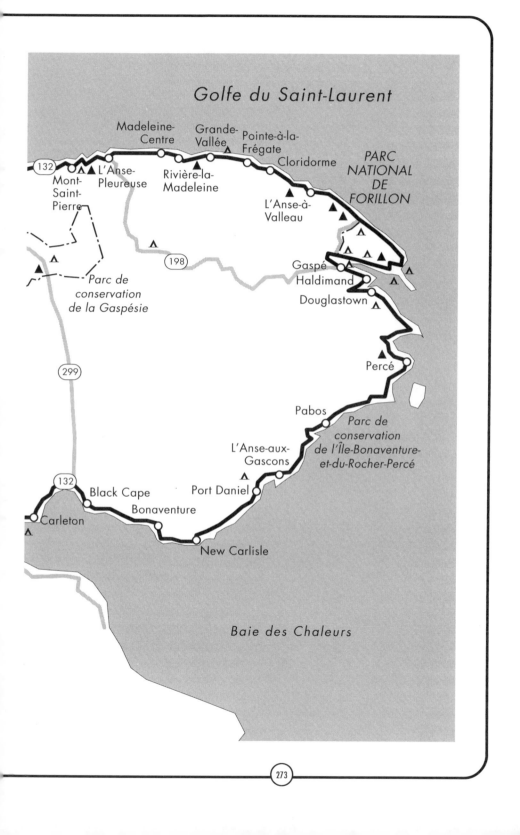

Golfe du Saint-Laurent

Madeleine-Centre

Grande-Vallée

Pointe-à-la-Frégate

Cloridorme

PARC NATIONAL DE FORILLON

L'Anse-Pleureuse

Rivière-la-Madeleine

Mont-Saint-Pierre

132

L'Anse-à-Valleau

Gaspé

Haldimand

Douglastown

Parc de conservation de la Gaspésie

198

Percé

299

Pabos

Parc de conservation de l'Île-Bonaventure-et-du-Rocher-Percé

L'Anse-aux-Gascons

132

Black Cape

Port Daniel

Bonaventure

Carleton

New Carlisle

Baie des Chaleurs

THE ROUTE:

0 km (0 miles) Mont-Joli

This tour follows Highway 132 for almost its entire route.

70 km (43 miles) Matane

From Mont-Joli, overlooking the St. Lawrence River, ride along the shore for 70 km (43 miles) to Matane, which is known for its shrimp and salmon. The name comes from a Micmac word meaning "beaver breeding ground."

Leaving Matane, the route is more hilly. At Grosses-Roches there are imposing lone rocks rising up out of the water.

117 km (73 miles) Les Méchins

The fishing village of Les Méchins, where each street is named after a fisherman's boat, is 47 km (29 miles) from Matane.

158 km (98 miles) Ste-Anne-des-Monts

At Capucins and Cap-Chat are beaches. The name Cap-Chat comes from a rock resembling a crouching cat, near the lighthouse, 2 km (1.2 miles) west of the village. Near Cap-Chat you can see the peaks of the Chic-Chocs Mountains.

Keep riding to Ste-Anne-des-Monts, 41 km (25 miles) from Les Méchins.

Side trip: Ste-Anne-des-Monts to Gaspésie Provincial Park, 39 km (24 miles) each way

You can take a side trip inland via Highway 299 to scenic Gaspésie Provincial Park, 39 km (24 miles) away.

Gaspésie Park's Chic-Chocs Mountains reach 1,270 meters (4,166 feet). Part of the Appalachian Mountain chain, the Chic-Chocs are the highest mountains in southern Québec. Moose, wood caribou and Virginia deer inhabit the forest. The park offers hiking trails, fishing and canoeing, as well as campgrounds and an inn.

Main tour continues from Ste-Anne-des-Monts

215 km (134 miles) Mont-St-Pierre

Back on Highway 132, ride to Mont-St-Pierre, 57 km (35 miles) from Ste-Anne-des-Monts. The route is steep at first, and skirts picturesque bays.

Mont-St-Pierre is the glider capital of eastern Canada. You can ride on the road to the top of the 430-meter (1,410-foot) mountain, which has a panoramic view and glider launching pads.

250 km (155 miles) Madeleine-Centre

Much of the 35 km (22 miles) from Mont-St-Pierre to Madeleine-Centre is flat with paved shoulders and meanders beside the cliffs.

L'Anse-Pleureuse, meaning "Crying Cove," is named for the cries of shipwrecked ghosts.

273 km (170 miles) Grande-Vallée

Ride to Rivière-la-Madeleine, you will find camping and hotels. At the mouth of Rivière Madeleine is a 1,300-meter (4,265-foot) long sand spit.

From Rivière-la-Madeleine the road climbs over a 2-km (1.2-miles) stretch. This is followed by a series of descents and climbs.

Continue on Highway 132 and descend along almost 3 km (1.8 miles) to Grande-Vallée, 23 km (14 miles) from Madeleine-Centre. As its name implies, Grande-Vallée is situated in a wide valley. In the village is the covered Galipean Bridge.

288 km (174 miles) Pointe-à-la-Frégate

From Grande-Vallée, ride 15 km (9 miles) along the bluffs and through rolling hills to Pointe-à-la-Frégate, where there is camping.

320 km (199 miles) L'Anse-à-Valleau

From Pointe-à-la-Frégate, Highway 132 climbs steeply and goes along the bluff with good views of the Gulf of Saint Lawrence. The road then descends over 3 km (1.8 miles) to the fishing village of Cloridorme.

From Cloridorme to L'Anse-à-Valleau are several climbs and descents, and flat stretches along the bluffs and lakeshore. The route then turns inland through rolling hills.

L'Anse-à-Valleau, 34 km (21 miles) from Pointe-à-la-Frégate, has hotels and campgrounds.

336 km (209 miles) Entrance of Forillon National Park

From l'Anse-à-Valleau, it's 16 km (10 miles) of steep climbs and descents to the entrance of Forillon National Park. There are many good views of the ocean.

Forillon Park is at the eastern end of the Gaspé Peninsula, sep-arating the Gulf of St. Lawrence and Gaspé Bay.

Covering 238 square km (92 square miles) in area, Forillon Park's eastern coast is dominated by 180-meter (600-foot) limestone cliffs. The southern shore facing Gaspé Bay has pebble beaches and small coves interspersed by rocky headlands. The hills in the park's interior reach almost 540 meters (1,800 feet).

Harbor seals and several species of whales can be seen in the waters near the park. The network of over 55 km (34 miles) of trails follows the valleys and highland routes through the park's interior.

Side trip: Highway 197 across the tip of the Gaspé Peninsula, 15 km (9 miles)

If you don't want to tour Highway 132 through Forillon Park you can take Highway 197 across the peninsula and save approximately 33 km (21 miles).

Main tour continues through Forillon Park

409 km (254 miles) Village of Gaspé

From the park entrance, ride 73 km (45 miles) along hilly Highway 132 through Forillon Park and on to the village of Gaspé. The village is situated on a headland overlooking a spectacular bay that provides an immense natural harbor into which three salmon rivers flow. The name Gaspé comes from a Micmac word meaning "land's end."

433 km (269 miles) Douglastown

South of the village of Gaspé, are the beaches at Sandy Beach and Haldimand, popular for wind surfing. Continue to Douglastown, a small Loyalist stronghold with a scenic sandbar, 24 km (15 miles) from Gaspé.

483 km (300 miles) Percé

Another 50 km (31 miles) brings you to Percé, which is dominated by Percé Rock: the Gaspé's most famous attraction for tourists and artists.

You can walk to Percé Rock at low tide or go by boat at other times. Do take the boat to L'île-Bonaventure bird sanctuary with its thousands of gannets and seagulls. At Percé, there is an art center and a theater.

523 km (325 miles) Pabos

Leaving Percé you ride on the southern side of the Gaspé Peninsula, and the terrain is less hilly.

At Pabos, 40 km (25 miles) away, is a beach and camping.

564 km (350 miles) Port-Daniel

Continuing on Highway 132, you pass through many small villages. In L'Anse-aux-Gascons is a white sand beach. Craftsmen make little wooden boats, which they sell at roadside stands.

Port-Daniel, 41 km (25 miles) from Pabos, is at the end of a deep bay and has a sandy beach. Tuna fishing, unusual in the Gaspé, is carried on here.

600 km (373 miles) New Carlisle

From Port-Daniel to the old Loyalist village of New Carlisle is 36 km (22 miles) of relatively flat terrain.

645 km (401 miles) Black Cape

From New Carlisle to Black Cape, 45 km (28 miles) away, the road follows the coast of the Baie des Chaleurs.

Bonaventure, 15 km (9 miles) from New Carlisle, is an Acadian farming center. Many Acadian refugees settled here in 1755.

687 km (427 miles) St-Omer

Cycling from Black Cape to St-Omer you have a view of the coast of New Brunswick. Along the way you pass through several villages including Carleton, which was founded in 1756 by Acadian refugees.

St-Omer offers good bird-watching and clam-digging, as well as hotels and campgrounds.

750 km (466 miles) Matapédia

From St-Omer it's 65 km (40 miles) to Matapédia, at the head of the Baie des Chaleurs and the New Brunswick border.

Option: Northeast Coast tour in New Brunswick

Here you connect with the Northeast Coast Tour in New Brunswick (described in the New Brunswick chapter).

Main tour continues from Matapédia

From Matapédia, the Gaspé loop tour goes inland on Highway 132 through the valley of the Matapédia River.

829 km (515 miles) Amqui

You pass through Causapscal and Amqui, 77 km (48 miles) from Matapédia.

854 km (530 miles) Sayabec

Go along Lac Matapédia to Sayabec, a farming and forestry village at the head of Lac Matapédia, 25 km (15 miles) from Amqui.

903 km (561 miles) Mont-Joli

From Sayabec you continue through an agricultural area for 49 km (30 miles) to Mont-Joli, this tour's starting point.

More Information: Gaspésie Provincial Park, P.O. Box 550, 10 Ste-Anne Blvd., Ste-Anne-des-Monts, Québec G0E 2G0, telephone (418) 763-3301. Forillon National Park, P.O. Box 1220, Gaspé, Québec G0C 1R0, telephone (418) 368-5505. Gaspé Tourism Association, 357 Route de la Mer, Ste-Flavie, Québec G0J 2L0, telephone (418) 775-2223.

ÎLES-DE-LA-MADELEINE

Length: 60 km (37 miles) each way north of Cap-aux-Meules; 25 km (16 miles) each way south of Cap-aux-Meules

Time: One day

Rating: Easy

Terrain: Along flat sandy beaches

Roads: No shoulders

Traffic: Light

Start: Cap-aux-Meules is reached by the ferry M.V. *Lucy Maud Montgomery*, which operates every day except Tuesdays from Souris, Prince Edward Island (cruising time 5 hours), and by the weekly *CTMA Voyageur* ferry from Montréal (cruising time 48 hours). The îles-de-la-Madeleine are also accessible by air.

Overview: An archipelago of islands in the center of the Gulf of St. Lawrence, the îles-de-la-Madeleine (also called the Magdalen Islands) have fine, white sandy beaches washed by warm gulfstream water. They are also noted for their green rolling hills, red cliffs, sand dunes, blue ocean and hillsides of dense, stunted forest.

The islands are 290 km (180 miles) east of the Gaspé, 120 km (75 miles) north of Prince Edward Island and 100 km (60 miles) off the coast of Cape Breton.

The ocean has carved the cliffs, forming magnificent caves which you can explore on foot at low tide at Dune-du-Sud, or by boat at Gros-Cap. You can also see how the constant wind has slowed the growth of trees and transformed the sand dunes.

Over the centuries the islands have been responsible for countless shipwrecks and many of the shipwrecked mariners settled here. In the fishing villages you can meet their

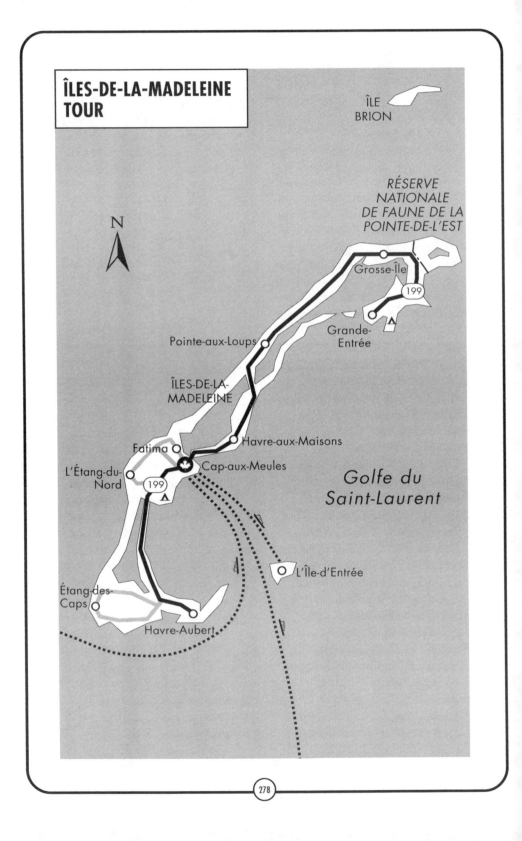

ÎLES-DE-LA-MADELEINE
TOUR

ÎLE
BRION

RÉSERVE
NATIONALE
DE FAUNE DE LA
POINTE-DE-L'EST

N

Grosse-Île

199

Pointe-aux-Loups

Grande-
Entrée

ÎLES-DE-LA-
MADELEINE

Fatima

Havre-aux-Maisons

L'Étang-du-
Nord

Cap-aux-Meules

Golfe du
Saint-Laurent

199

L'Île-d'Entrée

Étang-des-
Caps

Havre-Aubert

descendants and see lighthouses, boats and seabirds. There is also fishing and diving.

During the summer months the water temperatures reach 17 degree Celsius (62 degrees Fahrenheit), which is pleasant for swimming. The islands have a maritime climate with cooler temperatures in summer and milder temperatures in winter. The cycling season begins in June and ends in mid-September. The islands experience a lot of wind. Try to do your bicycling touring on days when the wind is not strong so you won't have to deal with blowing sand.

Camping is not permitted on the beaches. Four campgrounds, as well as motels and inns, are available. Since the Magdalen Islands are small, it's easier to stay at one accommodation and explore the islands on day tours.

THE ROUTE:

0 km (0 miles) Cap-aux-Meules

Highway 199 is the main road connecting the islands. The ferry takes you to Cap-aux-Meules near the mid-point of the islands. Here you can see a diversity of ocean vessels, sailboats and fishing boats.

Going east from Cap-aux-Meules

8 km (5 miles) île du Havre-aux-Maisons

Ride east on Highway 199 from Cap-aux-Meules to île du Havre-aux-Maisons, a charming rural village.

At Dune-du-Sud, a roadside rest area leads to the beach, bordered by magnificent cliffs and caves sculpted by the sea. You can explore them at low tide.

46 km (29 miles) Grosse-île

Continuing on Highway 199, go through Grosse-île, a fishing community of Scottish descent. Here are miles of beautiful deserted beaches.

Nearby, at Pointe-de-l'Est Reserve, you can see native flora and wildlife.

60 km (37 miles) île de la Grande-Entrée

Île de la Grande-Entrée is a lobster fishing port.

Going west from 0 km (0 miles) Cap-aux-Meules

25 km (15 miles) île du Havre-Aubert

Ride west from Cap-aux-Meules along Highway 199 to île du Havre-Aubert, the oldest of the villages on the islands. Near the marine museum are boutiques and restaurants.

More Information: The M.V. *Lucy Maud Montgomery* ferry is operated by CTMA, P.O. Box 245, Cap-aux-Meules, Magdalen Islands, Québec G0B 1B0, telephone in Cap-aux-Meules (418) 986-3278; in Souris (902) 687-2181.

For reservations for the *CTMA Voyageur*, contact Inter-Voyage Agency, 1253 McGill College Street, Montréal, Québec H3B 2Y5, telephone (514) 866-1944; in Cap-aux-Meules (418) 986-4224.

Îles-de-la-Madeleine Tourism Association, Box 1028, Cap-aux-Meules, îles-de-la-Madeleine, Québec G0B 1B0, telephone (418) 986-2245.

ACROSS QUÉBEC

Length: 534 km (332 miles)
Time: Four to six days
Rating: Intermediate
Terrain: Flat and hilly
Roads: Unpaved shoulders
Traffic: Heavier near Montréal and Québec, tourist traffic during summer
Connects with: Across Ontario and Across New Brunswick tours
Start: Montréal
Overview: If you're traveling across Québec, you can link several of the tours in this chapter.

THE ROUTE:
0 km (0 miles)
260 km (162 miles) Québec
  Ride the Montréal to Québec City tour.
434 km (270 miles) Rivière-du-Loup
  Then follow the Québec City to Mont-Joli tour for 174 km (108 miles) to Rivière-du-Loup.
534 km (332 miles) New Brunswick border
  From Rivière-du-Loup, take Highway 185—the Trans Canada Highway—east for 100 km (60 miles) to New Brunswick.

GUIDEBOOKS

Cycling the Islands: P.E.I. and The Magdalen Islands, by Campbell Webster. Available from: Breakwater Books, 100 Water Street, P.O. Box 2188, St. John's, Newfoundland A1C 6E6, telephone (709) 722-6680; $9.95.

Eastern Townships Touring Guide. Available from: Vélo Québec, 3575 Boulevard St. Laurent, Bureau 310, Montréal, Québec H1V 3R2, telephone (514) 847-VELO; $12.79.

Great Montréal Bicycling, and in French as *Montréal et les alentours à velo*, by Elliott Katz. Available from: Great North Books, 60 Bayhampton Crescent, Thornhill, Ontario L4J 7G9; $7.95.

Pédaler Montréal (in French). Available from: Vélo Québec; $6.37.

Québec à Vélo map (in French). Available from: Vélo Québec; $4.57.

25 Randonnées à Vélo au Québec (in French). Available from: Vélo Québec; $18.14.

Répertoire des sentiers de vélo de montagne (in French). Available from: Vélo Québec; $18.14.

Hopewell Cape Rocks
(Tourism New Brunswick)

New Brunswick

Fishing villages, the world's highest tides, charming historic towns, sand dunes and beaches are just some of the attractions of New Brunswick, the gateway to Atlantic Canada.

New Brunswick's variety of bicycling opportunities are not as well known outside the province as those of neighboring Nova Scotia and Prince Edward Island, but are well worth exploring.

Tourist Information: General tourism information, including an accommodation guide listing campgrounds, bed-and-breakfasts, motels and hotels, a provincial road map and several bicycle tour maps are available from Tourism New Brunswick, P.O. Box 12345, Fredericton, New Brunswick E3B 5C3, or call toll-free from Canada and the United States 1-800-561-0123; from New Brunswick 1-800-442-4442.

Roads: Most main routes have paved shoulders.

Weather: The interior of New Brunswick has a continental climate of hot summers. The coast has more temperate weather due to the moderating influence of the ocean. Average summer temperatures range from 13 to 26 degrees Celsius (55 to 78 degrees Fahrenheit) at Fredericton in the interior, and from 12 to 21 degrees Celsius (54 to 70 degrees Fahrenheit) at Saint John on the Bay of Fundy.

Hostels: For a list of hostels in New Brunswick, write to the Canadian Hostelling Association/New Brunswick Region, 150 Leeds Drive, Fredericton, New Brunswick E3B 4S8, telephone (506) 454-9950.

Trains: For information on VIA Rail service, call in Moncton (506) 857-9830; in Saint John (506) 642-2916; elsewhere in New Brunswick call toll-free 1-800-561-3952.

Airports: The main centers in New Brunswick are Moncton, Fredericton and Saint John. All are served by major airlines.

Bicycling: For information on cycling clubs, contact: Velo New Brunswick, Sports Branch, P.O. Box 6000, Marysville Place, 20 McGloin Street, Fredericton, New Brunswick E3B 5H1, telephone (506) 453-2928.

Area: At 73,437 square km (28,354 square miles), New Brunswick is the largest of the three Maritime provinces (the other two are Nova Scotia and Prince Edward Island).

Terrain: New Brunswick has 2,250 km (1,400 miles) of coastline and is surrounded on three sides by water. Over 85 per cent of the province is covered by forests and a vast array of rivers, lakes and streams. The province's highest point is Mount Carleton, which is 820 meters (2,690 feet) high; the lowest is sea level along the northern and eastern coasts.

Population: Of New Brunswick's population of 723,900 (1991 census), almost 34 per cent are French speaking. Of the remaining English speaking population, many are descendants from United Empire Loyalists who migrated northward following the American Revolution. New Brunswick is Canada's only officially bilingual (English and French) province.

Capital: Fredericton is New Brunswick's third-largest city after Saint John and Moncton.

History: New Brunswick was originally inhabited by Micmac and Malacite Natives. Pierre de Gua and Samuel de Champlain sailed into the Bay of Fundy in 1604 and claimed the territory for France. The Treaty of Utrecht of 1713 then ceded the land to Britain. From 1713 to 1784 New Brunswick and neighboring Nova Scotia were known as Acadia.

In 1784 the British divided the territory at the Chignecto Isthmus and created New Brunswick. In 1867, New Brunswick was one of the four original provinces that came together to found Canada. Today, the province's economy is based largely on the timber industry, agriculture and tourism.

FUNDY TIDAL COAST

Length: 228 km (142 miles)
Time: Three days
Rating: Moderate to challenging
Terrain: Hilly, twists
Roads: Highways 127 and 770 have good surfaces but no paved shoulders; caution is advised.
Traffic: Heavy traffic in summer
Connects with: Across New Brunswick, Grand Manan Island
Start: Fredericton, served by VIA Rail, buses and an airport
Overview: The highest tides in the world, seascapes, rugged shorelines and quiet coves are seen on this tour of the southern shore of New Brunswick along the Bay of Fundy. The communities in this area were largely settled by United Empire Loyalists following the American Revolution and many of their historic homes have been preserved.

THE ROUTE:

0 km (0 miles) Fredericton
140 km (88 miles) Saint John

From Fredericton take Highway 102 along the Saint John River to Saint John.

Canada's oldest incorporated city and New Brunswick's largest, Saint John has marked walking tours to help you ex-

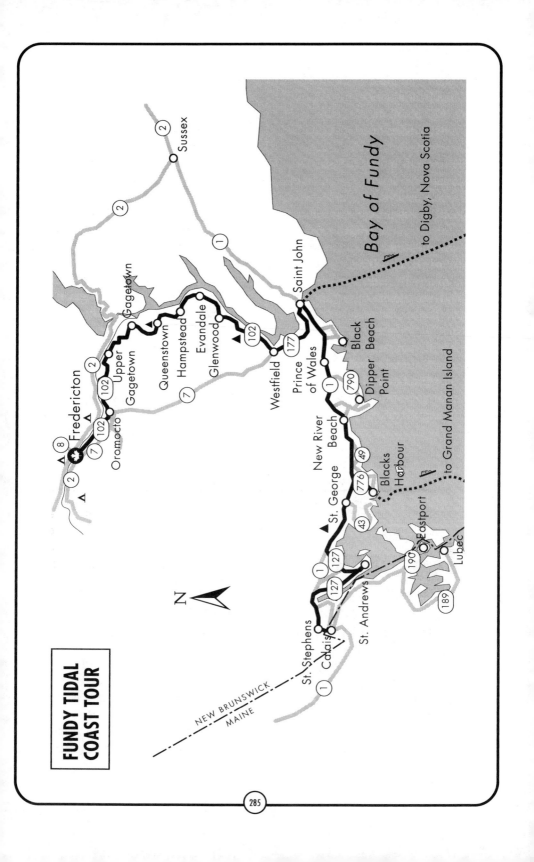

FUNDY TIDAL COAST TOUR

Sussex

Bay of Fundy

to Digby, Nova Scotia

Saint John

Gagetown

Evandale

Queenstown

Hampstead

Glenwood

Upper
Gagetown

Fredericton

Oromocto

Westfield

Prince
of Wales

Black
Dipper
Beach
Point

New River
Beach

Blacks
Harbour

to Grand Manan Island

St. George

Eastport

Lubec

St. Andrews

N

St. Stephens

Calais

NEW BRUNSWICK
MAINE

plore the city's restored historic areas. The city is also known for the Reversing Falls, which occur twice a day when the Bay of Fundy's high tides force the Saint John River to flow upriver. Rockwood Park, in the heart of Saint John, has a good viewpoint. The park also offers camping.

From Saint John take Highway 1 west along the Bay of Fundy coast. This road has a 0.3- to 0.6-meter (1- to 2-foot-) wide paved shoulder.

Option: Ferry to Grand Manan Island

Black's Harbour, situated just off Highway 1 on Route 776, is the ferry terminal for Grand Manan Island (a bicycle tour of the island is described in this chapter).

Main tour

Continue west on Highway 1. In Lake Utopia, near the town of St. George, a sea monster is said to live. Sighting over the past 100 years claim the monster has crawled inland.

199 km (124 miles) St. Andrews

Turn off Highway 1 onto Route 127 to St. Andrews, 96 km (60 miles) from Saint John. The route is very hilly in places but makes for great cycling as it visits many picturesque fishing villages.

St. Andrews is a popular resort town with a charming New England atmosphere. The town was founded in 1783 by United Empire Loyalists and many of the buildings date from that period. Whale-watching cruises are available from the St. Andrews wharf.

228 km (142 miles) St. Stephen

Take Route 127 back to Highway 1 and continue west to the town of St. Stephen, 29 km (18 miles) away. St. Stephen is a major entry point from Maine.

GRAND MANAN ISLAND

Length: 29 km (18 miles)
Time: Half-day of cycling; plan some time for hiking Grand Manan's trails
Rating: Moderate difficulty
Terrain: Rolling hills
Roads: Roads have gentle curves, no major grades
Traffic: Little
Connects with: Fundy Tidal Coast tour

Start: North Head, the terminal for the ferry from Blacks Harbour.
Overview: Grand Manan is the largest and most remote of the Bay of Fundy Isles situated off New Brunswick's southwest coast. The island is 35 km (22 miles) long and 10 km (6 miles) across at its widest point. Grand Manan's eastern side has several villages and long sandy beaches.

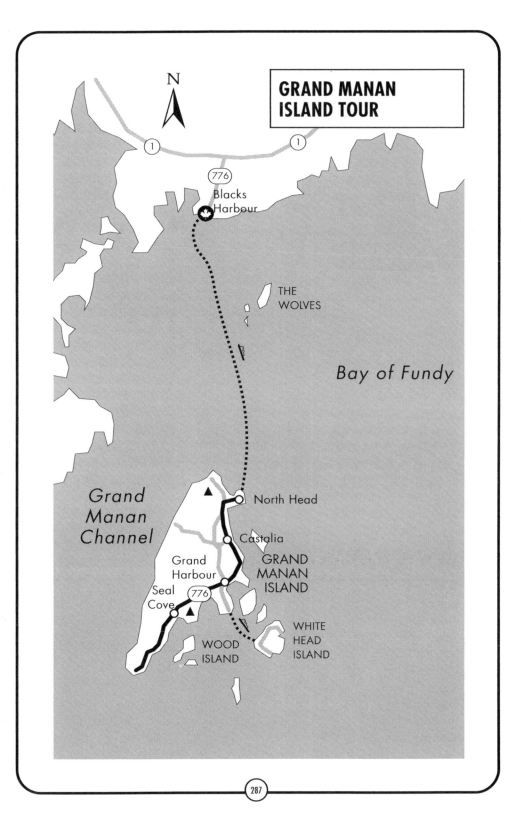

N

GRAND MANAN ISLAND TOUR

1

1

776

Blacks Harbour

THE WOLVES

Bay of Fundy

Grand Manan Channel

North Head

Castalia

Grand Harbour

GRAND MANAN ISLAND

Seal Cove

776

WHITE HEAD ISLAND

WOOD ISLAND

The uninhabited western side, where the edible dulse seaweed is harvested, is characterized by craggy 90-meter (300-feet) cliffs.

More than 275 species of birds have been sighted here and ornithologist James Audubon did many of his sketches here. There are nineteen nature trails along the shore and beach. Cruises to Machias Seal Island to see whales and birds are also popular.

THE ROUTE:

0 km (0 miles) North Head

Grand Manan Island has only one main road, which is 29 km (18 miles) long and runs along the sea for the entire length of the island. Along the way are quaint villages, country inns, lighthouses and magnificent seascapes. Off the main road are gravel roads into the island's interior.

22 km (14 miles) Seal Cove

Near Seal Cove is Anchorage Provincial Park and a bird sanctuary. A free ferry crosses a narrow channel to White Head Island.

More Information: Grand Manan Island ferry service is operated by Coastal Transportation Limited, Box 26, Saint John, New Brunswick E2L 3X1, (506) 657-3306. Anchorage Provincial Park, Seal Cove, Grand Manan Island, New Brunswick E0G 3B0, (506) 662-3215.

NORTHEAST NEW BRUNSWICK

Length: 428 km (265 miles)
Time: Four to five days
Rating: Easy and enjoyable
Terrain: Flat, Highway 134 hugs the coast as it goes through the villages and past beaches.
Roads: Highway 134 has alternating paved shoulders—paved on one side for a distance then paved on the other side. The newer Highway 11 has 0.6- to 1.2-meter- (2- to 4-foot-) wide shoulders, but narrower Route 134 has scenic views of the Baie des Chaleurs.
Traffic: Highway 134 is the old road that has been bypassed by Highway 11, which is a limited-access road. As a result Highway 134 has little through traffic.
Connects with: Gaspé Peninsula tour (described in Québec chapter), ferry to Prince Edward Island, Across Nova Scotia tour.
Start: Campbellton, located just east of Matapédia, Québec. Campbellton can be reached by VIA Rail.
Overview: New Brunswick's northeastern shores is a region of many rivers, beaches, sandbars and historic Acadian settlements. If you want to cross New Brunswick along the coast, this is the route, especially if you're coming into New Brunswick from the Gaspé Peninsula.

THE ROUTE:

0 km (0 miles) Campbellton

Campbellton is at the western tip of the Baie des Chaleurs near the mouth of the Matapédia and Restigouche rivers. Here is scenic Sugarloaf Provincial Park.

22 km (14 miles) Dalhousie

From Campbellton follow Route 134 along the coast through the communities for 22 km (14 miles) to Dalhousie.

Continue on Route 134 through Belledune. The route has scenic views of the Baie des Chaleurs.

114 km (70 miles) Bathurst

Route 134 takes you through the neighboring villages of Pointe-Verte, Petit-Rocher, Nigadoo and Beresford, to Bathurst, 92 km (57 miles) from Dalhousie.

131 km (81 miles) Janeville

From Bathurst, take Highway 134 for 17 km (10.5 miles) to Janeville. Just before Janeville, Highway 134 links with Highway 11.

177 km (110 miles) Caraquet

Ride Highway 11 northeast along the coast, passing through fishing villages like Grande-Anse to Caraquet, 46 km (28 miles) from Janeville. Highway 11 has a 15- to 30-cm- (6-inch to 1-foot-) wide paved shoulder. Between Grande-Anse and Caraquet is the Acadian Historical Village, telling the story of the early Acadian settlers in this region.

288 km (179 miles) Chatham

Just beyond Caraquet, Highway 11 turns south to Tracadie, Neguac and Chatham. From here, there are two routes to Kouchibouguac National Park. (The km/mileage log here took the shorter route.)

Option: Kouchibouguac National Park via Highway 11, 42 km (26 miles)

From Chatham, ride Highway 11 for 42 km (26 miles) through St. Margarets to the village of Kouchibouguac and the entrance to Kouchibouguac National Park.

Option: Kouchibouguac National Park via Route 117, 98 km (60 miles)

From Chatham, follow Route 117 around the coast and enter the park near Pointe-Sapin, 67 km (41 miles) from Chatham. From Pointe-Sapin it's 31 km (19 miles) through the park on Route 117 to the park entrance near the village of Kouchibouguac.

Main tour

330 km (205 miles) Kouchibouguac National Park

Situated on 26 km (16 miles) of the shore of the Northumberland Strait, 238-square-km (92-square-mile) Kouchibouguac Park has sand dunes formed by the sea and wind, secluded beaches, rivers, lagoons and a mixed forest. Kouchibouguac Park has a 25-km (15-mile) bicycle trail system with its own campsites.

351 km (218 miles) Rexton

After visiting Kouchibouguac

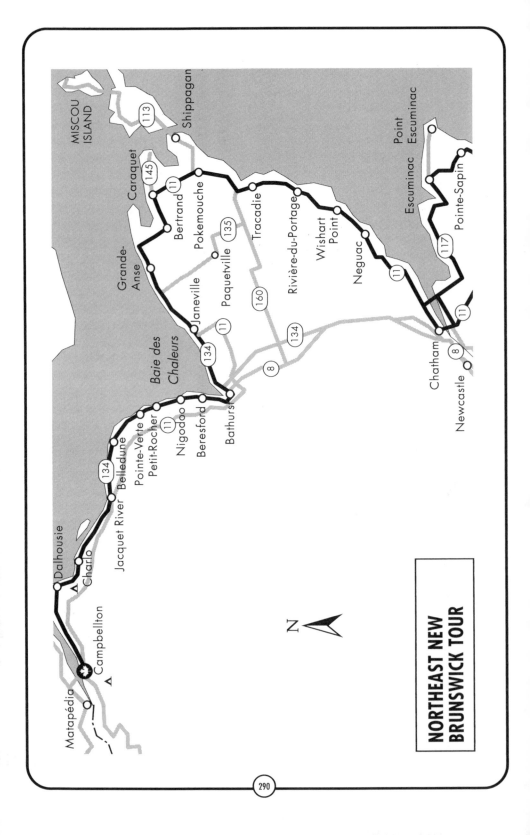

MISCOU
ISLAND

Shippagan

Point
Escuminac

(113)

(145)

Caraquet

Escuminac

Bertrand (11)

Pointe-Sapin

Pokemouche

Grande-
Anse

(135)

Tracadie

(117)

Janeville

Paquetville

(160)

Rivière-du-Portage

Wishart
Point

(11)

Neguac

(11)

Baie des
Chaleurs

(134)

(11)

(134)

Bathurst

(8)

Beresford

(11)

Chatham

Nigodoo

(8)

Petit-Rocher

Newcastle

Pointe-Verte

Belledune

(134)

Jacquet River

Dalhousie

Charlo

Campbellton

Matapédia

N

NORTHEAST NEW
BRUNSWICK TOUR

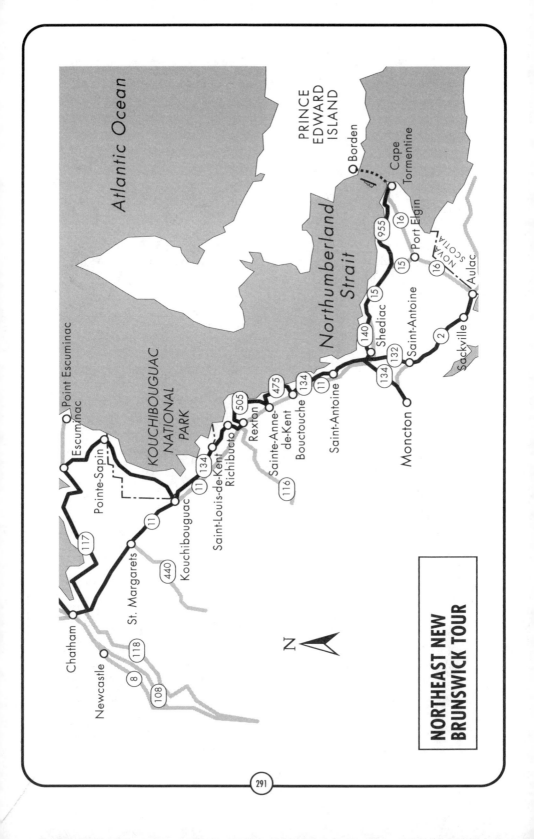

Atlantic Ocean

PRINCE EDWARD ISLAND

Borden

Cape Tormentine

Northumberland Strait

Point Escuminac

Escuminac

KOUCHIBOUGUAC NATIONAL PARK

Pointe-Sapin

955

16

Port Elgin

15

16

NOVA SCOTIA

Aulac

15

Shediac

Saint-Antoine

2

Sackville

140

132

134

Moncton

475

134

Bouctouche

11

505

Sainte-Anne-de-Kent

Saint-Antoine

Rexton

Richibucto

134

Saint-Louis-de-Kent

116

11

Kouchibouguac

11

440

St. Margarets

117

Chatham

118

Newcastle

8

108

N

NORTHEAST NEW BRUNSWICK TOUR

Park, ride Route 117 to the junction with Route 134. Go south on Route 134 for 21 km (13 miles) to Rexton.

395 km (245 miles) Boutouche

From Rexton follow the picturesque coastline along Route 505 and then Route 475 for 44 km (27 miles) to Boutouche.

428 km (265 miles) Shediac

From Boutouche, ride Highway 134 for 33 km (20 miles) to Shediac. (If you're in a hurry you can take the Highway 11 bypass route, which has 0.6- to 1.2-meter- (2- to 4-foot-) wide shoulders from Rexton to Shediac.)

Option: Shediac to Moncton, 20 km (12 miles)

From Shediac, if you want to go to Moncton take Route 134 for 20 km (12 miles).

Option: Shediac to Prince Edward Island ferry, 74 km (46 miles)

If you want to head to the ferry for Prince Edward Island, take Route 140 for 17 km (10.5 miles) to Highway 15, which has a wide shoulder. Ride Highway 15 for 25 km (15.5 miles) to Route 955 and take Route 955 for 32 km (16 miles) to the Cape Tormentine ferry terminal.

Option: Shediac to Nova Scotia, 55 km (34 miles)

Take Route 132 south for 13 km (8 miles) to Highway 2 (the Trans Canada Highway) and continue east for 42 km (26 miles) to the Nova Scotia border.

More Information: Kouchibouguac National Park, Kent County, Kouchibouguac, New Brunswick E0A 2A0, (506) 876-2443.

ACROSS NEW BRUNSWICK: ST. JOHN RIVER VALLEY AND SOUTHEAST SHORES

Length: 538 km (334 miles)

Time: Six to eight days

Rating: Moderate to challenging

Terrain: Flat and then hilly

Roads: Highways 105 and 114 don't have a shoulder; caution is advised. The Trans Canada Highway through New Brunswick has a 0.6- to 1.2-meter- (2- to 4-foot-) wide paved shoulder.

Traffic: Highway 105 has light traffic; the Trans Canada Highway has heavier traffic.

Connects with: Across Québec tour, Across Nova Scotia tour, Across Prince Edward Island Tour.

Start: The Trans Canada Highway at the Québec–New Brunswick border.

Overview: Known as "the Rhine of North America," the picturesque Saint John River Valley is the first part of this tour across New Brunswick. Along the river's course, through highlands and rolling farmlands, is the magnificent cataract at Grand Falls and the famous Reversing Falls.

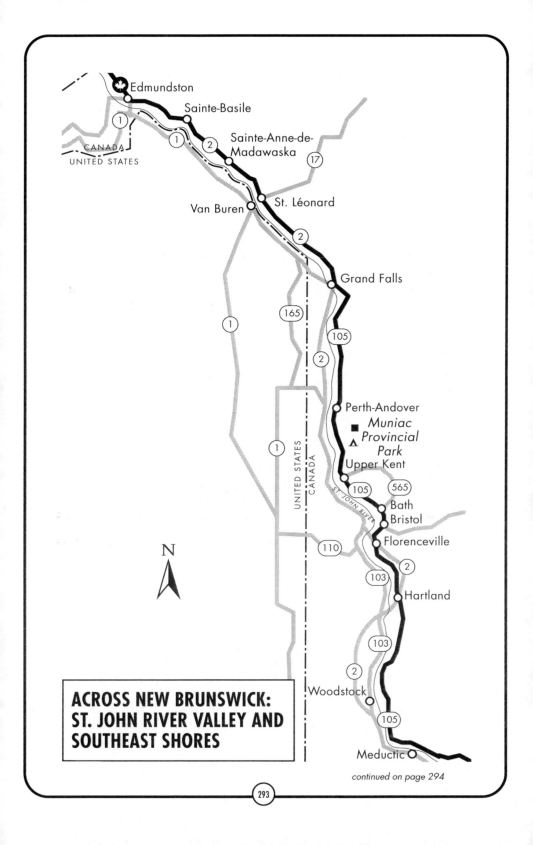

N

**ACROSS NEW BRUNSWICK:
ST. JOHN RIVER VALLEY AND
SOUTHEAST SHORES**

Edmundston
Sainte-Basile
Sainte-Anne-de-Madawaska
St. Léonard
Van Buren
Grand Falls
Perth-Andover
Muniac Provincial Park
Upper Kent
Bath
Bristol
Florenceville
Hartland
Woodstock
Meductic

CANADA
UNITED STATES

UNITED STATES
CANADA

ST. JOHN RIVER

continued on page 294

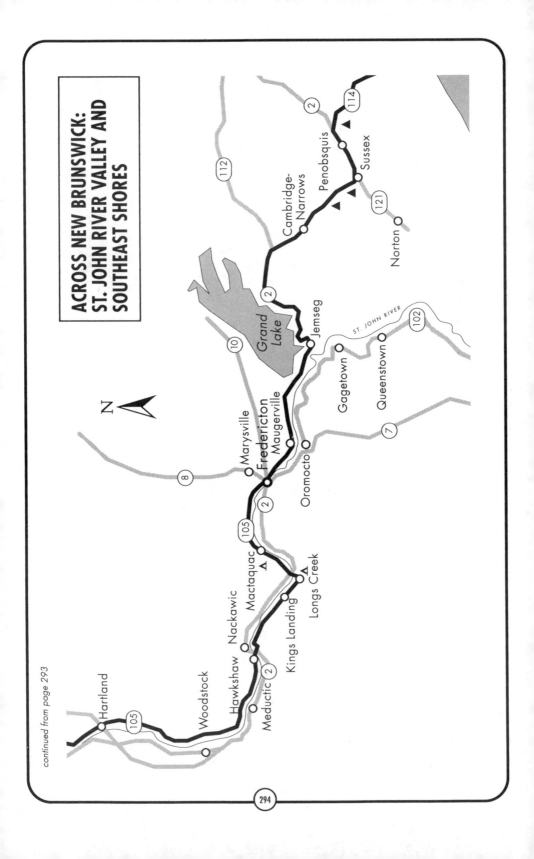

ACROSS NEW BRUNSWICK:
ST. JOHN RIVER VALLEY AND
SOUTHEAST SHORES

continued from page 293

N

ST. JOHN RIVER

Hartland
Woodstock
Hawkshaw
Nackawic
Meductic
Kings Landing
Mactaquac
Longs Creek
Marysville
Fredericton
Maugerville
Oromocto
Gagetown
Queenstown
Jemseg
Grand Lake
Cambridge-Narrows
Penobsquis
Sussex
Norton

105
2
8
105
2
10
112
2
114
121
7
102

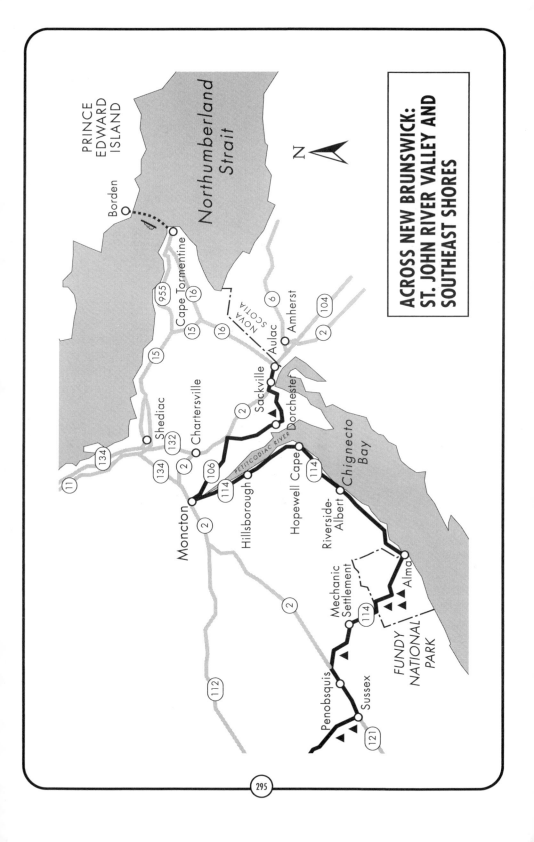

ACROSS NEW BRUNSWICK:
ST. JOHN RIVER VALLEY AND
SOUTHEAST SHORES

PRINCE
EDWARD
ISLAND

Northumberland Strait

N

Borden

Cape Tormentine

955

16

15

16

NOVA SCOTIA

Amherst

104

6

2

Aulac

15

Shediac

134

132

Chartersville

2

Sackville

Dorchester

2

106

114

PETITCODIAC RIVER

Chignecto Bay

Hopewell Cape

114

134

11

Hillsborough

Moncton

2

Riverside-Albert

Alma

Mechanic Settlement

114

FUNDY NATIONAL PARK

2

112

Penobsquis

Sussex

121

First traveled by the Native Indians and explorers, the Saint John River was a vital communication link between the Maritime provinces and the rest of Canada. A variety of settlers including Acadians, United Empire Loyalists, Scots and Danes traveled the river to their new homes and you can see their influence. Numerous historic sites are found along the river's shore. Thirty-two covered bridges are found in the valley and you'll cross some on this route.

THE ROUTE:

0 km (0 miles) Québec-New Brunswick border

Crossing the border with the province of Québec, the Trans Canada Highway becomes Highway 2 in New Brunswick. At the border is a provincial tourist information center.

20 km (12 miles) Edmunston

Ride east on the Trans Canada Highway to Edmundston, at the junction of the Madawaska and St. John rivers.

Edmundston is known as the capital of the Republic of Madawaska. The republic was formed by nineteenth-century inhabitants, who were tired of being pawns in border negotiations between Canada and the United States.

73 km (45 miles) Grand Falls

Continue east for 53 km (33 miles) past Saint Leonard and to Grand Falls (Grand-Sault in French) where you can see its 41-meter (135-foot) waterfalls, one of the largest cataracts east of Niagara Falls.

113 km (70 miles) Perth-Andover

At Grand Falls turn off the Trans Canada Highway and take Highway 105 along the east side of the St. John River. This more leisurely highway has less traffic than the Trans Canada Highway and some spectacular views of the waterway. The two highways have several junctions as they follow the course of the river. Perth-Andover is 40 km (25 miles) from Grand Falls.

127 km (79 miles) Muniac Provincial Park

Ride 14 km (9 km) east to camping at Muniac Provincial Park.

136 km (85 miles) Upper Kent

Continue on Highway 105 for 9 km (5.5 miles) to Upper Kent.

Side trip: To Monquart River covered bridge

19 km (12 miles)

At Upper Kent you can take a side trip on Route 565 to a covered bridge spanning the Monquart River. Continue on Route 565 and rejoin Route 105 at Bath.

Main tour

148 km (92 miles) Bath

If you stay on Highway 105, Bath is 12 km (7 miles) south of Upper Kent.

158 km (98 miles) Florenceville

From Bath, cycle 10 km (6 miles) south to Florenceville, named in honor of Florence Nightingale, heroine of the Crimean War.

177 km (110 miles) Hartland

Hartland is 19 km (12 miles) farther at one of the junctions of Highway 105 and the Trans Canada Highway and is the site of the world's longest covered bridge. Built in 1899, the bridge stretches 391 meters (1,282 feet) across the Saint John River.

194 km (120 miles) Woodstock

Woodstock, 17 km (10.5 miles) from Hartland, has a summer farmers' market. The Old County Court House is open to the public.

234 km (145 miles) Hawkshaw

Staying on Highway 105, continue south and then east along the Saint John River for 40 km (25 miles) to Hawkshaw.

261 km (162 miles) King's Landing

Cross the Saint John River at Hawkshaw, and ride on Highway 2 (the Trans Canada Highway) for 27 km (17 miles) to King's Landing. This historical settlement's sixty restored buildings recreate a 1790–1880 Loyalist town.

273 km (169 miles) Mactaquac

Ride along Highway 2 for 4 km (2.5 miles) to Longs Creek, where there is a wildlife park, a campground and a beach. Cross the Saint John River here and continue east on Route 105 to Mactaquac. Mactaquac Provincial Park evolved as a result of establishing a major hydro generating station. The 567-hectare (1,400-acre) park offers camping, swimming, nature trails and fishing for smallmouth bass.

303 km (189 miles) Fredericton

Stay on Highway 105 for 30 km (19 miles) to Fredericton, the provincial capital. This gracious city with tree-lined streets and small town charm has many historic buildings and museums. Be sure to visit the Beaverbrook Art Gallery and take a walking tour of the city center.

332 km (206 miles) Sussex

From Fredericton follow Highway 2—the Trans Canada Highway past Maugerville, around the southern end of Grand Lake, to Sussex, a dairy center, 129 km (80 miles) beyond Fredericton.

387 km (240 miles) Alma in Fundy National Park

Continue on the Trans Canada Highway. Near Penobsquis, take Highway 114 through Fundy National Park to park headquarters at Alma, 55 km (34 miles) from Sussex. (If you're in a hurry, you can stay on the Trans Canada Highway straight into Moncton.)

Fundy National Park covers 207 square km (80 square miles) on the Bay of Fundy. Known for its rugged coastline and abundant wildlife, the park has more than 100 km (60 miles) of hiking trails through its wooded interior and along the coast. The Bay of Fundy is famous for having the world's highest tides, up to 16 meters (53 feet). At low tide you can explore the tidal flats and see periwinkles, barnacles, sea anemones and sandhoppers.

427 km (265 miles) Hopewell Cape

Continue on Route 114 for 40 km (25 miles) to the Flowerpot

Rocks at Hopewell Cape near the mouth of the Petitcodiac River. At high tide these mushroom-like columns look like islands, but at low tide you can descend at the Rocks Provincial Park to see them from the bottom.

469 km (291 miles) Moncton

Ride 45 km (28 miles) to Moncton, the major center in southeastern New Brunswick.

Moncton's Magnetic Hill is one of nature's contradictions. Your bike seems to coast uphill backward. The tidal bore which has some of the highest tides in the world, surges twice a day up the Petituodiac River. It can be seen from Bore Park in downtown Moncton.

528 km (328 miles) Sackville

From Moncton, take Highway 106 for 59 km (37 miles) to the university town of Sackville.

538 km (334 miles) Aulac

Continue on Highway 106 for 5 km (3 miles) to Highway 2 and then go east on Highway 2 for 5 km (3 miles) to Aulac.

Option: Prince Edward Island ferry, 52 km (32 miles)

Just east of Aulac you can take Highway 16 to the Cape Tormentine terminal for ferries to Prince Edward Island.

Option: Amherst, Nova Scotia, 7 km (4 miles)

If you're headed for Nova Scotia, continue east on Highway 2 to Amherst, Nova Scotia.

More Information: Fundy National Park, Alma, New Brunswick E0A 1B0, (506) 887-2000.

GUIDEBOOKS

Bicycle tour maps and guide brochures describing day tours in the Upper Saint John River Valley; Baie des Chaleurs, Campbellton, Bathurst and Caraquet Area; Moncton and Area; and South Central Area, are available free from Tourism New Brunswick, P.O. Box 12345, Fredericton, New Brunswick E3B 5C3, or call toll-free from Canada and the United States 1-800-561-0123; from New Brunswick 1-800-442-4442. For overseas calls (506) 465-5011.

Cape Breton Highlands
(Nova Scotia Tourism and Culture)

Nova Scotia

In Nova Scotia you cycle beside sandy beaches and ride along rocky shorelines where the waves crash against the cliffs. You visit picturesque fishing communities in quiet coves that have centuries of history. The magnificent scenery, along with plentiful campgrounds and accommodations including charming bed-and-breakfasts, have made Nova Scotia one of the continent's most popular cycling areas.

Known as Canada's ocean playground, Nova Scotia is almost completely surrounded by water. Its western shores are washed by the Bay of Fundy, which has the world's highest tides. To the north are Northumberland Strait and the Gulf of St. Lawrence, and to the south and east is the Atlantic Ocean.

Although no part of Nova Scotia is more than 56 km (35 miles) from the sea, the province is more than just shoreline. The province's interior contains rugged mountains, rolling farmland and orchards.

Roads: Most of the province's roads are narrow, winding, picturesque and paved. Traffic on these roads is generally light. The 100 series roads are straight and have paved shoulders, but they carry faster traffic and are not recommended for bicycle touring. The signposted routes such as the Sunrise Trail and the Glooscap Trail are keyed to the Nova Scotia tourist guide and maps.

Weather: The weather is maritime and subject to the frequent changes the sea can bring. Average annual precipitation is 89 cm (35 inches). Expect and be prepared for rain. Have fenders on your bike. Summer temperatures range from 12 degrees Celsius (53 degrees Fahrenheit) at night, occasionally dipping to 5 degrees Cel-sius (40 degrees Fahrenheit), to a daytime high of 30 degrees Celsius (86 degrees Fahrenheit). Sea breezes from the Bay of Fundy or the Atlantic Ocean keep summer daily temperatures averaging around 21 degrees Celsius (70 degrees Fahrenheit). In summer, banks of fog drift inland an average of thirty-eight days during June, July and August, but rarely remain all day. Spring arrives late in Nova Scotia, but the autumn season is long.

Tourist Information: For general tourist information and accommodation reservation contact: Nova Scotia Tourism, Box 130, Halifax, Nova Scotia B3J 2M7 or call toll-free from Canada 1-800-565-0000; in the United States 1-800-341-6096; in Maine 1-

800-492-0643; in Halifax/Dartmouth or from overseas (902) 425-5781; or fax (902) 425-6924.

This is also the number to reach Check In, a reservation service for hotels, motels and campgrounds.

Accommodations: The whole range of accommodation from campgrounds and bed-and-breakfasts to luxury hotels is generally available in every part of the province. Use the tourism information telephone numbers above to reach the Check In reservation service.

Use the Nova Scotia Tourism guide to select the accommodation and campgrounds in the places along these tours. Information on bed-and-breakfasts is also available from the local and regional tourist associations.

Hostels: Information on hostels can be obtained from Nova Scotia Tourism or from the Canadian Hostelling Association/Nova Scotia Region, Sport Nova Scotia Centre, 5516 Spring Garden Road, P.O. Box 3010 South, Halifax, Nova Scotia B3J 3G6, telephone (902) 425-5450, fax (902) 425-5606.

Airports: Nova Scotia is served by airports at Halifax, Sydney and Yarmouth. The airports handle bicycles at an extra charge.

Trains: VIA Rail trains in Nova Scotia have baggage cars and will transport bicycles. For more information contact your local VIA Rail agent or telephone in Halifax (902) 429-8421, elsewhere in Nova Scotia, call toll-free 1-800-561-3952.

Buses: Acadian Bus Lines serves most of the larger towns in the province, but will take bikes only if there is room. Don't depend on taking your bike on the bus during peak travel times. For more information, contact Acadian Bus Lines, 6040 Almon Street, Halifax, Nova Scotia B3K 1T8, (902) 454-9321.

Ferries: All ferries take bicycles at a small or no additional charge. **Bar Harbor, Maine to Yarmouth, Nova Scotia:** In the United States, contact Marine Atlantic, Bar Harbor, Maine 04609; in Canada, contact Marine Atlantic, Box 250, North Sydney, Nova Scotia B2A 3M3; or telephone (902) 794-5700. **Portland, Maine to Yarmouth, Nova Scotia:** In the United States, contact Prince of Fundy Cruise Limited, P.O. Box 4216, Station A, Portland, Maine 04101, or call toll-free 1-800-341-7540, in Maine 1-800-482-0955; in Canada, contact Prince of Fundy Cruise, P.O. Box 609, Yarmouth, Nova Scotia B5A 4B6, or in Nova Scotia, New Brunswick and Prince Edward Island call toll-free 1-800-565-7900. **Saint John, New Brunswick to Digby, Nova Scotia;** and **Port aux Basques and Argentia, Newfoundland to North Sydney, Nova Scotia:** Marine Atlantic, Box 250, North Sydney, Nova Scotia B2A 3M3, telephone (902) 794-5700. **Wood Islands, Prince Edward Island to Caribou, Nova Scotia:** Northumberland Ferries, Box 634, Charlottetown, Prince Edward Island C1A 7L3, or call from Prince

Edward Island and Nova Scotia toll-free 1-800-565-0201; from other areas, call (902) 566-3838.

Bicycling: Bicycle Nova Scotia, P.O. Box 3010 South, Halifax, Nova Scotia B3J 3G6, (902) 425-5450.

Terrain: Nova Scotia's highest point is in the Cape Breton Highlands at 532 meters (1,745 feet); lowest point is sea level. Nova Scotia is a peninsula almost entirely surrounded by the sea and linked to the rest of Canada by the Isthmus of Chignecto. Cape Breton Island is part of the Appalachian Mountain Range. Nova Scotia's southern coast is hilly with elevations reaching 450 meters (280 feet).

Area: 55,491 square km (21,425 square miles), ninth of Canada's ten provinces

Capital: Halifax, the largest city in Atlantic Canada (which comprises the provinces of Nova Scotia, New Brunswick, Prince Edward Island and Newfoundland)

Population: 899,942 (1991 census), seventh largest in population; over 93 per cent have English as their mother tongue, 3.5 per cent are French speaking

History: Micmac Indians were Nova Scotia's original inhabitants. In 1497 John Cabot landed on Cape Breton Island. The first European settlement took place in 1604 when the French sailed into the Bay of Fundy and settled on the island of Ste. Croix. In 1605, after a harsh winter, those who survived resettled at Port Royal, and called the territory l'Acadie. Port Royal is now known as Annapolis Royal (visited on two of these tours).

Over the next one hundred years the French settlements were captured three times by the British and later returned. After the fourth capture in 1710, the 1713 Treaty of Utrecht passed the territory to the British. France kept Cape Breton Island and built the Louisbourg Fortress in the 1720s. Tensions between the English and French led to the expulsion of 6,000 Acadians in 1755 to British colonies on the American coast. Many later returned.

During the eighteenth century there was an influx of immigration from Scotland, Ireland and Germany. Following the American Revolution of 1776, thousands of Loyalists—including many freed slaves—came north and settled in Nova Scotia.

BICYCLING IN HALIFAX/DARTMOUTH

Halifax—the largest city in Atlantic Canada—and Dartmouth surround one of the world's largest harbors. There is no bicycle access to the bridges between the cities, but you can walk your bike 1.7 km (1.05 miles) across the Angus L. MacDonald Bridge. The ferry between Halifax and Dartmouth, which operates daily except Sunday mornings in summer and daily except Sunday in winter, accepts bicycles only on weekdays. There is no extra charge for bicycles. The Halifax/Dartmouth area has no bicycle roadways, pathways or lanes, except a few unmaintained relics in the suburbs.

SUNRISE TRAIL

Length: 131 km (81 miles); plus 10-km (6-mile) side trip
Time: Two to three days
Rating: Easy
Terrain: Flat roads with few hills
Roads: Two-lane road, no shoulders
Traffic: Light
Connects with: Along this route is the Caribou terminal for ferries to Prince Edward Island. This tour also can be linked with the Cape George tour (described in this chapter).
Start: Amherst is on the Trans Canada Highway just east of the New Brunswick boundary. Amherst can be reached by VIA Rail.
Overview: On the relatively flat shore of the Northumberland Strait, the Sunrise Trail takes you to picturesque seascapes and some of the warmest saltwater beaches north of the Carolinas. Average water temperature in the summer is 21 degrees Celsius (70 degrees Fahrenheit). In the summer months, Scottish heritage festivals are held in towns and villages along this route.

The Sunrise Trail extends from Amherst to Auld Cove on the Strait of Canso. This cycling tour, however, ends at Pictou, the approximate midpoint of the trail. The tour generally follows flat roads with few hills, fine ocean views and many long sandy beaches. Lorneville, Amherst Shore and Northport are summer colonies on some of the finest beaches north of Cape Cod.

Campgrounds are located at Tidnish, Northport, near Pugwash, in Wallace, Tatamagouche, Brule, Seafoam and at Caribou outside Pictou.

THE ROUTE:
0 km (0 miles) Amherst
18 km (11 miles) Tidnish

Leaving Amherst on Highway 6 east, turn off onto Highway 366, which meets the Northumberland Strait 18 km (11 miles) at Tidnish, a Native Indian name

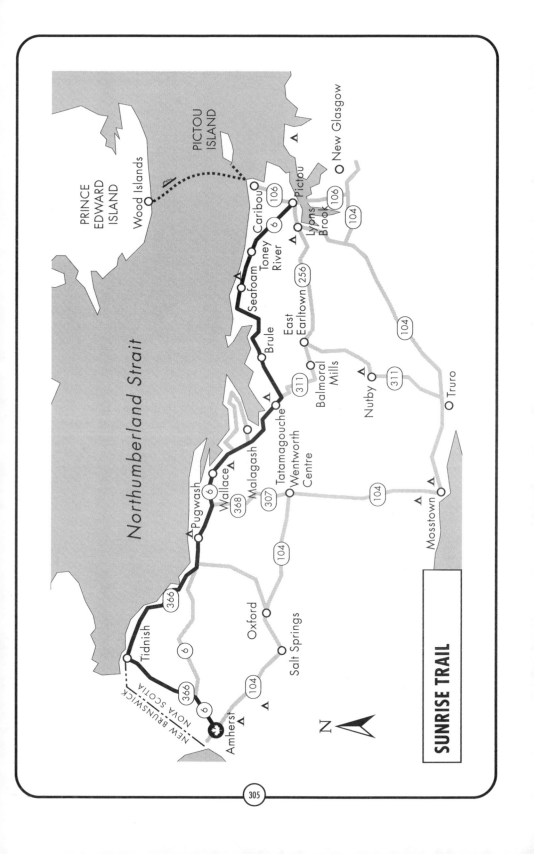

SUNRISE TRAIL

meaning "a paddle." Here are the remains of the uncompleted Chignecto Ship Railway, begun in 1890, intended to haul schooners and boats across the isthmus to the Bay of Fundy.

43 km (26 miles) Pugwash

From Tidnish, follow the shore. There are many ocean views, beaches and usually strong in-shore breezes. Ride 25 km (15 miles) to Pugwash.

Pugwash is a popular tourist spot on the Sunshine Trail. Its harbor handles both fishing boats and large freighters carrying lumber and salt. A Scottish "Gathering of the Clans" festival is held annually in July.

58 km (36 miles) Wallace

Ride 15 km (9 miles) farther to Wallace, a fishing and farming community on Wallace Bay and once a source of sandstone used in building Province House in Halifax and the Parliament Buildings in Ottawa.

A few kilometers beyond Wallace is the North Shore Road, which detours around the Malagash peninsula, the site of abandoned salt mines.

78 km (48 miles) Tatamagouche

Continue 20 km (12 miles) along Highway 6 to Tatamagouche, which was an Acadian settlement until 1755, when a detachment of New Englanders sacked the town and expelled its residents. The Sunrise Trail Museum, which has exhibits on the region's history, is located here.

Side trip: Tatamagouche to Balmoral Mills, 10 km (6 miles)

An interesting 10-km (6-mile) side trip from Tatamagouche leads to Balmoral Mills just off Highway 311, where you can see one of the few grist mills still in operation in Nova Scotia. After your visit, retrace your route back to Tatamagouche.

Main tour continues from Tatamagouche

131 km (81 miles) Pictou

Continue on Highway 5 through Brule, Seafoam and Toney River, which all have long beaches. At Toney River you can see Prince Edward Island 22 km (14 miles) away.

This tour's endpoint is Pictou, the largest community on the Northumberland Strait and 53 km (33 miles) from Tatamagouche. Pictou is called "the birthplace of New Scotland." In 1773, Scottish Highlanders arrived here to begin the wave of Scottish immigration that has built the province. The town is famous for its church lobster suppers.

Option: Pictou to Truro train station, 60 km (37 miles) or 70 km (43 miles)

From Pictou you have several options. To catch the train to Halifax or another destination, the nearest VIA Rail train station is in Truro. If you're in a hurry, ride 60 km (37 miles) to Truro via Highways 376 and 104. If you have the time, you can take the more leisurely 70-km (43-mile) route to Truro via Highway 256 from Lyons Brook and turn onto Highway 311 at East Earltown.

Option: Pictou to Prince Edward Island, 8 km (5 miles)

If you want to continue to Prince Edward Island, take Highway 106 for 8 km (5 miles) to Caribou, where ferries provide frequent daily service to Wood Islands, Prince Edward Island. (See the Prince Edward Island chapter for more information on the ferry service.)

Option: Continue on Sunrise Trail, 54 km (3.3 miles)

To continue riding along the Sunrise Trail, follow the scenic Highway 245 at Sutherland River 8 km (5 miles) through Merigomish and Arisaig. At Malignant Cove you connect with the Cape George Tour described in this chapter.

CAPE GEORGE TOUR

Length: 71 km (44 miles) loop
Time: One day
Rating: Difficult, challenging
Terrain: Hilly
Roads: Two-lane road, no shoulder
Traffic: Very light
Connects with: This tour can be a continuation of the Sunrise Trail tour
Start: Antigonish, the major center in this region of Nova Scotia, is the starting and end point of this loop tour.
Overview: This tour follows the coast of the Northumberland Strait. Described as a mini Cabot Trail, the Cape George tour traverses hilly terrain and is considered strenuous. The descent from Cape George is exhilarating.

THE ROUTE:

0 km (0 miles) Antigonish

20 km (12 miles) Malignant Cove

Ride out of Antigonish on Highway 245. An almost flat 20 km (12 miles) brings you to the sea at Malignant Cove. The town took its name from the British man-of-war H.M.S. *Malignant*, wrecked here on its way to Québec during the American Revolution.

At Malignant Cove, turn right onto Highway 337, part of the Sunrise Trail. Here the scenery changes dramatically. Houses perch precariously on round, sometimes treeless hills, or nestle in quiet coves. Bicycling alternates between strenuous climbs and exhilarating glides.

The tour follows the shore of St. George's Bay through Ballantyne's Cove. The lighthouse here, first built in 1895, is situated 300 meters (1,000 feet) above St. George's Bay. From this vantage point on a clear day, you can see Prince Edward Island and Cape Breton Island.

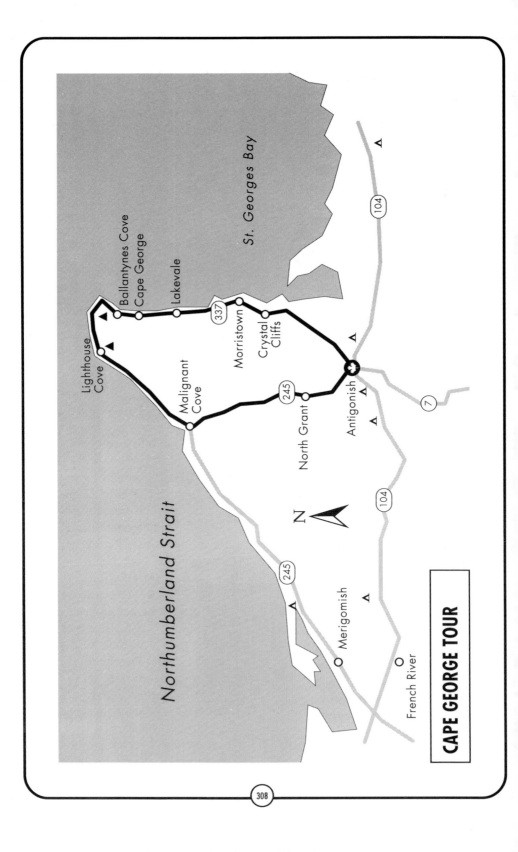

St. Georges Bay

Ballantynes Cove
Cape George
Lakevale

337

Morristown

Crystal
Cliffs

Lighthouse
Cove

Malignant
Cove

245

North Grant

Antigonish

7

104

104

245

N

Northumberland Strait

245

Merigomish

French River

104

CAPE GEORGE TOUR

71 km (44 miles) Antigonish

Continue riding through the communities of Cape George, Lakevale, Morristown and Crystal Cliffs to Antigonish. Since 1861 Antigonish has hosted the Highland games, which are the oldest celebration of Scottish music, dance and sport in North America.

CABOT TRAIL

Length: 294 km (183 miles)

Time: Three to four days

Rating: Challenging, for experienced cyclists

Terrain: Mountainous including three steep climbs of over 400-meter (1,300-foot) climbs

Roads: Mostly two lanes, no shoulders, Highway 105 has paved shoulders

Traffic: Mixed, heavy on holiday weekends

Connects with: Across Nova Scotia tour

Start: Baddeck. The description here goes in a clockwise direction on the Cabot Trail.

Overview: "I have traveled around the globe. I have seen the Canadian and American Rockies, the Andes and the Alps and the Highlands of Scotland, but the simple beauty of Cape Breton outrivals them all," observed Alexander Graham Bell.

The famous Cabot Trail on Nova Scotia's Cape Breton Island is the province's best-known cycling route. This spectacular tour gives you vast panoramas of blue ocean as you ride through mountainous terrain and rolling meadows. You pass along cliffs, lakes, rivers gorges, sand beaches, rocky coves and rugged coastline. Picturesque vistas unfold from the top of each hill. The Cape Breton villages are known for their traditional fiddlers and folk singers.

THE ROUTE:

0 km (0 miles) Baddeck

In Baddeck is the Alexander Graham Bell National Historic Park, on a hill overlooking Bras D'Or Lake. The museum building is a unique structure—its design incorporates tetrahedra, a favourite of Bell's. The museum displays many of Bell's inventions and artifacts of his work in communication, aviation and medicine.

8 km (5 miles) Cabot Trail

From the Bell Museum, go south on the Trans Canada Highway 105 and turn north onto the Cabot Trail. The road follows part of the low rolling and flat Middle River valley.

40 km (25 miles) Northeast Margaree

Ride over several hills to Northeast Margaree, 32 km (20 miles) from the Trans Canada Highway, At Northeast Margaree is the Salmon Museum where ex-

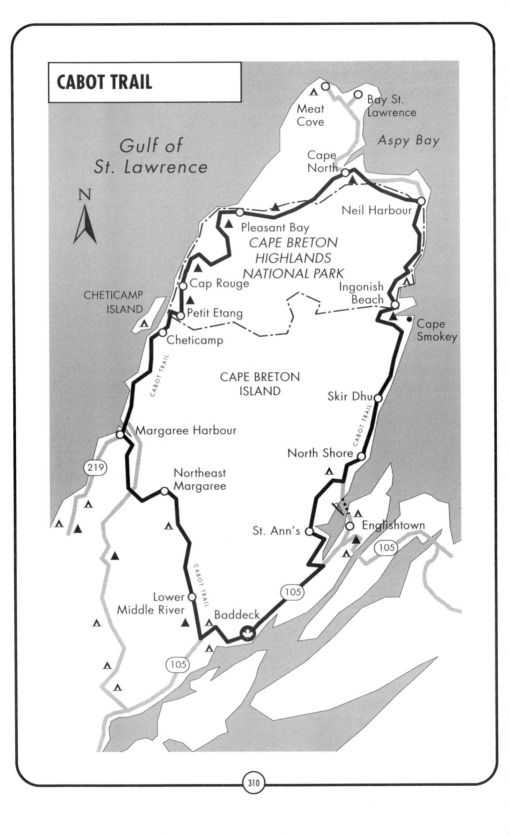

CABOT TRAIL

Gulf of
St. Lawrence

N

Meat Cove

Bay St. Lawrence

Aspy Bay

Cape North

Neil Harbour

Pleasant Bay

CAPE BRETON
HIGHLANDS
NATIONAL PARK

Cap Rouge

CHETICAMP
ISLAND

Ingonish Beach

Petit Etang

Cheticamp

Cape Smokey

CABOT TRAIL

CAPE BRETON
ISLAND

Skir Dhu

CABOT TRAIL

Margaree Harbour

North Shore

219

Northeast
Margaree

Englishtown

St. Ann's

105

CABOT TRAIL

105

Lower
Middle River

Baddeck

105

hibits describe the Margaree River, known among fishermen as one of Eastern Canada's finest salmon rivers.

58 km (36 miles) Margaree Harbour

Continue through farmland to Margaree Harbour on the coast. Here you can get a view of the Northumberland Strait.

85 km (53 miles) Cheticamp

Turn north and cycle 27 km (16 miles) through rolling hills to Cheticamp, a French Acadian fishing village. Stock up on food here before riding to Cape Breton Highlands Park. Inquire locally about whale-watching boat trips. At Petit Etang is the Acadian Trail, a four-hour hiking trail to the top of the Highlands and a panoramic view of the Cheticamp area.

90 km (56 miles) Cape Breton Highlands National Park

The entrance to Cape Breton Highlands National Park is 5 km (3 miles) north of Cheticamp and is free for people entering on bicycles.

Inside the park you enter a narrow valley and climb up Cap Rouge, the first major ascent. Several look-outs give you views of Cheticamp and the surf below. On French Mountain the road climbs steeply inland from the ocean. Ride along the high plateau and gradually descend to the top of MacKenzie Mountain at the end of the plateau. Along the way you can hike a boardwalk winding through a bog full of native flora.

129 km (80 miles) Pleasant Bay

Descend steeply from MacKenzie Mountain via a series of switchbacks to the village of Pleasant Bay, 44 km (28 miles) from Cheticamp.

From here the road is mostly flat and goes along the Grand Anse River. You gradually climb up the valley to the Lone Sheiling, 6 km (4 miles) beyond Pleasant Bay. Lone Sheiling is a replica of the stone huts used by the Scottish crofters, the region's first settlers, to protect themselves against the blast of the North Sea while tending their sheep.

Beyond this is the ascent up North Mountain, the most strenuous climb of the entire Cabot Trail, followed by another breathtaking descent. The road hugs the cliffs that line the gorge of the North Aspy River valley. You then come to the famous view, seen on the tourist brochures, of the Sunrise Valley with rolling meadows and green valleys bordered on the west by Cape North Mountain and stretching out to Aspy Bay to the northeast.

158 km (98 miles) Cape North

Ride in a flat valley through rolling hills to the town of Cape North, 29 km (18 miles) from Pleasant Bay. Cape North is the northernmost point on the Cabot Trail.

177 km (110 miles) Neil's Harbour

From Cape North, turn east and gradually climb over the next 19 km (12 miles) to the turn-off for Neil's Harbour. Turning south, the route climbs and then descends to Black Brook on Cape Breton Island's east coast. At Black Brook there are campgrounds and a popular sandy beach. You'll find the climbs shorter along Cape Breton's rocky east coast than on the island's western coast.

200 km (124 miles) Ingonish

Ride through Ingonish, a popular resort area, which includes the provincially owned Keltic Lodge.

Ingonish is one of the oldest settled areas on the Atlantic seaboard. Portuguese fishermen wintered here as early as 1521. There are beaches, parks, hiking trails and scenic lookouts. Ingonish Beach offers swimming in the ocean and at a nearby freshwater lake.

The route gradually climbs over the next 6 km (4 miles) to Cape Smokey, a towering 360-meter (1,200-foot) promontory often capped by white mist. The Cape Smokey ski area has Atlantic Canada's only double chair lift. During summer it takes visitors to an unforgettable view of the Atlantic and the rocky Cape Breton coast.

From Cape Smokey the road steeply descends some 360 meters (1,200 feet) in less than 3.2

km (2 miles) and then straightens out and continues along the rugged coastline.

It passes through the small fishing villages such as Skir Dhu (Gaelic for "black rock"), population ten.

At North Shore is Plaster Provincial Park, a picnic area with a short but steep walking trail to the cliff. From here you can view the Bird Islands, where many seabirds nest from early June to late July.

Option: Ferry to Englishtown

An alternative is to turn off the Cabot Trail onto Route 312, situated between North Shore and St. Ann's. Ride Route 312 and take the ferry to Englishtown. Here you can see the burial place of Angus MacAskill, "the Cape Breton Giant." Standing 213 cm (7 feet 9 inches) tall and weighing 192 kg (425 pounds), MacAskill was famous as a strongman with the P.T. Barnum Circus during the nineteenth century.

From Englishtown, ride south to Highway 312 to the Trans Canada Highway. Then proceed to Baddeck to end your tour.

Main tour continues

263 km (163 miles) St. Ann's

From the junction of the Cabot Trail and Route 312, continue on the Cabot Trail along the mostly flat Barachois River Valley, followed by a climb and descent to the hilly North River Valley.

Ride to St. Ann's, 63 km (39 miles) from Ingonish Beach.

At picturesque St. Ann's is the Gaelic College, which preserves the region's Highland heritage with courses in bagpipe playing, clan lore and Gaelic singing. Visitors are invited to observe classes held both outside and inside the college.

294 km (183 miles) Baddeck

Continue on the Cabot Trail to the Trans Canada Highway 105, which has 1- to 2-meter- (3- to 6-feet-) wide paved shoulders. Ride mostly flat Highway 105 to Baddeck, 31 km (19 miles) from St. Ann's.

More Information: Cape Breton Highlands National Park, Ingonish Beach, Cape Breton, Nova Scotia B0C 1L0, (902) 285-2270.

PEGGY'S COVE TOUR

Length: 45 km (28 miles)
Time: One day
Rating: Easy
Terrain: The tour has two hills
Roads: Two lane, no shoulders
Traffic: Some traffic leaving Halifax, then tour bus traffic
Connects with: Other tours starting from Halifax
Start: Halifax, reached by VIA Rail train, international airport and bus.
Overview: A picturesque fishing community centered around a narrow ocean inlet, Peggy's Cove is one of Nova Scotia's best-known tourist attractions. The town is dominated by a lighthouse perched high up on huge, wave-washed granite boulders.

THE ROUTE:

0 km (0 miles) Halifax

Leave Halifax via the Armdale Rotary traffic circle, and take Route 3—St. Margarets Bay Road. Just beyond Second Chain Lake, take Highway 333 through Goodwood, Whites Lake, Shad Bay, East Dover and West Dover. At Whites Lake two interesting side routes go to Terence Bay and to Prospect.

45 km (28 miles) Peggy's Cove

Continue on Highway 333 to Peggy's Cove.

When you've seen Peggy's Cove, continue on through Glen Margaret and Seabright to Upper Tantallon.

Option: Return to Halifax quickly via Highway 103, 23 km (14 miles)

From Upper Tantallon you can return to Halifax quickly via Highway 103.

Option: Return to Halifax leisurely on Highway 3, 23 km (14 miles)

Or, take a more leisurely and more interesting ride on Highway 3 through Five Island Lake and Timberlea.

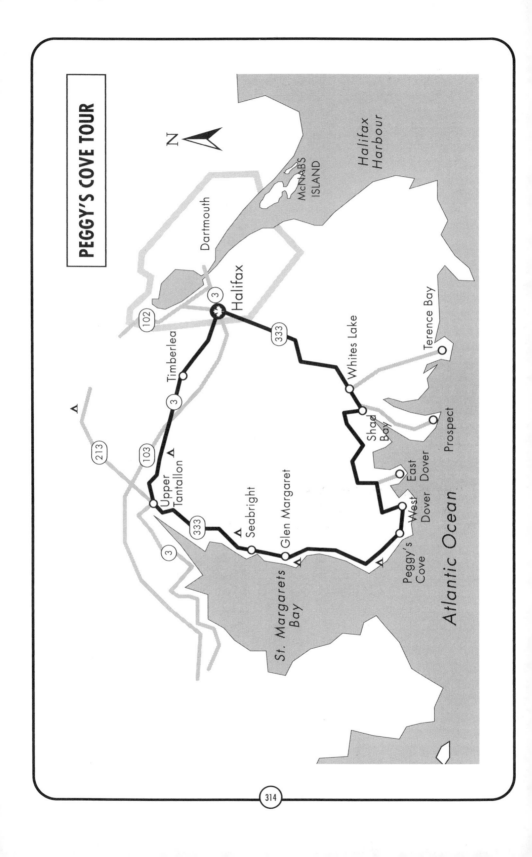

PEGGY'S COVE TOUR

N

Dartmouth

Halifax

Halifax Harbour

McNAB'S ISLAND

102

3

Timberlea

333

103

Upper Tantallon

213

3

333

Seabright

Glen Margaret

St. Margaret's Bay

Peggy's Cove

West Dover

East Dover

Shad Bay

Whites Lake

Prospect

Terence Bay

Atlantic Ocean

HALIFAX TO CHESTER BEACH

Length: 84 km (50 miles)
Time: One or two days
Rating: Intermediate
Terrain: Rolling with several hills
Roads: Two lanes, no shoulders
Traffic: Summer traffic near beaches can be heavy
Connects with: Other tours starting in Halifax
Start: Halifax, the capital of Nova Scotia, and a major center served by VIA Rail, an international airport and buses.
Overview: This tour takes you to beautiful scenery and beaches. A return trip can be done in one day but take at least two to have time to enjoy it all. It's great for a hot summer weekend.

THE ROUTE:

0 km (0 miles) Halifax

Leave Halifax via Quinpool Road, through the Armdale Rotary traffic circle, and take Highway 3—St. Margarets Bay Road. You encounter the steepest hills on your way out of Halifax. Follow Highway 3 inland and pass Lakeside, Beechville and Timberlea.

20 km (12 miles) Upper Tantallon

At Upper Tantallon, 20 km (12 miles) from Halifax, the tour starts to follow the bays and inlets of the South Shore.

Near Head of St. Margaret's Bay is the start of the Bowater Mersey Hiking Trail. At Black Point, Queensland and Hubbards are popular sand beaches.

41 km (25 miles) Hubbards

Just past Hubbards, about 21 km (13 miles) from Upper Tantallon, turn left onto Highway 329. Here the route detours around the Aspotogan Peninsula. Near the tip of the peninsula is Bayswater Beach Provincial Park, offering a sand beach and a picnic area. Next is the town of Blandford, the former site of a whaling industry. From the shoreline you can see the Tancook Islands in Mahone Bay. The detour around the peninsula is about 35 km (22 miles).

76 km (47 miles) East River

Continue to East River, where you rejoin Highway 3, which has several steep hills. Nearby Graves Island Provincial Park is a particularly beautiful oceanside campground and picnic site.

84 km (52 miles) Chester

Chester, 8 km (5 miles) from East River, offers swimming, sport fishing and sailing. Boat trips to Big and Little Tancook Islands can be arranged.

To have time to enjoy the beaches and scenery, camp at Hubbards or on Grave's Island, or stay in one of the many accommodations in the area.

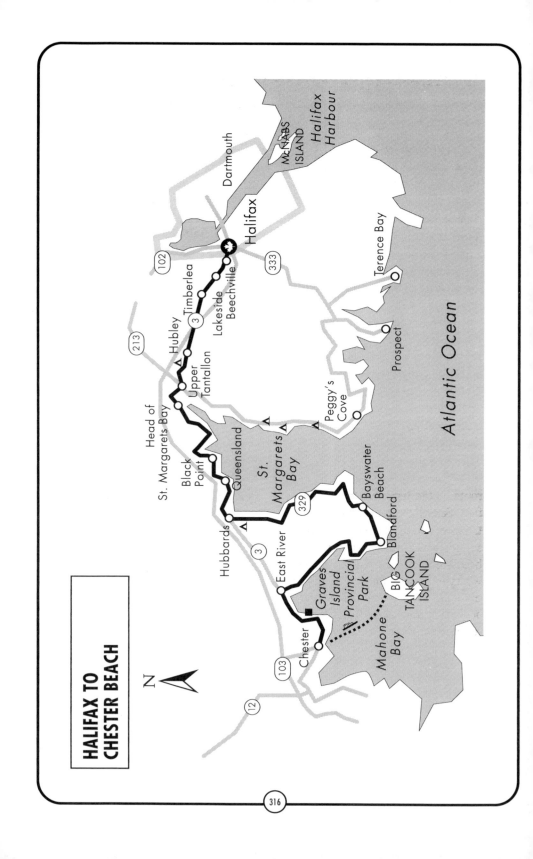

HALIFAX TO
CHESTER BEACH

N

Halifax

Dartmouth

Halifax Harbour

McNABS ISLAND

102

Timberlea

Lakeside
Beechville

333

3

Hubley

213

Upper
Tantallon

Head of
St. Margarets Bay

Black
Point

Queensland

St.
Margarets
Bay

Peggy's
Cove

Prospect

Terence Bay

Atlantic Ocean

Hubbards

East River

3

329

Bayswater
Beach

Blandford

BIG
TANCOOK
ISLAND

Graves
Island
Provincial
Park

Chester

103

12

Mahone
Bay

SOUTHWESTERN NOVA SCOTIA

Length: 494 km (307 miles); plus 21-km (13-mile) side-trip

Time: One week, take ten days to two weeks to explore the many attractions

Rating: Intermediate

Terrain: Rolling with occasional hills; if you do the tour in a counterclockwise direction you miss the long steep climb from Annapolis Royal to Milford.

Roads: Part of tour is on two-lane road with no shoulder, other part on four-lane road with shoulders.

Traffic: Two-lane roads have light traffic, four-lane roads have heavy traffic.

Connects with: Annapolis Royal tour

Start: Yarmouth can be reached by road or ferry from Bar Harbor or Portland, Maine. Digby, along this route, is the terminus for the ferry from Saint John, New Brunswick.

Overview: Rugged coastline, white sand beaches, crashing surf, lighthouses and colorful fishing villages with wharves piled high with lobster traps are some of the sights as you begin this tour along Nova Scotia's south coast. From the Atlantic shore you ride through the rolling fertile farmland of the Annapolis Valley, to Kejimkujik National Park. Along the Bay of Fundy you explore historic Acadia. On the way are places with stories of buried treasure and ghost ships.

THE ROUTE:

0 km (0 miles) Yarmouth

Yarmouth, known as "the gateway to Nova Scotia," has a shipping tradition dating from the days of wind and sail. Exhibits at the Yarmouth County Historical Society Museum reflect this tradition. Just outside Yarmouth is Cape Forchu, named by Champlain in 1604, and site of the Yarmouth Light, built in 1840.

The tour from Yarmouth to Liverpool follows the scenic Lighthouse Route along the Atlantic coast, with many bays and points to discover.

76 km (47 miles) Doctor s Cove

Follow the Lighthouse Route along Route 3 to Doctor s Cove 76 km (47 miles) from Yarmouth.

Side trip: Cape Sable Island, 21 km (13 miles)

Just 1.5 km (0.9 miles) beyond Doctor s Cove, you can take a 21-km (13-mile) return side trip on Route 330 to Cape Sable Island. Nova Scotia's southernmost point, Cape Sable Island is reached by a 1,200-meter (4,000-foot) causeway.

Main tour continues

Continue cycling on the Lighthouse Route. If you want to save time you can take Highway 103 from just beyond Crowell to Shelburne, a short cut saving 40 km (25 miles). Highway 103 is

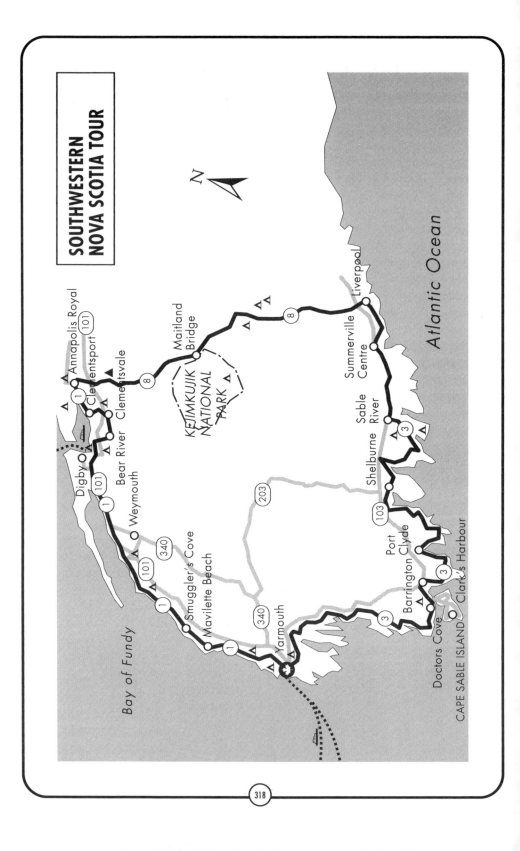

SOUTHWESTERN
NOVA SCOTIA TOUR

N

Atlantic Ocean

Annapolis Royal
Clementsport
101
Clementsvale

Maitland Bridge

8

Digby
1
101
Bear River
Weymouth

KEJIMKUJIK
NATIONAL
PARK

8

Liverpool

Summerville Centre

Sable River

Shelburne

3

Smuggler's Cove
340
Mavilette Beach
101
1

340
Yarmouth

203

103

Port
Barrington Clyde
3

3

Doctors Cove
CAPE SABLE ISLAND
Clark's Harbour

Bay of Fundy

quicker, but much less interesting.

157 km (97 miles) Shelburne

A major tourist center on the Lighthouse Route, Shelburne was settled by United Empire Loyalists, and is now a shipbuilding and fishing community.

227 km (141 miles) Liverpool

Liverpool, 70 km (44 miles) beyond Shelburne, is a pretty town with tree-lined streets and many historic buildings. Deepsea fishing trips can be arranged locally.

294 km (183 miles) Kejimkujik National Park

From Liverpool go north on Highway 8 inland through farm and forest land for 67 km (42 miles) to Kejimkujik National Park.

At Kejimkujik National Park, you can swim in the freshwater lakes, rent a canoe for a wilderness trip on rivers once used by the Micmac Indians or hike along some of the more than 100 km (60 miles) of wooded trails.

344 km (214 miles) Annapolis Royal

Ride 50 km from Kejimkujik Park to Annapolis Royal where the tour connects with the Annapolis Royal tour (described in this chapter).

Annapolis Royal, founded in 1605, is the oldest European settlement in Canada. Here is Fort Anne National Historic Park, dating from 1643, and the Port Royal Habitation, the oldest permanent settlement by Euro-

peans north of the Gulf of Mexico. Nearby is the unique Fundy Tidal Power Project and the Lequille hydro-electric plant housed in a seventeenth-century-style building.

373 km (231 miles) Bear River

Leave Annapolis Royal on Highway 1. Ride through farmland and meadows to Clementsport, 13 km (8 miles) from Annapolis Royal. Just over the bridge at Clementsport, turn left and ride about 8 km (5 miles) toward Clementsvale.

At Clementsvale, take the road for 8 km (5 miles) to the village of Bear River. Situated in a valley surrounded by steep wooded hills, Bear River is known as the Switzerland of Nova Scotia.

388.5 km (241 miles) Digby

Take the road that runs beside the Bear River for 5 km (3 miles) over rolling hills. Rejoin Highway 1, which winds through the hills.

You soon merge with Highway 101. After 7.5 km (4.6 miles) on Highway 101 you reach the junction with Route 217.

Three km (1.8 miles) off Highway 101 on Route 217 is Digby, the terminus for the Marine Atlantic ferry to Saint John, New Brunswick. Among the services offered at Digby is the provincially owned resort, The Pines.

418.5 km (260 miles) Weymouth

Continue on Highway 101 to

Weymouth, 30 km (19 miles) from Digby, then rejoin Highway 1. From Weymouth to Yarmouth Highway 1 becomes the longest main street in Canada as it passes through many coastal villages. This is the center of the French Acadian culture in Nova Scotia. Try some native Acadian cuisine, especially "rappie pie," at one of the family-run restaurants.

493.5 km (307 miles) Yarmouth

Continue on Highway 1 for 75 km (46 miles) to Yarmouth. Expect occasional heavy traffic in areas where Highway 101 has not yet been completed. If you encounter heavy traffic take a break in one of the many small villages along the route.

More Information: The ferries from Bar Harbor, Maine, to Yarmouth, and from Saint John, New Brunswick are operated by Marine Atlantic. The ferry from Portland, Maine, to Yarmouth is operated by Prince of Fundy Cruises Limited. For details on ferry services, see the beginning of this chapter. Kejimkujik National Park, Box 36, Maitland Bridge, Annapolis County Nova Scotia B0T 1N0, (902) 242-2770.

ANNAPOLIS VALLEY: ANNAPOLIS ROYAL TO WOLFVILLE

Length: 109 km (68 miles); plus side trips of 36 km (22 miles), 5 km (3 miles) and 11 km (7 miles)
Time: One to two days
Rating: Intermediate
Terrain: Mostly flat; side trips over North Mountain have steep climbs and descents
Roads: Two lanes, no shoulders
Traffic: Moderate; a lot of tourist traffic on summer weekends
Connects with: Southwestern Nova Scotia tour, Blomidon Peninsula tour
Start: Annapolis Royal
Overview: The famous fruit-growing region of the Annapolis Valley is sheltered from heavy winds and fog by mountains on both sides.

The steep North Mountain separates the valley from the Bay of Fundy. On the other side of the valley is South Mountain. This tour is fairly level unless you cross North Mountain.

In late May you can see the apple blossoms. In summer there are seasons of strawberries, raspberries, plums and cherries. October is apple-picking season and the woods are ablaze with fall colors.

Annapolis Royal, where this tour begins, is one of Canada's most historic regions. In addition to Fort Anne National Historic Park and the Port Royal Habitation, there are many other restored buildings and historic gardens. There are approx-

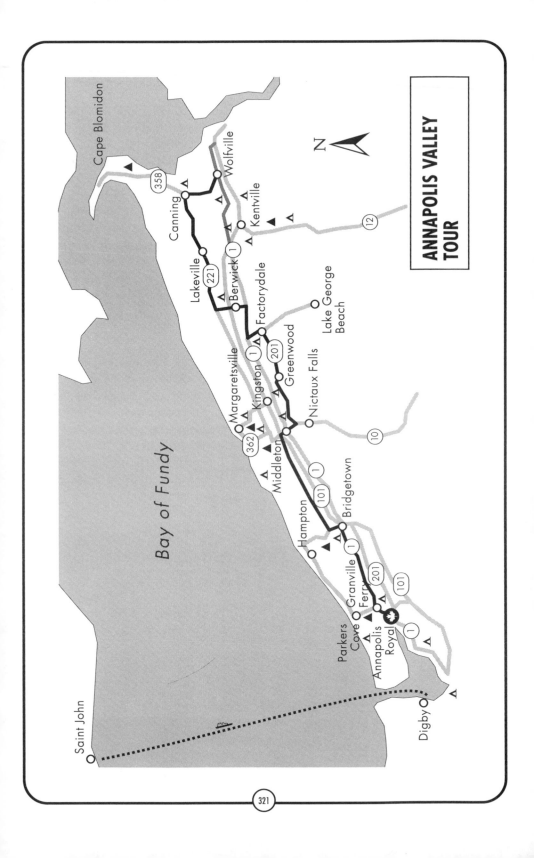

ANNAPOLIS VALLEY
TOUR

N

Cape Blomidon

Wolfville

358

Canning

Kentville

Lakeville

12

221

Berwick 1

Factorydale

Lake George
Beach

201

Bay of Fundy

Greenwood

Margaretsville

Kingston 1

Nictaux Falls

362

Middleton

10

Bridgetown

1

Hampton

101

Parkers
Cove

Granville
Ferry

1

201

Annapolis
Royal

101

1

Saint John

Digby

321

imately ten popular bed-and-break-fasts in the area.

THE ROUTE:

0 km (0 miles) Annapolis Royal

After visiting Annapolis Royal, ride east on either Highway 1 or Parallel Highway 201 (Highway 1 has more traffic but is flatter) to Bridgetown.

Side trip: Annapolis Royal to Bridgetown via North Mountain, 36 km (22 miles)

For a side trip with a long climb and descent over the North Mountain, take Highway 1 from Annapolis Royal past Granville Ferry. Ride north to Parkers Cove on the Bay of Fundy. Go right and cycle along the coast road to Hampton. You may notice a drop in temperature between the valley and the Fundy shore.

Turn right just past Hampton to return to Highway 1 at Bridgetown.

Main tour continues

24 km (15 miles) Bridgetown

Above Bridgetown is Valleyview Provincial Park, a picnic park with a panoramic view of the Annapolis Valley.

46 km (29 miles) Middleton

North of Bridgetown, you take the Clarence Road, which runs east along the base of the hills. Middleton is 22 km (14 miles) farther.

Option: Middleton to Canning, 56 km (35 miles)

From Middleton take Highway 221 for 56 km (35 miles) to Canning at the east end of the Annapolis Valley where the North Mountain comes to a dramatic end at Cape Blomidon.

Option: Middleton to Kingston, 37 km (23 miles)

Another option near Middleton is to take Route 362 over Mount Hanley. Ride east along the Bay of Fundy to East Margaretsville. Then cycle south to Kingston.

Side trip: Middleton to Nictaux Falls, 5 km (3 miles)

South of Middleton, you can ride Highway 10 to Nictaux Falls. There is a pond above the dam on the Nictaux River where you can swim.

Main tour from Middleton

71 km (44 miles) Factorydale

From Middleton continue on Highway 201 past the air base at Greenwood to Factorydale, 25 km (15 miles) away.

Side trip: Factorydale to Lake George Provincial Park, 11 km (7 miles) each way

From Factorydale, turn south to Morristown. A paved road up the South Mountain leads to Lake George Provincial Beach Park at Lake George. Take this road back through Factorydale to Highway 1.

Main tour continues from Factorydale

81 km (50 miles) Berwick

From Factorydale ride 10 km (6 miles) north to Highway 1 and into Berwick. East of Berwick, take Highway 360 north and turn right onto Highway 221. Ride Highway 221 east. You pass a small lake for swimming at Lakeville and reach the scenic village of Canning. From here you can take the Blomidon-

Scots Bay tour (described in this chapter).

109 km (68 miles) Wolfville

From Canning, take Highway 358 through farmland to Wolf-ville, a university town that was settled in the 1760s. Wolfville is 28 km (17 miles) from Berwick.

BLOMIDON PENINSULA LOOP

Length: 75 km (47 miles)
Time: One day
Rating: Intermediate
Terrain: Hilly; several very steep hills
Roads: Two lane, no shoulders
Traffic: Light
Connects with: Annapolis Valley: Annapolis Royal to Wolfville tour
Start: Kentville
Overview: The Blomidon Peninsula was the home of the Micmac god Glooscap who is said to have created the Annapolis Valley and other natural features. This tour can be done on its own or as a continuation of the Annapolis Valley tour. You pass farmland and orchards and reach the cliffs, trails and beaches of Blomidon Provincial Park.

THE ROUTE:

0 km (0 miles) Kentville

8 km (5 miles) Port Williams

From Kentville, take the road for Port Williams through the dykelands of "Glooscap Country," past farms with apple orchards.

Go through Port Williams, where freighters loading barrels of fresh apples sit high and dry beside the wharf at low tide.

25 km (15 miles) Blomidon

Follow the coast road to Blomidon, past the wide red mud flats of Minas Basin—if the 8- to 12-meter (26- to 39-foot) tide is out.

Blomidon Provincial Park, a few kilometers past Blomidon, offers picnic grounds, hiking trails, beaches and cliffs.

28 km (17 miles) Scots Bay Road

There is a 3-km (1.8-mile) gravel road, which climbs North Mountain to the Scots Bay Road.

40 km (25 miles) End of Scots Bay Road

Turn right on Scots Bay Road (Route 358) and cycle 12 km (7 miles) through Scots Bay to the end of the road.

In Scots Bay is the start of the 13-km (8-mile) hiking trail to a spectacular cliff at Cape Split, known for its strong tides, fierce winds and thousands of sea-birds.

53 km (33 miles) The Lookoff

Return 13 km (8 miles) along the Scots Bay Road to the village of The Lookoff where there is a famous view of the Annapolis Valley and the Minas Basin.

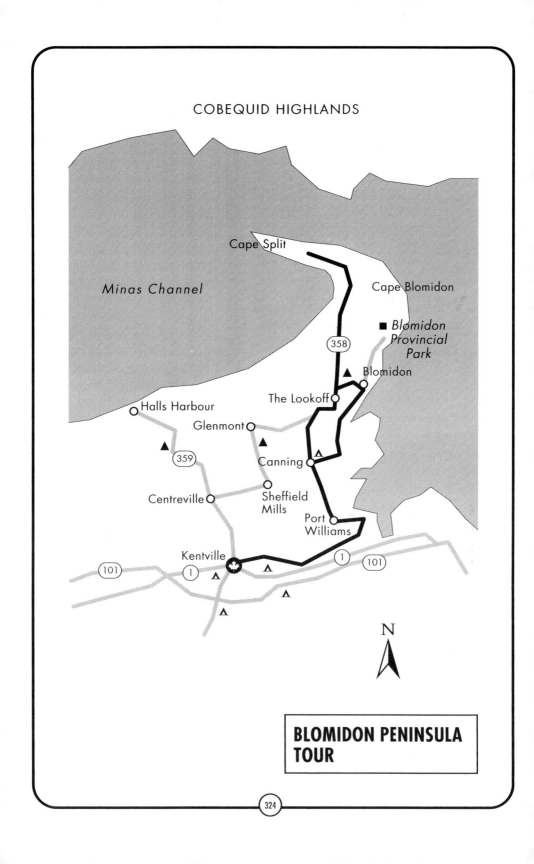

COBEQUID HIGHLANDS

Minas Channel

Cape Split

Cape Blomidon

■ Blomidon
Provincial
Park

358

Blomidon

The Lookoff

Halls Harbour

Glenmont

359

Canning

Centreville

Sheffield
Mills

Port
Williams

Kentville

101

1

1

101

N

**BLOMIDON PENINSULA
TOUR**

Option: Retrace route to Kentville,
22 km (14 miles)

From here you can go south on Route 358 to Canning and retrace your route for 22 km (14 miles) to Kentville.

Option: Return to Kentville via North Mountain,
20 km (12 miles)

From the Lookoff, ride west for 5 km (3 miles) on gravel along the North Mountain to Glenmont. From Glenmont, an exhilarating winding road, descends beside Sleepy Hollow Brook, through Sheffield Mills and Centreville and along Route 359, for 15 km (9 miles) back to Kentville, the starting point of this tour.

EVANGELINE COUNTRY TOUR

Length: 24 km (15 miles) loop

Time: Half-day

Rating: Easy

Terrain: Flat, with one hill

Roads: Mostly two-lane paved road with no shoulder, part of route is on gravel road.

Traffic: Light

Connects with: Annapolis Valley: Annapolis Royal to Wolfville tour

Start: Grand Pré National Historic Park, 5 km (3 miles) east of Wolfville

Overview: Grand Pré National Historic Park commemorates the British expulsion of the French Acadians in 1755. This event was immortalized in Henry Wadsworth Longfellow's poem "Evangeline," the story of young lovers separated by the deportation.

In late May the apple blossoms turn the orchards along this route a snowy white. In late September the boughs are bent with fruit.

THE ROUTE:

0 km (0 miles) Grand Pré National Historic Park

5 km (3 miles) Wolfville

From Grand Pré Historic Park ride up the slight rise to Highway 1, turn right and continue into Wolfville.

In Wolfville, turn left onto Gaspereau Avenue.

After a steep climb, you are rewarded by a panoramic view of the valley. You then have an exciting descent. Turn right before reaching the Gaspereau River onto the White Rock road, a quiet road beside the river.

Ride to White Rock, where you can see the hydro station from the road. Turn left across the river and left again to follow the river back to Gaspereau.

24 km (15 miles) Grand Pré

Continue through the villages of Melanson and Wallbrook, where signs lead you back to Grand Pré.

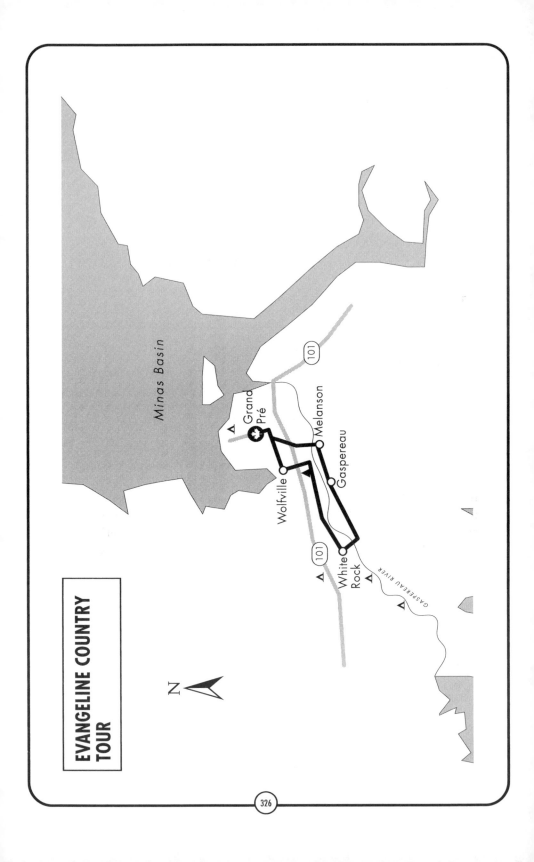

EVANGELINE COUNTRY
TOUR

N

Minas Basin

Grand
Pré

101

Melanson

Gaspereau

Wolfville

White
Rock

101

GASPEREAU RIVER

GLOOSCAP TRAIL

Length: 246 km (153 miles)
Time: Three to four days
Rating: Intermediate
Terrain: Rolling and a very hilly side trip
Roads: Two lane, no shoulder
Traffic: Light
Connects with: Across Nova Scotia tour, Across New Brunswick tour
Start: Amherst, situated on the Trans Canada Highway just east of the New Brunswick–Nova Scotia border. Amherst can be reached by VIA Rail.
Overview: The Glooscap Trail scenic route follows near the shores of Chignecto Bay and the Minas Basin. This tour follows parts of the Glooscap Trail from Amherst to Truro before branching off to Dartmouth.

Along the way you can explore beaches with semi-precious stones, the traditional Micmac hunting and fishing grounds, and a historic port of call.

Glooscap, the Micmac Indians' legendary man-god who lived on Blomidon, claimed this land hundreds of years ago. According to Micmac legend, when the beaver taunted his people, Glooscap threw five handfuls of mud at him. These clumps of mud became the Five Islands near Parrsboro.

THE ROUTE:

0 km (0 miles) Amherst

Start on Highway 2 out of Amherst and turn right onto Route 302 to the communities of Nap-

pan and Maccan. At Nappan Station is a federal Agricultural Experimental Station open to visitors. Just before Athol, ride Little Forks Road as it turns east to reach Highway 2 near Springhill Junction.

24 km (15 miles) Springhill

Ride Highway 21 east to Springhill, 24 km (15 miles) from Amherst. Springhill is situated on the northeastern slope of a rounded hilltop. Large-scale coal mining began here in 1872. The 1,230-meter (4,000-foot) deep No. 2 mine was once the deepest in Canada. Tragedy struck Springhill in 1891 when an underground disaster took the lives of 125 miners; in 1956 when an explosion took 39 more; and in 1958 when a massive earth disturbance in No. 2 mine claimed 76 lives. The mines are now closed, but a Miner's Museum perpetuates the memory of the miners with underground tours and exhibits.

44 km (27 miles) Southampton

Continue on Highway 2 through Mapleton, a center for maple sugar and maple syrup production, to Southampton, 20 km (12 miles) from Springhill.

70 km (43 miles) Parrsboro

The 26-km (16-mile) ride from Southampton to Parrsboro is especially beautiful in the autumn when the maple trees turn to

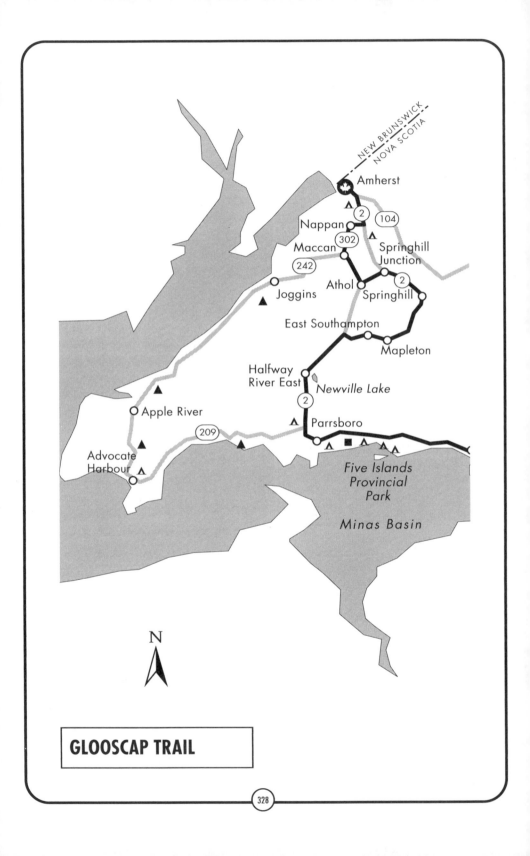

GLOOSCAP TRAIL

N

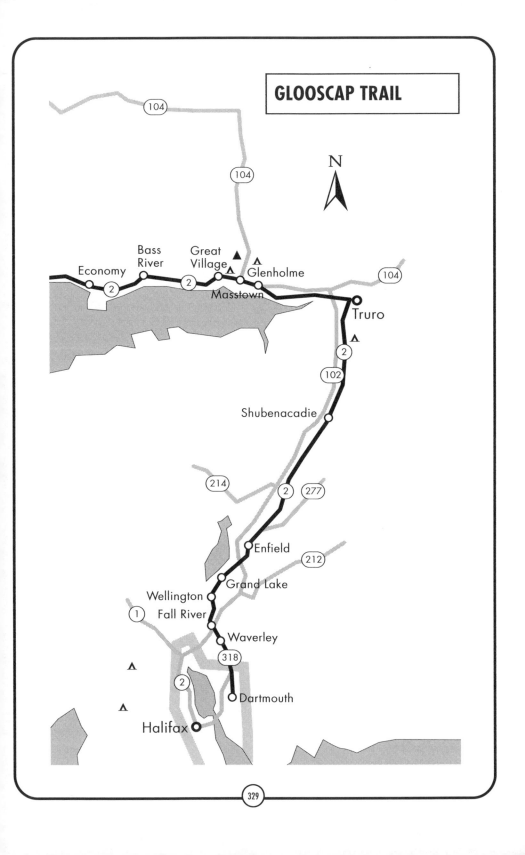

GLOOSCAP TRAIL

N

Economy — 2 — Bass River — 2 — Great Village — Glenholme
Masstown

Truro
2
102

Shubenacadie

214   2   277

Enfield
212
Grand Lake
Wellington
1   Fall River
Waverley
318
2
Dartmouth

Halifax

104

scarlet and yellow. Near Half-way River East the road goes along Newville Lake between the Canaan Mountains and the Boar's Back Ridge, which contains interesting rock formations. Continue on Highway 2 to Parrsboro.

Option: Maccan to Parrsboro via Apple River, 116 km (72 miles)

An alternative route for adventurous cyclists is to ride from Maccan to the coastal town of Joggins on Highway 242. Then take the road between the coast and the Chignecto Game Sanctuary to Apple River. Highway 209 from Apple River follows the coast of the Minas Channel through Advocate Harbour to Parrsboro.

The route is hilly, going from sea level to elevations of 230 meters (750 feet). The scenic winding route is often compared to the Cabot Trail. From Parrsboro, continue following the rest of this tour.

Main tour continues at Parrsboro

Parrsboro is the largest town on the northern shore of Minas Basin and a major tourist center. On the town's beaches and cliffs you can find amethyst, agates and other semi-precious stones. You can also see them in the Geological Museum. Around the corner from the museum is a giant statue of Glooscap, the Micmac god whom legend says created the Fundy tides and scattered the gems, his grandmother's jewelry, along the Minas shore.

94 km (58 miles) Five Island Provincial Park

Highway 2 continues east through a narrow gorge between high wooded hills. Five Islands is a popular tourist destination. The best view of the five offshore islands is from Five Islands Provincial Park, a campground and picnic area on the Minas Basin 24 km (15 miles) east of Parrsboro.

Economy Mountain, the only major hill on the tour, rises 215 meters (705 feet) above the Minas Basin and provides a panoramic view of the countryside. The name is from the Micmac word *Kenomee*, meaning "a long point jutting out into the sea."

157 km (97 miles) Truro

Continue on Highway 2 to Bass River where you can fish for striped bass near the mouth of the river. Ride on through Great Village, an important shipbuilding community and port of call during the nineteenth century. Many fine old sea captains' mansions remain.

Continue through the farming communities of Glenholm and Masstown to Truro.

Truro is at the junction of Highways 102, 2, 104 and 4, and is on the VIA Rail line. Take a break from bicycling and stroll through the 405-hectare (1,000-acre) Victoria Park where there are hiking trails and a deep gorge with two waterfalls.

The Salmon River in the north end of Truro, experiences a tidal bore. This wall of water, up to half a meter (18 inches) high, moves upstream against the current and can be seen from several viewing places. For tide times call DIAL-A-TIDE at (902) 426-5494.

190 km (118 miles) Shubenacadie

South of Truro, continue on Highway 2 towards Halifax. Along the way you go through the fertile Stewiacke River Valley, a traditional Micmac fishing and hunting territory. Near Shubenacadie, 33 km (20 miles) from Truro, is a provincial wildlife park where native birds and animals may be seen.

210 km (130 miles) Enfield

Ride 20 km (12 miles) on Highway 2 to Enfield near Halifax International Airport, which can be reached by Highway 102. Highway 2 crosses Highway 102 on an overpass.

219 km (136 miles) Grand Lake

At Grand Lake 9 km (5 miles) farther, Oakfield Park provides picnic facilities, while Laurie Provincial Park offers camping, swimming and fishing for salmon, trout and striped bass in Grand Lake.

231 km (143 miles) Highway 318 near Waverley

Ride Highway 2 for 12 km (7 miles) through Wellington and Fall River to Waverley.

246 km (153 miles) Dartmouth

From Waverley, take Highway 318, a tree-lined road that winds along the chain of lakes that make up what was once the Shubenacadie Canal. This road takes you into Dartmouth, 15 km (9 miles) from Waverley.

ACROSS NOVA SCOTIA

Length: 461 km (290 miles)
Time: Five to six days
Rating: Intermediate
Terrain: Rolling, hilly sections near Canso Causeway to Cape Breton Island.
Roads: Sections on four-lane roads have wide shoulder; other sections are on two-lane roads with no shoulder.
Traffic: Four-lane roads have heavy traffic, two-lane roads have light to moderate traffic.
Connects with: Glooscap Trail, Sunrise Trail, Cape George, Cabot Trail
Start: Amherst, just east of the New Brunswick–Nova Scotia boundary. Amherst can be reached by VIA Rail.
Overview: If you're crossing Nova Scotia en route from New Brunswick to North Sydney and the ferry to Newfoundland, you can combine

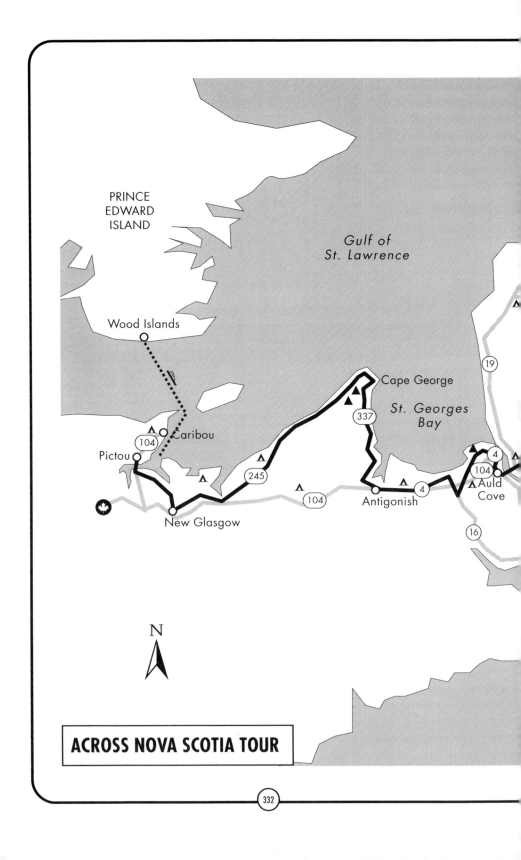

PRINCE
EDWARD
ISLAND

Gulf of
St. Lawrence

Wood Islands

Cape George

St. Georges
Bay

19

337

104
Caribou

Pictou

245

104

New Glasgow

Antigonish

4

104

Auld
Cove

16

N

ACROSS NOVA SCOTIA TOUR

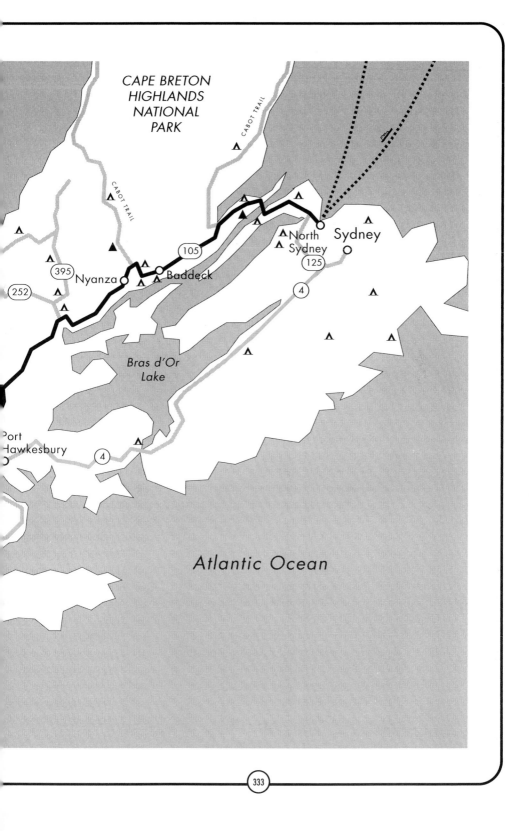

CAPE BRETON
HIGHLANDS
NATIONAL
PARK

CABOT TRAIL

CABOT TRAIL

105

395

252

Nyanza

Baddeck

North
Sydney

Sydney

125

4

Bras d'Or
Lake

Port
Hawkesbury

4

Atlantic Ocean

some of the tours here for a more scenic—though longer—route than taking the Trans Canada Highway.

THE ROUTE:

0 km (0 miles) Amherst

316 km (196 miles) Canso Causeway

From Amherst, ride the Sunrise Trail tour (described in this chapter) to Pictou.

Continue on the Sunrise Trail to the Cape George tour (also described in this chapter) and take that route to Antigonish.

Stay on the Sunrise Trail to Auld Cove on the Strait of Canso.

461 km (290 miles) North Sydney ferry terminal

Cross the Canso Causeway, which at a depth of 67 meters (217 feet) is the world's deepest causeway.

From the Canso Causeway cycle 151 km (94 miles) on Highway 105 (the Trans Canada Highway) to the North Sydney ferry terminal.

The road winds along the base of the Creignish Hills and crosses several brooks and rivers coming down from the mountains.

The highway then proceeds along Bras d'Or Lake, a vast inland sea connected to the Atlantic by the fjord-like channels, Great Bras d'Or and Little Bras d'Or to the northeast, and by St. Peter's Canal to the south.

At the town of Nyanza is a Micmac Indian reserve.

At Baddeck you connect with the Cabot Trail tour (described in this chapter).

Stay on Highway 105 to North Sydney, and the terminal for the ferry to Newfoundland.

GUIDEBOOKS

Bicycle Tours in Nova Scotia. Available from Bicycle Nova Scotia, P.O. Box 3010 South, Halifax, Nova Scotia B3J 3G6; $5.

Nova Scotia by Bicycle by Walton Watt. Available from Bicycle Nova Scotia; $25 includes postage, handling and GST.

The Nova Scotia Bicycle Book by Gary Conrod. Available from Atlantic Canada Cycling Festival, P.O. Box 1555, Station M, Halifax, Nova Scotia B3J 2Y3; $24.95 (or $21.95 U.S.) plus postage of $4.50, $9 for first class, or $7 for overseas.

Covehead Lighthouse
(Paul Demone)

Prince Edward Island

"The fairest land 'tis possible to see," was how sixteenth-century French explorer Jacques Cartier described Prince Edward Island. The Micmac Indians called it *Abegweit*, meaning "land cradled on the waves."

The Garden of the Gulf, as Prince Edward Island is now known, has a gentle coastline with long stretches of red and white sand beaches washed by warm ocean waves. The flat, leisurely country roads take you through red-soiled farmland, along wooded lots and past protected harbors with brightly colored fishing boats. Separated by 15 km (9 miles) of water from the mainland, PEI has a distinct rural character with a slower pace of life.

Excellent camping facilities, bed-and-breakfasts, farm accommodations and lobster dinners have made Prince Edward Island very popular with cyclists. Described here are tours of one day, two days, four days and six days. Most start in Charlottetown, the Island's largest city and the provincial capital. Some of the routes overlap.

Tourist Information: General tourism information including a map, and the *Visitors Guide* listing attractions, campgrounds and the full range of accommodations including bed-and-breakfasts, is available from: Prince Edward Island Tourist Information Center, Box 940, Charlottetown, Prince Edward Island C1A 7M5, or call toll-free 1-800-565-7421 in Prince Edward Island, Nova Scotia and New Brunswick; or 1-800-565-0267 from the rest of Canada and from the United States.

Accommodations: Prince Edward Island offers a variety of accommodation including bed-and-breakfasts, cottages, country inns, hotels, motels and tourist homes. The bed-and-breakfasts in towns and on farms are popular with cyclists as they offer good affordable accommodation and a true taste of the Island way of life.

Terrain: Low and rolling; PEI's highest point is in central Queens County at only 152 meters (500 feet) above sea level; lowest point is sea level.

Area: Canada's smallest province, PEI is only 224 km (140 miles) long and 6 to 64 km (4 to 40 miles) wide. Its 5,660 square km (2,185 square miles) comprises 0.1 per cent of Canada. Cycling distances are therefore quite short.

Roads: Prince Edward Island has the most miles of paved road per capita in the country. Routes 1 and 1A, and parts of Route 2 and 3 have paved shoulders. The generally low volume of traffic on most secondary roads provides safe and scenic bicycle touring routes.

The province has signposted three scenic routes: Blue Heron Drive, Kings Byway and Lady Slipper Drive. The tours in this chapter follows parts of these routes.

Weather: Prince Edward Island has a temperate climate; extreme and sudden changes in temperature are rare. The island gets more summer sunshine than the other Maritime provinces and is free of fog as it is sheltered from the Atlantic by Nova Scotia and Newfoundland. Summer days are generally warm, with an average high of 22.6 degrees Celsius (73 degrees Fahrenheit). Breezes are light but constant, averaging 22 km/hour (13 mph).

Nights are cool due to sea breezes. Morning dew is heavy and keeps the grass damp until around 10:00 a.m. Average annual precipitation is 110.5 cm (43.5 inches). Bring clothing for cool nights and occasional rain. The cool and dry autumn season is also pleasant for cycling.

Hostels: Prince Edward Island Hostel Association, 153 Mount Edward Road, P.O. Box 1718, Charlottetown, PEI, C1A 7N4, (902) 894-9696.

Ferries: Two ferry services connect Prince Edward Island to the mainland. **Cape Tormentine, New Brunswick to Borden, Prince Edward Island:** Marine Atlantic, P.O. Box 250, North Sydney, Nova Scotia B2A 3M3 or call from North Sydney, Nova Scotia (902) 794-5700; from St. John's Newfoundland (709) 772-7701; from Port aux Basques, Newfoundland (709) 695-7081; from Bar Harbor, Maine toll-free 1-800-341-7981. **Caribou, Nova Scotia to Woods Island, Prince Edward Island:** Northumberland Ferries Ltd., P.O. Box 634, Charlottetown, Prince Edward Island C1A 7L3, telephone (902) 566-3838; from Nova Scotia, New Brunswick and Prince Edward Island, call toll-free 1-800-565-0201. **Souris, Prince Edward Island to the Magdalen Islands, Québec:** See the Magdalen Islands tour in the Québec chapter.

Airports: Charlottetown is served by Air Canada and Canadian Airlines International.

Trains: There is no train service on Prince Edward Island. However, VIA Rail operates a bus service between Charlottetown, PEI and Moncton, New Brunswick via the Borden-Cape Tormentine ferry. This bus service does not take bicycles. To get information on VIA Rail service when on Prince Edward Island, call toll-free 1-800-561-3952.

Bicycling: Prince Edward Island Cycling Association, P.O. Box 2487, Charlottetown, PEI C1A 8C2, telephone (902) 566-5836.

Capital: Charlottetown, the provincial capital, is also PEI's largest city. In 1986 its population was 15,776.

Population: 129,765 (1991 census), the smallest population of Canada's ten provinces. Most Islanders are of British origin, approximately 12 per cent are of Acadian descent. There are also small Dutch, Lebanese and Micmac communities.

History: Micmac natives have lived on PEI for 2000 years. Following Jacques Cartier's landing in 1534, French and Basque fishermen visited the Island's harbors and bays. In 1720 French settlement began on PEI. The Treaty of Paris of 1763 gave PEI to the British. In 1864 the Charlottetown Conference was called to discuss the union of Prince Edward Island, Nova Scotia and New Brunswick. Representatives from Québec and Ontario (then called Lower Canada and Upper Canada) promoted the confederation of all the colonies of British North America. On July 1, 1867, the other colonies joined in the new federation. PEI did not join until 1873.

PRINCE EDWARD ISLAND NATIONAL PARK

Length: 37 km (27 miles)
Time: Day tour
Rating: Easy
Terrain: Flat route along spectacular beaches and sand dunes
Roads: Cycling is very popular along the Gulf Shore Parkway's two-meter- (6.5-foot-) wide paved shoulder. A 5.7-km (3.5-mile) cycling trail explores the Cavendish area.
Traffic: Busy in July and August, low during off-season
Connects with: Charlottetown to PEI National Park tour, Central Beach tour, and Eastern Kings tour all go through the park. The route is described here in more detail.
Start: Dalvay Beach, headquarters of Prince Edward Island National Park, is located 25 km (15 miles) from Charlottetown.
Overview: Red sandstone cliffs, sand dunes, marshes, ponds and 40 km (25 miles) of saltwater beaches dominate Prince Edward Island National Park's 32 square km (12 square miles) on the Gulf of St. Lawrence coast. The magnificent white sand dunes contrast to the clear blue ocean. In July and August, water temperatures average in the 20 degrees Celsius (70 degrees Fahrenheit) range, some of the warmest salt water north of the Carolinas.

There are national park campgrounds at Stanhope, Rustico Island and Cavendish, in addition to several private campgrounds in the area. The park has several nature trails. Supervised beaches are found at Cavendish, North Rustico, Brackley, Stanhope and Dalvay.

THE ROUTE:

0 km (0 miles) Dalvay Beach

Dalvay Beach got its name from Alexander MacDonald, a business associate of John D. Rockefeller. In 1898 MacDonald built a summer home here which he called Dalvay-by-the-Sea, after his ancestral home in Scotland. The residence is now a hotel near Dalvay Beach.

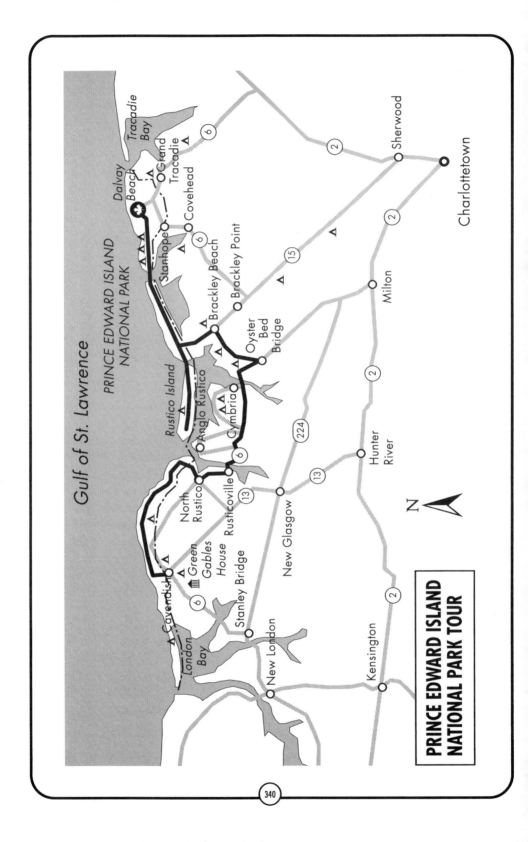

Gulf of St. Lawrence

PRINCE EDWARD ISLAND
NATIONAL PARK

Tracadie Bay

Dalvay Beach
Stanhope
Grand Tracadie
Covehead

Brackley Beach
Brackley Point

Rustico Island

Oyster Bed Bridge

Anglo Rustico
Cymbria

North Rustico
Rusticoville

Green Gables House

Cavendish
London Bay
Stanley Bridge

New London

Kensington

New Glasgow

Hunter River

Milton

Sherwood

Charlottetown

6

2

2

2

15

224

13

13

6

6

N

**PRINCE EDWARD ISLAND
NATIONAL PARK TOUR**

340

10 km (6 miles) Brackley Beach

From Dalvay, ride west on the Gulf Shore Parkway along the beaches and sand dunes of Stanhope Beach to Brackley Beach. On the way is the Brackley Marsh, a stopover for migrating birds in August.

Side trip: Brackley Beach to Rustico Island, 6 km (4 miles) each way

From Brackley Beach you can ride over the causeway to Rustico Island, a 6-km (4-mile) ride each way from Brackley Beach.

At one time, cranberries grown here were shipped all over eastern North America. Rustico Island is now home to a protected colony of Great Blue Herons.

Main tour

27 km (17 miles) North Rustico

From Brackley Beach, take Highway 15 and exit from this section of the park. After 2.5 km (1.5 miles), turn right onto Highway 6 (Blue Heron Drive scenic route) and ride Highway 6 for 14.5 km (9 miles) to North Rustico, one of the island's most picturesque villages.

37 km (23 miles) Cavendish

Re-enter Prince Edward Island National Park. Turn left and ride 10 km (6 miles) along the shore of the Gulf of St. Lawrence, past some of the Island's most spectacular coastal scenery.

You pass North Rustico Beach, Cape Turner and Orby Head on the way to Cavendish.

On the beach you may see "mossers," people who rake the Irish moss from the beach and load it into horse-drawn carts. Irish moss is a marine red algae containing carrageenin, used as an emulsifier and thickener in toothpastes, puddings and ice cream.

Cavendish is at the western end of the park. Here is a 5.7-km (3.5-mile) loop cycling trail.

At Cavendish is the Anne of Green Gables House, the home of Lucy Maud Montgomery and now a museum. Cavendish has been immortalized by Lucy Maud Montgomery in her "Anne" books.

The Cavendish cliffs erode at a rapid pace, up to 5 meters (15 feet) per year, by the action of wind and waves.

More Information: Prince Edward Island National Park, Box 487, Charlottetown, Prince Edward Island C1A 7L1, (902) 672-2211.

CHARLOTTETOWN TO PRINCE EDWARD ISLAND NATIONAL PARK

Length: 101 km (63 miles)
Time: One to two days
Rating: Leisurely, easy
Terrain: Gently rolling farmland, beaches
Roads: Route 2 has a paved shoulder, Route 6 has no shoulder
Traffic: Generally low traffic although Route 6 is busy especially during July and August.
Connects with: PEI National Park tour, Central Beach tour, Eastern Kings tour
Start: Charlottetown
Overview: This tour leads from Charlottetown across the island through gently rolling terrain dotted with picturesque farm buildings, to Prince Edward Island National Park. Ride along the park's sand dunes, white sands beaches and redstone cliffs. Return to Charlottetown through the island's rural interior.

THE ROUTE:

0 km (0 miles) Charlottetown

From Charlottetown, leave by St. Peter's Road, which becomes Highway 2 (signposted as the Kings Byway scenic route).

24 km (15 miles) Prince Edward Island National Park

After 14 km (9 miles) turn left onto Highway 6 and cycle 10 km (6 miles) to an entrance of Prince Edward Island National Park (see the Prince Edward Island National Park tour for a more detailed description).

Enter the park and ride along Dalvay Beach, Stanhope Beach and Brackley Beach on the Gulf of St. Lawrence. Be sure to stop and enjoy a swim.

National park campgrounds are located at Brackley Beach and private campgrounds at Stanhope Beach.

36 km (22 miles) Brackley Beach

After exploring the park, turn onto Highway 15 to the community of Brackley Beach. It's a 12 km (7 miles) ride from the eastern park entrance to Brackley Beach.

63 km (39 miles) Cavendish

Go right onto Highway 6 (the Blue Heron Drive scenic route) to North Rustico. Here is the western part of Prince Edward Island National Park. Ride along North Rustico Beach and Orby Head on the Gulf of St. Lawrence to the town of Cavendish, 27 km (17 miles) from Brackley Beach. There are numerous campgrounds along this part of the route.

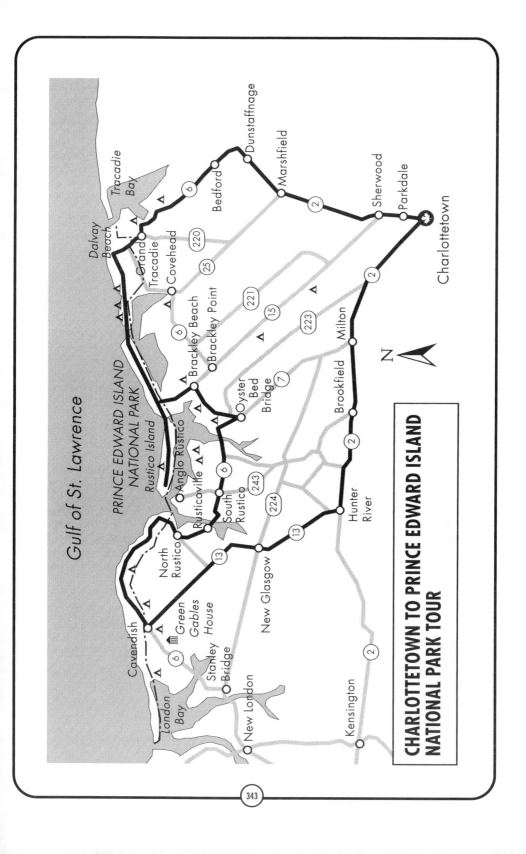

Gulf of St. Lawrence

Tracadie Bay

Dunstaffnage

Marshfield

Sherwood

Parkdale

Bedford

6

2

Dalvay Beach

Grand Tracadie

Covehead

220

25

Charlottetown

Brackley Beach

Brackley Point

221

15

223

2

6

PRINCE EDWARD ISLAND NATIONAL PARK

Rustico Island

Oyster Bed Bridge

7

Milton

Anglo Rustico

Rusticoville

6

Brookfield

2

South Rustico

243

224

Hunter River

N

North Rustico

13

New Glasgow

13

Cavendish

Green Gables House

Stanley Bridge

New London

London Bay

Kensington

2

6

CHARLOTTETOWN TO PRINCE EDWARD ISLAND NATIONAL PARK TOUR

79 km (49 miles) Hunter River

From Cavendish, go inland on Highway 13 for 16 km (10 miles) to Hunter River.

101 km (63 miles) Charlottetown

Then turn left onto Highway 2 for 22 km (14 miles) to Charlottetown.

CENTRAL BEACH LOOP

Length: 168 km (104 miles)
Time: Four days
Rating: Easy to moderate
Terrain: Gently rolling farmland, flat route along south shore
Roads: The Trans Canada Highway—Highway 1 and Highways 1A and 2 have good shoulders; all others are without shoulders.
Traffic: The Trans Canada Highway is busy; all other roads have low traffic
Connects with: West Prince Tour, PEI National Park tour, Charlottetown to PEI National Park tour, Eastern Kings tour
Start: Charlottetown
Overview: Cycling through central Prince Edward Island you explore the Island's red shores in the south and the white sand beaches and dunes of Prince Edward Island National Park along the north shore. While crossing the island, you ride through rolling fields where the famous PEI potatoes are grown, and on winding roads through the wooded Bonshaw Hills.

Part of this tour follows the Blue Heron Drive, where, as its name suggests, you can see blue herons in the tidal marshes. Along this route is the Borden terminus for the ferry from Cape Tormentine, New Brunswick. If you're arriving by this ferry, you can start this loop tour from there.

THE ROUTE:

0 km (0 miles) Charlottetown

11 km (7 miles) Cornwall

Leave Charlottetown via University Avenue, which becomes Highway 1 (the Trans Canada Highway and here part of the Blue Heron Drive). Ride Highway 1 for 11 km (7 miles) to Cornwall.

26 km (16 miles) Fort Amherst National Historic Park

Follow Highway 19 (Blue Heron Drive) another 15 km (9 miles) to Fort Amherst National Historic Park.

After the British won control of the island in 1758, they built Fort Amherst on the site of the French settlement of Port LaJoie founded in 1720.

60 km (37 miles) Victoria

After visiting Fort Amherst Park, continue cycling on Highway 19 along the shores of Hillsborough Bay to Canoe Cove on Northumberland Strait. At DeSable, turn left and follow

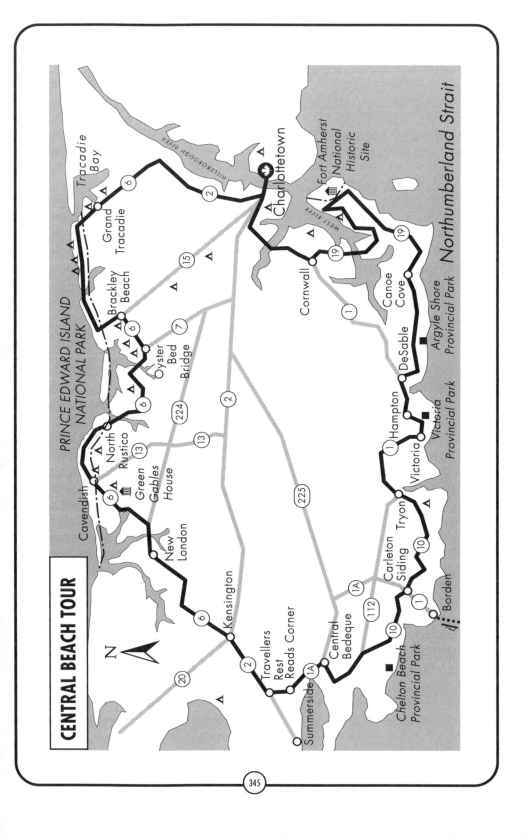

CENTRAL BEACH TOUR

N

PRINCE EDWARD ISLAND NATIONAL PARK

Northumberland Strait

Tracadie Bay

Grand Tracadie

Brackley Beach

Oyster Bed Bridge

Cavendish

Green Gables House

North Rustico

New London

Kensington

Travellers Rest

Reads Corner

Summerside

Central Bedeque

Carleton Siding

Chelton Beach Provincial Park

Borden

Tryon

Victoria

Victoria Provincial Park

Hampton

DeSable

Argyle Shore Provincial Park

Canoe Cove

Cornwall

Charlottetown

Fort Amherst National Historic Site

HILLSBOROUGH RIVER

WEST RIVER

Highway 1 (the Trans Canada Highway and Blue Heron Drive) to Hampton. At Hampton, turn left onto Route 231 and ride to the picturesque seaside village of Victoria, a 34-km (21-mile) ride from Fort Amherst. Nearby are private campgrounds, inns and cottages. Sailing excursions can be arranged in Victoria.

67 km (41 miles) Tryon

From Victoria, continue on Highway 1 (the Trans Canada Highway and Blue Heron Drive), to Tryon, 7 km (4 miles) away.

78 km (48 miles) Carleton Siding

From Tryon follow Highway 10 (Blue Heron Drive) another 11 km (7 miles) to Carleton Siding.

Option: Borden ferry terminal, 3 km (2 miles)

From Carleton Siding, Highway 1 goes south 3 km (2 miles) to Borden and the terminus for the ferry to Cape Tormentine, New Brunswick.

Main tour continues

81 km (50 miles) Central Bedeque

From Carleton Siding, continue on Highway 10 (Blue Heron Drive) for 3 km (8 miles) to Central Bedeque.

89 km (55 miles) Reads Corner

Then ride for 8 km (5 miles) on Highway 1A into Reads Corner.

91 km (56 miles) Travellers Rest

From Reads Corner, cycle 2 km (1.2 miles) on Highway 1A (Blue Heron Drive) to Travellers Rest.

99 km (61 miles) Kensington

Turn right onto Highway 2 for 8 km (5 miles) to Kensington.

110 km (68 miles) New London

From here take Highway 6 for 11 km (7 miles) to New London. Along the way are several artists' communities.

121 km (75 miles) Cavendish in PEI National Park

Continue on Highway 6 (it rejoins Blue Heron Drive), for 11 km (7 miles) to Cavendish.

131 km (81 miles) North Rustico

Ride into Prince Edward Island National Park and along Cavendish Beach and North Rustico Beach on the Gulf of St. Lawrence. (See the Prince Edward Island National Park tour for a more detailed description of this part of the route.)

There is a national park campground at Cavendish Beach and several private campgrounds along the way. It's 10 km (6 miles) from Cavendish to the village of North Rustico.

141 km (88 miles) Oyster Bed Bridge

At North Rustico, you leave the western section of Prince Edward Island National Park, and ride 10 km (6 miles) on Highway 6 (Blue Heron Drive) to Oyster Bed Bridge.

144 km (89 miles) Brackley Beach

Continue on Highway 6 for 3 km (1.8 miles) to Highway 15 and turn left to Brackley Beach and the eastern part of Prince Edward Island National Park. You ride along Brackley Beach, Stanhope Beach and Dalvay Beach.

168 km (104 miles) Charlottetown

Exit from the park and turn left onto Highway 6 (part of the Kings Byway scenic route). Ride Highway 6 and then turn right onto Highway 2 and cycle into Charlottetown, 24 km (15 miles) farther.

EASTERN KINGS TOUR

Length: 305 km (190 miles)
Time: Six days
Rating: Easy; cool winds near East Point and along the North Shore can be challenging.
Terrain: Flat, some small hills
Roads: Trans Canada Highway—Highway 1—has a good shoulder, the others don't have shoulders
Traffic: Trans Canada Highway and Highway 1A can be busy during the summer and commuting hours; the other areas have fairly low traffic.
Connects with: Prince Edward Island National Park tour, Charlottetown to Prince Edward Island National Park. Along this route is Souris, terminus for the ferry to the Magdalen Islands of Québec (described in the Québec chapter).
Start: Charlottetown
Overview: Explore the tall capes, long white beaches, deep inlets and harbors of eastern Prince Edward Island on the first part of this tour. You ride through charming towns with an old-world flavor, lively fishing ports and villages settled by Scottish and French pioneers.

At East Point you can see Nova Scotia. The tour then turns west and goes along the spectacular beaches of Prince Edward Island National Park on the Gulf of St. Lawrence.

THE ROUTE:

0 km (0 miles) Charlottetown

5 km (3 miles) Cross Roads

Leave Charlottetown by going east on Highway 1 (the Trans Canada Highway and the Kings Byway scenic route), across the Hillsborough Bridge, for 5 km (3 miles) to Cross Roads.

17 km (11 miles) Highway 1 near Mount Mellick

From Cross Roads, take Highway 1A (Kings Byway), to Tea Hill. At the top of Tea Hill you have a spectacular view of Northumberland Strait and Governor's Island. Follow Highway 1A through strawberry country to Highway 1 near Mount Mellick, a ride of 12 km (7 miles) from Cross Roads.

29 km (18 miles) Orwell

Go right and follow Highway 1 (the Trans Canada Highway and Kings Byway) for 12 km (7 miles) to Orwell. Here is Orwell Corner Historic Site, a

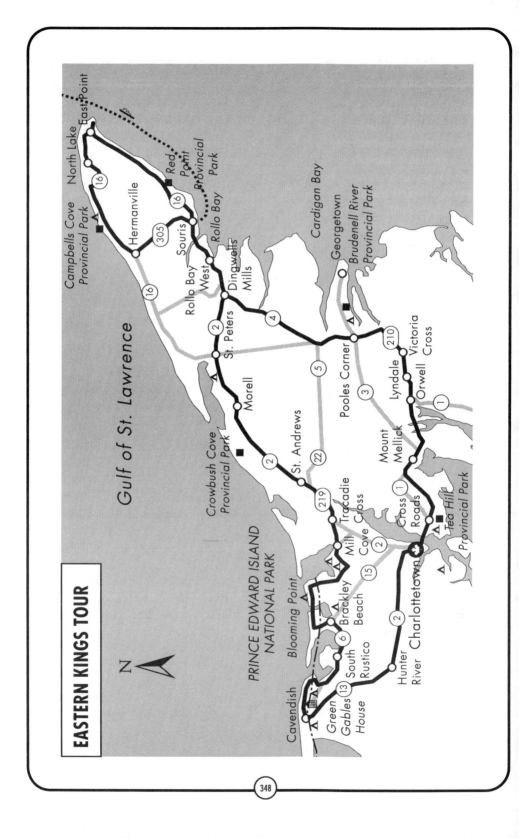

EASTERN KINGS TOUR

N

Gulf of St. Lawrence

East Point
North Lake
Campbells Cove Provincial Park
Red Point
Provincial Park
Hermanville
Rollo Bay
16
16
305
Souris
Rollo Bay West
Dingwells Mills
Cardigan Bay
Georgetown
Brudenell River Provincial Park
16
St. Peters
2
4
5
210
Victoria Cross
Pooles Corner
Lyndale
3
Orwell
1
Crowbush Cove Provincial Park
Morell
St. Andrews
22
Mount Mellick
2
PRINCE EDWARD ISLAND NATIONAL PARK
219
Tracadie Cross
1
Cross Roads
Tea Hill Provincial Park
Blooming Point
Mill Cove Cross
2
Brackley Beach
15
Charlottetown
6
South Rustico
13
Green Gables House
Cavendish
Hunter River
2

community restored to depict nineteenth-century Prince Edward Island life.

45 km (28 miles) Montague

From Orwell, take Secondary Highway 210. Go right on Highway 24 at Kinross and then left on Secondary Highway 210 through Lyndale and Victoria Cross to Montague, 16 km (10 miles) from Orwell.

The third-largest town on Prince Edward Island, Montague is the home of the Garden of the Gulf Museum. If you're camping, the nearest provincial park with camping is Brudenell River Provincial Park, 5 km (3 miles) along Highway 4 and right for another 5 km (3 miles).

79 km (49 miles) Rollo Bay West

Ride north from Montague along Highway 4 for 34 km (21 miles) to Rollo Bay West.

89 km (55 miles) Souris

Take Highway 2 (Kings Byway) to Souris, 10 km (6 miles) farther. Souris, the Island's fourth-largest town, is the terminus for the ferry to the Magdalen Islands of Québec (see the Magdalen Islands tour in the Québec chapter).

East Point Loop

From Souris, this tour loops around East Point and returns to Souris. You can use Souris as a base to leave some of your gear and ride with less weight.

119 km (74 miles) North Lake

Leave Souris and ride Secondary Highway 305 to Hermanville

on the Gulf of St. Lawrence. Turn right and follow Highway 16 (Kings Byway) along the north shore to North Lake, a distance of 30 km (18 miles) from Souris. North Lake is known for its tuna fishing.

129 km (80 miles) East Point

Ride another 10 km (6 miles) to East Point, from where you have a view of Cape Breton Island, 56 km (35 miles) away. At the tip of the point is the East Point Lighthouse, warning ships of the dangerous rock reef and turbulent waters below.

154 km (96 miles) Souris

Head west along Highway 16 to Basin Head, and past Red Point Provincial Park back to Souris, 25 km (15 miles) from East Point.

164 km (102 miles) Rollo Bay West

From Souris, ride for 10 km (6 miles) on Highway 2 (Kings Byway) to Rollo Bay West.

176 km (109 miles) St. Peters

Follow Highway 2 west for 19 km (12 miles) to St. Peters, which was founded by shipwrecked French sailors. St. Peters Provincial Park offers a good beach and campground. Many mussel lines demonstrating the success of commercial aquaculture can be seen in St. Peters Bay.

215 km (134 miles) Mill Cove

Continue on Highway 2 (here it rejoins the Kings Byway). At Tracadie Cross, turn right onto Secondary Highway 219 to Mill

Cove, a 39-km (24-mile) ride from St. Peters.

223 km (139 miles) Stanhope Beach in PEI National Park

Go right on Highway 6 to the Dalvay Beach entrance of Prince Edward Island National Park, and ride the park road along the Gulf of St. Lawrence to Stanhope Beach, 8 km (5 miles) from Mill Cove. (See the Prince Edward Island National Park tour for a detailed description of this part of the route.) At Stanhope Beach is a national park campground as well as a selection of private campgrounds.

236 km (147 miles) Brackley Beach

From Stanhope Beach ride along the shore for 13 km (8 miles) to Brackley Beach.

249 km (155 miles) North Rustico

Take Highway 15 and turn right onto Highway 6 and ride to North Rustico, another 13 km (8 miles).

257 km (160 miles) North Rustico Beach

From here, ride 8 km (5 miles) to North Rustico Beach.

267 km (166 miles) Cavendish Beach

Ride 10 km (6 miles) along the beaches on the Northumberland Strait to Cavendish Beach. A national park campground is situated here. There are also private campgrounds nearby.

283 km (176 miles) Hunter River

From Cavendish take Highway 13 for 16 km (10 miles) to Hunter River.

305 km (190 miles) Charlottetown

Turn left onto Highway 2 and ride 22 km (14 miles) into Charlottetown.

WEST PRINCE TOUR

Length: 359 km (223 miles)
Time: Eight days
Rating: Intermediate
Terrain: Generally flat with some rolling hills
Roads: Route 2 and the Trans Canada Highway—Highway 1—have good paved shoulders; the remaining roads don't have shoulders
Traffic: Busy near ferry terminal and around Summerside, low traffic otherwise

Connects with: Central Beach Tour
Start: Borden ferry terminal
Overview: This tour takes you along the scenic shores of Malpeque Bay, renowned for its oysters, through farming areas and fishing villages to North Cape. At North Cape the waters of the Gulf of St. Lawrence meet the Northumberland Strait, providing a spectacular scene. You then ride south along the cliffs and rolling fields of PEI's west coast. At Cedar

Dunes Park are the island's only cedar trees. From here, you can see New Brunswick's north shore.

After crossing red farmland near O'Leary, where more than half of PEI's potatoes are grown, you ride through central Prince County which was settled by Acadians in the mid-1700s.

THE ROUTE:

0 km (0 miles) Borden

28 km (17 miles) Summerside

Leaving Borden, follow Highway 1—the Trans Canada Highway. Go left on Highway 1A through Central Bedeque to Reads Corner. Turn left on Route 11 into Summerside.

33 km (20 miles) Miscouche

From Summerside, take Route 11 and turn left on Highway 2 for 5 km (3 miles) to Miscouche, home of the Acadian Museum.

37 km (23 miles) Route 122

Continue on Route 2 for about 6 km (4 miles) and turn right onto Route 122.

62 km (38 miles) Green Park

Ride Route 122, turn left onto Route 12. Ride Route 12 along the Grand River and Malpeque Bay for 25 km (15 miles) to Green Park, where there is a provincial campground. Nearby on Lennox Island is the Micmac Nation Reserve.

92 km (57 miles) Foxley River

Continue north on Route 12 (Lady Slipper Drive scenic route) for 30 km (19 miles). Keep left at Foxley River through Woodbrook and turn back onto Route 2.

107 km (66 miles) Mill River Provincial Park

Turn right at Portage, and ride 15 km (9 miles) to Mill River Provincial Park where camping and a resort are located.

108 km (67 miles) Route 172

From Mill River follow along Route 136 for about 1 km (0.6 mile) to Route 172.

110 km (68 miles) Route 12

Turn left on Route 172. Ride 2 km (1.2 miles) on Route 172 to rejoin Route 12.

127 km (79 miles) Jacques Cartier Park

Turn left and ride 17 km (11 miles) along Cascumpec Bay through Alberton past the Kildare River to Jacques Cartier Park. Here you can swim and visit a monument commemorating Cartier's sighting of PEI in 1534.

156 km (97 miles) North Cape

Then ride 29 km (18 miles) along the coast from Jacques Cartier Park, past the windswept red sandstone cliffs of Kildare Capes, and onto North Cape, site of an international wind generator test laboratory.

167 km (104 miles) Christopher Cross

From North Cape you travel 3 km (2 miles) along Route 12 to Route 14. Take Route 14 for 8 km (5 miles) to Christopher Cross.

175 km (109 miles) Skinners Pond

Continue riding on Route 14 for 8 km (5 miles) through Nail

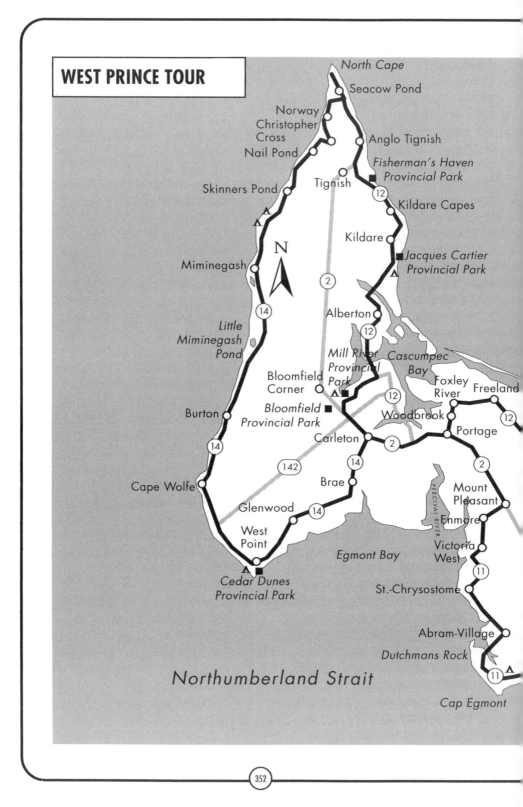

WEST PRINCE TOUR

North Cape
Seacow Pond
Norway
Christopher
Cross
Nail Pond
Anglo Tignish
*Fisherman's Haven
Provincial Park*
Skinners Pond
Tignish
(12)
Kildare Capes
Kildare
*Jacques Cartier
Provincial Park*
Miminegash
(2)
Alberton
(12)
N
(14)
*Little
Miminegash
Pond*
*Mill River
Provincial
Park*
*Cascumpec
Bay*
Foxley
River
Freeland
Bloomfield
Corner
(12)
Woodbrook
Burton
*Bloomfield
Provincial Park*
Carleton
(2)
Portage
(12)
(14)
(2)
(142)
(14)
Brae
Cape Wolfe
PERCIVAL RIVER
Mount
Pleasant
Glenwood
(14)
Enmore
West
Point
Victoria
West
Egmont Bay
(11)
St.-Chrysostome
▲■
*Cedar Dunes
Provincial Park*
Abram-Village
Dutchmans Rock
(11) ▲
Northumberland Strait
Cap Egmont

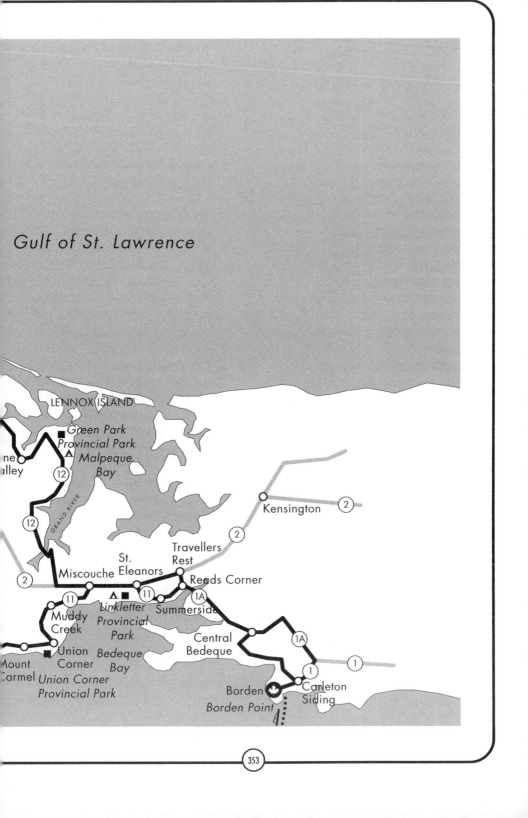

Gulf of St. Lawrence

LENNOX ISLAND

Green Park
Provincial Park

Malpeque
Bay

ne
lley

12

12

GRAND RIVER

2

Kensington

2

Travellers
Rest

St.
Eleanors

Miscouche

Reads Corner

2

11

11

Linkletter
Provincial
Park

Summerside

1A

Muddy
Creek

Central
Bedeque

1A

Union
Corner

Bedeque
Bay

Mount
Carmel

Union Corner
Provincial Park

Borden

Carleton
Siding

1

1

Borden Point

Pond to Skinners Pond. Camping within walking distance of the beach and harbor is available at Skinners Pond.

188 km (117 miles) Miminegash

Stay on Route 14 for 15 km (9 miles) through Miminegash.

223 km (138 miles) Cedar Dunes Provincial Park

Keep riding another 35 km (22 miles) to Cedar Dunes Provincial Park and West Point Lighthouse where a restored century-old lighthouse serves as a museum, dining room and guest house.

247 km (153 miles) Carleton

From West Point ride 24 km (15 miles) on Route 14 along the shore of Egmont Bay to Carleton and Route 2.

265 km (165 miles) Mount Pleasant

Go right (south) on Route 2 for 18 km (11 miles) to Mount Pleasant.

302 km (188 miles) Mont-Carmel

Turn right at Mount Pleasant, and follow Route 11—the Lady Slipper scenic route—for 37 km (23 miles) through Enmore, Victoria West and St. Chrysostome to Mont-Carmel. This scenic, flat tour along Cape Egmont is in the heartland of the island's Evangeline region.

At Mont-Carmel is an Acadian Pioneer Village and the grand spires of the Mont-Carmel church towering over the surrounding farm land. Camping, cottages and cabins are available near Mont-Carmel.

320 km (199 miles) Miscouche

From Mont-Carmel, continue on Route 11 for 18 km (11 miles) through Union Corner and Muddy Creek to Miscouche. Camping is available at Union Corner Provincial Park.

331 km (206 miles) Travellers Rest

Turn right on Route 2 for 11 km (7 miles) to Travellers Rest.

359 km (223 miles) Borden ferry terminus

From Travellers Rest, take Highway 1A for 11 km (7 miles) to Central Bedeque.

Then take Highway 10 for 13 km (8 miles) through to Carleton Siding at the junction with Highway 1.

Take Highway 1 south for 4 km (3 miles) to the Borden ferry terminus, this tour's starting point. From here the ferry crosses the Northumberland Strait to Cape Tormentine, New Brunswick.

Option: Travellers Rest to Kensington on Central Beach tour

From Travellers Rest, you can continue on Highway 2 for 8 km (5 miles) to Kensington and link with the Central Beach tour (described in this chapter).

ACROSS PRINCE EDWARD ISLAND

If you're crossing Prince Edward Island from its western ferry terminus at Borden to its eastern ferry terminus at Woods Island as part of a cross country cycling tour, the quickest route across the island is the Trans Canada Highway. You should, however, definitely consider spending more time exploring this picturesque island.

Length: 115 km (71 miles)

Start: Borden, terminus of the Marine Atlantic ferry from Cape Tormentine, New Brunswick.

THE ROUTE:

0 km (0 miles) Borden

54 km (33 miles) Charlottetown

From Borden, follow Highway 1 (the Trans Canada Highway) for 54 km (33 miles) through farmland to Charlottetown.

115 km (71 miles) Woods Island

From Charlottetown, ride east for 61 km (28 miles) on Highway 1 along Hillsborough Bay and Northumberland Strait to Woods Island, the terminus for the ferry to Caribou, Nova Scotia.

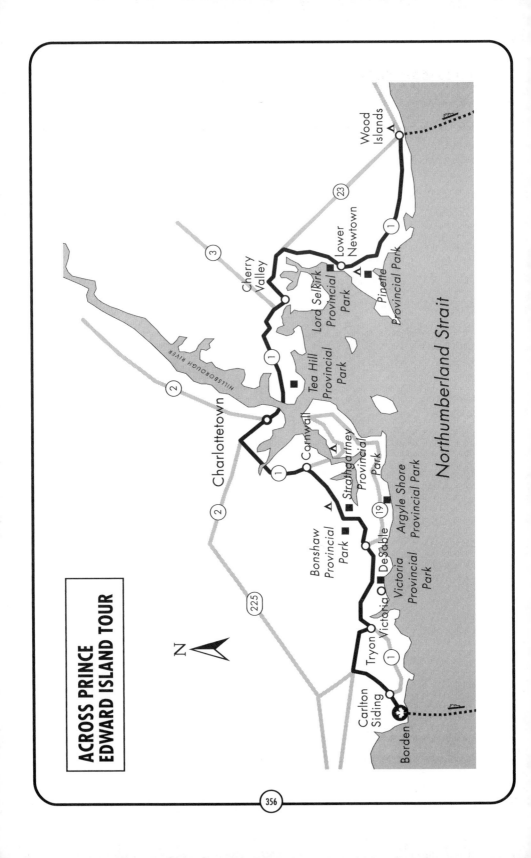

ACROSS PRINCE EDWARD ISLAND TOUR

Wood Islands

23

1

Lower Newtown

Cherry Valley

3

Lord Selkirk Provincial Park

Pinette Provincial Park

1

Tea Hill Provincial Park

Northumberland Strait

2

HILLSBOROUGH RIVER

Charlottetown

1

Cornwall

Strathgartney Provincial Park

1

Argyle Shore Provincial Park

2

Bonshaw Provincial Park

DeSable

19

Victoria Provincial Park

225

Victoria

Tryon

1

N

Carlton Siding

Borden

GUIDEBOOKS

Cycling the Islands: PEI and the Magdalen Islands, by Campbell Webster. Available from Breakwater Books Ltd., P.O. Box 2188, St. John's, Newfoundland A1C 6E6, telephone (709) 722-6680; $9.95.

Western Brook Gorge, Gros Morne Park
*(Courtesy of Department of Tourism and Culture,
Government of Newfoundland and Labrador)*

Newfoundland and Labrador

A rugged rocky island in the Atlantic Ocean, Newfoundland is Canada's eastern-most province. The 112,293-square-km (43,359-square-mile) island has been isolated for much of its history, and many of the outport communities were cut off from each other, except by coastal boat, until relatively recently. Many areas still have an old-world atmosphere.

The island of Newfoundland is a continuation of the Appalachian Mountain chain. The Long Range Mountains on the northern peninsula rise abruptly from the west coast. Newfoundland's rugged southern and eastern coasts are laced with islets, filigree bays and coves.

The coast of Labrador is on the Canadian mainland. The island of Newfoundland is separated from Labrador by the Strait of Belle Isle, which is 17 km (11 miles) wide at its narrowest point.

Newfoundland's unique bicycling opportunities have yet to be discovered by many cyclists. There is a lot more to cycling in Newfoundland than crossing the island via the Trans Canada Highway. The cycling tours here explore secondary roads, taking you to picturesque outport communities and spectacular scenery. In many settlements are hospitality homes, offering accommodation with a Newfoundland family. If you're planning to cross Newfoundland, take a side trip on one of these tours on secondary roads.

Tourist Information: For a current accommodation guide that includes campgrounds, road map and other tourist information, contact: Newfoundland Tourism, P.O. Box 8730, St. John's, Newfoundland A1B 4K2, toll-free 1-800-563-6353.

Weather: In early summer, floating ice moves southward producing fog and cool weather on the island. Average summer temperatures range from 11 to 21 degrees Celsius (52 to 70 degrees Fahrenheit) in St. John's. Newfoundland experiences frequent high winds, and on the east coast precipitation is heavy. St. John's experiences rain or snow an average of 201 days per year and has an average total precipitation of 137 cm (54 inches) per year.

Hostels: Newfoundland Hostelling Association, P.O. Box 1815, St. John's, Newfoundland A1C 5P9, telephone (709) 739-5866.

Roads: Most of the highways on the island of Newfoundland are paved two-lane roads, but not all of them have paved shoulders. Over an extended period of time, the Trans Canada Highway through Newfoundland is being improved to include passing lanes, wider lanes and paved shoulders.

The rugged and isolated coast of Labrador has approximately 80 km (50 miles) of road, about 40 km (30 miles) of which are paved.

Ferries: Marine Atlantic provides ferry service from North Sydney, Nova Scotia to Channel-Port aux Basques and Argentia, as well as serving Newfoundland outports. Some cycling tours include ferries.

If you want to take the ferry, make reservations well in advance and be sure to ask for the extra cost of transporting your bike.

For more information and reservations, contact: Marine Atlantic, P.O. Box 250, North Sydney, Nova Scotia B2A 3M3; telephone from North Sydney, Nova Scotia (902) 794-5700; from St. John's Newfoundland (709) 772-7701; from Channel-Port aux Basques, Newfoundland (709) 695-7081; from Bar Harbor, Maine toll-free 1-800-341-7981.

Trains: There is no passenger train service in Newfoundland. For information on VIA Rail service when you're in Newfoundland, call toll-free 1-800-561-3926.

The rail tracks on Newfoundland have been removed and consideration is now being given to making the corridor a recreational trail. The provincial cycling association was one of the first to propose this change.

Airports: Canada's major airlines serve Gander and St. John's. Regional airlines serve smaller centers in Newfoundland, Labrador and the island.

Buses: Bus service on the island is provided by Terra Transport Roadcruiser Services, 495 Water Street, P.O. Box 310, St. John's, Newfoundland A1C 5K1 (709) 737-5912.

Bicycling: The Newfoundland and Labrador Cycling Association, P.O. Box 2127, Station C, St. John's, Newfoundland A1C 5R6.

Capital: St. John's, Newfoundland's largest city, is a historic port on the Avalon peninsula. Near St. John's is Cape Spear, the easternmost point in North America. It's closer to Ireland than to Winnipeg or Miami.

Area: 404,517 square km (156,144 square miles) of which 112,299 square km (43,347 square miles) is the island of Newfoundland, and 292,218 square km (112,796 square miles) are in Labrador.

Terrain: On the island of Newfoundland's west coast are the Long Range Mountains. Gros Morne Mountain, the island's second highest peak, reaches 795 meters (2,651 feet). The interior is a plateau covered with forests and crossed by rivers. The northeast coast on the Atlantic has many bays, islands and headlands. The south coast is characterized by rocky headlands and hidden shoals.

On the mountainous and fjord-indented coast of Labrador is Newfoundland's highest point, 1,652-meter (5,420-foot) Mount Caubvick in the Torngat Mountains.

Population: 568,474 (1991 census),

ninth-largest of Canada's ten provinces.

History: Newfoundland may well have been the first part of North America seen by Europeans. Vikings from Iceland and Greenland settled at L'Anse aux Meadows in northern Newfoundland during the tenth century. In the fifteenth century the Grand Banks, the fishing grounds off southeastern Newfoundland, were visited by Basque, French and Portuguese fishermen. Settlement of Newfoundland began by the British in 1583 and continued during the 1600s.

Newfoundland rejected joining Canada in 1867, and remained a British Colony until 1948 when, in a referendum, a majority of voters indicated they wanted to join Canada. In 1949 Newfoundland joined Canadian confederation. The economy, once based on fishing, mining and forestry, is increasingly directed to tourism and oil exploration.

CHANNEL-PORT AUX BASQUES TO CRABBES RIVER

Length: Main tour is 90 km (56 miles); with side tours 45 km (28 miles), 36 km (22 miles), 13 km (8 miles) and 5 km (3 miles)

Time: One or two days

Rating: Intermediate

Terrain: Rises gradually as you travel northeast

Roads: All are paved with good surfaces

Traffic: Light except near ferry departures

Connects with: Across Newfoundland tour

Start: Channel-Port aux Basques, the Marine Atlantic terminus for the ferry from North Sydney, Nova Scotia.

Overview: The southwestern coastal plains of Newfoundland are the first part of Newfoundland that many visitors see. The rugged coast here has dark cliffs pounded by waves. Most of the tour follows the Trans Canada Highway, with side trips along secondary roads.

THE ROUTE:

0 km (0 miles) Channel-Port aux Basques

Port aux Basques was named by Basque fishermen as long ago as the sixteenth century.

Side trip: Channel-Port aux Basques to Rose Blanche 45 km (28 miles)

A side trip can be made east along the coast of Cabot Strait. Ride 27 km (16 miles) east on Route 470 to Otter Bay Provincial Park, which has campsites and a swimming area.

Along the way is Isle aux Morts, French for "Island of the Dead," so named because of the more than 40 shipwrecks that lie in the waters of Cabot Strait.

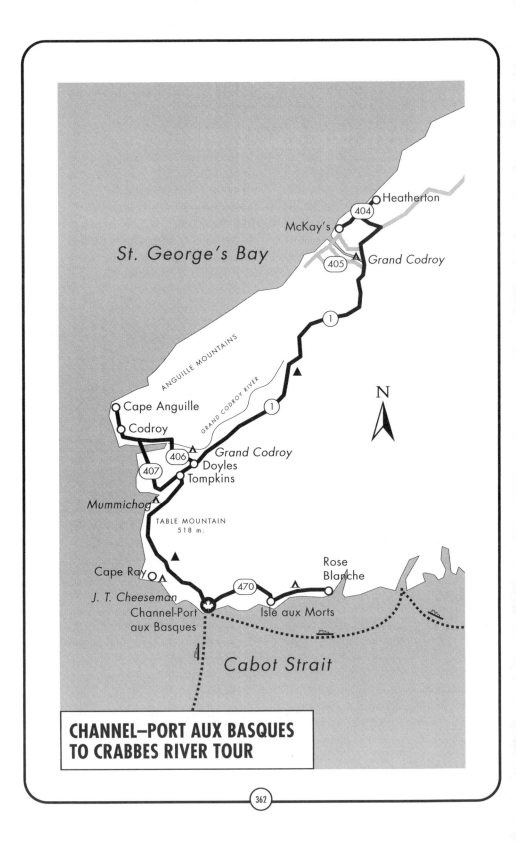

St. George's Bay

Heatherton

McKay's

404

405 Grand Codroy

1

ANGUILLE MOUNTAINS

GRAND CODROY RIVER

1

N

Cape Anguille

Codroy

406 Grand Codroy

407 Doyles

Tompkins

Mummichog

TABLE MOUNTAIN
518 m.

Cape Ray

Rose
Blanche

J. T. Cheeseman

Channel-Port
aux Basques

470 Isle aux Morts

Cabot Strait

CHANNEL–PORT AUX BASQUES
TO CRABBES RIVER TOUR

At Rose Blanche, 18 km (11 miles) east of Otter Bay, is a stone lighthouse, dating from 1856, with a good view of the Cabot Strait.

Main tour begins

From Channel - Port aux Basques, start riding on the Trans Canada Highway—Highway 1.

2.5 km (1.5 miles) John Cheeseman Provincial Park

At John Cheeseman Provincial Park and Cape Ray Sands are sandy beaches.

At 518-meter (1,700-foot) Table Mountain, part of the Long Range Mountains, is a hiking trail to a scenic viewpoint.

20.5 km (13 miles) Mummichog Provincial Park

Ride to Mummichog Provincial Park, 18 km (11 miles) from John Cheeseman Park, which has 15 km (9 miles) of beach and a 2-km (1.2-mile) nature trail. It's a good spot for birdwatching.

26.5 km (16 miles) Tompkins

Ride to Tompkins, 6 km (4 miles) farther.

Side trip: Tompkins through Codroy Valley to Doyles, 36 km (22 miles)

At Tompkins, take Route 407 to through Millville, Codroy a picturesque farming area and other communities to reach Cape Anguille, Newfoundland's most westerly point. Cape Anguille is located 20 km (12 miles) from Tompkins.

To return, take Route 406 to the community of Doyles at the junction with the Trans Canada Highway, 16 km (10 miles) from Cape Anguille.

Along the way is Grand Codroy Provincial Park (day-use only), 3 km (1.8 miles) from the Trans Canada Highway.

Main tour continues

35 km (22 miles) Doyles

If you stay on the Trans Canada Highway instead of the above side trip, ride 10 km (6 miles) from Tompkins to Doyles.

90 km (56 miles) Crabbes River Provincial Park

Ride along the Trans Canada Highway for 55 km (34 miles) from Doyles to Crabbes River Provincial Park, which has swimming in the river and camping.

Side trip: Trans Canada Highway to St. Fintan's, 5 km (3 miles)

Here you can turn off the Trans Canada Highway and ride 5 km (3 miles) on Route 405 to explore the community of St. Fintan's. You can buy fresh fish from the local fishermen.

Side trip: Trans Canada Highway to Heatherton, 13 km (8 miles)

Another 3 km (2 miles) on the Trans Canada Highway past Crabbes River Provincial Park, you can take Route 404 to the scenic fishing and farming communities of McKays and Heatherton.

DEER LAKE TO GROS MORNE NATIONAL PARK

Length: 100 km (62 miles)
Time: One day
Rating: Intermediate
Terrain: Undulating barren hills, with some stiff climbs
Roads: Paved; paved shoulder in Gros Morne Park
Traffic: Many recreational vehicles during June to August
Connects with: Viking Trail from Gros Morne National Park to St. Anthony tour, across Newfoundland tour.

Start: Deer Lake is at the junction of the Trans Canada Highway and Route 430, which leads to Newfoundland's northern peninsula and southern Labrador. The community is served by an airport with interprovincial flights. Terra Transport Trans Island Motorcoaches also makes routine stops but carry bicycles on a space-available basis only.

Overview: The highest and most spectacular portion of the Long Range Mountains is found in 1,812-square-km (700-square-mile) Gros Morne National Park on Newfoundland's west coast, one of the province's most scenic areas. Gros Morne's coastal Long Range Mountains are indented by huge fjords with cliffs rising 600 meters (1,968 feet) above the water. The shoreline varies from boulders to fine sandy beaches. The coastal tidal pools support crabs, starfish, chitons, mussels, barnacles, periwinkles, hermit crabs, sea urchins and sea anemones. There are campsites and beaches along the shores of Deer Lake and Upper Humber.

THE ROUTE:

0 km (0 miles) Deer Lake

23 km (14 miles) Wiltondale

Take Route 430, known as The Viking Trail, out of Deer Lake and ride 23 km (14 miles) of long steep hills to Wiltondale, near the entrance to Gros Morne National Park.

50 km (31 miles) Turn-off for Rocky Harbour in Gros Morne National Park

Continue on Route 430. The road winds up steep climbs, flattens out and then descends. There are passing lanes along the steep climbs.

The road then skirts the shore of Bonne Bay's East Arm.

After 27 km (17 miles) take the turn-off which leads 5 km (3 miles) to Rocky Harbour, a fishing village and headquarters of Gros Morne National Park. Gros Morne's main campground, Berry Hill, is 4 km (2.5 miles) north of Rocky Harbour.

54 km (34 miles) Lobster Head Cove

Ride north along flat and rolling hills to Lobster Cove Head, 6 km (4 miles) north of the Rocky Harbour. Located at the entrance to Bonne Bay, Lobster Head Cove has a lighthouse with marine displays.

64 km (40 miles) Green Point

Route 430 follows the rugged

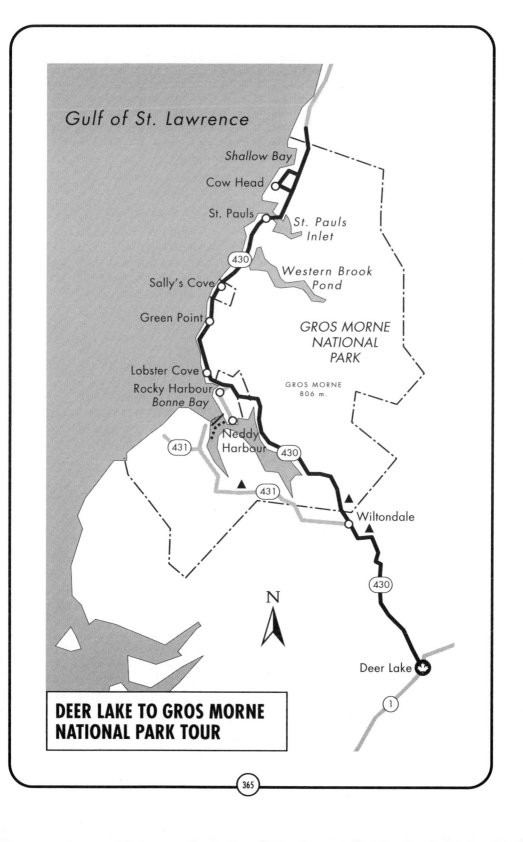

Gulf of St. Lawrence

Shallow Bay

Cow Head

St. Pauls

St. Pauls Inlet

430

Western Brook Pond

Sally's Cove

Green Point

GROS MORNE NATIONAL PARK

GROS MORNE 806 m.

Lobster Cove

Rocky Harbour

Bonne Bay

431

Neddy Harbour

430

431

Wiltondale

430

N

Deer Lake

1

DEER LAKE TO GROS MORNE NATIONAL PARK TOUR

coast for 10 km (6 miles) to Green Point, where there is a primitive campground near the ocean.

69 km (43 miles) Sally's Cove

Continue on Route 430 for 5 km (3 miles) to Sally's Cove, in a wind-swept cove where lobster fishing is a way of life.

74 km (46 miles) Western Brook Pond

Ride another 5 km (3 miles) to the spectacular Western Brook Pond, a 19-km (12-mile) inland fjord set between 600-meter (2,000-foot) cliffs. To explore the pond, walk 2 km (1.2 miles) along the trail to the nearest shore where boats take you to the end of the pond.

79 km (49 miles) Mouth of Western Brook

Another scenic spot is 5 km (3 miles) north on Route 430 at the mouth of Western Brook. Here, the river twists through high dunes and runs out by sandy beaches.

86 km (53 miles) St. Paul's Inlet

Follow Route 430 north for 7 km (4 miles) to St. Paul's Inlet. It is believed French explorer Jacques Cartier anchored nearby in 1534.

102 km (63 miles) Cow Head

Turn inland along rolling hills for 16 km (10 miles) to Cow Head where there are several views of the coast.

109 km (68 miles) Shallow Bay

Another 7 km (4 miles) is Shallow Bay, off Route 430 past Cow Head. There is a campground and a driftwood-strewn sand beach here.

Gros Morne's Park northern boundary is just beyond the bay.

Option: Continue on Viking Trail to St. Anthony

The Viking Trail from Gros Morne National Park to St. Anthony tour (described in this chapter) begins north of the park.

THE VIKING TRAIL: GROS MORNE NATIONAL PARK TO ST. ANTHONY

Length: 355 km (221 miles)
Time: Three to four days
Rating: Experienced
Terrain: Barren terrain; no severe hills; winds can be very strong.
Roads: Paved; unpaved shoulders; short side trips on gravel roads
Traffic: Recreational vehicles during June to August; no major impediments

Connects with: Deer Lake to Gros Morne National Park tour; ferry to Labrador Coast tour.
Start: Parson's Pond, near the northern boundary of Gros Morne National Park.
Overview: The site of the only known Viking colony in North America, L'Anse aux Meadows is along this tour of Newfoundland's Great

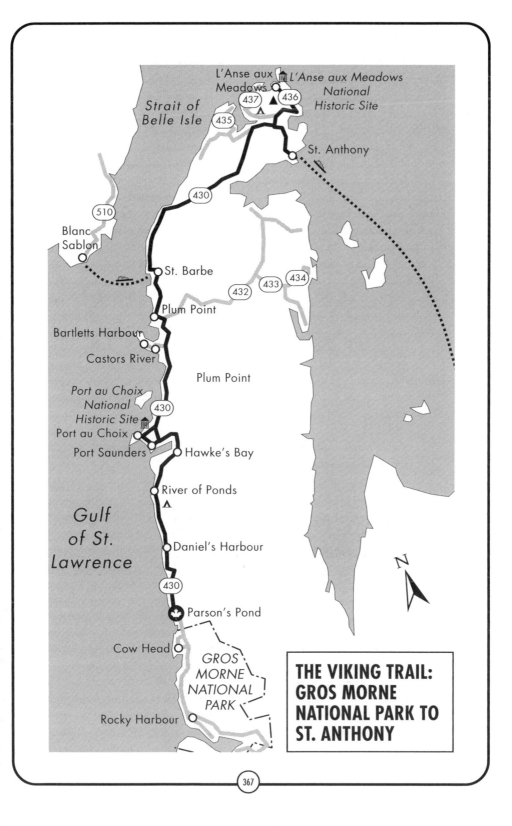

Strait of
Belle Isle

L'Anse aux
Meadows

437

435

436

L'Anse aux Meadows
National
Historic Site

St. Anthony

430

Blanc
Sablon

510

St. Barbe

432 433 434

Plum Point

Bartletts Harbour

Castors River

Plum Point

Port au Choix
National
Historic Site

430

Port au Choix

Port Saunders

Hawke's Bay

River of Ponds

Gulf
of St.
Lawrence

Daniel's Harbour

430

Parson's Pond

Cow Head

GROS
MORNE
NATIONAL
PARK

Rocky Harbour

N

**THE VIKING TRAIL:
GROS MORNE
NATIONAL PARK TO
ST. ANTHONY**

Northern Peninsula. To ride this tour without having to retrace your route, take the Marine Atlantic ferry from St. Anthony at the tip of the Northern Peninsula to Lewisporte. Make reservations in advance and schedule your trip so you won't have a long wait in St. Anthony for the ferry.

L'Anse aux Meadows, one of the most historically significant areas in North America, is believed to be the site of Leif Eriksson's colony around the year 1000. Sod buildings here recreate the earliest known European structures in North America. In 1978 L'Anse aux Meadows was named the first UNESCO World Heritage Site.

THE ROUTE:

0 km (0 miles) Parson's Pond

From Parson's Pond, ride Route 430 north.

10 km (6 miles) The Arches

A short road leads to "The Arches," two massive arches carved by the action of the sea.

22 km (14 miles) Daniel's Harbour

Continue on Route 430 for 12 km (7 miles) to Daniel's Harbour, a fishing, lumbering and mining town offering stores and two motels.

57 km (35 miles) River of the Ponds Provincial Park

Ride 35 km (22 miles) north from Daniel's Harbour to River of Ponds Provincial Park, which offers camping and swimming areas. The park has several upstream trout pools.

72 km (48 miles) Hawkes Bay

Another 15 km (9 miles) is Hawkes Bay, midway between Deer Lake and St. Anthony. The nearby East River and Torrent River are popular for salmon fishing.

91 km (57 miles) Port Saunders

Approximately 19 km (12 miles) farther, at Port Saunders, are general stores and a hospital.

101 km (63 miles) Port au Choix

Port au Choix, 10 km (6 miles) from Port Saunders, has a national historic park with archaeological artifacts from a prehistoric Dorset Inuit community.

A short ride on an unpaved road takes you back to Route 430.

156 km (97 miles) Plum Point

Continue north on Route 430 for 65 km (40 miles) past Castors River and Bartletts Harbour to Plum Point, where many buildings and traditions remain of the French occupation.

171 km (106 miles) St. Barbe

At St. Barbe, 15 km (9 miles) from Plum Point, is the terminal for the ferry across to Labrador (a Labrador cycling tour is described in this chapter).

194 km (121 miles) Flowers Cove

Continue 23 km (14 miles) on Route 430 to Flowers Cove, a fishing community with the Grenfell Mission nursing station.

287 km (178 miles) Route 436

Continue north on Route 430 for 93 km (58 miles) as the road turns inland to the junction with Route 436.

315 km (196 miles) L'Anse aux Meadows

Ride 28 km (17 miles) on un-paved Route 436 to L'Anse aux Meadows, site of the only known Viking colony in North America.

343 km (213 miles) return to Route 430

After visiting L'Anse aux Meadows, return to Route 430.

355 km (221 miles) St. Anthony

Continue for 12 km (7 miles) to St. Anthony, the largest town on the Northern Peninsula and the headquarters of the International Grenfell Association, which still provides some medical services to Newfoundland's isolated communities. Grenfell Handicrafts are known for their hand-embroidered parkas. The town has a hospital, a grocery store and hotels.

Option: Ferry from St. Anthony to Lewisporte

St. Anthony is a port of call for the Marine Atlantic ferry serving coastal communities between Lewisporte and Goose Bay. Take the ferry to Lewisporte.

Continue cycling on Route 340 for 14 km (9 miles), to the Trans Canada Highway—Highway 1.

Option: Airplane

Several regional airlines have flights within Newfoundland and Labrador.

More Information: Marine Atlantic coastal ferries, P.O. Box 250, North Sydney, Nova Scotia B2A 3M3; telephone from North Sydney, Nova Scotia (902) 794-5700; from St. John's, Newfoundland (709) 772-7701; from Port aux Basques, Newfoundland (709) 695-7081; from Bar Harbor, Maine toll-free 1-800-341-7981.

LABRADOR COAST FROM BLANC SABLON TO RED BAY

Length: 80 km (50 miles)
Time: One day
Rating: Intermediate
Terrain: No severe climbs
Roads: Paved
Traffic: Light
Connects with: Ferry from the Viking Trail: Gros Morne National Park to St. Anthony tour
Start: Blanc Sablon in Québec just 5 km (3 miles) west of the Labrador boundary. Take the ferry from St. Barbe in northern Newfoundland across the Strait of Belle Isle to Blanc Sablon.

Overview: The Labrador coast, the part of Newfoundland on mainland Canada, is an adventure for cyclists who want to explore a remote region of rugged, unspoiled terrain. Labrador is separated from the island of Newfoundland by the 18-km- (11-

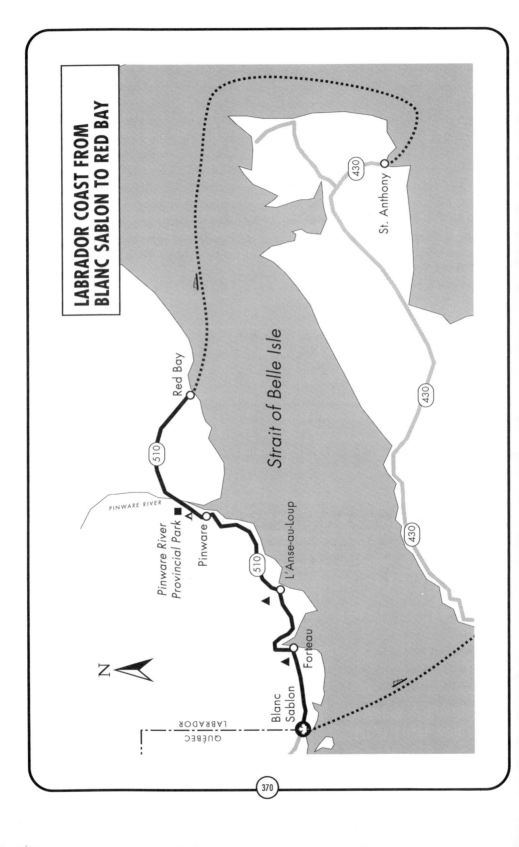

LABRADOR COAST FROM
BLANC SABLON TO RED BAY

N

QUÉBEC
LABRADOR

Blanc
Sablon

Forteau

L'Anse-au-Loup

Pinware

Pinware River
Provincial Park

PINWARE RIVER

510

510

Red Bay

Strait of Belle Isle

430

430

430

St. Anthony

mile-) wide Strait of Belle Isle. In the communities of Forteau, West St. Modeste and Red Bay are the descendants of fishermen who first traveled from the island of Newfoundland to the lucrative fishing grounds off Labrador centuries ago.

You can see whales, icebergs drifting southward from the Arctic and a variety of birds. There is also hiking and fishing. Local art and crafts are available.

THE ROUTE:

0 km (0 miles) Blanc Sablon

From Blanc Sablon, take Route 510 for 5 km (3 miles) east to the Labrador boundary.

Continue along Route 510 to Forteau, which has good salmon and trout fishing. At L'Anse Amour is a Maritime Archaic Indian burial site 7,500 years old.

40 km (25 miles) Pinware

Around Pinware in August you can pick "bakeapples" or cloudberries, considered a delicacy by the locals. The Pinware River has good salmon fishing. Pinware River Provincial Park has camping and is a good base for exploring the area.

80 km (50 miles) Red Bay

Red Bay is the site of a sixteenth-century Basque whaling station.

Retrace your route to Blanc Sablon and take the ferry back to St. Barbe.

More Information: The Strait of Belle Isle ferry is operated by Puddister Trading Co. Ltd., 23 Springdale Street, P.O. Box 38, St. John's, Newfoundland A1C 5H5, (709) 722-4000.

BISHOP'S FALLS TO ENGLISH HARBOUR WEST

Length: 150 km (93 miles)
Time: One day
Rating: For experienced cyclists prepared for a long exposed ride with no habitation.
Terrain: Intermediate
Roads: Paved, but broken surface in places
Traffic: Light but fast
Connects with: Across Newfoundland tour and Burin Peninsula tour
Start: Bishop's Falls, near the junction of the Trans Canada Highway and Route 360.

Overview: Route 360 links with the Trans Canada Highway near Bishop's Falls and goes through the unspoiled interior wilderness to remote communities on Newfoundland's south coast.

Cycling the South Coast of Newfoundland is a journey back into a rich unspoiled part of the province's traditions and folklore. The people

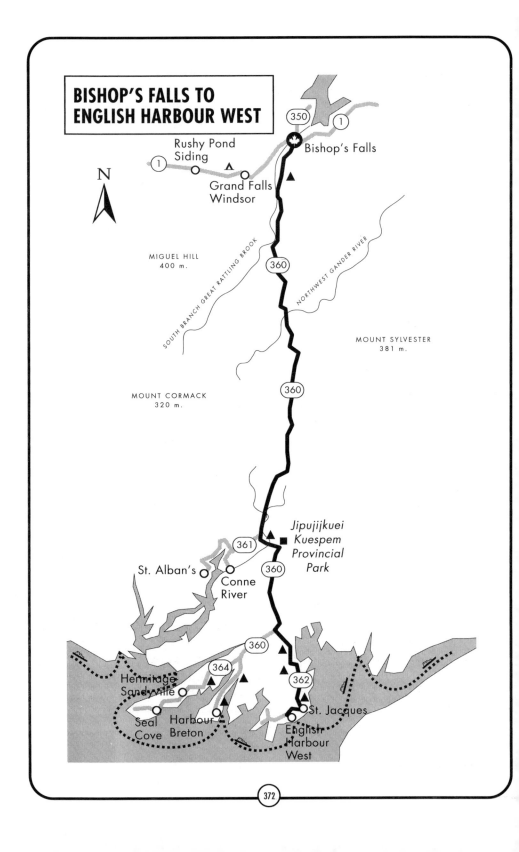

here depend for their livelihood on the sea off one of the roughest coasts in North America.

THE ROUTE:

0 km (0 miles) Trans Canada Highway

80 km (50 miles) Jipujikuei Kuespem Provincial Park

From the Trans Canada Highway, ride south for 80 km (50 miles) on Route 360 to Jipujikuei Kuespem Provincial Park (its name means Little River Pond). The park is on Route 360 just a few kilometers past the junction of Route 361.

This area is part of the traditional hunting grounds of the Micmac Indians, whose ancestors were brought to Newfoundland from Nova Scotia by the French in the eighteenth and nineteenth centuries.

115 km (71 miles) Route 362

Continue south on Route 360 for 35 km (22 miles) to the junction with Route 362.

150 km (93 miles) English Harbour West

From here, ride another 35 km (22 miles) of gravel Route 362, through several settlements on ruggedly beautiful bays, to English Harbour West, a port of call for a Marine Atlantic ferry service.

Option: Ferry to Burin Peninsula

From English Harbour West, you can travel by Marine Atlantic ferry (make enquiries and reservations well in advance) to Terrenceville on the Burin Peninsula. From Terrenceville, you can explore the Burin Peninsula (described in this chapter).

More Information: Marine Atlantic coastal ferries, P.O. Box 250, North Sydney, Nova Scotia B2A 3M3; telephone from North Sydney, Nova Scotia (902) 794-5700; from St. John's, Newfoundland (709) 772-7701; from Channel-Port aux Basques, Newfoundland (709) 695-7081; from Bar Harbor, Maine toll-free 1-800-341-7981.

TERRA NOVA NATIONAL PARK AND THE BONAVISTA PENINSULA

Length: 293 km (162 miles); with 2-km (1.2-mile) and 11-km (7-mile) side trips

Time: Well worth three days of cycling

Rating: Intermediate

Terrain: A lot of short hills in and out of the communities

Roads: Paved; good surface; paved shoulders in Terra Nova Park

Traffic: Never heavy, except in Terra Nova Park where there are adequate paved shoulders.

Connects with: Across Newfoundland tour

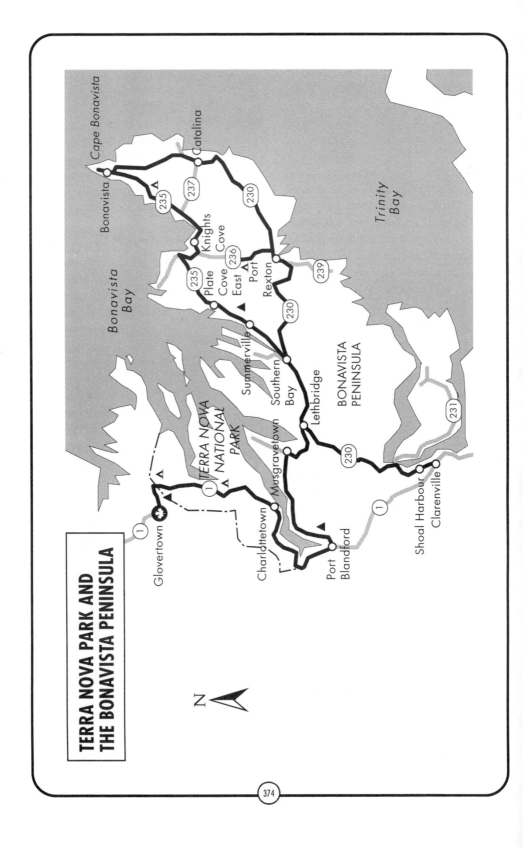

TERRA NOVA PARK AND
THE BONAVISTA PENINSULA

N

Cape Bonavista

Catalina

Bonavista

235

237

230

Knights Cove

236

Plate Cove East

Port Rexton

239

235

230

Trinity Bay

Bonavista Bay

Summerville

Southern Bay

Lethbridge

BONAVISTA PENINSULA

231

Musgravetown

TERRA NOVA NATIONAL PARK

1

Charlottetown

Port Blandford

230

1

Shoal Harbour

Clarenville

Glovertown

1

Start: Terra Nova National Park, on the Trans Canada Highway 78 km (48 miles) southeast of the town of Gander, the location of North America's easternmost international airport.

Overview: Canada's easternmost national park, Terra Nova is situated on the Appalachian mountain range. The park encompasses 400 square km (155 square miles) of deep rocky fjords, rolling crested hills, inland ponds and a deeply indented coastline on the shores of Bonavista Bay and the Labrador Sea. It offers hiking, swimming, canoeing, scuba diving and sailing. Scenery is typical of Newfoundland's east coast. From the park, this tour explores the Bonavista Peninsula.

The cold Labrador current gives the area cool, wet summers. Icebergs, a variety of whales and seals can occasionally be seen off the coast during the summer. Fishing for brook trout and Arctic char in the ponds, streams and lake is excellent. Saltwater fish in the area include cod, mackerel, herring, lumpfish and capelin. Blue mussels, barnacles and periwinkles can be found on coastal rocks while crabs and lobsters thrive in deeper water.

THE ROUTE:

0 km (0 miles) Terra Nova National Park

Ride along the Trans Canada Highway through Terra Nova Park. The road is hilly but moderately graded and has a paved shoulder. This part of the Appalachian Mountains system has spectacular views. The park's two main campgrounds are at Newman Sound and Malady Head.

Side trip: Charlottetown, 2 km (1.2 miles)

Take a 2-km (1.2-mile) side trip to Charlottetown, a tiny community on the Atlantic coast, where you can observe varied wildlife—you may even see bald eagles or whales.

59 km (37 miles) Port Blanford and Route 233

After exploring Terra Nova Park head toward the Bonavista Peninsula by riding 10 km (6 miles) past the park boundary to Route 233 at Port Blanford.

84 km (52 miles) Musgravetown

Take Route 233 east for 25 km (15 miles) to Musgravetown. Communities along this route are situated so close together that you're seldom cycling long stretches of lonely highway.

91 km (57 miles) Route 230

Ride 7 km (4 miles) to Route 230 near Southwest Brook.

135 km (84 miles) Trinity

Take Route 230 east for 44 km (27 miles) through Lethbridge, past the Rattle Falls viewpoint and Southern Bay to Route 239. Turn south on Route 239 to Trinity, considered one of the oldest European settlements in North America.

Portuguese explorer Gaspar Corte Real sailed into the harbor here on Trinity Sunday in A.D. 1500. Trinity became one of the mercantile capitals of the fish trade in the New World. In addition to historic buildings here, there is boating, whale watching and scuba diving.

140 km (87 miles) Port Rexton

After visiting Trinity, ride north on Route 239 for 3 km (2 miles) to Route 230, and go east on Route 230 for 2 km (1.2 miles) to Port Rexton.

Side trip: Port Rexton to Lockston Path Provincial Park, 6 km (4 miles)

To reach Lockston Path Provincial Park, which has sheltered campsites and a freshwater beach, continue east on Route 230. Just past Port Rexton, turn north on gravel Route 236 for 6 km (4 miles) to the Lockston Path Park. You can camp at the park and use it as a base to visit Port Union and Catalina.

Main tour continues on Route 230 near Port Rexton

Continue riding east on Route 230 to the historic communities of Port Union and Catalina, 27 km (16 miles) from Port Rexton.

187 km (116 miles) Bonavista

Keep riding Route 230 for 20 km (12 miles) to Bonavista, where accommodation is available.

Nearby Cape Bonavista is believed to be the place where John Cabot first saw the New World on June 24, 1497. Bonavista is the largest community on Newfoundland's east coast, and entirely dependent on the fishing industry. Places of interest include the restored lighthouse and White Rock, which offers a panoramic view of the surrounding countryside and ocean.

198 km (123 miles) Knights Cove

Take Route 235 for 31 km (19 miles) along the Bonavista Bay coast through Amherst Cove to Knights Cove.

238 km (148 miles) Southern Bay, junction with Route 230

Continue on Route 235 for 40 km (25 miles) past Plate Cove east, to Southern Bay.

261 km (162 miles) Clarenville

Connect here with Route 230 and travel 23 km (14 miles) through Lethbridge and Southwest Brook.

Option: Return to Trans Canada Highway at Port Blanford via Route 233

From Southwest Brook, you can take Route 233 and retrace the part of this tour to Port Blanford on the Trans Canada Highway.

Main tour continues along Route 230

293 km (162 miles) Clarenville

Keep riding on Route 230 for 32 km (20 miles) through Milton to arrive at the Trans Canada Highway at Clarenville. Clarenville, a distribution center for the Bonavista Peninsula, has hotels, restaurants, banks and a shopping center.

BURIN PENINSULA AND ST. PIERRE-MIQUELON

Length: 365 km (227 miles)

Time: Four full days of cycling, excluding the time on St. Pierre-Miquelon

Rating: Intermediate to experienced; long periods of riding in exposed areas

Terrain: Rolling

Roads: Good pavement all the way

Traffic: Recreational vehicles add to traffic from June to August

Connects with: Across Newfoundland tour

Start: The junction of the Trans Canada Highway and Route 210. For a shorter circuit, start at Marystown for a circuit of the lower Burin Peninsula.

Overview: The picturesque Burin Peninsula has its history tied to the fishery on the Grand Banks. A rich fishing ground, the Grand Banks attracted Europeans to these shores as early as the 1500s when French, English and Portuguese came in the summer to fish and dry their catch before returning home in the fall. The islands of St. Pierre and Miquelon, territories of France, are a two-hour ferry ride from Fortune.

This tour follows Route 210 south from the Trans Canada Highway. The route is open and exposed to wind and rain but the scenery is spectacular.

THE ROUTE:

0 km (0 miles) Trans Canada Highway

18 km (11 miles) Swift Current

From the Trans Canada Highway, go south on Route 210 through mountain scenery to Swift Current.

35 km (22 miles) Pipers Hole River Picnic Park

Pipers Hole River Picnic Park, in a carpet of heath surrounded by distant hills, is 17 km (10.5 miles) farther.

145 km (90 miles) Marystown

Ride 110 km (73 miles) from Pipers Hole River Picnic Park to Marystown on Placentia Bay. Along the way are gravel roads leading to outport communities.

In Marystown, the largest community on the Burin Peninsula, deep-sea fishing trawlers were built.

From Marystown, start the circuit of the historic Burin Peninsula. Take Route 210 to Winterland.

185 km (115 miles) Frenchmans Cove Provincial Park

Then ride Route 213 west to Frenchmans Cove Provincial Park, where there are camping and swimming facilities. The park is approximately 40 km (25 miles) from Marystown.

239 km (149 miles) Grand Bank

Turn onto Route 220 and ride to Grand Bank, 54 km (33 miles) from Marystown. At Grand

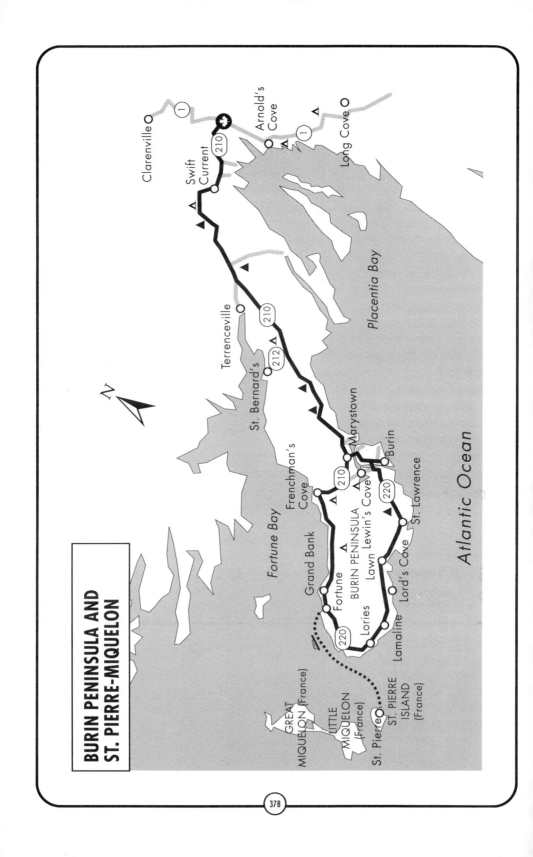

BURIN PENINSULA AND
ST. PIERRE-MIQUELON

N

Clarenville

Arnold's Cove

Swift Current

Long Cove

Terrenceville

Placentia Bay

St. Bernard's

Frenchman's Cove

Marystown

Burin

Fortune Bay

Grand Bank

BURIN PENINSULA

Lawn Lewin's Cove

St. Lawrence

Fortune

Lories

Lord's Cove

Lamaline

GREAT
MIQUELON (France)

LITTLE
MIQUELON (France)

ST. PIERRE
ISLAND (France)

St. Pierre

Atlantic Ocean

Bank you can visit the Seaman's Museum.

245 km (152 miles) Fortune

Ride Route 220 for 6 km (4 miles) past Grand Bank to Fortune.

Option: Ferry from Fortune to St. Pierre and Miquelon

From Fortune, you can take the ferry, a two-hour ride, to the French islands of St. Pierre and Miquelon, a part of France situated 18 km (11 miles) offshore.

Once off the ferry, you're in a real French town with French gendarmes, cuisine, wines, perfumes, clothes and, of course, the French language.

St. Pierre is a busy fishing port with only 3 km (1.8 miles) of road. Miquelon is a picturesque island where several hundred people live by fishing and farming.

Main tour continues from Fortune

320 km (199 miles) St. Lawrence

From Fortune, continue on Route 220 for 75 km (47 miles) through the picturesque coastal villages of Lories, Lamaline, Taylor's Bay, Lords Cove and Lawn to St. Lawrence. St. Lawrence was once the site of a large fluorspar mine. Here you can visit the Miner's Museum.

355 km (221 miles) Burin

Continue for 35 km (22 miles) on Route 220 to Route 22, and then Route 221 along the bay to Burin, built along a series of cliffs. Here are docking facilities for fishing trawlers.

365 km (227 miles) Marystown

Return along Route 221 through Creston for another 10 km (6 miles) and you're back at Marystown.

More Information: The ferry from Fortune to St. Pierre is operated by Lake and Lake Limited, P.O. Box 98, Fortune, Newfoundland A0E 1P0, telephone (709) 832-0429; from St. John's call (709) 738-1357.

ST. JOHN'S AND THE SOUTH AVALON PENINSULA LOOP

Length: 322 km (200 miles)
Time: Four days
Rating: Difficult
Terrain: Hills, barren terrain, hilly highland
Roads: All paved with good surface; little shoulder
Traffic: Light

Connects with: Across Newfoundland tour
Start: St. John's, the capital of the province of Newfoundland
Overview: This circuit explores the Avalon Peninsula, the easternmost part of Newfoundland. The area has some of the oldest European settle-

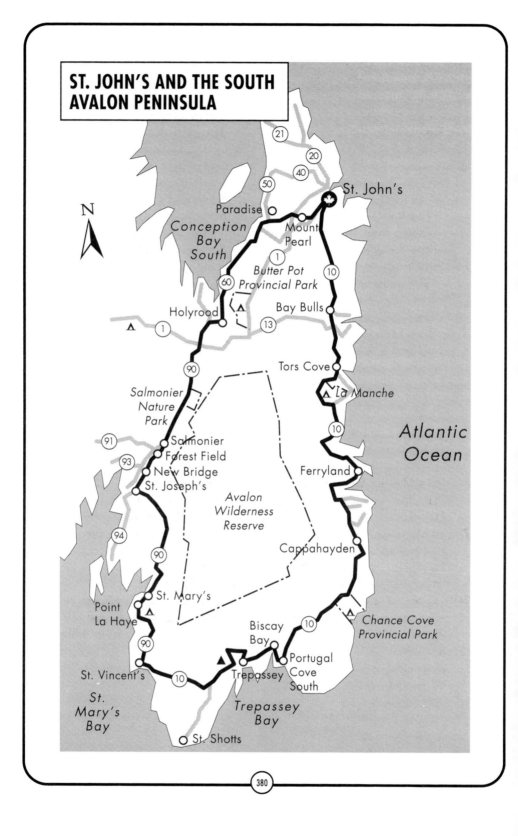

ST. JOHN'S AND THE SOUTH AVALON PENINSULA

St. John's

㉑
⑳
㊵
㊿

Paradise ○

Conception
Bay
South

Mount Pearl

①

Butter Pot
Provincial Park

⑩

㊿

Bay Bulls

Holyrood ○

①

⑬

Tors Cove

La Manche

Salmonier
Nature
Park

⑩

Atlantic Ocean

㉑

Salmonier ○
Forest Field
New Bridge
St. Joseph's

㊳

Avalon
Wilderness
Reserve

Ferryland

㊹

⑩

Cappahayden

St. Mary's

Point
La Haye

⑩

Biscay
Bay

⑩

Chance Cove
Provincial Park

St. Vincent's

⑩

Trepassey

Portugal
Cove
South

St.
Mary's
Bay

Trepassey
Bay

St. Shotts ○

ments in North America. This tour follows Highway 10, known as the Southern Shore. Many tales of shipwrecks are told here.

THE ROUTE:

0 km (0 miles) St. John's

31 km (19 miles) Bay Bulls

Ride on Route 10 south from St. John's to the fishing community of Bay Bulls.

Dating from 1638, Bay Bulls is one of Newfoundland's oldest settlements. In the deep waters of Bay Bulls lies the wreck of the H.M.S. *Sapphire* sunk in battle in 1696.

40 km (25 miles) Tors Cove

Keep riding Route 10, which is hilly but has good views of the coast.

At Tors Cove, 13 km (8 miles) from Bay Bulls, is Witness Bay Ecological Reserve, an offshore bird sanctuary, which extends to the La Manche Valley.

La Manche Valley Provincial Park has swimming and a hiking trail.

71 km (44 miles) Ferryland

At Ferryland, 31 km (19 miles) from Tors Cove, is a battle site and an early settlement.

149 km (93 miles) Trepassey

Ride the 78 km (48 miles) from Ferryland through Cappahayden, Portugal South Cove and Biscay Bay to Trepassey. Much of the route crosses barren terrain. You cross traces of the old railway that once served the coast.

Trepassey means "the dead" or "dead souls"; it was settled by the Welsh in the 1620s. It was the starting point for trans-Atlantic flights in the 1920s.

185 km (115 miles) St. Vincent's

Cycle west from Trepassey across the highland. There are a lot of hills on this stretch of road.

Ride 36 km (22 miles) on Route 10 to St. Vincent's, a sheep-raising community.

200 km (124 miles) St. Mary's

From St. Vincent's, cycle north on Route 90 through low barren hills. At Point La Haye, 13 km (8 miles) from St. Vincent's, is a beach.

At St. Mary's, 2 km (1.2 miles) north of Point La Haye, is the turn-off for Holyrood Pond Provincial Park, which offers camping facilities.

244 km (152 miles) Salmonier

Continue north on Route 90 through the communities of St. Joseph's, New Bridge and Forest Field to Salmonier, a distance of 44 km (27 miles) from St. Mary's.

274 km (170 miles) Holyrood

From Salmonier, ride 30 km (19 miles) along Route 90 past Salmonier Nature Park to Holyrood.

322 km (200 miles) St. John's

From Holyrood, take Route 60— the Conception Bay Highway— for 48 km (30 miles) back to St. John's.

NORTH AVALON PENINSULA: CONCEPTION BAY AND TRINITY BAY

Length: 349 km (217 miles)
Time: Three full days
Rating: Difficult
Terrain: Mostly level
Roads: Paved; little shoulder
Traffic: Heavy during rush periods
Connects with: Across Newfoundland tour
Start: Topsail, located 12 km (7.5 miles) west of St. John's. From St. John's take the Topsail Road, which is Route 60, to the village of Topsail.
Overview: If one area could portray Newfoundland, it must be Conception Bay, west of the city of St. John's.

This tour explores this area from Topsail on Conception Bay's Eastern Arm, to Grates Cove on the western tip. It then continues to the Trinity Bay coast.

THE ROUTE:

0 km (0 miles) Topsail
25 km (15 miles) Holyrood

Start your tour with a view of Conception Bay and its islands, by climbing Topsail Head. From Topsail, take Route 60 south along the Conception Bay coast.

From Topsail through Long Pond and Kelligrews to Holyrood is along fairly even terrain. The road is busy at times, and rough pavement edges are frequent.

At Holyrood is a municipal park and Butter Pot Provincial Park with camping facilities. To get to the Butter Pot Park, take the Trans Canada Highway, which intersects with Route 60 south of Holyrood.

36 km (22 miles) Avondale

From Holyrood, ride Route 60 as it turns north along the winding coast. The road borders the sea around the Arm and goes over a series of hills through Harbour Main and Avondale, 11 km (7 miles) from Holyrood.

52 km (32 miles) turn-off for Cupids

Ride along Route 60 over the Barrens to the turn-off for Brigus and 1 km (0.6 mile) farther on Route 60 is the turn-off for Cupids. Cupids was the first settled place in Newfoundland.

67 km (42 miles) Spaniard's Bay

Continue riding north on Route 60 to South River and take Route 70 to the turn-off for Bay Roberts. Accommodation in hotels and hospitality homes is available in Bay Roberts.

Continue north on to Spaniard's Bay, 15 km (9 miles) from the turn-off for Cupids.

78 km (48 miles) Harbour Grace

From Spaniard's Bay, ride north for 11 km (7 miles) on hilly Route 70 through several communities to Harbour Grace, the

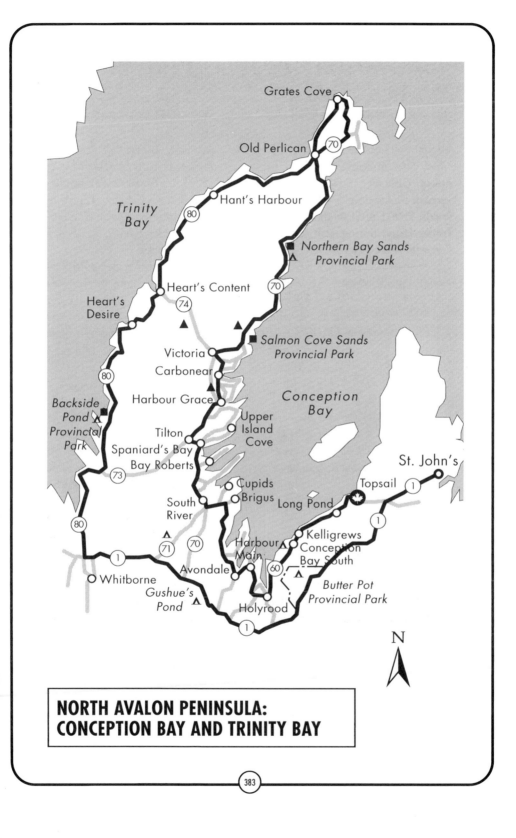

Grates Cove

Old Perlican
70

Trinity
Bay

80 Hant's Harbour

■ Northern Bay Sands
▲ Provincial Park

Heart's Content
70

74

Heart's
Desire

▲ ▲

Victoria ■ Salmon Cove Sands
Carbonear Provincial Park

80

Harbour Grace ▲ Conception
Bay

Backside
Pond ■
Provincial ▲ Upper
Park Tilton Island
Cove

Spaniard's Bay
73 Bay Roberts

Cupids St. John's
Brigus

South Long Pond Topsail 1
River
Kelligrews 1

Whitborne 80 Harbour ▲ Conception
71 70 Main Bay South
Avondale 60 ▲ Butter Pot
Provincial Park
Gushue's ▲ 1
Pond Holyrood

1

N

**NORTH AVALON PENINSULA:
CONCEPTION BAY AND TRINITY BAY**

haven of seventeenth-century pirate Peter Easton. Here is Newfoundland's oldest stone church and a museum in the old Customs House.

83 km (52 miles) Carbonear

Keep riding to Carbonear, a 5 km (3 miles) past Harbour Grace.

122 km (76 miles) Northern Bay Sands Provincial Park

Continue north on Route 70 through Victoria. Along Route 70 is a sandy beach at Salmon Cove Sands Provincial Park, and both sandy beaches and camping at Northern Bay Sands Provincial Park, 39 km (24 miles) from Carbonear.

155 km (96 miles) Grates Cove

Keep riding north for 33 km (21 miles) to Grates Cove, at the windy western tip of Conception Bay.

211 km (131 miles) Hearts Content

From Grates Cove, turn south onto Route 80 along Trinity Bay to Hearts Content, a distance of 56 km (35 miles).

At Hearts Content was the first successful landing of the Trans-Atlantic telegraphic cable. The old cable station is preserved as a historic site.

236 km (147 miles) Backside Pond Provincial Park

Ride farther down Route 80 on the Trinity Bay coast through Hearts Desire, Hearts Delight and Cavendish to Backside Pond Provincial Park with camping and swimming, a distance of 25 km (15 miles) from Hearts Content.

269 km (167 miles) Trans Canada Highway

Continue on Route 80 for 33 km (20 miles) to the Trans Canada Highway.

349 km (217 miles) St. John's

From here, you can return 80 km (50 miles) to St. John's via Highway 1—the Trans Canada Highway.

ACROSS NEWFOUNDLAND

Length: 905 km (562 miles)
Time: Seven to nine days
Rating: Intermediate
Terrain: Ranges from hilly to mountainous
Roads: Paved; good surface
Traffic: Recreational vehicle traffic during June to August
Connects with: Most of the other tours in this chapter

Start: Channel-Port aux Basques ferry terminal
Overview: Following the Trans Canada Highway—Highway 1—takes you across the island of Newfoundland from Channel-Port aux Basques to St. John's. There are provincial parks and private campgrounds a day's ride apart, and motels and hotels in the larger towns.

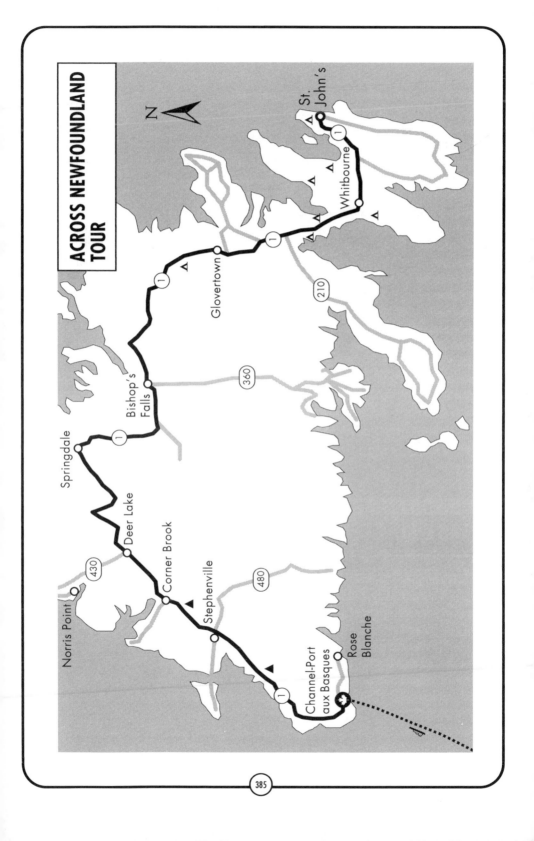

ACROSS NEWFOUNDLAND TOUR

N

St. John's

Whitbourne

210

Glovertown

360

Bishop's Falls

Springdale

Deer Lake

430

Corner Brook

Norris Point

Stephenville

480

Channel-Port aux Basques

Rose Blanche

The other tours in this chapter are segments of this Across Newfoundland tour but include secondary roads to coastal communities. Be sure to take the time to explore some of these other tours.

THE ROUTE:

0 km (0 miles) Channel-Port aux Basques

218 km (135 miles) Corner Brook

From Port aux Basques to Corner Brook the Trans Canada Highway follows the coast.

496 km (308 miles) Bishop's Falls

From Corner Brook, the 278 km (173 miles) to Bishop's Falls the terrain is more hilly and becomes mountainous between Deer Lake and South Brook. Climbs tend to be long and gradual.

905 km (562 miles) St. John's

The 409 km (254 miles) from Bishop's Falls to St. John's is rolling coastal to hilly terrain.

GUIDEBOOKS

Newfoundland By Bicycle, by Audrey Porter and Tom Sandland. Available from: Newfoundland and Labrador Cycling Association, P.O. Box 2127, Station C, St. John's, Newfoundland A1C 5R6; free.

Index